TOWARDS IMPLEMENTING UNIVERSAL HUMAN RIGHTS

FESTSCHRIFT FOR THE TWENTY-FIFTH ANNIVERSARY OF THE HUMAN RIGHTS COMMITTEE

THE RAOUL WALLENBERG INSTITUTE
HUMAN RIGHTS LIBRARY
VOLUME 18

TOWARDS IMPLEMENTING UNIVERSAL HUMAN RIGHTS

FESTSCHRIFT FOR THE TWENTY-FIFTH ANNIVERSARY OF THE HUMAN RIGHTS COMMITTEE

EDITED BY

NISUKE ANDO
ON BEHALF OF THE COMMITTEE

THE RAOUL WALLENBERG INSTITUTE HUMAN RIGHTS LIBRARY
VOLUME 18

MARTINUS NIJHOFF PUBLISHERS
LEIDEN/BOSTON
2004

A C.I.P. Catalogue record for this book is available from the Library of Congress.

Printed on acid-free paper.

ISBN 90-04-14078-6 (HB)
ISBN 90-04-14080-8 (PB)

Brill Academic Publishers incorporates the imprint Martinus Nijhoff Publishers.
http://www.brill.nl

Printed and bound in The Netherlands

TABLE OF CONTENTS

PART III: ACTIVITIES OF THE HUMAN RIGHTS COMMITTEE (1) – GENERAL ISSUES

PART IV: ACTIVITIES OF THE HUMAN RIGHTS COMMITTEE (2) – SPECIFIC ISSUES

TABLE OF CONTENTS

PREFACE

Professeur Abdelfattah Amor

Président
Comité des droits de l'homme

Les présents 'Mélanges' célébrant les vingt-cinq années d'exercice du Comité des droits de l'homme, soit un quart de siècle, nous permettent d'apprécier l'impact du Pacte international relatif aux droits civils et politiques, et le chemin encore à parcourir pour une meilleure protection des droits de l'homme.

Le Pacte international relatif aux droits civils et politiques a introduit un élément nouveau à l'édifice des droits de l'homme, en ce qu'il a porté création d'un organe d'experts indépendants chargé d'en surveiller l'application: le Comité des droits de l'homme.

Parmi les principales fonctions de cet organe de traité, la procédure d'examen des rapports des Etats parties sur les mesures prises pour donner effet aux droits énoncés dans le Pacte et aboutissant à la formulation par le Comité de recommandations spécifiques – dénommées observations finales – à l'attention des Etats parties, a connu des innovations récentes majeures. Le Comité a, en effet, joué un rôle pionnier dans l'établissement d'une procédure de suivi, ceci à travers la création du mandat de Rapporteur spécial chargé du suivi des observations finales du Comité. Afin, par ailleurs, de remédier aux problèmes de non-présentation des rapports par les Etats parties ou de présentation tardive, le Comité a adopté et mis en œuvre une nouvelle procédure permettant l'examen, à la lumière du Pacte, de situations dans les Etats parties n'ayant pas présenté leurs rapports. Les résultats de cette nouvelle procédure depuis 2001 ont été prometteurs.

L'interprétation du Pacte permettant de préciser le champ d'application et le sens de ses articles est devenue également l'une des tâches importantes du Comité, dont les observations générales guident les Etats parties dans l'application des dispositions du Pacte et dans l'établissement de leurs rapports. Parmi les trente observations générales du Comité, l'on pourra se référer notamment à l'Observation générale N° 29 relative à l'article 4 du Pacte précisant les dérogations aux obligations prévues par le Pacte lors d'un danger public exceptionnel menaçant l'existence de la nation et dans la stricte mesure où la situation l'exige. Cette Observation générale s'est révélée des plus pertinentes dans l'examen de la légalité des mesures prises au nom de la lutte contre le terrorisme depuis les évènements du 11 septembre, et qui dans de nombreux pays, se sont traduites, en réalité, par de graves violations des droits de l'homme.

Concernant les plaintes individuelles – communément dénommées communications – au titre du Protocole facultatif se rapportant au Pacte, cette fonction essentielle a contribué à la juridictionnalisation croissante du Comité. Certes, ce dernier ne constitue pas un tribunal en tant que tel, telles que le reflètent en particulier deux caractéristiques de la procédure des plaintes, à savoir d'une part, l'examen des communications sur la base de soumissions écrites de l'Etat partie et du requérant, plutôt qu'au travers de procédures contradictoires devant le Comité, et d'autre part l'adoption par le Comité à l'issue de cet examen de constatations n'étant pas juridiquement contraignantes.

Cependant, le travail du Comité sur les plaintes s'est rapproché, au fil du temps, du processus de décision juridictionnel: dans des cas concrets relatifs à un individu ou un groupe de personnes, le Comité, à travers une procédure contradictoire, décide si l'Etat partie en question a violé les droits de l'homme du requérant. En d'autres termes, le Comité applique les dispositions du Pacte et du Protocole facultatif dans un esprit juridique. Par ailleurs, les constatations du Comité ne constituent pas de simples recommandations, mais des interprétations juridiques du Pacte faisant autorité de la part d'un organe quasi-judiciaire d'experts indépendants établi et élu par les Etats parties à cette fin.

A partir de ces constatations, la jurisprudence du Comité s'est considérablement enrichie au cours de ces dix dernières années. L'on constate également, toujours dans ce processus de juridictionnalisation, le phénomène de 'la perméabilité de l'ordre juridique interne et de l'ordre juridique international en matière de droits de l'homme'. En effet, le Comité des droits de l'homme tend à développer sa jurisprudence dans un esprit de cohérence avec les précédents jurisprudentiels des instances régionales, voire même des juridictions nationales, ceci lorsqu'il est amené à se prononcer sur une question d'interprétation d'une des dispositions du Pacte.

Un phénomène analogue se dessine de la part des instances régionales, dont la Cour européenne des droits de l'homme et la Commission Inter-Américaine ainsi que des plus hautes juridictions des Etats parties, ces dernières invoquant de plus en plus souvent les décisions du Comité. Bien qu'il s'agisse là d'un phénomène récent, il est d'autant plus remarquable dans la mesure où il contribue au renforcement de la jurisprudence internationale et de la cohérence dans le domaine des droits de l'homme. Finalement et surtout, la procédure des plaintes individuelles a permis de rendre justice à de nombreuses victimes, et sous diverses formes, qu'il s'agisse de la suspension de peines de mort, de modifications législatives, de changements dans les pratiques administratives, de la réintégration de personnes dans leurs fonctions, ou du paiement de compensations financières aux victimes de violations des droits de l'homme. La procédure de suivi des constatations du Comité à travers l'établissement du mandat de Rapporteur spécial chargé du suivi des constatations a considérablement facilité la mise en œuvre de nombreuses décisions depuis 1991.

L'attention croissante des médias à la jurisprudence du Comité au titre du Protocole facultatif a accrû la visibilité de cette fonction du Comité, et surtout de vulgariser auprès du grand public cette procédure de plaintes, et donc de rendre plus courante son utilisation.

Le présent ouvrage publié grâce au concours de l'Institut Raoul Wallenberg et aux contributions d'anciens et actuels membres du Comité vise, à travers la célébration du 25ème anniversaire du Comité des droits de l'homme, à une meilleure connaissance de ce mécanisme de protection des droits de l'homme auprès de tout un chacun et pourra constituer, c'est notre vœu, un guide aux acteurs impliqués dans le champ des droits de l'homme. Contribuer, sans cesse et sans relâche, au renforcement de l'édifice des droits de l'homme face aux défis toujours plus grands se posant à la promotion et à la protection des droits de l'homme, tel est notre credo et notre engagement.

EDITOR'S NOTES

As noted in the Preface, the Human Rights Committee established under the International Covenant on Civil and Political Rights celebrated the 25th anniversary of its activities in 2002. To commemorate that occasion the Committee decided to publish a book (Festschrift, mélange) reflecting various aspects of the Committee and its activities comprised of articles contributed exclusively by its members, past and present. All together sixteen members submitted their contributions, nine in English, four in French and three in Spanish.

During the summer session of 2002 the Bureau of the Committee asked me to work as the editor of the Festschrift. My first problem was to raise funds for the publication as well as to find a publisher willing to publish the sixteen articles in their respective original languages. Fortunately, the Raoul Wallenberg Institute of Human Rights and Humanitarian Law agreed to publish the Festschrift (with each article in its original language) in its Library Series with Martinus Nijhoff Publishers under the imprint of Brill Academic Publishers as the publisher.

Several Committee members with English, French or Spanish as a mother tongue volunteered to language edit the articles where appropriate. The Committee's Secretariat, under the leadership of Dr. Markus Schmidt, carefully checked the cases cited in the articles, although I decided not to adopt a uniform style of case citations.

In editing the Festschrift I divided the sixteen articles into five chapters. Chapter I is comprised of four articles dealing with the UN system of human rights protection in general and the role and work of the Human Rights Committee in particular. Chapter II contains two articles on the historical aspects of the Committee, both in retrospect and prospect. Chapter III covers three articles, each generally dealing with the Committee's different activities, whereas Chapter IV includes six articles, each analyzing specific Committee activities. Chapter V is composed of only one article, a case study of the domestic implementation of the Covenant. For details, please kindly consult the Table of Contents.

Considering the character of the Festschrift, I have decided not to attach any Index.

Last but not least, I would like to thank the Raoul Wallenberg Institute for making possible the publication of this Festschrift, those Committee members who undertook the language editing, and the Secretariat for checking the cases in the articles.

Nisuke Ando

Committee member in charge of editing this Festschrift

CONTRIBUTORS' AFFILIATION WITH THE HUMAN RIGHTS COMMITTEE (IN ALPHABETICAL ORDER)

MR. ABDELFATTAH AMOR (TUNISIA)	*(Member, 1999–present; Vice-Chair, 1999–2002; Chairperson, 2003–2004)*
MR. NISUKE ANDO (JAPAN)	*(Member, 1987–present; Rapporteur, 1991–1992; Chairperson, 1993–1994)*
MR. NEJIB BOUZIRI (TUNISIA)	*(Member, 1979–1986; Vice-Chair, 1983–1984)*
MS. CHRISTINE CHANET (FRANCE)	*(Member, 1987–present; Rapporteur, 1999–2000; Chairperson, 1997–1998)*
MS. ELIZABETH EVATT (AUSTRALIA)	*(Member, 1993–2000; Rapporteur, 1997–1998; Vice-Chair, 1999–2000)*
MR. MAURICE GLÈLÈ-AHANHANZO (BENIN)	*(Member, 2001–present)*
MR. LOUIS HENKIN (UNITED STATES OF AMERICA)	*(Member, 1999–2002)*
MR. ECKART KLEIN (GERMANY)	*(Member, 1995–2002; Rapporteur, 2001-2002)*
MR. ANDREAS MAVROMMATIS (CYPRUS)	*(Member, 1977–1996; Chairperson, 1977– 1986)*
MR. JULIO PRADO VALLEJO (ECUADOR)	*(Member, 1977–1996; Vice-Chair, 1979–1986; Chairperson, 1987–1988)*
MR. RAFAEL RIVAS POSADA (COLOMBIA)	*(Member, 2001–present; Vice-Chair, 2003–2004).*
SIR NIGEL RODLEY (UNITED KINGDOM OF GREAT BRITAIN AND NORTHERN IRELAND)	*(Member, 2001–present; Vice-Chair, 2003–2004)*
MR. MARTIN SCHEININ (FINLAND)	*(Member, 1997–present)*
MR. IVAN SHEARER (AUSTRALIA)	*(Member, 2001–present; Rapporteur, 2003–2004)*
MR. HIPOLITO SOLARI-YRIGOYEN (ARGENTINA)	*(Member, 1999–present; Vice-Chair, 2001–2002)*
MR. CHRISTIAN TOMUSCHAT (GERMANY)	*(Member, 1976–1986; Vice-Chair, 1981–1982, 1985–1986)*

Part I

United Nations Protection of Human Rights and the Human Rights Committee

UNITED NATIONS HUMAN RIGHTS TREATY BODIES AND SPECIAL PROCEDURES OF THE COMMISSION ON HUMAN RIGHTS – COMPLEMENTARITY OR COMPETITION?

Sir Nigel Rodley[*]

INTRODUCTION

For historical reasons, the United Nations (UN) is presently endowed with two sets of human rights monitoring procedures: those established under human rights treaties and those set up by the UN Commission on Human Rights, variously called 'special procedures', 'extra-conventional mechanisms' or 'Charter-based bodies'.[1] The latter may be divided into country-specific and thematic mechanisms.[2] It is the

---

[*] I am grateful to Jan Doerfel for his diligent research assistance for this essay which began as a talk to an International Law Association (British Branch) Regional Seminar, University of Nottingham, 2 May 2001. I am also indebted to Daniel Atchebro, Christina Saunders and Markus Schmidt, all of the Office of the UN High Commissioner for Human Rights, for providing me with important information. This chapter seeks to take account of developments as of 31 May 2002.

[1] The treaties and treaty bodies are: International Convention on the Elimination of All Forms of Racial Discrimination, 660 UNTS 195 (ICERD)/Committee on the Elimination of Racial Discrimination (CERD); International Covenant on Economic, Social and Cultural Rights, 993 UNTS 3 (ICESCR)/Committee on Economic, Social and Cultural Rights (CESCR); International Covenant on Civil and Political Rights, 999 UNTS 171 (ICCPR)/Human Rights Committee (HRC); Convention on the Elimination of All Forms of Discrimination against Women, 1249 UNTS 13 (CEDAW)/Committee on the Elimination of Discrimination against Women (CEDAW Committee); Convention against Torture and Other Cruel, Inhuman or Degrading Treatment or Punishment, 1465 UNTS 85 (CAT)/Committee against Torture (CAT Committee); Convention on the Rights of the Child, 1577 UNTS 3 (CRC)/Committee on the Rights of the Child (CRC Committee). A seventh treaty, the International Convention on Protection of the Rights of All Migrant Workers and Members of Their Families (MWC), adopted by General Assembly res. 45/158, 18 Dec 1990, is not yet in force. It too has a Committee, bearing the same title, which will doubtless share subject-matter jurisdiction with the Special Rapporteur on the human rights of migrants. While it will not be further studied here, what is said about existing relationships will be relevant to that one. The following works deal with the treaty system as a whole: P. Alston and J. Crawford (eds.), *The Future of Human Rights Treaty Monitoring* (Cambridge University Press, Cambridge, 2000); A. Bayefsky (ed.), *The UN Human Rights System in the 21st* Century (Kluwer, The Hague, 2000); A. Bayefsky, *The UN Human Rights Treaty System* (Transnational, Ardsley, NY, 2001).

[2] The following thematic mandates are in existence at the time of writing: Working Group on Enforced or Involuntary Disappearances, Working Group on Arbitrary Detention, Special Rapporteur on extrajudicial, summary or arbitrary executions, Special Rapporteur on the

thematic mechanisms that are most relevant for the comparative analysis of this essay, the first of which (the Working Group on Enforced or Involuntary Disappearances) was not created until 1980, that is, some 35 years after the founding of the UN.

This delay reflected a belief by many of the states members of the Organization in its early days that scrutiny of any individual state's human rights practices constituted improper intervention in matters essentially within the domestic jurisdiction of states, as excluded by Article 2(7) of the Charter of the United Nations. Even though, as early as 1950, the bold and pioneering commentator Sir Hersch Lanterpacht argued that mere discussion of a state's human rights

---

independence of judges and lawyers, Special Rapporteur on the question of torture, Representative of the Secretary-General on internally displaced persons, Special Rapporteur on religious intolerance, Special Rapporteur on the question of the use of mercenaries, Special Rapporteur on the promotion and protection of the right to freedom of opinion and expression, Special Rapporteur on contemporary forms of racism, racial discrimination, xenophobia and related intolerance, Special Rapporteur on the sale of children, child prostitution and child pornography, Special Rapporteur on violence against women, its causes and consequences, Special Representative of the Secretary-General on the situation of human rights defenders, Special Rapporteur on the adverse effects of the illicit movement and dumping of toxic and dangerous products and wastes, Special Rapporteur on the human rights of migrants, Independent expert on structural adjustment and foreign debt, Special Rapporteur on the right to education, Special Rapporteur on the right to adequate housing as a component of the right to an adequate standard of living, Special Rapporteur on the right to food, Special Rapporteur on the situation of human rights and fundamental freedoms of indigenous people, Independent expert on the question of human rights and extreme poverty, independent expert on the right to development, Special Rapporteur on the right to health. The following country mandates are in existence at the time of writing: Special Rapporteur on the situation of human rights in Afghanistan, Special Rapporteur on the situation of human rights in Iraq, Special Rapporteur on the situation of human rights in Myanmar, Special Rapporteur on the situation of human rights in the Palestinian territories occupied by Israel since 1967, Special Rapporteur on the situation of human rights in Bosnia and Herzegovina and the Federal Republic of Yugoslavia, Special Rapporteur on the situation of human rights in the Democratic Republic of the Congo, Special Rapporteur on the situation of human rights in the Sudan, Special Rapporteur on the situation of human rights in Burundi, Special Representative of the Secretary-General for human rights in Cambodia, independent expert on the situation of human rights in Somalia, independent expert on the situation of human rights in Haiti. The following works deal with the special procedures system: J. Carey, *UN Protection of Civil and Political Rights*, (Syracuse University Press, New York, 1970); T. Zuijdwijk, *Petitioning the United Nations* (Gower/St Martins Press, Aldershot/New York, 1982); M. Tardu, *Human Rights: The International Petition System* (Oceana, Dobbs Ferry, NY, 1979-); A. Dormenval, *Procédures onusiennes de mise en oeuvre des droits de l'homme* (PUF, Paris, 1991); M. Lempinen, *Challenges Facing the System of Special Procedures of the United Nations Commission on Human Rights* (Institute for Human Rights, Abo Akademi University, Turku/Abo, 2001), whose chapter 8 also addresses the relationship between the special procedures and the treaty bodies.

performance was not precluded under the Charter's non-intervention rule, that view was not to prevail for some two decades.[3]

On the other hand, there could be no such problem if a state voluntarily agreed to the monitoring activity by means of adherence to a treaty that provided for it. In the words of one of the most renowned framers of the Universal Declaration of Human Rights,

> 'il aurait été difficile de contester que les Etats pouvaient par la voie d'instruments juridiques particuliers prendre des engagements qui faisaient ressortir les obligations qu'ils assumaient ainsi en matière des droits de l'homme du domaine de leur compétence interne.'[4]

Thus it was that supervisory procedures were envisaged as a necessary part of the two treaties that, with the Universal Declaration, were to complete the International Bill of Human Rights: the International Covenant on Economic Social and Cultural Rights (ICESCR)[5] and the International Covenant on Civil and Political Rights (ICCPR) (1966).[6] As it happened, the protracted process of agreeing on the Covenants made it possible for the specialized International Convention on the Elimination of All Forms of Racial Discrimination (ICERD) to be adopted a year earlier, with its own supervisory body.[7] The drafting of the three other specialized conventions now in force (the Convention on the Elimination of All Forms of Discrimination against Women (CEDAW)[8], the Convention against Torture and Other Cruel, Inhuman or Degrading Treatment or Punishment (CAT)[9] and the Convention on the Rights of the Child (CRC)[10]) began before the beginnings of the thematic special procedures.

As evidenced by the current debate as to whether the envisaged Convention against Enforced Disappearance should have its own supervisory body, it may be speculated whether the treaty bodies would have been created had extra-

---

[3] H. Lauterpacht, *International Law and Human Rights* (Stevens, London, 1950), pp. 168–73.

[4] R. Cassin, Hague Recueil 1951, 27, 310.

[5] *See* M. Craven, *The International Covenant on Civil and Political Rights* (Clarendon Press, Oxford, 1995).

[6] *See* D. McGoldrick, *The Human Rights Committee* (Clarendon Press, Oxford, 1991); I. Boerefijn, *The Reporting Procedure under the Covenant on Civil and Political Rights* (Intersentia/Hart, Antwerp, Groningen/Oxford, 1999).

[7] *See* N. Lerner, *The UN Convention on the Elimination of All Forms of Racial Discrimination* (Sijthoff and Noordhoff, Alphen aan den Rijn, 2nd edn., 1980).

[8] *See* L. Rehof, *Guide to the Travaux Préparatoires of the United Nations Convention on the Elimination of All Forms of Discrimination against Women* (Nijhoff, Dordrecht, 1993).

[9] *See* H. Burgers and H. Danelius, *The United Nations Convention against Torture* (Nijhoff, Dordrecht, 1988); A. Boulesbaa, *The UN Convention on Torture and the Prospects for Enforcement* (Nijhoff, The Hague, 1999).

[10] *See* A. G. Mower, *The Convention on the Rights of the Child* (Greenwood, Westport, Conn., 1997); S. Detrick, *A Commentary on the United Nations Convention on the Rights of the Child* (Nijhoff, The Hague, 1999).

conventional mechanisms with a comprehensive mandate been achievable at the birth of the UN.[11]

Similarly, the existence of the treaty bodies, once on the horizon, led to early concerns that special procedures should not duplicate their work and, indeed, that the very existence of the special procedures should be reviewed once the treaty bodies were in operation.[12]

In fact, we seem now to be at the stage where, despite periodic reviews of each of the two systems – treaty bodies[13] and special procedures[14] – there is no serious proposal to roll back one system in favour of the other. Rather the purpose of this essay is to explore to what extent the two systems act separately and act cooperatively. This will permit an evaluation that will conclude that by and large their activities are complementary.

SCOPE OF THE ANALYSIS

It would require a substantially deeper and broader examination than space here permits to consider every aspect of actual and potential overlap of the mandates of all six treaty bodies and twenty odd thematic special procedures. Indeed, the subject-matter of the mandates of the two general treaty bodies, the Human Rights Committee (HRC) established under the ICCPR and the Committee on Economic, Social and Cultural Rights (CESCR) established under the ICESCR, is potentially co-extensive with each a part of each special procedures mandate. However, as will appear, the functions and methods of operation of the two types of bodies are substantially different. To the extent of that difference, their work is manifestly complementary. It is also evident that any potential overlap is mainly applicable in respect of states parties to the treaties.

While some limited attention will be given to commonalities and differences between the work of the general treaty bodies and that of the special procedures, the main focus will be on the commonalities and differences where mandates appear substantially closer, namely, the CAT Committee and the Special Rapporteur on Torture; the CEDAW Committee and the Special Rapporteur on Violence against Women; the ICERD Committee (CERD) and the Special Rapporteur on contemporary forms of racism, racial discrimination, xenophobia and related intolerance; and the CRC Committee and the Special Rapporteur on the sale of

[11] *See* Report submitted by Mr Manfred Nowak, independent expert charged with examining the existing international criminal and human rights framework for the protection of persons from enforced or involuntary disappearances, pursuant to paragraph 11 of Commission [on Human Rights] resolution 2001/46: E/CN.4/2002/71, paras. 99–102.

[12] *See* Ecosoc res. 1235 (XLII), 6 Jun 1967, para. 4; and 1503 (XLVIII), 27 May 1970, para. 10.

[13] *See* the reports of Professor Philip Alston, in UN docs. A/44/68 (1989); A/CONF. 157/PC/62/Add. 11/Rev. 1 (1993); E/CN.4/1997/74 (1997).

[14] See Commission on Human Rights doc. 2000/109, 26 April 2000, and Annex (Report of the Intersessional open-ended working group on enhancing the effectiveness of the mechanisms of the Commission on Human Rights), together with Ecosoc res. 2000/3, 16 Jun 2000.

children, child prostitution and child pornography. If disproportionate attention seems to be given to the work of the CAT Committee and the Special Rapporteur on Torture, it is hoped that this may be as much a reflection of both mechanisms' consistent efforts at cooperation as the result of this writer's inevitably special familiarity with their respective activities.

PURPOSE OF ACTIVITIES

While there might be extensive overlap or potential overlap in the mandate of treaty bodies, on the one hand, and special procedures, on the other, there is little, if any, in their purpose.

The treaties are silent as to the purpose of the functions attributed to the treaty bodies, as are the resolutions establishing or continuing the mandates of the special procedures. Nevertheless, there are differences in context that clearly elucidate their respective purposes. Essentially, I suggest, the treaty bodies should be conceived of as functioning on a bilateral plane, while the special procedures operate on the multilateral plane. This is mainly a matter of formality, but it has substantive implications.

In formal terms, the treaty bodies are typically elected by one multilateral cluster and report to another. That is to say, they are elected by a meeting of states parties and report to the General Assembly.[15] Since the reports of the treaty bodies are not before the meetings of states parties (substantive items on their agendas are usually confined to electing the treaty bodies' members), it is understandable that those meetings not be concerned with the treaty bodies' conclusions and views of compliance or otherwise with the respective treaties.[16] Meanwhile, the General Assembly similarly ignores the country-specific substance of the reports. Arguably, it may be thought inappropriate, unless the treaty were to provide otherwise, for a body, like the Assembly, composed of members not confined to states parties, to take positions on the behaviour of those states that *have* assumed the respective treaty obligations.[17]

Accordingly, it may be inferred that the essential relationship as regards the treaties is that between the treaty bodies and each individual state party. This is a view underlined by the current core function of all of them, namely, the consideration, in dialogue with each state party, of the reports submitted to the treaty bodies by the states parties.

---

[15] The CESCR is anomalous in this respect, as it is established by the Economic and Social Council (Ecosoc), the original body designated to receive and consider states' periodic reports (ICESCR Articles 16, 17). Accordingly, it is elected by and reports to Ecosoc.

[16] It should be noted, however, that some members of the HRC have hinted that a more country-specific substantive role for the meetings could be appropriate: CCPR/C/SR. 1999 (2002).

[17] As the formally constituted treaty body for the ICESCR is Ecosoc, it evidently could have members not states parties reviewing reports of states parties.

By contrast, the special procedures are elected by and report to the same multilateral body, the Commission on Human Rights. Their reports frequently provide the subject matter of discussion, not least in respect of their country-specific reporting, which may even be invoked in debates on whether or not to adopt country specific resolutions.

In addition, as far as the thematic procedures are concerned, they are expected to make recommendations aimed at states generally (these are often reflected in resolutions on the subject matters of the mandates) and, through the Commission, to other parts of the UN and the international community, including non-governmental organizations.[18]

It is, of course, true that, in response to the political impossibility, in their early days, of the treaty bodies' adopting country specific observations, they developed the techniques of the general comment. These are expositions of the treaty body's understanding of the scope and nature of states' obligations under the treaty in question. They have proved to be important, authoritative guides to states, especially when preparing their periodic reports. As such they may cover similar territory to that covered by the special procedures in the recommendations that may be found in their annual reports.

Space does not allow for a detailed comparison of the two types of contribution. Any interested reader is invited to compare the HRC's general comment on ICCPR Article 7 with the compilation of recommendations made by the Special Rapporteur on torture[19], to perceive the different nature of both exercises. In brief, the general comment adopts an expository style, identifying key obligations perceived to be explicit or implicit in the prohibition of torture or cruel, inhuman or degrading treatment or punishment. The compilation of recommendations uses more lapidary language and goes into greater detail in respect of desirable measures. Indeed, the very fact that the Special Rapporteur's functions include, not just identifying the specifics of legal obligation, but also proposing the measures that might be considered good practice with a view to prevention, inevitably affects the content and nature of the two approaches.

So, while much of the work of the special procedures is carried out by means of bilateral communication between each special procedure and individual UN member or observer states, it is done with a view to informing the action of a multilateral body. That action may be country specific, but need not be. Equally, if not more, important is the procedures' function of permitting the Commission to understand certain phenomena on a comparative and global basis, for it then to be able further to address the phenomena on the same basis.

---

[18] *See, e.g.,* the compiled recommendations of the Special Rapporteur on Torture, in E/CN.4/2002/76, Annex I, and Commission on Human Rights res. 2002/38, 22 Apr 2002, especially paras. 1–15.

[19] *Ibid.* (for the compilation); HRC General Comment No. 20: HRI/GEN/1/Rev. 5 (26 April 2001), 139.

It is in this context – the essentially bilateral focus of the treaty bodies and the essentially multilateral focus of the special procedures – that an examination of working methods of both type of mechanism needs to be situated.

WORKING METHODS

It is through an examination of the working methods of each type of mechanism that it can be seen that there is little in the way of overlap and duplication of function.

The treaty bodies have up to four types of activity. First, all have a core function in common, that is, they examine reports to be submitted periodically by states parties. Second, three of them may consider interstate complaints: CERD, on an obligatory basis (ICERD Articles 11–13); the HRC (ICCPR Articles 41–43) and CAT Committee (CAT Article 21), on an optional basis. Third, four of them may on an optional basis consider complaints of violations of the rights of individuals (CERD under ICERD Article 14, HRC under ICCPR Optional Protocol, CAT Committee under CAT Article 22, CEDAW Committee under CEDAW Optional Protocol). Fourth, two of them, the CAT Committee (CAT Article 20) and the CEDAW Committee (CEDAW Optional Protocol) may investigate *of their own motion* apparent systematic torture practices or violations of CAT and CEDAW respectively. These investigations may include on-the-spot visits to particular state parties, with the latters' permission.[20]

The special procedures that engage in systematic actions on alleged violations within their mandates typically undertake the following actions: first, transmittal of allegations of violations and legislative or institutional aspects conducive to violations to governments for their comments; second, sending urgent appeals (usually in individual cases) to prevent possible imminent violations; and, third, undertaking on-the-spot visits to countries with an apparent extensive problem, with the permission of the state in question.[21]

The interrelatedness or otherwise of the activities of both sets of bodies may best be understood by approaching them from three perspectives: general country work, case specific work and general overview activity.

General country work may itself be divided between routine work, investigation work – usually involving on-the-spot fact-finding missions – and, occasionally, urgent appeals. Beginning with *routine general country work*, it is evident that the styles of work between the two types of bodies are very dissimilar. The typical core work of the treaty bodies involves an examination of reports, article by article, submitted periodically by states parties. The reports, whose quality assuredly varies, are usually dealt with according to a standard formula. The

---

[20] While the CAT Article 20 procedure is automatically applicable in principle, it may be excluded by a reservation made under Article 28. Similarly, the CEDAW procedure may be excluded by means of a reservation made under Optional Protocol Article 10.

[21] The technique may also be used for more general urgent matters: *see* fn. 33 below and accompanying text.

committee in question or a designated sub-group will approve written questions to the government of the state party which then sends a delegation to a session of the committee to present the report and respond to the questions, as well as to oral questions members may choose to put by way of follow-up. Thus, the report is the basis of the exercise and the main formal source of information.

Except for the CESCR and the CRC Committee, NGOs will have no formal role and their information no formal status. In practice, the Secretariat makes arrangements to facilitate the transmission of NGO information to individual committee members and to permit NGOs to brief interested committee members.[22] It is evident that the NGO information looms large in the ability of the committee and its members to pose the kinds of questions necessary to elicit from the state party's delegation a fuller sense than typically apparent from its report, of the actual practice in that state. The questions, particularly written ones, will normally be formulated in general terms, although they may well be based on individual cases. Of course, individual cases taken up by the committees that have dealt with such cases in their optional procedures may well figure in the questions. Despite having no formal status, NGO information effectively provides a sort of continuing education or refresher course to enhance the expertise of committee members for the purposes of the exercise at hand. As will be seen below, treaty bodies or, at least, their members increasingly have access to other independent sources of information, such as the findings of other treaty bodies and of the special procedures themselves.

The centrepiece of the exercise is the dialogue with the government delegation.[23] In response to the written and oral questions, the delegation is able to clarify legal and factual questions and give important contextual orientation. Follow-up oral questions can elicit direct responses, prevarication or no response, all of which permit the committee in question to assess the reality sought to be elucidated by the questions.

Even in the days before the committees began formulating concluding observations on the basis of the exchange, there were, as there remain, at least three important outcomes of the exercise. One was the learning process for the state party, through the process of preparing the report, involved in examining its own legal system from the perspective of the requirements of a seriously undertaken international instrument. The second was having to submit to and absorb critical reactions by members from all parts of the world, to whose election they had been a party. The third, however intangible and unsusceptible of measurement, yet perhaps

[22] This of itself represents an evolution: in the early days of the HRC, for example, NGOs had to post or distribute personally to individual members willing to receive it, any material they wished to be considered; the argument was that since the material had no official status, the Secretariat should not be involved in processing or disseminating it; *see* Boerefijn, *supra* note 6, pp. 216–220.

[23] There has been a tentative trend towards conducting a review where the state party fails over a long period to submit a due report or where it constantly delays sending a delegation. The main purpose here is to prod the state into submitting the report or appearing, not to have a hearing in absentia: see HRC Rules of Procedure (CCPR/C/3/Rev. 6), Rules 69A and 68(2).

the most important, was the dialogue itself. A delegation, typically consisting of senior officials responsible for law enforcement and the administration of justice and diplomats, flanks the Committee chairperson and faces the Committee in a formally arranged chamber; it has come for the purposes of undergoing an act of formal and public accountability regarding the extent to which the state party it represents has given effect to a set of obligations that it has solemnly assumed by ratifying or acceding to the treaty in question. No individual Special Rapporteur, special representative or advisory services expert under the special procedures system has anything comparable. Certainly, the few special procedures working groups may, like their one-person counterparts, have meetings with representatives of states, in respect of which they are seeking to elucidate facts or arrange possible missions. But these are *ad hoc*, informal and private. They have nothing of the ceremonial nature of the reviews by treaty bodies of state reports.

For the last ten or so years, there has been a much more concrete outcome of the review process carried out by the treaty bodies, namely, the concluding observations.[24] The crucial parts of these are their findings under the notion of 'subjects of concern' and the recommendations made to the state party to address the concerns. Where the concerns relate to factually contested matter, they will usually refer to 'allegations' of violations rather than to 'violations' *tout court*. Nevertheless, the very inclusion of the allegations will at least signify that the state party has failed effectively to refute their credibility. Moreover, in the practice of at least one committee, the HRC, the seriousness of the concerns will be reflected in the follow-up information or action requested of the state party in the concluding observations. The actual follow-up may also affect the timing of the subsequent periodic report.[25]

The approach of the action-oriented special procedures is very different. Most of the material they transmit to governments is in the form of individual case allegations, to which the governments may or may not respond. The main source, which will be authorized as a source by the resolutions establishing their mandates, will be NGOs.[26] Where the allegations they receive include general material, for instance, assessing the scope of the practice or describing legal impediments to the prevention of the phenomenon, then states will also be invited to comment on these. In the early years of their mandates, the country entries in their reports to the Commission on Human Rights tended to restrict themselves to a summary of allegations transmitted and any replies received. To the extent that this represented a dialogue, it was primarily a written one. Many subsequently formulated observations

[24] Until 1992, the HRC was not prepared to interpret its power to make 'general comments', under ICCPR Article 40(4), as empowering it to make country-specific comments, as opposed to comments of a general nature: *see* Boerefijn, *supra* note 6, ch. XIV and pp. 303–6.

[25] *See* HRC Rules of Procedure (CCPR/C/3/Rev. 6), Rule 70A.

[26] For example, by Ecosoc res. 1982/35, 7 May 1992, which, on the recommendation of the Commission, established the mandate of the Special Rapporteur on summary or arbitrary executions, the Special Rapporteur would seek and receive information from governments and international governmental and non-governmental organisations.

on the correspondence, in the way of provisional judgment and rather general recommendations. These generally consist of a few sentences. They are inevitably limited by the fluctuating information they may receive in any given year and the limited nature of the information on the political and legal context in which the allegations of individual violations are said to occur. Accordingly, while their reporting is annual, they have little of the sustained consideration of the issues that the treaty bodies' reviews of periodic reports evince. On the other hand, the wealth of case specific material can give a sense of the scope and gravity of a problem that is missing from the process of periodic reporting to the treaty bodies.

Only two of the treaty bodies are expressly empowered to engage in *investigative country work*, including the use of on-the-spot visits. So any area of potential overlap with the special procedures only applies to the CAT Committee (Article 20) and the CEDAW Committee (Optional Protocol). The latter so far has no experience since the power has only recently been granted and that only in respect of the as yet small number of states parties to the Optional Protocol. The CAT Committee's power applies to all states parties except the few which have availed themselves of the option in CAT Article 28 to exclude the power. Yet, here too the experience is limited. It is understood that there have been six enquiries into suspected systematic practices of torture. The summary reports of three are in the public domain: Turkey,[27] Egypt[28] and Peru.[29] The reports on Turkey and Peru are based on on-the-spot fact-finding visits. That on Egypt is not, the government having availed itself of the right to refuse to receive a committee delegation.

The three published reports show the value of sustained study. They deal with a broad range of allegations and consider in detail the legal and institutional framework in which the problem is manifested. The Turkey and Peru reports suggest that the in-country experience permits the committee to make less tentative conclusions (the Egypt report makes greater use of 'allegations' to qualify its assessment), more detailed analysis of the legal issues and more specific recommendations reflecting the greater understanding of the local scene. In sum, they demonstrate the undoubted value of an on-the-spot visit to come to grips with the legal and practical realities of the human rights situation.

The country visit has become routine for most special procedures. Of course, states remain free to refuse access, but a substantial number set a more positive example. Indeed, there is now a practice of states' giving blanket prior agreement to visits by any special procedure, some 38 having done so at the time of writing.[30] The interest of the special procedures in country visits is assuredly because of the benefits described above. Direct access to civil society and most relevant levels of officialdom permits an 'immersion course' in the historical, constitutional, legal and operational framework of the problems being studied. Insistence on the conditions of access contained in the standard terms of reference for fact-finding visits make

---

[27] UN doc. A/48/44A (1994).
[28] UN doc. A/51/44 (1996), ch. V B.
[29] UN doc. A/56/44 (2001), ch. V B.
[30] *See* website of the Association for the Prevention of Torture: <www.apt/ch/un/hrc58.htm>.

possible, in this writer's experience, substantial uncovering of those aspects of the reality that governments prefer to conceal and which, indeed, may be unknown to important higher-level decision makers, whether by preference or inadvertence.

So far the potential for overlap has applied only to the CAT Committee acting under CAT Article 20 and the Special Rapporteur on torture. Any such overlap or duplication has been avoided by the Special Rapporteur's policy of not seeking to visit a country in respect of which the CAT Committee has initiated an Article 20 enquiry. On the other hand, there is evidently room for complementary action. Thus, in 1997, five years after the CAT Committee visited Turkey, the Special Rapporteur also sought a visit, which took place in 1998.[31] Since neither mechanism has the resources that would make follow-up visits practicable, the Special Rapporteur's visit was able to serve as a *de facto* follow-up to the Committee's visit. More recently, the CAT Committee is understood to have engaged in a mission to a country previously visited by the Special Rapporteur, with potentially equally symbiotic effect. In addition, in the light of Egypt's refusal of access to the Committee, the Special Rapporteur did not hesitate to seek an invitation to visit that country, albeit no such invitation was forthcoming.[32]

One final aspect of special procedure activity relevant to general country work, for which there is no counterpart in the methods of the treaty bodies, is the urgent appeal. As will be noted below, urgent appeals are normally used by special procedures in individual cases, by way of seeking to avert harm to individuals feared to be at risk. However, the technique may occasionally be resorted to for a more general purpose. For instance, four procedures jointly appealed to Peru to refrain from adopting a constitutional amendment aimed at permitting an amnesty for crimes committed by security forces in counter-emergency operations.[33] The only analogous treaty body measure available is the request for a special report from the state party.[34]

To the extent that some treaty bodies and several special procedures are engaged in **case specific work**, this at first sight could be a source of overlap and duplication. A closer look reveals that the perception is largely illusory. The area of potential overlap is, in any event, limited. It covers only individual cases that could be the subject of communications to the Human Rights Committee in respect of state parties to the Optional Protocol to the ICCPR, to the CAT Committee in respect of states parties that have made the requisite declaration under CAT Article 22, to the

[31] UN doc. E/CN.4/1999/61/Add. 1. The Special Rapporteur sought the invitation in 1995: E/CN.4/1996/35, para. 178. The Committee's visit had taken place in 1992.

[32] The Committee reported in 1996 (*see supra* note 28) and the Special Rapporteur sought the invitation in 1997: UN doc. E/CN.4/1998/38, para. 4.

[33] The four procedures were the Working Group on Enforced or Involuntary Disappearances and the Special Rapporteurs on extrajudicial, summary or arbitrary executions, on torture, and on the independence of judges and lawyers: UN doc. E/CN.4/1996/35, paras. 133–6.

[34] *For example*, the Committee against Torture sought a special report from Israel in 1996, which was submitted in 1997: UN doc. CAT/C/33/Add. 2/Rev. 1.

CERD in respect of states parties that have made the requisite declaration under ICERD Article 14 and to the CEDAW Committee in respect of states parties to the CEDAW Optional Protocol.

Moreover, the nature of the activity of the two types of mechanisms is generally different. The treaty bodies, when considering individual cases, do so for the purpose of formulating 'views' as to whether or not there has been a violation. This is the practice of only one of the special procedures. While, as noted earlier, they seek information from states in respect of allegations of individual violations, they do so in the framework of reporting the dialogue and perhaps making observations on the problem in general in the state. Except for the Working Group on Arbitrary Detention, they do not systematically engage in formulating judgmental conclusions on each case. The Human Rights Committee, tellingly, does not generally consider the activities of the special procedures as 'procedures of international investigation or settlement', as precluded by ICCPR Optical Protocol Article 5(2)(a).[35]

The Working Group, on the other hand, has from the beginning had a specific mandate of 'investigating' cases of arbitrary detention.[36] In the light of this wording, it does make reasoned findings (currently called 'opinions'[37]) on whether the case involves a violation of the right not to be subjected to arbitrary detention. This could evidently involve overlap with a case coming before the Human Rights Committee, especially under ICCPR Article 9. Indeed, in respect of one case submitted to both bodies, the Working Group transmitted the case to the Human Rights Committee, once it became aware of the situation.[38] It is also understood that attempts are made in the Secretariat to steer cases in the right direction. For example, in a case where domestic remedies have been exhausted the Secretariat may process it under the Optional Protocol, while in one where they have not, it may be processed for the attention of the Working Group. Here, however, much will depend on the familiarity of staff members with the different procedures, a task rendered more difficult by the fact that the relevant staff work in separate branches.

As far as the treaty bodies and special procedures are concerned, the duplication is not of function, but of potential inconvenience to a state receiving multiple requests. This can be a problem within the cluster of special procedures, as well as between them and the treaty bodies. Ideally, systems in the Secretariat would ensure that in such cases, states are invited to make their responses to each of the mechanisms involved.

---

[35] *For example*, the HRC was not precluded from dealing with a case also under study by the Special Rapporteur on summary or arbitrary executions: *Baboeram et al* v. *Suriname* (146/1983 and 148-54/1983), A/40/40 (1985) Annex X, para. 9.1.

[36] Commission res. 1991/42, 5 Mar 1991.

[37] Commission res. 1997/50, 15 Apr 1997, para. 7, required the Group to give 'views', rather than 'decisions'. In response, it has chosen the word 'opinions'.

[38] *Arredondo Guevara* v. *Peru*, Opinion 4/2000, UN doc. E/CN.4/2001/14/Add. 1, 61; the HRC considered that the case remained admissible in the light of the Group's reference of the case to the HRC without any expression of its views: UN doc. A/55/40, Vol. II (2000), Annex IX E.

As noted earlier, the special procedures have developed the method of issuing urgent appeals to states in circumstances where a violation within their mandates is feared to be about to take place or to be taking place. They constitute routine preventive work for several of the procedures that use them, especially the Working Group on Enforced or Involuntary Disappearances, the Special Rapporteurs on extrajudicial, arbitrary or summary executions, and on torture, and the Special Representative on Human Rights Defenders.[39]

The only comparable measure currently used by the treaty bodies is the interim measure, whereby the body seeks suspension of a formal measure believed to be imminent in a state party, pending its consideration of the substance of the complaint. Thus, for example, the Human Rights Committee, through its Special Rapporteur on New Communications, is empowered under Rule 86 of its Rules of Procedure to request interim measures by a state party to avoid irreparable damage, for instance an execution taking place before the HRC is able to assess the compatibility of the penalty with the state party's obligations under the ICCPR.[40] The HRC and CAT Committee act similarly in the case of threatened expulsions from states parties to states where the alleged potential victim would be at risk of torture.[41]

It is not impossible to conceive that the treaty bodies, resources permitting, might adopt an urgent appeals system similar to that of the special procedures. However, it is unlikely that they would do so outside the formal framework of action on individual cases pursuant to the optional individual complaints procedures. Since the latter involves compliance with the rule of exhaustion of domestic remedies and the maintenance of confidentiality until the case is either declared inadmissible or is the subject of final views, any urgent action would presumably be likely to be constrained by the domestic remedies rule and the same confidentiality. For the special procedures, there are no similar constraints. They can take up a case, regardless of the stage it may be at in the domestic legal system. They may, following a mandated requirement to use 'discretion' in their work,[42] not usually report publicly on the actions until they issue their annual reports, but there is no

---

[39] Office of the High Commissioner for Human Rights, Seventeen Frequently Asked Questions about United Nations Special Rapporteurs, Fact Sheet No. 27 (2001), 9; N. Rodley, 'Urgent Action', in G. Alfredsson, J. Grimheden, B. Ramcharan and A. de Zayas (eds.), *International Human Rights Monitoring Mechanisms - Essays in Honour of Jakob Th. Möller* (Nijhoff, The Hague/Boston/London, 2001), pp. 279–83.

[40] A. de Zayas, 'The Examination of Individual Complaints by the United Nations Human Rights Committee under the Optional Protocol to the International Covenant on Civil and Political Rights', in G. Alfredsson, J. Grimheden, B. Ramcharan and A. de Zayas, *supra* note. 39, pp. 67, 79–81.

[41] Pursuant to Rule 108(9) of the CAT Committee's Rules of Procedure; *see, e.g.,* Case No. 121/1998 (*S. H.* v. *Norway*), UN doc. A/55/44 (2000), Annex VIII. B. 4, para. 1.2.

[42] *See, e.g.*, Commission on Human Rights res. 1985/33, para. 6 (establishing the mandate of the Special Rapporteur on torture).

rule of confidentiality and some have also used press releases to draw public attention to the appeal. Indeed, if the work of the treaty bodies is one that is, as has been seen, characterized by its formality, that of the special procedures is more notable for its flexibility.

EXTENT OF DIRECT COOPERATION

One factor representing a pull towards common endeavour is the very existence of the relevant treaties. These establish the mandates of the treaty bodies, but they are also essential sources of legitimacy for the activities of the special procedures. Thus, the CAT will frequently be invoked by the Special Rapporteurs on torture and on violence against women, as will the ICERD by the Special Rapporteur on Racial Discrimination and the CRC by the Special Rapporteur on the sale of children.[43] Of course, it is essential that the special procedures not seem to arrogate to themselves the role of guardians of the treaties, a role that belongs to the treaty bodies. Rather, they base themselves on general international law or normative standards. These may be reflected in various sources, such as declarations, resolutions and other manifestations of acceptable state practice. For example, the Special Rapporteur on torture will frequently invoke the 1975 General Assembly Declaration against Torture,[44] especially vis-à-vis states not party to the CAT, as well as other 'soft-law' instruments.[45] Yet, where a particular rule or type of recommended behaviour promoted by the Special Rapporteur is covered by the CAT, it would be perverse for him to refrain from invoking the relevant CAT provision in communication with states that are, in fact, parties to the Convention. Certainly, a special procedure should be careful in adopting a controversial interpretation of a human rights treaty monitored by a treaty body, especially if that interpretation is at odds with that of the treaty body. Yet, the silence of the treaty body need not necessarily preclude the special procedure from staking out a position. For instance, the Special Rapporteur, where constrained to address the appropriateness of including corporal punishment within his mandate, could not but explore the relevance of the CAT in support of his

[43] UN doc. E/CN.4/2001/66/Add. 2, paras. 149–51 (Special Rapporteur on torture, report on visit to Brazil); UN doc. E/CN.4/2000/68/Add. 3, para. 76 (Special Rapporteur on violence against women, report on visit to Haiti); UN doc. E/CN.4/1994/66, para. 10 (Special Rapporteur on racism, annual report, describing ICERD as 'the basic international legal instrument' relevant to his mandate); UN doc. E/CN.4/2002/88, para. 13 (Special Rapporteur on sale of children, annual report, describing the CRC and its Optional Protocol on the sale of children, child prostitution and child pornography as 'the foundation for determining and developing the scope of the mandate').

[44] These references will be in letters transmitting allegations to governments, but do not appear in the heavily summarised versions found in the annual reports; it also figured in his analysis of the relevance of his mandate to the problem of corporal punishment: UN doc. E/CN.4/1997/7, para. 6.

[45] *E.g.,* UN doc. E/CN.4/1994/31, para. 135, referring to the Body of Principles for the Protection of All Persons under Any Form of Detention or Imprisonment (GA res. 43/173, 9 Dec 1988).

contention that the practice did fall within the mandate.[46] The CAT Committee appears subsequently to have taken the same view.[47]

The special procedures also typically promote ratification of the treaties of most concern to their mandates, with some also advocating acceptance of their optional complaints procedures.[48] This is a role proper to them that would be minimally appropriate for the treaty bodies themselves. In doing so, they are inevitably promoting the importance of the work of the treaty bodies. After one visit (to Sierra Leone), the Special Rapporteur on violence against women even recommended that the authorities submit a report to the CEDAW.[49]

While they may not formally invoke the country-specific findings of the special procedure, the treaty bodies routinely have access to and cite in the oral dialogue the findings of special procedures. This is especially the case where the findings are those of a country-specific special procedures or of a thematic one which has recently reported on a country visit. For example, the report of the Special Rapporteur on torture on his visit to Brazil in 2000 was referred to in the CAT Committee's dialogue with that country in 2001.[50] While, in view of the confidentiality of Committee discussions of the list of issues to be presented to a state party in advance of the review and of their concluding observations, the point cannot be documented, it is my experience of the Human Rights Committee that the findings and recommendations of these special procedures reports will also influence the issues identified in the list of issues and recommendations in the concluding observations. It is my understanding that the same is true for other treaty bodies, notably the CAT Committee.

The work of the treaty bodies may also inform that of the special procedures. Thus, the findings of the CAT Committee's mission to Turkey and its concluding

---

[46] UN doc. E/CN.4/1997/7, paras. 6–8.

[47] *See* Concluding Observation on the Initial Periodic Report of Saudi Arabia: CAT/C/XXVIII/CONCL. 6 (2002), para. 4(b).

[48] *E.g.*, UN doc. E/CN.4/1997/Add. 2, para. 102 (Special Rapporteur on torture, visit to Pakistan: CAT and ICCPR and Optional Protocols); UN doc. E/CN.4/1999/15/Add. 1, para. 90(6) (Special Rapporteur on racism, visit to South Africa: ICERD); UN doc. E/CN.4/2000/68/Add. 3, para. 76 (Special Rapporteur on violence against women, report on visit to Haiti: CAT); UN doc. E/CN.4/1997/95/Add. 2, ch. VII (Special Rapporteur on the sale of children, visit to United States of America: CRC); inexplicably the former Special Rapporteur on the sale of children omitted to recommend that the Russian Federation ratify the Optional Protocol to the Convention on the Rights of the Child on the sale of children, child prostitution and child pornography, adopted by GA res. 263, 25 May 2000, after her visit to that country in October 2000 (UN doc. E/CN.4/2001/78/Add. 2).

[49] UN doc. E/CN.4/2002/83/Add. 2, para. 115.

[50] CAT/C/SR. 471 (2001), para. 39 (Ms Gaer); in its concluding observations, the Committee requested 'information concerning measures taken by the public authorities to implement throughout the country, the recommendations … of the Special Rapporteur on torture to which the State party delegation referred during the dialogue with the Committee': A/56/44 (2001), para. 120(i).

observations on Mexico loomed large in his discussions with the authorities during the visit of the Special Rapporteur on torture to those countries.[51] The same Special Rapporteur has routinely included in his observations at the end of country visits entries in his annual report reference to the findings of the HRC and the CAT Committee in their concluding observations.[52] While this may not be standard practice for the special procedures, the work of the treaty bodies may inform their recommendations in other ways. For instance, in the report of her visit to Colombia, the Special Rapporteur on violence against women urged the government to comply with the CEDAW recommendations after its review of Colombia's fourth periodic report.[53] On the other hand, the CERD in 1999 took the unusual step of publicly lamenting that the Special Rapporteur on racism 'appears to completely overlook the relevance' of the ICERD.[54] While it is unfortunately true that he had apparently overlooked the CERD's concluding observations in the reports on several country visits,[55]in that very year he did refer to them in his annual report in respect of the scheduled tribes and castes of India.[56] It may be speculated whether this reflected an awareness of the concern within CERD. Certainly, by 2001, the report of his visit to Australia made reference to CERD's concluding observations.[57]

As far as direct contact between the special procedures and the treaty bodies is concerned, it appears that only the Special Rapporteur on torture and the CAT Committee consistently have joint meetings.[58] The main topic of these is to ensure precisely that the two mechanisms maximise the complementarities of their work and minimize duplication. On one occasion, responding to a Committee member's question, the Special Rapporteur gave reasons why he thought there would be difficulties for the Special Rapporteur to submit situations that the Committee might study under CAT Article 20.[59] At their most recent meeting, cooperation in respect of Article 20 was further explored.[60] Another topic of the meetings has become

[51] E/CN.4/1999/61/Add. 1, para. 104 (visit to Turkey); the report of the visit to Mexico (E/CN.4/1998/38/Add. 2) is, regrettably, silent on the point, which is a matter of my personal recollection.

[52] *E.g.,* most recently, E/CN.4/2001/66, paras. 50 (Argentina), 63 (Armenia), 68 (Australia), 167 (Belarus), 231 (Cameroon), 235–6 (Chile), 330-31 (China), 349 (Congo), 475–6 (Egypt), 688 (Kyrgyzstan), 843 (Peru), 857 (Portugal), 1223 (United States of America).

[53] UN doc. E/CN.4/2002/Add. 2, para. 120.

[54] UN doc. A/52/18, para. 666; see K. Boyle and A. Baldaccini, 'A Critical Evaluation of International Human Rights Approaches to Racism', in S. Fredman (ed.), *Discrimination and Human Rights – The Case of Racism* (OUP, Oxford, 2001), pp. 135, 183–4.

[55] T. Van Boven, 'United Nations Strategies to Combat Racism and Racial Discrimination: A Sobering but not Hopeless Balance Sheet', in M. Castermans et al. (eds.), *The Role of the Nation-State in the 21st Century* (Kluwer, The Hague, 1998), pp. 251, 261.

[56]UN doc. E/CN.4/1999/15, paras. 88–100.

[57] E/CN.4/2002/24/Add. 1, para. 1.

[58] *See, e.g.*, UN doc. E/CN.4/1995/34, para. 6; UN doc. A/55/40 (2000), para. 17.

[59] CAT/C/SR. 187 (1994), paras. 19–21.

[60] United Nations Press Release, CAT, 28th session, 25 May 2002, morning: 'Committee against Torture holds dialogue with Special Rapporteur on torture'.

agreeing on a joint text, together with the Voluntary Fund for Victims of Torture and the High Commissioner for Human Rights, to commemorate the International Day in Support of Victims of Torture (June 26).[61] However, the new Special Rapporteur on the sale of children recently had a meeting with the CRC Committee with a view to seeking closer cooperation with the Committee and attended a thematic meeting convened by the Committee.[62] His predecessor had attended similar thematic meetings.[63]

In general, a recent study considers the cooperation between both Special Rapporteurs and both Committees to be an exception.[64] It finds that the same does not apply to the relationship between the CEDAW Committee and the Special Rapporteur on violence against women or that between CERD and the Special Rapporteur on racism.[65] The same source indicates dissatisfaction by these treaty bodies with the absence of contact,[66] although it is my understanding that the Special Rapporteur on violence against women has sought such contact with the CEDAW Committee.[67] It is hoped that by 2003 a meeting may take place. Except for an initial, apparently positive, exploratory meeting in 1995,[68] the only contact between CERD and the Special Rapporteur on racism that I have been able to identify is the attendance by the former at a one-day meeting on Roma convened in 2001 by the CERD.[69] On the other hand, the Special Rapporteur apparently had a meeting in 2001 with the Secretary of the CERD which considered ways and means of enhancing cooperation between them.[70] In the light of the positive relationship between the torture-related and child-related mechanisms, it is difficult to comprehend why that of the others should not be similar. It cannot be excluded that a (misplaced) perception of potential competition is a factor.

There is no doubt that the Human Rights Committee has not sought systematic contacts with the special procedures, respectful as it may be of their contribution, through their reports, to its work. Since most of them are relevant to its work, a practice of holding meetings with them would be an added burden on an already overcharged agenda. Presumably juridical considerations do not loom large. It is true that there is nothing in the ICCPR envisaging such contacts, but a similar

---

[61] *See, e.g.*, UN doc. A/55/44 (2000), paras. 17–8 and Annex V.

[62] UN doc. E/CN.4/2002/88, para. 34; CRC/C/111 (2001), para. 670.

[63] *E.g.,* she attended the CRC Committee's day of discussion on state violence against children: UN doc. E/CN.4/2001/78, para. 6; so did the Special Rapporteur on torture: UN doc. E/CN.4/2001/66, para. 15.

[64] A. Bayefsky, *The UN Human Rights Treaty System* (Transnational, Ardsley, NY, 2001), 56.

[65] *Ibid.*

[66] *Ibid.*

[67] Information kindly provided by the human rights officer who services the mandate of the Special Rapporteur, on file with the author.

[68] UN doc. A/50/476 (1995), paras. 26–32; see K. Boyle and A. Baldaccini, *supra* note 54.

[69] UN doc. A/55/304 (2000), para. 19.

[70] Information kindly provided by the human rights officer who services the mandate of the Special Rapporteur, on file with the author.

absence in the ICERD, CAT and the CRC has not prevented the contacts referred to. Certainly, the CESCR, as a sub-organ of ECOSOC has no formal inhibitions, nor does it apparently have practical ones. In 2001 it had an exchange of views with the Special Rapporteur on adequate housing 'with a view to exploring the scope of appropriate cooperation between the Committee and the Special Rapporteur'.[71] In the same year, evidencing that this was no isolated incident, the Committee announced that it would

> 'look into ways of further strengthening its cooperation with the relevant special rapporteurs of the Commission on Human Rights (including the special rapporteurs on adequate housing, on the right to education, on the right to food, on violence against women, its causes and consequences, on the sale of children, child prostitution and child pornography and on the human rights of migrants) and with its independent experts (on the right to development, on the question of human rights and extreme poverty and on structural adjustment and foreign debt . . .'[72]

What is clear is that at the group level both sets of procedures have been keen to develop an annual consultation. Starting with the attendance in 1996 of the chairperson of the third annual meeting of special procedures at the seventh session of the meeting of persons chairing human rights treaty bodies,[73] the chair of that session of the treaty body meeting attended the fourth special procedures meeting in 1997, as did the chair of the CESCR.[74] So, the following year did the chair of the Committee against Torture.[75] By 1999, the scheduling of both meetings was such as to permit the first joint session of the chairs of treaty bodies and the special procedures, of which by the time of writing there have been a further two.[76]

It is beyond the scope of this essay to examine the details of this evolving cross-system dialogue. Perhaps the most significant aspect of it is that it manifestly corresponds to a shared perceived need. One facet of the need is that of improving mutual knowledge and understanding of each group of mechanisms. Inevitably, the meetings can only help partially: each of the six treaty bodies can convey what it wishes to the assembled special procedures, but not all the special procedures can do the same in a brief meeting, nor can the treaty body chairs reasonably be expected to be an effective conduit to the whole membership of the Committee he or she represents. Moreover, the regular turnover of special procedures mandate holders and treaty body chairs limits the possibility of entrenching the information and ideas exchanged.

---

[71] UN doc. E/2002/22; UN doc. E/C.12/2001/17, para. 1066.

[72] *Ibid.,* para. 1050. I am grateful to my University of Essex colleague Professor Paul Hunt, who is also Rapporteur of the CESCR, for providing me with this information.

[73] UN doc. A/51/482 (1996), paras. 8, 53.

[74] UN doc. E/CN.4/1998/45, paras. 9, 34–43.

[75] UN doc. E/CN.4/1999/3, paras. 10, 33–42.

[76] UN doc. E/CN.4/2000/5, paras. 30–1 (first); UN doc. E/CN.4/2001/6, paras. 71–6 (second); UN doc. E/CN.4/2002/14, paras. 69–75 and Appendix V (third).

The constant theme to be found in the reports of their first three joint meetings is the intense focus on the importance of promoting full awareness by mechanisms of each group of the activities and output of the mechanisms of the other group. The key role of the Secretariat in making that happen is evidenced by increasingly insistent demands for feedback on the recommendations, notably, those requesting the Secretariat to put in place systems that would facilitate the desired information exchange.[77]

The joint meetings have, with some nuance that doubtless reflects a certain diffidence by some treaty bodies, given their blessing in principle to the notion of bilateral meetings between treaty bodies and relevant special procedures. In the words of the recommendation from the first meeting:

> 'The joint meeting encouraged the treaty bodies to call, as they felt necessary, for the cooperation of the special procedures, including the possibility of a direct exchange of information during their respective sessions.'[78]

By the third joint meeting, the tone, albeit in the passive voice, seemed somewhat less doubtful: 'Increased emphasis should be placed on organising meetings between special procedures mandate holders and the treaty bodies'.[79]

In terms of the overall theme of this essay, the will towards cooperation rather than competition was best stated in the first sentence of the first recommendation of the first joint meeting: 'The joint meeting emphasised that the work of each group of mechanisms is equally and mutually important'.[80]

CONCLUSION

It may be that, had the UN from the beginning been ready to establish a human rights monitoring system analogous to that found in the current special procedures system, it might not have then gone on to create the system of treaty bodies. Yet the existence of the two systems cannot be properly understood as creating duplication and overlap.

The implicit purpose of each system is substantially different. The structural features of the elective and reporting constituencies of type of mechanism places them on essentially separate planes: bilateral for the treaty bodies, multilateral for the special procedures. This is connected with a different style of communication; characterized by dialogue, in the case of the treaty bodies, and fact-elucidation, in the case of the special procedures. The main focus of the treaty bodies, particularly through their core function of reviewing states' reports is to promote enhanced

---

77 *Ibid.*

78 UN doc. E/CN.4/2000/5, para. 31(b). The present author chaired that year's meeting of Special Rapporteurs and co-chaired the joint meeting.

79 UN doc. E/CN.4/2002/14, Appendix V.

80 UN doc.E/CN.4/2000/5. para. 31(a).

respect for the human rights enshrined in the treaty obligations, with general comments being merely an attendant product aiming to give states guidance on the nature and scope of other obligations for their reports. A main focus, if not the only one, of the thematic special procedures is to provide the whole UN membership with comparative and global understanding of the human rights problem in question, as well as with guidance on how to deal with it.

As far as actual working methods are concerned, there is surprisingly little overlap. The special procedures have no equivalent of the treaty bodies' review of periodic reports. The concluding observations of the treaty bodies at the close of the review is of a much more sustained analysis of the country's human rights problems and recommendations to address them, than the observations in the country entries in the special procedures' annual reports. Meanwhile, the special procedures are able to engage in yet more sophisticated fact-finding (and consequent recommendation-making) through the use of on-the-spot visits. Only the CAT and CEDAW Committees have similar powers, the former exercising them sparingly, the latter not yet having had the chance to test them. Any overlap or duplication was avoided by the Special Rapporteur on torture's refraining from seeking to visit a country subject to a CAT Article 20 inquiry by the CAT Committee.

As far as casework is concerned, the special procedures, with one exception (the Working Group on Arbitrary Detention) do not pursue individual cases to a formal conclusion on whether or not there has been a violation, whereas the treaty bodies do just that. In the case of the exception, the problem has been solved in the one case it has arisen, by the Working Group on Arbitrary Detention's deferring the case to the HRC. If that had not happened, it cannot be excluded that such an incident could lead to the HRC's considering the case to be inadmissible by reason of having been submitted to an alternative procedure of international investigation or settlement. That no such thing happens in respect of cases submitted to the other special procedures, testifies to the difference in function between the two types of procedure. Also, improved information management systems within the Secretariat can contribute substantially to the avoidance of duplicative casework.

By contrast the special procedures' use of urgent appeals has no real counterpart in the treaty bodies' methods. In the rare cases where an apparent similar practice exists, it is used by the treaty bodies to preserve the possibility of determining whether or not a violation could occur. The purpose of the special procedures' urgent appeals is to prevent, inhibit or stop any feared violations.

In general, the activities of the treaty bodies reflect the formality of the solemn legal instruments that gave birth to them; those of the special procedures have the flexibility appropriate to their genesis in a UN political body. This does not mean that the special procedures should consider themselves free to act inconsistently, without an established (common or procedure-specific) methodology. Rather, a key aspect for the special procedures is to seek to have some effect and give some guidance in a short or relatively short time frame, whereas for the treaty bodies the very nature of periodic reports and the necessarily protracted process of reaching views on individual cases require a longer term perspective.

This analysis suggests that any area of potential overlap and duplication of work between the two types of mechanism is largely illusory. Where occasionally, it is real, it is avoidable by the application of the treaties' rules on admissibility, by improved information management systems in the Secretariat and by a spirit of cooperation, whereby the special procedures defer to the activities of the treaty bodies.

Underlying any legitimate concern of potential cross-system duplication and overlap is the assumption that the state whose activity in question is a party to the relevant treaty and that, where optional, it has accepted the treaty bodies' scrutinising or complaints functions. It is, therefore, axiomatic that there can be no such duplication or overlap in respect of states that have not adhered to the treaty or accepted the optional procedures. That acceptance would also have to be, as is not presently the case, irrevocable.[81]

Pursuing the same logic, it would also be necessary for the treaty bodies that do not at present engage in on-the-spot fact-finding visits to do so. This would raise the question as to whether they have the implied power to do so or would need a treaty amendment or optional protocol to give them that power (the CEDAW Optional Protocol may be invocable as suggesting, *a contrario*, that there is no such implied power.) The treaty bodies would also have to be able to engage in urgent appeals beyond those merely aimed at preserving their adjudicative functions.

It will be evident that this sort of evolution would in fact involve a transformation in the nature of the treaty body system to approximate that of the special procedures system. Any transformation of this sort cannot reasonably be expected in the near future. More universal ratification of the treaties is still a depressingly distant-goal, despite sustained attempts at promoting it.[82] Presumably acceptance of the optional procedures is yet further off.

So, it would appear that, for the foreseeable future, the two systems will remain what they have been so far, highly complementary means of promoting accountability for compliance with human rights norms. The complementarity is increased by the ability of each system to build on the work of the other. Of course, from the perspective of the state, interest from more than one body, however different the basis of that interest, represents probably unwanted, increased pressure

[81] *For example*, Guyana, Jamaica and Trinidad and Tobago have denounced the Optional Protocol to the ICCPR.

[82] Most recently, the strategy of promoting urgent ratification of the six principal human rights treaties; see Road map towards the implementation of the United Nations Millenium Declaration; Report of the Secretary-General: UN doc. A/56/326 (2001), para. 204.

to address the problem. The human rights perspective must, however, particularly in view of the non-coercive nature of the actions, be that of the potential victim. From that perspective, multiple activity can only help.

LA PROTECCIÓN INTERNACIONAL DE LOS DERECHOS HUMANOS Y EL COMITÉ

Julio Prado Vallejo

I. EVOLUCIÓN DE LOS DERECHOS HUMANOS

El esfuerzo de la humanidad por consagrar los derechos humanos tiene lejanas raíces pero es a partir de la Carta de las Naciones Unidas y de la Declaración Universal de Derechos Humanos que se inicia el desarrollo de un sistema que progresivamente va perfeccionándose y definiendo el alcance y consagración a nivel regional y universal de los derechos humanos.

Una de las tareas más nobles y permanentes de la humanidad ha sido promover y hacer efectivos los derechos inherentes a la persona humana. Largos y penosos años de lucha, sacrificios, angustias y dolores han precedido para que se abra paso y se consagre una nueva concepción de vida cimentada y enaltecida por los Derechos Humanos. En la etapa histórica que hoy vive el mundo, el reconocimiento de los Derechos Humanos iguales e inalienables de todos los miembros de la familia humana es la base de la libertad, la justicia y la paz en el mundo, como lo declara la Carta de las Naciones Unidas.

Los Derechos Humanos no son producto de una ley ni originarios de un sistema jurídico ni otorgados por un gobierno. Ellos valen por si mismos y nacen de la naturaleza del hombre. Lo que hace un sistema jurídico es reconocerlos, garantizarlos, promoverlos. Rigen en cualquier condición en la que el individuo se encuentre y la personalidad jurídica de todo ser humano los torna inalienable, imprescriptibles e irrenunciables. Por un lado, la igualdad jurídica del hombre establece la universalidad de lo Derechos Humanos, y por otro, un ordenamiento jurídico da fe de su existencia, promueve su vigencia, los garantiza en cuanto a su ejercicio o goce, tutelando su respeto, pero los Derechos Humanos son en sí anteriores a toda ley positiva.

La Declaración Universal de Derechos Humanos señala que el desconocimiento y el menosprecio de los Derechos Humanos han originado actos de barbarie ultrajantes para la conciencia de la humanidad y proclama que los Derechos Humanos deben ser 'protegidos por un régimen de derecho, a fin de que el hombre no se vea compelido al supremo recurso de rebelión contra la tiranía y opresión'. La evolución progresiva del derecho internacional consagró como uno de los más relevantes principios de convivencia en el mundo que los Derechos Humanos deben ser protegidos por ley internacional. Esta es la orientación vigente que norma la conducta de la comunidad de naciones.

De esta manera el sistema universal y los sistemas regionales perfeccionan el derecho internacional haciendo efectivo el principio de la Declaración Universal que considera 'esencial que los derechos humanos sean protegidos por un régimen de derecho' y se establece la jurisdicción internacional para su protección (en ambos sistemas) constituyéndose en el mecanismo idóneo para la promoción y defensa de los derechos humanos. Así queda perfectamente establecido por un lado, la armonía y complementación entre lo universal y lo regional, y por otro, la concepción integral de los derechos humanos como un todo indivisible y esencial, entre derechos civiles y políticos junto a los derechos económicos, sociales y culturales.

Los derechos humanos no constituyen una graciosa concesión de un Estado ni de un orden jurídico determinado sino que se desprenden de la dignidad inherente a la persona humana y representan valores anteriores y superiores al Estado.

Los Derechos Humanos pertenecen a la categoría de JUS COGENS porque son principios morales y fundamentales que la comunidad internacional considera esenciales para su existencia. Es evidente que su validez como JUS COGENS nace de la práctica de los Estados, de la jurisprudencia internacional, de la doctrina y tratados internacionales, así como de las resoluciones y declaraciones de los organismos internacionales.

Como dice la proclamación de Teherán del 13 de mayo de 1968 'la creciente disparidad entre los países económicamente desarrollados y los países en desarrollo impide la realización de los derechos humanos en la comunidad internacional'. Esta es una triste y dolorosa realidad que todavía subsiste y que aún no se puede superar por la ceguedad y resistencia de los países ricos e industrializados. La cooperación internacional todavía no se da en condiciones satisfactorias que permita eliminar esta disparidad.

II. EL PACTO Y EL COMITÉ

El esfuerzo de las Naciones Unidas para promover el respeto a los valores de la persona humana y avanzar por el camino que permita la debida protección a los derechos humanos se concretó de manera positiva con la aprobación del Pacto Internacional de Derechos Civiles y Políticos que entró en vigencia el 23 de marzo de 1976 y que marca una etapa histórica importante en este proceso de evolución de los derechos humanos. El Pacto estableció el Comité de Derechos Humanos con 18 miembros elegidos a título personal para aplicar el Pacto y durante veinticinco años ha venido desarrollando una magnifica labor en el cumplimiento de sus altas responsabilidades

El Pacto establece con claridad, objetividad y precisión los derechos humanos que están garantizados y el mecanismo del Protocolo Facultativo establece los medios y las instancias para la protección de los derechos individuales de las víctimas de violación. De conformidad con el Pacto los Estados asumen obligaciones que deben ser cumplidas permanentemente de buena fe y asumen responsabilidades ante la comunidad internacional.

El Pacto de Derechos Civiles y Políticos a través de la acción del Comité de Derechos Humanos viene ejecutándose hace 25 años y durante este cuarto de siglo ha servido para que la conciencia universal se proyecte con decisión y claridad en la exigencia de que todos los gobiernos inspiren su conducta en los principios y normas proclamados por el Pacto. Este valioso instrumento internacional ha hecho realidad la Declaración Universal de Derechos Humanos y los propósitos enunciados en la Carta de las Naciones Unidas. Han sido por lo tanto 25 años de una importante labor a través de los cuales representantes de las diversas regiones del mundo han sido rotativamente elegidos para integrar el Comité de Derechos Humanos. Esos miembros electos con un sentido geográfico y considerando sus meritos personales han actuado con gran sentido jurídico y una inquebrantable decisión de promover una sociedad internacional en la cual los derechos humanos ocupen el núcleo central de preocupación en el desarrollo de la vida política de los Estados.

Desde sus primeras sesiones el Comité ha cumplido a cabalidad sus inmensas responsabilidades y ha logrado crear conciencia de la obligación de todos los gobiernos y los Estados de respetar los derechos humanos y de cumplir las instancias internacionales de protección, establecidos por el Protocolo Facultativo que forma parte integrante del Pacto. Consecuentemente en este cuarto de siglo el Comité ha alcanzado un avance fundamental en el cumplimiento de las aspiraciones proclamadas por la Declaración Universal de derechos humanos y ha conseguido crear conciencia universal sobre los principios y normas que deben ser cumplidos por los Estados encaminadas al respeto y protección de los derechos humanos.

Este objetivo ha sido posible alcanzarlo a través de la acción del Comité mediante los procedimientos adoptados: Observaciones Generales, los diálogos con los Representantes de los Estados sobre los informes y las decisiones adoptadas por el Comité durante el examen de los casos según el Protocolo Facultativo.

a) Observaciones Generales

Las Observaciones Generales adoptadas por el Comité a lo largo de los periodos de sesiones han constituído un mecanismo central y muy efectivo a través de los cuales el Comité buscó ayudar a los Estados Partes a cumplir de la mejor manera las obligaciones que les incumben en la preparación y presentación de los informes al Comité. Por otro lado estos Informes son documentos muy importantes para que los Estados precisen el alcance y contenido de su legislación en el campo de los derechos humanos y del cumplimiento de los mecanismos de acción y garantía establecidos en el Protocolo Facultativo. De esta manera esas Observaciones Generales han llegado a constituir un elemento fundamental para interpretar los derechos protegidos por el Pacto y un sistema abierto a los individuos para hacer respetar los a través de la instancia internacional en el evento de que tales derechos hubieren sido violados por el Estado.

b) Los diálogos con los Representantes de los Estados

Los diálogos del Comité con los Representantes de los Estados han constituído un mecanismo idóneo, práctico y eficaz para que los gobiernos examinen los procedimientos internos de sus países que han generado problemas con los derechos humanos y los actos de conducta que han sido contrarios a las normas del Pacto de Derechos Civiles y Políticos. Este diálogo ha permitido además que los Estados reconozcan la competencia del Comité y acepten las insinuaciones, las críticas, los planteamientos formulados por los Miembros de Comité a través del intercambio de ideas y del análisis de la problemática de un Estado. Este sistema, que ha venido aplicando el Comité a lo largo de los años, ha constituído evidentemente un valioso mecanismo para la protección de los derechos humanos, para promover las rectificaciones legales de las legislaciones internas que han generado actos censurables y para incentivar una conducta de los Estados de acuerdo al Pacto, inclusive ha permitido que los Estados anuncien cambios legislativos y en los informes sucesivos den cuenta de los esfuerzos de aplicación del Pacto y de los avances internos para asegurar el respeto y la vigencia de los derechos humanos en sus países.

c) Decisiones del Comité

Las decisiones adoptadas por el Comité frente a los casos individuales que le han sido sometidos en virtud del Protocolo Facultativo han constituido también medios adecuados para asegurar el cumplimiento del Pacto y exigir que los Estados apliquen los tres principios básicos en caso de una denuncia sobre violación de un derecho humano: investigación, sanción al culpable e indemnización a la víctima o sus familiares. En este sentido los avances que han sido posible conseguir en virtud de la acción del Comité de Derechos Humanos han sido muchos e importantes, todo lo cual ha permitido crear conciencia sobre la obligación internacional de respetar los derechos humanos y aceptar las responsabilidades de los Estados establecidos en el Pacto de Derechos Civiles y Políticos.

Este accionar del Comité de Derechos Humanos le ha prestigiado a este organismo internacional. Las sociedades nacionales y los ciudadanos de los diversos países conocen que existe un recurso eficaz al cual se puede acudir si un Estado ha violado cualquiera de los derechos garantizados por el Pacto.

Este conocimiento permite además crear opinión publica interna e internacional para que los Estados rectifiquen procedimientos internos y legislaciones que de alguna manera afectan o contradicen los derechos humanos y los mecanismos internacionales de defensa y que asuman sus responsabilidades en el caso de que efectivamente se hayan producido esas violaciones que exigen una acción inmediata del Estado.

El desempeño a lo largo de los años del Comité ha permitido igualmente que se difundan los mecanismos y procedimientos establecidos por el Protocolo Facultativo, y que para iniciar un proceso legal la víctima tenga conciencia de que primero debe agotar los recursos internos, en el entendido de que si no se resuelve el problema de violación es posible acudir a la instancia internacional que constituye el Pacto de Derechos Civiles y Políticos junto con el Protocolo Facultativo.

III. EL RECURSO INTERNACIONAL

Cualquier violación de los Derechos Humanos por parte de un Estado afecta a todos los demás Estados y fundamenta la acción de la comunidad internacional para eliminar esa situación. Así, la protección internacional de los Derechos Humanos a la luz del nuevo derecho de gentes no implica intervención ilícita. Ya nadie puede poner en duda el derecho de todos los pueblos a oponerse a las violaciones sistemáticas y flagrantes de los Derechos Humanos.

La soberanía del Estado ya no es reinado absoluto e impenetrable. En el Derecho Internacional contemporáneo la soberanía estatal está limitada en función de otros elementos que han advenido con la transformación de la comunidad de naciones y el régimen jurídico internacional.

Hoy existen con sentido obligatorio, deberes y derechos proclamados en la sociedad de naciones independientemente de si un Estado quiera admitirlos. La transformación internacional ha sido tan profunda hacia el reconocimiento de la subjetividad del individuo, que hoy nadie duda que el hombre es un sujeto del Derecho Internacional.

Todo este proceso de transformación histórica desplaza el origen de los derechos individuales de la voluntad omnímoda del soberano al del orden natural intrínseco de la persona humana.

Esta realidad jurídica se ha desenvuelto a lo largo de la vida de la humanidad. Basta recoger las iluminadas palabras del filósofo y jurista español Francisco de Victoria, quien proclamó hace varios siglos: 'la voluntad de la comunidad internacional en su conjunto (totus orbis) no sólo tiene fuerza de pacto y convención, sino fuerza de ley'.

Una de las grandes conquistas del Derecho Internacional contemporáneo, es el principio ya consagrado positivamente de que un individuo que se siente víctima de la violación de uno de sus Derechos Humanos puede tener el recurso de queja para acudir a la instancia internacional y reclamar a su propio gobierno. Con todo aún existen Estados que se resisten a aceptar esa posibilidad, pero evidentemente, el Derecho Internacional ha dado un paso que confirma la aspiración de la comunidad de los pueblos para actuar solidariamente en caso de violaciones de los Derechos Humanos y buscar el restablecimiento de la norma y reparación consiguiente. De acuerdo con el Protocolo Facultativo del Pacto Internacional de Derechos Civiles y Políticos, se reconoce la competencia del Comité de Derechos Humanos para recibir y considerar comunicaciones de individuos que se hallen bajo la jurisdicción de un Estado Parte y que aleguen ser víctimas de una violación de cualquiera de los derechos enunciados en el Pacto. Esto permite al individuo que alegue tal violación y que antes haya agotado todos los recursos internos disponibles, someter su reclamo al Comité de Derechos Humanos.

Mediante este procedimiento, los individuos que sientan menoscabados o violados sus derechos por actos imputables a un gobierno o a leyes nacionales, tienen abierta la instancia internacional para exigir una rectificación del gobierno y reclamar la debida reparación del Estado. Igualmente un Estado puede declarar que reconoce la competencia del Comité para conocer denuncias de otro Estado Parte sobre violaciones a los Derechos Humanos.

IV. ACCIÓN DE LOS ESTADOS

La protección de los Derechos Humanos, en lo nacional, está dada por el poder judicial y los mecanismos legales internos. Con la firma del Pacto de Derechos Civiles y Políticos la acción de los Estados se proyecta al campo internacional y asumen la obligación de adoptar, con arreglo a sus procedimientos constitucionales estos y a las disposiciones del mismo Pacto, las medidas oportunas para dictar las disposiciones legislativas o de otro carácter que fueren necesarias para hacer efectivos los Derechos Humanos y que no estuviesen garantizados por disposiciones legislativas o de otro orden. De suerte que la armonización de la norma interna con la legislación internacional de los derechos humanos es una obligación ineludible de los Estados. No puede consecuentemente servir de pretexto para soslayar el respeto a un principio del Pacto, la disculpa de que en la ley interna del Estado no esta reconocido tal principio.

La obligación de los Estados no se limita al reconocimiento teórico de los Derechos Humanos, sino que los Estados Partes de acuerdo con los diversos Pactos Internacionales tienen el deber de avalar el goce de esos derechos a todas las personas que están sujetas a su jurisdicción garantizando un recurso efectivo para su protección.

Cuando surja una situación excepcional que amenace la vida de una nación y tal situación sea oficialmente proclamada, un Estado puede suspender momentáneamente de acuerdo con el Pacto algunos de los derechos en la medida estrictamente requerida. Tal suspensión debe ser excepcional y temporal y solo puede durar mientras corra peligro la vida de la nación sin afectar a los derechos que no pueden ser derogados ni objeto de suspensión tal como el derecho a la vida; ni del derecho a no ser sometido a torturas ni apenas o tratos crueles, inhumanos o degradantes, ni a esclavitud ni servidumbre, ni suspenderse el derecho a no ser encarcelado por el sólo hecho de no poder cumplir una obligación contractual ni ser condenado por actos u omisiones que en el momento de cometerse no fueron delictivos; ni suspenderse el derecho de todo ser humano al reconocimiento de su personalidad jurídica; ni por último afectar el derecho a la libertad de pensamiento, de conciencia o de religión. Tampoco el Estado puede adoptar medidas discriminatorias y debe, en todo caso, cumplir con el deber de informar acerca de la índole y el alcance de la suspensión de ciertos derechos según lo permite el Pacto.

Por desgracia han existido y existen gobiernos dictatoriales, abusivos o prepotentes, que declaran el estado de sitio o de emergencia y lo prorrogan sucesiva e indefinidamente. Y se han dado casos de Estados que han vivido por muchos años bajo esa situación excepcional.

V. DERECHOS PROTEGIDOS POR EL PACTO

Los derechos fundamentales de la persona humana están establecidos y protegidos por el Pacto. Y el Comité a lo largo de sus actuaciones y decisiones en sus 25 años de vida ha ayudado a fundamentar el alcance de los derechos protegidos y ha establecido entre otros los siguientes parámetros jurídicos y que sirven de base para determinar la responsabilidad de los gobiernos en el cumplimiento de las normas internacionales:

1. El derecho a la vida es el derecho supremo de toda persona humana y el fundamento de todos los demás derechos. No cabe suspensión alguna de este derecho ni aun en situaciones excepcionales que pongan en peligro la vida de la nación. Lamentablemente la guerra y otros actos de violencia masivos siguen siendo el peor flagelo de la humanidad y constituyen una denegación del derecho a la vida. Por lo tanto la suprema obligación de los Estados es evitar las guerras que están al margen del derecho y tienen el deber de realizar todos los esfuerzos necesarios para fortalecer la paz y la seguridad internacionales. Consecuentemente la ley debe prohibir toda propaganda de guerra así como toda incitación a la violencia.

La Asamblea General de las Naciones Unidas declaró que 'el uso de armas nucleares y termonucleares es contrario al espíritu, a la letra y a los objetivos de la Carta de las Naciones Unidas y, por lo tanto, constituye una violación directa de la misma' y que todo Estado que utilice armas nucleares y termonucleares 'obra en contra de las leyes de la humanidad y comete un crimen contra la humanidad y la civilización'.

El genocidio ya sea cometido en tiempo de paz o en tiempo de guerra es un delito de lesa humanidad que la Comunidad de Naciones se ha comprometido a prevenir y sancionar. Se entiende por genocidio cualquier acto perpetrado con la intención de destruir total o parcialmente, a un grupo nacional, étnico, racial o religioso. Este delito no prescribe nunca.

Es obligación de los Estados tomar medidas para evitar y castigar los actos criminales que entrañen privación de la vida. De manera particular esa obligación tiene que ver con las propias Fuerzas de Seguridad y el Estado debe impedir que ellas priven arbitrariamente de la vida a cualquier persona. Igual obligación tienen los Estados para investigar y denunciar contra ellos sobre violaciones de derechos humanos.

Frente a violaciones graves y sistemáticas de derechos humanos por parte de Gobiernos represivos es necesaria una acción solidaria de todos los pueblos para detener y castigar esa conducta.

2. Nadie debe ser sometido a torturas ni a penas o tratos crueles, inhumanos o degradantes. Por tortura se entiende todo acto por el cual se infrinja intencionalmente a una persona dolores o sufrimientos graves ya sean físicos o mentales, con el fin de obtener de ella o de un tercero información o una confesión, de castigarla por un acto que haya cometido o se sospeche que ha cometido o de intimidar o coaccionar a esa persona o a otras o por cualquier razón basada en otro

tipo de discriminación, cuando dichos dolores o sufrimientos sean infligidos por un funcionario público u otra persona en el ejercicio de funciones públicas, a instigación suya, o con su consentimiento o aquiescencia. Esta es la legislación internacional recogida en la Convención contra la tortura. Todos los Estados tienen la obligación de adoptar medidas eficaces, legislativas, administrativas, judiciales o de otra índole, para impedir los actos de tortura. Ninguna circunstancia excepcional puede invocarse para justificar la tortura. Ni un estado de guerra, inestabilidad política o emergencia pública puede justificarla.

Las denuncias de torturas o malos tratos deben ser investigadas pronta y eficazmente por las autoridades competentes. Los culpables deben ser castigados y las victimas disponer de recursos legales, inclusive del derecho a obtener debida reparación. La tortura constituye una forma agravada y deliberada de trato o pena cruel, inhumano o degradante y todas esas categorías de tratamientos inhumanos han sido determinados como una ofensa a la dignidad humana y considerados como violación a los principios de la Carta de las Naciones Unidas y de los Derechos Humanos y libertades fundamentales.

3. Todo individuo tiene derecho a la libertad y seguridad personales. Es este un derecho básico que cubre un amplio esquema de garantías y que es aplicable a todas las formas de privación de la libertad. Uno de los aspectos fundamentales está dado por el derecho de toda persona a recurrir ante un tribunal a fin de que este decida sobre la legalidad de su prisión. Y esto junto al derecho para ser llevado 'sin demora' ante un juez que conozca y resuelva su caso. Esta garantía se refiere no solo al momento que debe comenzar un proceso, sino también a aquel en que debe concluir y pronunciarse la sentencia. Todos las fases del proceso, inclusive una apelación, deben desarrollarse sin dilaciones indebidas. Si la persona es juzgada en un plazo razonable tiene derecho a ser puesta en libertad.

4. En el caso de detención de una persona: a) no debe ser arbitraria; b) debe obedecer a causas fijadas por la ley; c) debe efectuarse con arreglo al procedimiento establecido en la ley; d) debe informarse sin demora a la persona de las razones de la detención y de la acusación formulada contra ella, en idioma que entienda; e) debe ser juzgada sin dilaciones indebidas; f) debe garantizársele plenamente el derecho de defensa; g) debe garantizársele el derecho a recurrir ante un tribunal; h) debe reconocérsele el derecho a exigir una reparación en caso de haberla. El derecho a ser informado 'sin demora' de la acusación exige que tal información proporcionada por la autoridad competente tan pronto como decida adoptar medidas procesales contra una persona sospechosa de haber cometido un delito o la designe públicamente como tal, indicando tanto la ley como los supuestos hechos en que se basa.

5. Toda persona privada de libertad será tratada humanamente y con el respeto debido a la dignidad inherente al ser humano. Es esto una norma básica de aplicación universal. No se refiere sólo a las condiciones materiales que dependen generalmente de los recursos económicos disponibles, sino a la forma y manera con que se trate al detenido y sin hacérsele objeto de discriminación en razón de la raza, color, sexo, religión, opinión política y de cualquier otra índole o condición social. En todo caso los procesados estarán separados de los condenados y los menores de

los adultos. Y el régimen penitenciario debe tender a la readaptación social de los penados.

6. Todas las personas son iguales ante los Tribunales y Cortes de Justicia y tienen derecho a ser oídos públicamente y con las debidas garantías por un tribunal competente, independiente e imparcial en la sustanciación de cualquier acusación de carácter penal formulada contra ella o para la determinación de sus derechos en obligaciones de carácter civil. La igualdad ante la ley es la base de los Derechos Humanos. Todos los hombres y mujeres son iguales y, por lo tanto, tienen derecho a igual protección de la ley en el goce de todos los derechos civiles y políticos. La igualdad es corolario de la universalidad. Por eso toda discriminación es condenable y requiere no solamente medidas legales de protección contra aquella sino una acción positiva destinada a garantizar el disfrute real de los derechos.

7. En la sustanciación de las causas penales y los procedimientos para determinar los derechos y obligaciones de carácter civil debe considerase que los individuos de cualquier condición tienen que estar amparados por: a) el derecho de acceso a los mecanismos judiciales; b) el derecho a un proceso público; c) el derecho a un proceso justo y rápido; d) la irretroactividad de las leyes y de las penas a menos que sea a favor del procesado y e) el derecho a una sentencia justa. Para eficacia de estos derechos el sistema judicial debe estar sustentado en la integración de los tribunales por magistrados competentes, independiente e imparciales. Y esta independencia tiene que ser completa, ya en lo que respecta a la manera como se nombran los jueces, a las calificaciones para su nombramiento, a la duración de su mandato, así como a las condiciones que rigen su ascenso, traslado o cesación de funciones. De acuerdo con el Comité de Derechos Humanos la independencia de los jueces debe ser efectiva tanto frente al Poder Ejecutivo como al Poder Legislativo. Hay que impedir legalmente la politización de los jueces y la integración de los tribunales en función de bloques políticos representados en un congreso o por razones de filiación partidistas. Por otro lado la transitoriedad de los jueces como aun existe en ciertos países impide la imparcialidad de la justicia y la transparencia de los tribunales, porque sufren la malsana influencia política.

Todo individuo tiene el derecho a ser juzgado por jueces competentes, independientes e imparciales, esto quiere decir que no caben tribunales de excepción o especiales, ni tribunales militares para juzgar a civiles. Generalmente las dictaduras pretenden mantenerse en el poder a base de la amenaza, y con este propósito establecen tribunales militares o especiales para juzgar y castigar a quienes se les oponen. Este procedimiento se halla en abierta contradicción con los principios de los Derechos Humanos y menoscaba las garantías que deben rodear a todo enjuiciamiento.

8. Junto al procedimiento judicial el individuo tiene que tener la garantía del derecho de defensa y de la presunción de inocencia mientras no se pruebe su culpabilidad conforme a la ley. En razón de la presunción de la inocencia no debe sufrir ningún tipo de pena o castigo sin sentencia firme. No debe tratársele como un 'presunto culpable' porque la culpabilidad debe probarse. La carga de la prueba

recae sobre la acusación y el acusado tiene el beneficio de la duda. No puede suponerse a nadie culpable a menos que se haya demostrado la acusación fuera de toda duda razonable. Por lo tanto las autoridades públicas tienen la obligación de no prejuzgar el resultado de un proceso. El derecho de defensa implica que el acusado disponga de tiempo y de los medios adecuados para la preparación de su defensa y a comunicarse con un defensor de su elección.

9. Nadie puede ser obligado a declarar contra si mismo ni a confesarse culpable. Para obtener confesiones o declaraciones de culpabilidad con frecuencia los gobiernos represivos utilizan métodos que violan estos principios. La ley debe establecer que las pruebas conseguidas por estos métodos o cualesquiera otras formas de coerción son enteramente inaceptables y no deben constituir testimonio contra el acusado. Toda persona declarada culpable de un delito tendrá derecho a que el fallo condenatorio y la pena que se le haya impuesto sean sometidos a un tribunal superior. Y esta garantía no se limita tan solo a las infracciones mas graves.

10. Tres libertades conforman una de las partes sensibles y esenciales de los Derechos Humanos garantizados por el Pacto de Derechos Civiles y Políticos: la libertad de pensamiento, la libertad de conciencia y la libertad religiosa. La primera, se refiere al conjunto de ideas y juicios que cualquier persona tiene sobre las realidades de la vida y del mundo, y que puede expresarla a través de cualquier medio de comunicación colectiva. La segunda comprende el juicio moral sobre las acciones propias al margen de toda acción por el Estado o la sociedad. Y la última tiene por objeto el respeto a la fe y a la práctica de la religión de acuerdo al fuero interno. Estos derechos incluyen la libertad de tener o adaptar la religión o las creencias de su elección, así como la libertad de manifestarlas individual o colectivamente, tanto en público como en privado, mediante el culto, la celebración de ritos, las prácticas y la enseñanza.

11. Nadie podrá ser molestado a causa de sus opiniones. Este derecho comprende no solamente la libertad de difundir informaciones e ideas de toda índole, sino también la libertad de buscarlas y recibirlas sin consideración de fronteras y por cualquier medio, ya sea oralmente, por escrito, o en forma impresa o artística o por cualquier otro procedimiento de elección personal. Este derecho entraña derechos y responsabilidades especiales y por consiguiente puede estar sujeto a ciertas restricciones pero estas no deben poner en peligro ese derecho en si mismo y en todo caso, deben estar expresamente fijadas en la ley. Tales restricciones no pueden ser otras que las necesarias para asegurar el respeto a los derechos o a la reputación de los demás: o para la protección de la seguridad nacional, el orden público o la salud o la moral públicas. Esas restricciones deben justificarse como necesarias para alcanzar uno de los indicados propósitos.

Entre los derechos fundamentales de toda persona humana está la libertad de expresión y de opinión. Sin ella, la personalidad intelectual del hombre no sería completa y no se realizarían plenamente sus virtualidades intelectuales y quedaría menoscabada su integración a la vida social.

El derecho a la libertad de expresión no sufre menoscabo con la prohibición que la legislación internacional sobre derechos humanos establece contra toda propaganda a favor de la guerra y contra toda apología del odio nacional, racial, o religioso que constituye incitación a la discriminación, la hostilidad o la violencia. Esa prohibición es plenamente compatible con el derecho a la libertad de expresión, toda vez que se trata de un derecho cuyo ejercicio implica deberes y responsabilidades especiales.

12. Un principio fundamental es el que asegura el derecho a la intimidad. Nadie será objeto de injerencias arbitrarias en su vida privada, su domicilio o su correspondencia, ni de ataques a su honra, o a su reputación. La ley debe proteger contra tales arbitrariedades que muchas veces se cometen en regímenes represivos que tratan de controlar indebidamente o de atemorizar a sus opositores políticos. La Declaración Universal de los Derechos Humanos establece la norma que 'en caso de persecución toda persona tiene derecho a buscar asilo y a disfrutar de él en cualquier país'

Es doloroso constatar que la situación mundial, las guerras, las represiones y las persecuciones han llevado a desplazamientos individuales y colectivos de una inmensa cantidad de mujeres, hombres y niños que buscan un lugar para asegurar su vida y su libertad. Es el cuadro tremendo ostracismo que viven los refugiados.

13. La familia es el elemento fundamental y la célula básica de la sociedad. Toda persona tiene derecho a constituir una familia y a recibir protección para ella. Este derecho no admite restricción alguna por motivos de raza, nacionalidad o religión. Y disfrutará de iguales derechos en cuanto al matrimonio, durante el matrimonio y en caso de disolución del matrimonio. La sociedad y el Estado tienen el deber de proteger la familia. Los derechos de los cónyuges son los mismos y tienen la misma fuerza. Constituye una injusticia y un hecho intolerable el conceder a terceros, sean padres, tutores u otra autoridad, el derecho a elegir la pareja para el matrimonio.

El consentimiento libre y pleno para el matrimonio abarca la libertad y anuencia de elección. La voluntad de hombres y mujeres que contraen matrimonio, de acuerdo con la ley, crea el vínculo jurídico que conlleva un conjunto de derechos y deberes. El Estado tiene que cumplir eficazmente su obligación de proteger a la familia, promoviendo su estabilidad, ayudando al desarrollo de la institución familiar con medidas de carácter social, económico y cultural y absteniéndose de actos que llevan a la separación de los cónyuges contra su voluntad. De conformidad con la legislación del Pacto de Derechos Civiles y Políticos los Estados se han comprometido a dictar medidas legales para asegurar la igualdad de derechos y de responsabilidades de ambos esposos en cuanto al matrimonio. Y en caso de disolución deberán adoptarse disposiciones que aseguren protección necesaria a los hijos.

14. Un principio fundamental de los Derechos Humanos es el que se refiere a la eliminación de todas las formas de discriminación contra la mujer que violan los principios de la igualdad de derechos y del respeto a la dignidad humana, dificulta la participación de la mujer, en las mismas condiciones que el hombre, en la vida política, social, económica y cultural, constituye un grave obstáculo para el aumento

de bienestar de la sociedad y de la familia y entorpece el pleno desarrollo de las posibilidades de la mujer para prestar servicios a su país y a la humanidad. Estos principios aceptados por el nuevo Derecho Internacional y proclamados por las Naciones Unidas inspiraron la Convención aprobada y vigente sobre la Eliminación de todas las Formas de Discriminación contra la Mujer.

Por desgracia, no todas las naciones del mundo han aprobado una legislación eficaz, justa y amplia, encaminada a poner en marcha una política de eliminación de todas las discriminaciones contra la mujer. Sin embargo, los Estados están obligados a adoptar todas las medidas apropiadas con ese propósito de acuerdo con los Convenios internacionales vigentes y las normas del Derecho Internacional.

15. El extranjero que se halla legalmente en el territorio de un Estado, sólo podrá ser expulsado en cumplimiento de una decisión adoptada conforme a la ley. Debe permitirse al extranjero que exprese las razones que lo asisten en contra de su expulsión, así como el poder someter su caso a revisión ante la autoridad competente. Por desgracia, no todos los Estados respetan este principio y en muchas oportunidades el extranjero no dispone de un recurso superior ante una decisión de expulsión y se encuentra en inferioridad de condiciones para hacer valer sus Derechos Humanos. En ningún caso el extranjero puede ser expulsado o devuelto a otro país, sea o no de origen, donde su derecho a la vida o a la libertad personal está en riesgo de violación a causa de raza, nacionalidad, religión condición social o de sus opiniones políticas. La legislación internacional de los Derechos Humanos condena la expulsión colectiva de extranjeros. Los Estados pueden imponer legítimamente restricciones a la actividad política de los extranjeros, sin que ello implique violación de la libertad de expresión o discriminación.

16. Las minorías étnicas, religiosas o lingüísticas tienen derecho a la protección del Estado y deben gozar de los Derechos Humanos fundamentales sin discriminación de ningún género.

A las personas que pertenezcan a dichas minorías debe reconocérseles el derecho que les corresponde, en común con los demás miembros de su grupo, a tener su propia vida natural a profesar y practicar su propia religión y a emplear su propio idioma. El Estado no debe hacer nada para destruir la personalidad de las minorías que viven en su territorio y, al contrario, está en el deber de reconocerles todos los Derechos Humanos fundamentales y de manera particular los que tienen relación con el mantenimiento de su integridad física, cultural, histórica, religiosa, lingüística, y demás que conforman su unidad étnica específica, ambiental y nacional.

Más tarde, el proceso de descolonización que es adoptado como un propósito esencial de la comunidad de naciones, cambia el mapa político del mundo y queda acogido como principio fundamental de la convivencia internacional el de la autodeterminación de los pueblos.

17. Toda persona tiene derecho a la libertad de reunión y de asociación pacífica. La reunión es un encuentro de personas para una finalidad determinada, en tanto que la asociación es una unión estable. Ambas son voluntarias y el fundamento de esos derechos está dado por la sociabilidad de los seres humanos. El ejercicio del derecho

de reunión sólo podrá estar sujeto a las restricciones previstas por la ley, de conformidad con las exigencias de la seguridad nacional, de la seguridad pública y del orden público y para proteger la salud o la moral públicas o los derechos y libertades de los demás. Toda persona tiene derecho a asociarse libremente con otras, inclusive el derecho a fundar sindicatos y afiliarse a ellos para la protección de sus intereses, y solamente puede aceptarse restricciones de acuerdo con la ley con los propósitos antes enunciados.

18. La Carta de las Naciones Unidas en su artículo 55 establece como uno de los principios fundamentales de la Organización Universal el de crear las condiciones de estabilidad y bienestar necesarias para las relaciones pacíficas y amistosas entre las naciones basadas en el respeto al principio de la igualdad de derechos y al de la libre determinación de los pueblos. Y declara que las Naciones Unidas promoverán el respeto universal a los derechos humanos y a las libertades fundamentales de todos sin hacer distinción por motivos de raza, sexo, idioma o religión y la efectividad de tales derechos y libertades.

La Asamblea General de las Naciones Unidas declaró que 'toda doctrina de diferenciación o superioridad racial es científicamente falsa, moralmente condenable, socialmente injusta y que nada permite justificar la discriminación racial ni en la teoría ni en la práctica'. Así, el Apartheid, la segregación o separación de razas, constituye un delito de lesa humanidad.

La comunidad internacional sufre con frecuencia por actos delictivos contra personas, en especial por actos de terrorismo y de secuestro, de extorsión y otros delitos comunes graves. Los hechos de terrorismo y la toma de rehenes constituyen delitos que afecta a los derechos esenciales a la persona humana. Por eso la comunidad internacional ha reaccionado y ha decidido poner en marcha la cooperación internacional para la prevención y sanción de tales actos.

VI. DERECHOS POLÍTICOS Y SOCIALES

El Pacto de Derechos Civiles y Políticos y el Pacto de Derechos Económicos, Sociales y Culturales consagran la legislación internacional sobre ambas categorías de derechos humanos y constituyen los dos lados de la misma medalla y no pueden sacrificarse los unos para garantizar exclusivamente a los otros. Ambas categorías de derechos tienen que ser respetadas, promovidas y consagradas por los Estados.

El primero de los Derechos Humanos Colectivos es el derecho de autodeterminación. La lucha contra el colonialismo llevó a los pueblos a consagrar el principio de la libre determinación como el fundamento del nuevo orden internacional. La vigencia de este derecho es la condición fundamental para una eficaz garantía y observancia de los derechos humanos individuales.

El Pacto de Derechos Civiles y Políticos, así como el Pacto de Derechos Económicos y Sociales establecen en el primero de sus artículos el derecho de libre determinación de los pueblos. Y las Naciones Unidas declararon que 'la sujeción de pueblos a una subyugación, dominación y explotación extranjeras constituye una denegación de los Derechos Humanos fundamentales, es contraria a la Carta de las Naciones Unidas y compromete la causa de la paz y de la cooperación mundiales'.

En virtud de este derecho los pueblos establecen libremente su condición política y proveen a su desarrollo económico, social y cultural. Para el logro de sus fines, todos los pueblos pueden disponer libremente de sus riquezas y recursos naturales. Este derecho entraña obligaciones correspondientes de todos los Estados y de la comunidad internacional.

El derecho de autodeterminación es un derecho humano fundamental y es la expresión más alta de la libertad de un pueblo. A través de su aplicación una colectividad humana decide sobre su futuro político. La autodeterminación es la antítesis del colonialismo.

Y para efectos de organizarse los pueblos tienen el derecho soberano e irrenunciable para elegir a sus legítimos mandatarios y representantes sin presiones ni interferencias que distorsionen la voluntad popular.

Tienen igualmente todos los ciudadanos derecho a votar y ser elegidos en elecciones periódicas, auténticas, realizadas por sufragio universal e igual y por voto secreto que garantice la libre expresión de la voluntad de los electores. Por último, todos los ciudadanos gozan del derecho a tener acceso, en condiciones generales de igualdad, a las funciones públicas de su país.

Sin embargo la convivencia entre los hombres no puede ser ordenada y fecunda si cada sociedad nacional no está estructurada en un ordenamiento jurídico interno y con una legítima autoridad que inspira sus actos en la razón y en el bien común. Todo hombre tiene derecho a participar en la vida pública y contribuir con su pensamiento y con su acción al bienestar general. La voluntad del pueblo es la base de la autoridad del poder público.

La mejor garantía, y quizá la única, para el respeto de los Derechos Humanos está dada por los gobiernos auténticamente democráticos, toda vez que en ellos la voluntad del pueblo es la base del poder público y consecuentemente tienen que acatar las limitaciones que surgen de los derechos individuales.

El Derecho Internacional está evolucionando hacia un nuevo orden en el campo de los Derechos Humanos. Este nuevo orden está sustentado en los valores universales, individuales y colectivos, ya reconocidos por todos los hombres y todos los pueblos y proyectado hacia cuatro nuevas dimensiones bien definidas: el derecho a la paz, el derecho al desarrollo, el derecho al medio ambiente y el derecho al aprovechamiento y respeto del patrimonio común de la humanidad.

Los Estados afrontan ante sí un objetivo esencial que no pueden renunciar y que está identificado con la firme defensa de los Derechos Humanos. Esta tarea debemos cumplirla todos individual y colectivamente desde nuestras distintas posiciones personales, profesionales, académicas y de trabajo frente a situaciones conflictivas internas y externas y a la promoción de esos valores irrenunciables y su indeclinable defensa.

VII. PROBLEMAS ACTUALES

Algunas conductas de ciertos Estados aplicadas en el momento actual contradicen las normas del Pacto de Derechos Civiles y Políticos y los avances internacionales de respeto a los derechos humanos. Los acontecimientos del 11 de septiembre del 2001 constituyeron actos repudiables de terrorismo que la comunidad internacional ha rechazado. Todas las naciones están llamadas a cooperar entre sí de la manera mas efectiva y responsable para combatir al terrorismo internacional. Pero esta acción de combate al terrorismo tiene también que encuadrarse en el respeto a los principios de los derechos humanos consagrados en los Pactos, Declaraciones y demás instrumentos internacionales de Derechos Humanos. En este sentido en el juzgamiento de los terroristas tiene que respetarse las normas del debido proceso, es decir tiene que ser un Tribunal imparcial, internacional y competente el que juzgue a los acusados de terrorismo. Estos procesos no pueden llevarse a cabo mediante juicios secretos porque el juzgamiento de todo delito debe ser público ante tribunales y cortes de justicia y deben además cumplirse todos los requisitos establecidos en el artículo 14 del Pacto de Derechos Civiles y Políticos. Todo acusado tiene el derecho de defensa y de la presunción de inocencia y deben respetarse las garantías mínimas establecidas, para el efecto, en el Pacto. Consecuentemente es inadmisible que se organicen tribunales especiales militares para juzgar a civiles acusados de terrorismo y que tales procesos judiciales sean secretos y ni siquiera se conozca el nombre de la persona involucrada en tal acusación.

Resulta igualmente inaceptable que, con motivo de los actos terroristas, se establezcan normas especiales que afectan a inmigrantes restringiendo sus derechos humanos y garantías legales. La lucha contra el terrorismo tiene que desarrollarse con la más amplia colaboración entre los Estados. Pero al mismo tiempo respetando en su integridad todos los principios básicos que la comunidad internacional ha proclamado en el campo de los derechos humanos. Sería un verdadero retroceso si después de 25 años de esfuerzo del Comité de Derechos Humanos por crear conciencia nacional e internacional para el respeto debido a las normas y principios del Pacto de Derechos Civiles y Políticos hoy se apliquen, con el pretexto de la lucha antéterrorista, sistemas y mecanismos que limitan las garantías de toda persona humana en cualquier caso y condición. Así como es necesario combatir el terrorismo de individuos o sociedades es también conveniente tomar posiciones contra todo terrorismo de Estado que igualmente afecta los principios por los cuales el Comité y otros organismos encargados de la promoción y defensa de los derechos humanos han desarrollado y alcanzado en los últimos 25 años.

LE COMITE DES DROITS DE L'HOMME DES NATIONS-UNIES – AUX CONFINS D'UNE JURIDICTION INTERNATIONALE DES DROITS L'HOMME?

Abdelfattah Amor

La protection des Droits de l'Homme, dans le cadre des Nations Unies, est assurée par différentes institutions ainsi que par des mécanismes aussi nombreux que variés et dont la plupart relèvent soit des mécanismes non conventionnels soit des mécanismes conventionnels.

Les mécanismes non conventionnels qui désignent 'les procédures spéciales' instituées par la Commission des Droits de l'Homme comportent quatre catégories de procédures ou de mandats[1]:

- Les mandats géographiques au nombre de 14, chacun portant sur un Etat ou des territoires particuliers[2],
- Les mandats thématiques au nombre de 15, chacun portant sur un thème particulier[3],

---

[1] Par commodité de langage on retiendra le terme mandat, étant entendu que celui-ci désigne dans la pratique onusienne tout mandat confié à un expert indépendant ou à un groupe d'experts indépendants menant, pour le compte et sous le contrôle de la Commission des Droits de l'Homme, des activités s'inscrivant dans le cadre de la protection et/ou, éventuellement, de la promotion des Droits de l'Homme.

[2] Ces mandats géographiques confiés à des Rapporteurs spéciaux portent en juin 2000 sur: L'Afghanistan; la Bosnie Herzégovine, la Croatie et la Yougoslavie; le Burundi; la République Démocratique du Congo; la Guinée Equatoriale; l'Iraq; la République Islamique d'Iran; le Myanmar; les Territoires palestiniens occupés; le Rwanda; le Soudan; le Cambodge; la Somalie et l'Haïti.

[3] Les mandats thématiques, confiés à des Rapporteurs spéciaux ou à des représentants du Secrétaire général ou à des groupes de travail, portent en juin 2000 sur:

1. les formes contemporaines de racisme, de discrimination raciale et de xénophobie,
2. les exécutions extrajudiciaires, sommaires ou arbitraires,
3. la liberté d'opinion et d'expression,
4. l'impact des conflits armés sur les enfants,
5. l'indépendance des juges et des avocats,
6. les personnes déplacées,
7. les mercenaires,
8. la liberté de religion ou de conviction,
9. la vente, la prostitution d'enfants et la pornographie,
10. la torture et autres traitements cruels, inhumains ou dégradants,
11. les déchets toxiques,
12. la violence contre les femmes, ses causes et ses conséquences,
13. la détention arbitraire,
14. les disparitions forcées ou involontaires.
15. défenseurs des droits de l'homme.

- Les mandats sur les droits économiques et sociaux, au nombre de sept, portent sur certaines questions à caractère économique et social particulièrement sensibles[4].
- Les mandats sur les programmes de coopération technique, au nombre de trois, portent sur trois Etats particuliers[5].

Les mécanismes conventionnels sont des mécanismes établis pour veiller au respect des conventions qui les instituent ou sur la base desquelles ils sont institués.

Il s'agit du comité pour l'élimination de la discrimination raciale[6], du Comité des droits économiques, sociaux et culturels[7] du Comité des Droits de l'Homme[8], du Comité pour l'élimination de la discrimination à l'égard des femmes[9] du Comité contre la torture[10] et du Comité des droits de l'enfant[11].

Le Comité des Droits de l'Homme est composé de 18 membres[12] ressortissants des Etats parties au pacte des droits civils et politiques[13] et qui 'doivent être des personnalités de haute moralité et possédant une compétence reconnue dans le domaine des Droits de l'Homme'[14]. L'article 28 du pacte ajoute qu' 'il sera tenu compte de l'intérêt que présente la participation aux travaux du Comité de quelques personnes ayant une expérience juridique'[15]. Les membres du Comité sont présentés

---

[4] Les mandats sur les droits économiques et sociaux, confiés à des experts, à des experts indépendants ou à des Rapporteurs spéciaux, portent en juin 2000 sur:

1. les effets de la dette extérieure,
2. la restitution, la compensation ou la réhabilitation pour les victimes de graves violations des Droits de l'Homme,
3. l'extrême pauvreté,
4. le droit à l'éducation,
5. le droit au développement,
6. l'ajustement structurel,
7. les droits des migrants.

[5] Ces mandats, confiés à un Représentant spécial et à deux experts indépendants, portent sur: le Cambodge, Haïti et la Somalie.

[6] Institué conformément à la convention internationale sur l'élimination de toutes les formes de discrimination raciale du 21 décembre 1965 (Art. 8).

[7] Créé sur la base du pacte international relatif aux droits économiques, sociaux et culturels du 16 décembre 1966.

[8] Institué par le pacte des droits civils et politiques du 16 décembre 1966 (Art. 28).

[9] Institué par la convention sur l'élimination de toutes les formes de discrimination à l'égard des femmes du 18 décembre 1979 (Art. 17).

[10] Institué par la convention contre la torture et autres peines ou traitements cruels, inhumains ou dégradants du 10 décembre 1984 (Art. 17).

[11] Institué par la convention relative aux droits de l'enfant du 20 novembre 1989 (Art. 43).

[12] Article 28, § 1 du pacte international relatif aux droits civils et politiques.

[13] A ce jour 148 Etats ont ratifié le pacte.

[14] Article 28, §2.

[15] *Ibid.*

par les Etats parties au pacte et élus par eux au scrutin secret[16] pour une période de quatre ans renouvelable[17]. Ils sont élus et siègent à titre individuel.[18]

Parmi les attributions et les activités du Comité, il y a lieu de souligner, notamment, l'examen des rapports d'Etats[19], l'élaboration et l'adoption d'observations générales[20] et l'examen des communications des particuliers.[21]

Il est indiscutable que le Comité des Droits de l'Homme occupe, en raison de la mission qui est la sienne et de l'importance particulière des droits concernés par son activité et de la formulation des normes qui le concernent, une place de premier plan parmi l'ensemble des mécanismes de protection des droits de l'homme.

Cette importance semble se renforcer de manière progressive, tant et si bien que le Comité – qui n'est pas une juridiction[22] – donne l'impression – notamment en

---

[16] Article 29, §1.

[17] Article 32, §1.

[18] Article 28, §3 du pacte.

[19] L'article 40, §1 du pacte énonce que 'les Etats parties... s'engagent à présenter des rapports sur les mesures qu'ils auront arrêtées et qui donnent effet aux droits reconnus dans le présent pacte et sur les progrès réalisés dans la jouissance de ces droits'. Le paragraphe 4 du même article charge le Comité d'étudier les rapports présentés par les Etats et de leur adresser ses propres rapports.

[20] Le Comité est habilité par l'article 40 du pacte à adresser aux Etats 'toutes observations générales qu'il jugerait appropriées'.

[21] L'article 1er du protocole facultatif se rapportant au pacte international relatif aux droits civils et politiques indique que: 'tout Etat-partie au pacte qui devient partie au présent protocole reconnaît que le Comité a compétence pour recevoir et examiner des communications émanant de particuliers relevant de sa juridiction qui prétendent être victimes d'une violation par cet Etat-partie de l'un quelconque des droits énoncés dans le pacte...'.
L'article 2 du même protocole précise que 'sous réserve des dispositions de l'article 1er, tout particulier qui prétend être victime d'une violation de l'un quelconque des droits énoncés dans le pacte et qui a épuisé tous les recours internes disponibles, peut présenter une communication écrite au Comité pour qu'il l'examine'.

[22] Quelle que soit la souplesse avec laquelle on peut envisager la notion de juridiction, il demeure très difficile -dans l'état actuel du droit de qualifier le Comité de juridiction. En s'arrêtant à la fonction, plutôt qu'à l'organe, l'on pourrait être tenté par la qualification juridictionnelle du Comité et trouver dans le protocole facultatif quelques éléments allant dans le même sens et tenant, notamment, à la fonction de dire de droit, relativement à des contestations, au fond, d'ordre juridique, examinées selon une procédure plutôt de nature juridictionnelle. Il demeure établi, quel que soit le degré d'obligation, notamment, des constatations du Comité, que celles-ci n'ont aucune autorité de la chose jugée, bien qu'elles soient juridiquement motivées et fondées sur l'appréciation de données factuelles à la lumière de normes juridiques.
Sur la notion de juridiction la littérature est abondante. Voir, notamment:

- J. Waline: *Préface à la première édition des grandes décisions au Conseil Constitutionnel* de L. Favoreu et L. Philippe, reproduite à la 9ème édition, Paris, Dalloz 1997, p. XI et seq.
- F. Luchaire, 'le Conseil Constitutionnel, Paris', *Economica* 1980, p. 33 et seq.
- D. Rousseau, *Droit du contentieux constitutionnel*, *Montchrestien*, 4ème édtion, 1996.

raison de la logique juridictionnelle dans laquelle il semble inscrire de plus en plus l'exercice de ses compétences – d'être, en quelque sorte, une juridiction, une cour internationale des Droits de l'Homme à l'état embryonnaire ou en état de formation.

Cette impression, ainsi énoncée, parce que n'étant pas à l'abri d'une certaine réversibilité, ne peut pas être confirmée facilement et totalement de nos jours. Il n'en demeure pas moins, cependant, qu'elle n'est pas dénuée, sinon de fondement, du moins d'une certaine réalité, d'une certaine existence qui pourrait précéder des évolutions ou peut être, même, les favoriser.

Il ne s'agit pas, ici, bien évidemment, de tenir un plaidoyer pour 'l'ivraie' aux dépens du 'bon droit'[23], mais de tenter d'examiner ce qui, à travers la pratique du Comité, semble contribuer à le situer sinon dans l'espace juridictionnel, du moins dans les confins d'une juridiction internationale des Droits de l'Homme dont il annoncerait l'avènement ou poserait l'équation.

Cet examen portera moins sur l'organe lui-même que sur ses fonctions. La discussion sur la nature du Comité n'est pas susceptible de rendre compte de la nature de ses fonctions. Par ailleurs, quel que soit le mode de recrutement des membres du Comité, il ne porte pas à conséquence sur le plan juridique quant à l'exercice ou non d'une fonction juridictionnelle: même si l'élection des membres et leur titre pour siéger au Comité sont à titre individuel et même si 'tout membre du Comité doit, avant d'entrer en fonctions, prendre en séance publique l'engagement solennel de s'acquitter de ses fonctions en toute impartialité et en toute conscience'[24]. C'est dire à quel point le statut des membres du Comité les prédispose à l'indépendance qui caractérise la condition des juges d'autant plus que la moralité, la compétence – et autant que possible l'expérience- juridique dont ils sont ou sont censés être porteurs, en font des êtres généralement à l'abri des influences. Mais tout cela reste d'une pertinence limitée.

Il y a donc lieu de rechercher des éléments de juridictionnalisation et c'est au niveau des fonctions que cela doit être tenté. De ce point de vue, et sans prétendre mener une analyse exhaustive, on pourrait susciter des interrogations au niveau de trois fonctions et d'une question particulière. Les fonctions tiennent à l'examen des

---

- S. Bastid, 'La fonction juridictionnelle dans les relations internationales', Les cours de droit, Paris, 1956-1957.
- A. Pellet, 'Le renforcement du rôle de la Cour en tant qu'organe judiciaire, principal des Nations Unies', dans *C.I./UNITAR*, (colloque du cinquantième anniversaire: Accroître l'efficacité de la Cour), 1997, Kluwer, Dordrecht.

[23] Sur ce type de démarche, voir la pertinente étude d'Alain Pellet: 'le bon droit' et 'l'ivraie', plaidoyer pour l'ivraie. Remarques sur quelques problèmes de méthode en droit international du développement', dans *Le droit des peuples à disposer d'eux-mêmes*. Méthodes d'analyse du droit international. Mélanges offerts à Charles Chaumont, Pédone, Paris, 1984, p.465 et seq.

[24] Article 38 du pacte. L'article 16 du règlement intérieur du Comité, reprenant les termes de l'article 38 du pacte, précise que tout membre du Comité doit, avant d'entrer en fonctions, prendre, en séance publique, l'engagement solennel ci-après: 'je m'engage solennellement à m'acquitter de mes fonctions de membre du Comité des Droits de l'Homme en toute impartialité et en toute conscience'.

rapports, à l'établissement d'observations générales et à l'examen des communications individuelles. La question particulière porte, quant à elle, sur l'approche de la question des réserves par le Comité.

L'EXAMEN DES RAPPORTS:

S'agissant de l'examen par le Comité des rapports des Etats il y a lieu de rappeler que l'article 2 paragraphe 1er du pacte des droits civils et politiques mets à la charge des Etats l'engagement de respecter et de garantir 'à tous les individus se trouvant sur leur territoire et relevant de leur compétence, les droits reconnus dans le pacte sans distinction aucune, notamment de race, de couleur, de sexe, de langue, de religion, d'opinion politique ou de toute autre opinion, d'origine nationale ou raciale, de fortune, de naissance ou de toute autre situation'.

Les Etats prennent, en outre, l'engagement de prendre les mesures 'propres à donner effet aux droits reconnus dans le pacte'.[25]

Tirant les conséquences pratiques de l'article 2, le premier paragraphe de l'article 40 fait obligation aux Etats parties de présenter des rapports sur 'les mesures qu'ils auront arrêtées' et qui 'donnent effet aux droits reconnus', dans le pacte. Les rapports doivent rendre compte des progrès réalisés dans la jouissance des droits ainsi que des facteurs et difficultés qui peuvent entraver la mise en œuvre du pacte. Les rapports doivent être présentés dans le délai d'un an à compter de l'entrée en vigueur du pacte pour chacun d'eux et par la suite chaque fois que le Comité le demande.

L'établissement du rapport, son examen, les observations finales auxquelles il donne lieu et son suivi se caractérisant par un rôle de plus en plus actif du Comité auquel les Etats ont de plus en plus de difficulté à échapper.

Relativement à l'établissement du rapport, déjà en 1981, lors de sa 13ème session, le Comité avait rappelé aux Etats ayant ratifié le pacte la nécessité de se 'préoccuper immédiatement de l'obligation qui leur est faite de présenter des rapports'[26]. Dans l'observation générale n° 2, adoptée au cours de la même session, le Comité avait défini des directives pour la présentation des rapports.[27] Dans ces directives, le Comité relève que certains rapports 'restent si succincts et si généraux qu'ils ne satisfont pas aux exigences en matière de rapports prévus à l'article 40'[28] et qu'ils se sont 'révélés incomplets sur le fond'.[29] D'après le contenu de certains d'entre eux 'il est difficile de juger … si les dispositions du pacte étaient appliquées'.[30] En conséquence le Comité 'considère que l'obligation de présenter

---

[25] Article 2, § 2 du pacte.

[26] Cf. Récapitulation des observations générales ou recommandations générales adoptées par les organes créés en vertu d'instruments internationaux relatifs au Droits de l'Homme – Nations Unies, HRJ/GE N/Rev. 3. Observation n°1 du Comité des Droits de l'Homme, p. 4.

[27] Observation n° 2, dans *Récapitulation*, *op. cit.*, p.5

[28] *Ibid.*

[29] *Ibid.*

[30] *Ibid.*

des rapports requiert que ceux-ci renseignent, non seulement sur les lois et autres règles se rapportant aux obligations contractées en vertu du pacte, mais aussi sur les pratiques des décisions des tribunaux et autres organes de l'Etat partie et sur tout autre fait de nature à indiquer le degré véritable de mise en œuvre et de jouissance des droits reconnus dans le pacte, les progrès accomplis et les facteurs et les difficultés qui affectent la mise en œuvre des dispositions du pacte'.[31]

Le Comité a eu à adopter plusieurs textes au sujet de la préparation des rapports.[32] Le dernier de ces textes, adopté par le Comité en dernière lecture le 18 octobre 1999 et applicable à parti du 1er janvier 2000 est intitulé 'directives unifiées concernant les rapports présentés par les Etats parties conformément au pacte international relatif aux droits civils et politiques.[33]

Ces directives, qui doivent être suivies par les Etats lors de l'établissement de leur rapport initial et de tous les rapports périodiques ultérieurs,[34] traitent des règles générales concernant le contenu des rapports ainsi que des règles spécifiques aux rapports initiaux d'un côté et aux rapports périodiques ultérieurs de l'autre. Se basant sur l'article 40 et sur l'idée qu'il se fait de ses compétences et de son rôle, le Comité ne s'adresse pas aux Etats en termes d'invitation, de recommandation et encore moins de prière. Les Etats sont rappelés à leurs devoirs nécessaires, aux obligations qu'ils ont souscrites, au respect des directives jugées appropriées.[35] Ils doivent expliquer, justifier, informer, fournir, suivre, etc.[36] c'est dire que, de ce point de vue, les Droits de l'Homme ne peuvent relever 'essentiellement de la compétence nationale d'un Etat',[37] que dans ce domaine l'espace est sinon un espace

---

[31] *Ibid.*

[32] Directives unifiées: CCPR/C/19/Rev. 1 du 26 août 1982; CCPR/C/5/Rev. 2 du 28 avril 1995 et annexe VIII au rapport présenté par le Comité à l'Assemblée générale en 1998 (A/53/40).

[33] Le texte des directives a été publié sous la cote suivante: CCPR/C/66/GUI-29 septembre 1999.

[34] Cf. les directives, *op. cit.*

[35] Directives – A2 (*s'appliqueront* à tous les rapports après le 31 décembre 1999), A3 (les Etats *devront*), B1 (les mesures qu'ils *auront adoptées*), C1(*devront*… être pris en compte), C3 (*devront être* indiquées en détail), C4 (le rapport *doit* décrire), C6 (le rapport *doit* décrire *suffisamment* de données), etc.

[36] C2 (toute réserve… devra être *expliquée* et sont maintien *justifié*), C4 (le rapport *doit décrire*…), C5 (il conviendra d'en *indiquer la nature et l'étendue*), C6 (le rapport *doit contenir suffisamment* de données statistiques), C7 (la situation… *doit être abordée spécifiquement*), C8 (les renseignements… *doivent*… être *mis à jour* dans le rapport), D1 (indiquer… *dans quelle mesure*…), D2.1 (fournir *des détails* sur la situation *concrète*… sur les *possibilités… application* et… *effets… donner des exemples*), D2.2 (indiquer les principales *mesures*… et l'éventail des *recours*…), D2.2 (expliquer *si le pacte… si… si*…), D2.3 (donner des *indications*), D2.4 (devra contenir des *informations*), D3.1 (le rapport devra être *accompagné*), E.2 (les rapports… devront être *structurés*), E.3 (se référer aux *règles générales*), F.1 (contenir des *informations* sur les *mesure* prises… *répondre à la préoccupation exprimée*), F.2 (la situation… *devra être expliquée*…), etc.

[37] Article 2, § 7 de la charte des Nations Unies.

d'intervention ou d'ingérence[38] du moins un *espace commun* aussi bien aux Etats qu'à la communauté internationale et que la souveraineté ne peut plus faire obstacle à la protection – et aussi à la promotion – des Droits de l'Homme.[39]

En somme tout se passe comme si l'Etat était encadré, au niveau de l'établissement de ses rapports, par le Comité. Cela n'a rien à voir avec l'action juridictionnelle. Mais le cadre se trouve ainsi posé, ainsi imposé. Il n'est pas sans conséquence sur *l'appréciation*, sur le *jugement*, que le Comité aura à porter sur l'Etat.

La procédure d'examen des rapports se caractérise par un certain nombre de temps forts qui témoignent du développement d'un processus qui, *sans être juridictionnel, s'y apparente de plus en plus.*

Sur la base des informations dont il dispose, qui proviennent des rapports et de bien d'autres sources dont, notamment, les organisations non gouvernementales, le Comité établit une liste de points qu'il communique à l'Etat concerné et sur lesquels portera, essentiellement, l'examen du rapport.

Pour l'examen de son rapport, l'Etat mets sur pied une délégation qui, de l'avis du Comité, doit être composée de manière à permettre un travail efficace et utile. 'Devront donc faire partie des délégations des personnes qui, grâce à leur connaissance approfondie de la situation des Droits de l'Homme dans l'Etat concerné et leur aptitude à expliquer cette situation, peuvent répondre aux questions orales et écrites ainsi qu'aux observations du Comité sur tout l'éventail des droits reconnus dans le pacte'.[40]

La délégation commence par répondre aux questions écrites ayant fait l'objet de la liste soumise à l'Etat. Elle répond, ensuite, aux questions additionnelles orales des

---

[38] Cf. Christine Chanet, 'Le Comité des Droits de l'Homme: méthodes de travail et cadre juridique d'activité' dans *La protection des Droits de l'Homme par le Comité des Droits de l'Homme des Nations Unies. Les communications individuelles*, sous la direction de F. Sudre, 1995, IDEDH, p. 4.

[39] C'est ainsi que le Secrétaire Général des Nations Unies Boutros Boutreos Ghali soutenait en 1993, devant la conférence de Vienne sur les Droits de l'Homme, que 'l'action internationale doit se poser lorsque les Etats se révèlent indignes de cette mission (protection des Droits de l'Homme), lorsqu'ils contreviennent aux principes fondamentaux de la charte et lorsque, loin d'être les protecteurs de la personne humaine, ils en deviennent les bourreaux…'

'Dans de telles circonstances, c'est à la Communauté internationale de prendre le relais des Etats défaillants, c'est-à-dire aux organisations internationales, universelles ou régionales. Il y a là une construction juridique et institutionnelle qui n'a rien de choquant et qui ne me semble pas attentatoire à la conception moderne que nous avons de la souveraineté. Car je pose –je vous pose la question: est-il en droit d'espérer le respect absolu de la communauté internationale, l'Etat qui ternit la belle idée de souveraineté en en faisant ouvertement un usage que la conscience universelle et que le droit réprouvent ? Lorsque la souveraineté devient l'ultime argument invoqué par les régimes autoritaires pour porter atteinte aux droits et libertés, des hommes, des femmes, des enfants, à l'abri des regards, alors –je le dis gravement – cette souveraineté-là *est déjà condamnée par l'histoire*'.

[40] Directives *op. cit.* G3.

membres du Comité et éventuellement réagit à leurs commentaires et observations et à leurs demandes d'actualisation ou d'information supplémentaires.

Le débat organisé avec la délégation se veut une 'discussion constructive' dans 'le but d'améliorer la situation des droits énoncés par le pacte dans l'Etat- partie'[41]. Ce n'est pas d'un débat contradictoire qu'il s'agit. Mais les rôles sont tels que le processus s'inscrit dans une stratégie au sein de laquelle un partenaire cherche à vérifier que le pacte n'est pas violé et l'autre partenaire cherche à prouver que le pacte est respecté. Deux perspectives qui découlent d'un positionnement différent, voire même contradictoire, qui atteste d'un 'rôle' et d'un 'contre-rôle', sans aller jusqu'à mettre en présence défense et accusation. Mais, de manière générale, l'*Etat* se trouve, quand même, dans la position de celui qui cherche à *prouver* et à *convaincre* alors que le *Comité* se trouve installé dans la condition de celui qui cherche à *s'assurer du bien fondé des informations et des affirmations* et à *se construire sa propre conviction, sa propre appréciation.*

Cela apparaîtra, clairement, à travers 'les observations finales'. Celles-ci constituent, en quelque sorte, l'appréciation finale *–le jugement?*- du Comité. 'Peu après l'examen du rapport, le Comité rendra publiques ses observations finales au sujet du rapport et du dialogue qui y fait suite avec la délégation'.[42]

'Les observations finales' comportent, généralement, outre une introduction, trois parties: la première porte sur 'les aspects positifs', la seconde sur 'les principaux sujets de préoccupation et recommandations' et la troisième sur 'la diffusion d'informations concernant le pacte'[43]. Dans la partie réservée aux aspects positifs, le Comité porte un jugement sur ce qu'il considère comme contribuant au respect du pacte et encourage l'Etat en conséquence. Les formules, à cet égard, sont variables: 'le Comité prend note avec satisfaction', 'le Comité se félicite', 'le Comité se réjouit', 'le Comité prend acte des changements positifs', 'le Comité rend hommage'...

Dans la partie réservée aux 'principaux sujets de préoccupation et recommandations', le Comité porte également un *jugement* sur des situations et recommande des changements en vue d'assurer le respect des dispositions du pacte. Là aussi, les formules sont diverses et varient en fonction de la gravité des atteintes au pacte. Le Comité 'regrette', 's'inquiète', 'constate', 'considère', 'réaffirme', 'constate avec préoccupation', 'note avec préoccupation', 'est toujours préoccupé', 'se déclare de nouveau préoccupé', 'est profondément préoccupé', 'note avec vive préoccupation', 'juge préoccupant', 'tient à souligner'... Lorsqu'il formule des recommandations, le Comité recourt, également, à des formules variables qui tiennent compte de la variété des situations et des questions examinées. C'est ainsi qu'il lui arrive, simplement, de 'recommander' ou 'd'encourager', de 'prier instamment' de demander à l'Etat de 'veiller', de l'inviter à 'prendre', à 'modifier', à

---

[41] Directives, *op. cit.* G1.

[42] *Ibid* G4.

[43] Voir, à titre d'exemples récents, les 'observations finales' sur:

- Trinité et Tobago, l'Argentine, le Venezuela et la République dominicaine in Rapport du Comité des droits de l'homme à l'Assemblée générale A/56/40 Vol. 1.

'adopter', à 'aligner', à 'supprimer', à 'mettre sur place', à 'poursuivre'. Le Comité peut être plus ferme en demandant que 'l'Etat fasse', en disant qu'il 'doit communiquer', qu'il 'doit prendre les mesures nécessaires', qu'il 'a l'obligation de veiller', qu'il doit fournir 'davantage d'effets' ou 'prendre des mesures nécessaires'…

La partie 'diffusion d'informations concernant le pacte' fixe 'la date du prochain rapport', 'appelle à tenir compte tout particulièrement des questions soulevées' dans les observations finales et demande la plus large diffusion possible tant des observations finales que du prochain rapport.[44] Par ailleurs, les observations finales sont publiées dans le rapport annuel du Comité à l'Assemblée Générale[45], après avoir fait l'objet de diffusion par voie de presse.[46]

Il reste que l'Etat aura à rendre compte des suites qu'il aura données aux observations finales à l'occasion de son prochain rapport. 'La liste des points à traiter' transmise à l'Etat concerné fait généralement référence aux recommandations au sujet des précédents rapports.[47]

Il est évident que l'ensemble des procédures relatives à l'examen des rapports fait ressortir une logique qui n'est ni administrative ni politique et qui, sans être juridictionnelle par sa portée notamment, n'en est pas moins proche.

A observer de près l'action du Comité dans ce domaine, telle qu'elle se développe concrètement, on finit par avoir l'impression qu'il y a des évolutions qui semblent s'inscrire, d'ores et déjà, dans la sphère du 'non encore achevé' lequel se caractérise par des balbutiements, naturellement hésitants et imparfaits, mais aussi parfois même par de francs propos juridictionnels y compris sur 'l'autorité de la chose observée' par le Comité. Les observations générales qu'adopte le Comité sont de nature à conforter cette impression.

L'ETABLISSEMENT D'OBSERVATIONS GENERALES :

Aux termes de l'article 40 paragraphe 4, le Comité des Droits de l'Homme 'adresse aux Etat-parties . . . toutes observations générales qu'il juge appropriées'.

Par la technique des observations générales, le Comité procède à l'interprétation du pacte, à l'actualisation des interprétations et va parfois même jusqu'à préciser sa

---

[44] Les directives, (*op. cit.*), précisent, en outre, dans le point G4 que 'le Comité attend de l'Etat-partie qu'il diffuse ces observations finales, dans toutes les langues voulues, à des fins d'information générale et pour susciter un débat public'.

[45] Voir les observations finales indiquées à la note 43.

[46] Il est de tradition qu'à la fin de chaque session, le bureau du Comité tienne une conférence de presse au cours de laquelle il présente, notamment, les observations finales au sujet de l'examen des rapports des Etats.

[47] Voir, à titre d'exemples, les listes des points à traiter transmises:

- au Guyana (CCPR/C/68/L/GUY – 3 décembre 1999),
- à la Mongolie (CCPR/C/68/L/MNG – 3 décembre 1999),
- au Venezuela (CCPR/C/68/L/VEN – 3 décembre 1999)…

pensée relativement à des questions qui ne sont pas liées à un article particulier du pacte.

Jusqu'à présent, 29 observations générales ont été établies.[48]

Les premières observations générales ont été d'un apport juridique très limité et attestaient plutôt d'une certaine timidité du Comité. Mais, progressivement, les observations générales sont devenues plus consistantes, plus précises, traçant, parfois, de véritables lignes de comportement pour les Etats. D'avance le Comité indique aux Etats le contenu des dispositions du pacte, leur portée ainsi que leurs limites.

Ce rôle que le Comité se reconnaît pour 'dire le droit' lui permet non seulement de faire œuvre d'interprétation mais également de développement des dispositions dont il doit assurer le respect. Le développement, le Comité le veut continu puisqu'il procède à la révision et à l'actualisation de ses propres observations générales comme cela a été le cas notamment pour l'article 3 qui a fait l'objet de l'observation générale n° 4 (1981) révisée et remplacée par l'observation générale n° 28 (1999). Tout semble se passer, donc, comme s'il s'agissait d'un processus de développement continu, de création du droit, rappelant ainsi, de certains points de vue, les arrêts de règlement que rendaient, avant la révolution, les anciens parlements en France.

Le Comité met souvent, par ailleurs, ses observations générales à contribution lors de l'établissement des observations finales sur les rapports des Etats ou lorsqu'il doit se prononcer sur les communications individuelles qui lui sont soumises.[49] Ce mouvement peut être réversible et il arrive, tout aussi souvent, que les principes

---

[48] Les observations ont concerné l'obligation de faire rapport (n° 1 – 1981), les directives pour la présentation des rapports (n° 2 – 1981), l'article 2 (n° 3 –1981), l'article 3 (n° 4 –1981), l'actrice 4 (n° 5 – 1981), l'article 6(n° 6 – 1982), l 'article 7 (n° 7 – 1982), l'article 9 (n° 8 – 1982), l'article 10 (n° 9 – 1982), l'article 19 (n° 10 –1983), l'article 20 (n° 11-1983), l'article 1er (n° 12 –1984), l'article 14 (n° 13 – 1984), l'article 6 (n° 14 – 1984), la situation des étrangers au regard du pacte (n° 15 –1986,) l'article 17 (n° 16 – 1988), l'article 24 (n° 17-1989), la non-discrimination (n° 18-1989), l'article 23 (n° 19-1990), l'article 7 (n° 20-1992), l'article 10 (n° 21-1992), l'article 18 (n° 22-1993), l'article 27 (n° 23-1994), la question touchant les réserves formulées au moment de la ratification du pacte ou des protocoles facultatifs y relatif ou de l'adhésion à ces instruments ou en rapport avec des déclarations formulées au titre de l'article 41 du pacte (n° 24-1994), l'article 25 (n° 24-1996), la continuité des obligations en vertu du pacte (n° 26-1997(, l'article 12 (n° 27-1999), l'article 3 (observation générale n° 28 révisant et remplaçant l'observation générale n°4-1999), et l'article 4 (observation générale n° 29). Les autres observations générales que le Comité a décidé de rédiger porteront sur les articles, 2, 21 et 22.

[49] Voir, à titre d'exemple, la référence que fait le Comité à l'observation générale n° 8 dans l'affaire n° 732/1997 B. Whyte c. Jamaïque –27 juillet 1998 dans *Rapport du Comité des Droits de l'Homme* volume 2 –supplément n° 40/A/53/40. les auteurs des communications et les Etats se réfèrent, également, assez souvent aux observations générales. Les cas sont nombreux à cet égard. Cf. le document ci-dessus référencé. Voir relativement aux observations finales et à titre d'exemples, les observations finales sur les rapports du Gabon, du Pérou et de la Syrie in Report of the Human Rights Committee A/56/40 Vol 1p. 41 et ss, p.45 et ss et p.70 et ss.

dégagés à l'occasion de l'examen des communications individuelles servent de sous-bassement à des observations générales[50]. Ainsi la jurisprudence du Comité alimente ses observations générales et celles-ci soutiennent sa jurisprudence.

Le Comité n'estime pas devoir limiter ses observations générales à des dispositions spécifiques du pacte. L'observation générale n° 24 portant sur les réserves ne traite pas d'une disposition spécifique du pacte mais se préoccupe, plus généralement du but et de l'objet du pacte. Des orientations sont ainsi données aux Etats quant à leur adhésion au pacte ou quant aux réserves qu'ils peuvent observer. Comme on le soulignera, ultérieurement, la question des réserves a eu des répercussions pratiques y compris sur les communications individuelles.[51]

Quelles conclusions tirer de la technique des observations générales ? D'abord que les Etats ne sont plus totalement souverains pour interpréter le pacte. Que le Comité institué spécialement à l'effet de veiller au respect du pacte est autrement habilité à l'interpréter et à en définir la portée et les limites. Que les interprétations sont imputables au pacte et que les Etats ne peuvent, en conséquence, s'y soustraire à moins d'une réserve jugée acceptable par le Comité lui-même. Que, ce faisant, le Comité fait œuvre juridique, ce qui n'est pas sans rappeler celle qu'assure le juge dans le cadre de l'accomplissement de sa fonction et qui lui permet par la technique de l'interprétation de faire, aussi, œuvre de création de normes.[52]

Mais le rapprochement entre le Comité des Droits de l'Homme et les juridictions ne prend toute sa signification qu'à la lumière de la question de l'examen des communications individuelles.

L'EXAMEN DES COMMUNICATIONS INDIVIDUELLES :

Le protocole facultatif se rapportant au pacte international relatif aux droits civils et politiques[53] avait été établi à l'effet de 'mieux assurer l'accomplissement des fins du pacte… et l'application de ses dispositions'.[54] Il était venu donner compétence au Comité pour 'recevoir et examiner les communication émanant de particuliers qui

---

[50] Cf., par exemple l'observation générale n° 27 qui se réfère notamment aux communications n° 456/1991 (*Calepli c/ Suède*), Constatations adoptées le 18 juillet 1994, UN doc. A/49/40 vol. II, p. 165, n° 138/1983 (*Mpandajila c/Zaïre*), Constatations adoptées le 26 mars 1986, *Sélection des décisions du Comité des droits de l'homme prises en vertu du Protocole Facultatif*, vol. 2, p. 172, n° 157/1983 (*Mpaka-Nsusu c/Zaïre*), Constatations adoptées le 26 mars 1986, *Sélection des décisions du Comité des droits de l'homme*, vol. 2, p 196 et n° 241/1987 et 242/1987 (*Birhashwirwa/Tshisekedi c/Zaïre*), Constatations adoptées le 2 novembre 1989, NU doc. A/45/40 vol. II, p. 77.

[51] Cf. *infra*.

[52] Voir, à cet égard, notamment, la thèse de Sadok Belaïd: *Essai sur le pouvoir créateur et normatif du juge*, Publication de l'Université de Tunis, Faculté de Droit et des Sciences Politiques et Economiques de Tunis, 8ème série, Volume 1, 1973.

[53] Il s'agit en réalité du premier protocole facultatif auquel est venu s'ajouter un second portant sur l'abolition de la peine de mort qui a été ratifié, jusque-là, par 45 Etats.

[54] Préambule du protocole facultatif.

prétendent être victimes d'une violation de l'un des droits énoncés dans le pacte'[55]. Il ne peut en être ainsi, cependant, que si l'Etat-partie au pacte a accepté la compétence ainsi donnée au Comité, en devenant partie au protocole facultatif.[56] Au 27 juillet 2001, 98 Etats sont parties au protocole facultatif, entré en vigueur, déjà, le 23 mars 1976, en même temps que le pacte lui-même. Par ailleurs, une communication ne peut être déclarée recevable que si, notamment, toutes les voies de recours disponibles ont été épuisées[57] et qu'elle n'est pas soumise à un autre mode international de règlement.

L'examen des communications individuelles revêt un caractère confidentiel et se fait à huis clos.[58] Les décisions finales, qu'il s'agisse de décisions de cesser l'examen ou, de décisions d'irrecevabilité et les constatations, sont rendues publiques.[59]

Jusqu'au 27 juillet 2001, 1004 communications ont été enregistrées. Elles concernent 69 Etats. 368 d'entre elles ont abouti à des constatations dont 282 concluant à des violations du pacte. 300 ont été déclarées irrecevables. 142 ont été classées ou retirées et 194 sont encore en cours d'examen.[60]

Au cours des cinq dernières années le nombre de nouvelles affaires enregistrées, autant que celui des affaires en suspens n'a cessé d'augmenter. Cela s'explique, notamment, d'une part par l'augmentation du nombre d'Etats parties au protocole facultatif et d'autre part par une meilleure circulation de l'information au sujet de la procédure des communications individuelles.[61]

La procédure d'examen des communications est établie par le règlement intérieur du Comité[62] en ses articles 78 à 97. Le règlement définit les règles de transmission des communications, les dispositions générales régissant l'examen des communications par le Comité ou par ses organes subsidiaires, la procédure visant à déterminer la recevabilité, la procédure d'examen des communications quant au fond et les règles de confidentialité.

De manière générale, les règles posées par le règlement intérieur ne s'écartent pas sensiblement des règles générales du droit judiciaire. Le Comité, qui jusqu'en

---

[55] *Ibid.* voir, également art. 1 du protocole.

[56] Art. 1er du protocole.

[57] Art. 2 du protocole.

[58] l'article 96 du règlement intérieur du Comité indique que les débats oraux et les comptes rendus analytiques des séances sont confidentiels (§1). Cependant l'auteur d'une communication ou l'Etat-partie intéressé conserve le droit de rendre publique toutes déclarations, observations ou informations ayant trait à la procédure à moins que le Comité ne les prie d'en respecter, totalement ou partiellement le caractère confidentiel (§3). Pour plus de détails voir l'ensemble de l'article 96 du règlement intérieur.

[59] Etant entendu que les noms des auteurs sont divulgués à moins que le Comité n'en décide autrement.

[60] Ces statistiques ont été fournies à la suite de la clôture de la 72ème session du Comité des Droits de l'Homme.

[61] Pour de plus amples informations sur les communications traitées jusqu'en 2001, voir le dernier rapport du Comité à l'Assemblée générale. Document 40 (A/56/40).

[62] Cf. CCPR/C3/Rev. 6 and Corr. 1. Report A/56/40 Vol 1, pp.168 à 192.

1997 devait disjoindre les question de recevabilité et de fond, est en mesure, aujourd'hui, de procéder à l'examen des deux questions à la fois.[63] Les règles de transmission des observations par l'auteur de la communication ou par l'Etat-partie témoignent d'une démarche plutôt de nature juridictionnelle. La procédure se caractérise par l'intervention d'un rapporteur spécial pour les nouvelles communications[64] d'un groupe de travail des communications[65] et enfin du Comité lui-même. Les constatations et les décisions sont théoriquement prises par consensus, mais la règle de la majorité est de plus en plus courante comme en témoigne le développement des opinions individuelles.[66]

S'agissant, des décisions et constatations, elles sont construites sous forme juridictionnelle et comportent, bien évidemment, des motifs et des dispositifs[67]. Rien, ne distingue, du point de vue formel, les constatations des décisions juridictionnelles. Après le visa ayant trait à l'institution du Comité, à la date de sa réunion, à la fin de l'examen de la communication, aux informations communiquées par l'auteur, son conseil et l'Etat-partie, interviennent successivement le rappel des faits présentés par l'auteur, la teneur de la plainte, les observations de l'Etat-partie et le commentaire de l'auteur ou de son Conseil. Par la suite le Comité se livre à l'analyse des considérations relatives à la recevabilité et à l'examen quant au fond avant d'adopter les décisions ou les constatations qui lui semblent devoir s'imposer et qui se terminent, lorsqu'il y a violation de l'une des dispositions du pacte, généralement par ce qui suit: 'Aux termes de l'article 2 du pacte, l'*Etat-partie s'est engagé à garantir* à tous les individus se trouvant sur son territoire et relevant de sa juridiction *les droits reconnus dans le pacte et à assurer un recours utile et*

---

[63] Cela découle des modifications du nouveau règlement intérieur adoptées le 1er août 1997.

[64] Le Rapporteur Spécial pour les nouvelles communications est chargé de traiter les communications nouvelles au fur et à mesure qu'elles parviennent au secrétariat. Il les transmet aux Etats parties intéressés en leur demandant de soumettre des renseignements ou des observations tant sur la recevabilité que sur le fond. Le Rapporteur Spécial est, également, habilité, dans certains cas, à formuler, adopter ou retirer, conformément à l'article 86 du règlement intérieur, des demandes de mesures provisoires de protection.

[65] Le groupe de travail des communications, constitué conformément à l'article 89 du règlement intérieur, est chargé notamment de se prononcer sur la recevabilité des communications et sur leur examen quant au fond. Il peut déclarer une communication recevable si ses 5 membres y sont favorables. En dehors de cette hypothèse, le groupe renvoie la question au Comité. Il ne peut pas déclarer une communication irrecevable mais peut toujours faire une recommandation en ce sens au Comité. Il est à signaler par ailleurs que le Comité avait décidé, à sa 55ème session, que chaque communication doit être confiée à l'un de ses membres en tant que 'rapporteur de la communication' au groupe de travail et en séance plénière.

[66] Sur le développement des opinions individuelles voir les sept derniers rapports du Comité à l'Assemblée générale 40 (A/50/40); 40 (A/51/40); 40 (A/52/40); 40 (A/53/40); 40 (A/54/40); 40(A/55/40) et 40 (A/56/40).

[67] Voir l'ensemble des rapports du Comité à l'Assemblée générale. Voir, également, Comité des Droits de l'Homme. Sélection de décisions prises en vertu du protocole facultatif, Volume 1 CCPR/C/OP/1 et Volume 2 CCPR/C/OP/2.

exécutoire lorsqu'une violation a été établie. Le Comité souhaite recevoir de l'Etat-partie, *dans un délai de 90 jours* des renseignements sur *les mesures prises pour donner effet à ses constatations*'.

L'examen des constatations 'rendues' par le Comité témoigne d'une très haute qualité d'analyse juridique, d'une grande variété de questions traitées et d'une remarquable aptitude à assurer, conformément au pacte, le développement continu du droit international des Droits de l'Homme. La consultation du dernier rapport du Comité à la 56ème session de l'Assemblée générale peut être fort instructive.[68]

A titre d'illustration et s'agissant des questions de procédure, le Comité a eu à adopter des constatations sur les points suivants: qualité de l'auteur, irrecevabilité 'rationnae temporis', communication sans fondement, communications incompatibles avec les dispositions du pacte, examen de la même affaire par une autre instance internationale d'enquête ou de règlement, règle de l'épuisement des recours internes, et mesures provisoires.[69]

Au titre des questions de fond le rapport rend compte de constatations où les points suivants ont été examinés: droit à la vie, droit de ne pas être soumis à la torture, ni à des peines ou traitements cruels, inhumains ou dégradants, liberté et sécurité de la personne, traitement en prison, garanties d'un procès équitable, droit à la liberté d'opinion et à la liberté d'expression, droit à l'égalité devant la loi et interdiction de la discrimination…[70]

S'agissant du suivi des constatations du Comité, il y a lieu de rappeler, d'abord, que le paragraphe 4 de l'article 5 du protocole facultatif énonce que 'le Comité fait part des ses constatations à l'Etat-partie intéressé et au particulier'. Tirant les suites logiques de la compétence de 'faire-part', le Comité à établi en 1990 une procédure de suivi en créant la fonction de rapporteur spécial pour le suivi des constatations.[71]

Depuis 1991 des demandes d'informations sur les suites des constatations concluant à une violation du pacte sont présentées aux Etats. Jusqu'en juillet 1999 des informations ont été communiquées relativement à 152 constatations. Quatre-vingt-quatre constatations n'avaient suscité aucune réponse. 'Pour 9 d'entre elles le délai de réception des informations n'était pas encore expiré'. 'Environ 30% des réponses reçues peuvent être considérées comme satisfaisantes en ce sens qu'elles

---

[68] Rapport du Comité des Droits de l'Homme, volume 1, Assemblée générale – 56ème de session supplément n° 40 (A/56/40).

[69] Cf. à titre d'exemple 40 (A/54/40) pp. 77 à 80.

[70] *Ibid.*, pp. 80 à 87.

[71] L'article 95 du règlement intérieur dispose, à ce égard, ce qui suit:

' 1 Le Comité désigne un rapporteur spécial chargé du suivi des constatations adoptées au titre du paragraphe 4 de l'article 5 du protocole facultatif, afin de vérifier que les Etats parties ont pris des mesures pour donner effet à ses constatations'.

' 2-Le Rapporteur spécial peut établir les contacts et prendre les mesures appropriées pour s'acquitter dûment de ce mandat'.

' 3 Le Rapporteur spécial fait périodiquement rapport au Comité sur les activités de suivi'.

' 4 Le Comité consigne dans son rapport annuel les informations sur les activités de suivi'.

montrent que l'Etat partie est prêt à donner suite aux constatations du Comité ou à accorder réparation au plaignant'.[72]

L'auteur d'une étude sur 'la portée et le suivi des constatations du Comité des Droits de l'Homme des Nations Unies', Markus, Schmidt,[73] indique que jusqu'en janvier 1995, sept ou huit réponses se sont explicitement opposées aux recommandations du Comité dont une émanant de la Jamaïque au sujet de l'affaire Hamilton (n° 333/1988). La Jamaïque avait informé le Comité qu'elle n'était pas disposée à suivre ses recommandations préconisant la relaxe de M. Hamilton, condamné à mort dont le procès n'avait pas été jugé équitable.

Dans l'affaire Campbell c/Jamaïque (n° 248/1987) la Jamaïque souligne 'que la communication demeure irrecevable eu égard, au non-épuisement des recours internes par l'auteur... Néanmoins par respect pour le Comité l'Etat... a examiné le fond de l'affaire et conclu que les faits ne permettent pas d'étayer les violations constatées par le Comité'. Suite à une affaire concernant l'enseignement religieux et le principe de non-discrimination[73 bis] le Canada a fait savoir qu'il ne lui était pas possible de mettre en œuvre les constatations du Comité en raison du fait que les questions d'éducation relèvent des provinces, étant pourtant précisé que l'article 50 du pacte s'applique sans limitation, ni exception aucune, à toutes les unités constitutives des Etats fédératifs.

Dans de nombreux cas, cependant, les suites données aux constatations sont parfaitement satisfaisantes.[74]

Suite aux constatations sur l'affaire Ortega (n° 481/1991), le gouvernement de l'Equateur a conclu un accord avec le représentant de l'auteur dans lequel il reconnaissait sa responsabilité internationale pour la violation des articles 7 et 10 paragraphe 1. Il acceptait, en conséquence, de verser à la victime, dans un délai de 90 jours, 25 000 dollars américains de dommages intérêts. L'Etat-partie a accepté, en outre, 'd'engager des poursuites civiles et pénales et une procédure administrative à l'encontre des personnes qui avaient commis les violations et de prendre les dispositions nécessaires pour les déférer à la justice, en se réservant le droit de leur réclamer le remboursement du montant versé à titre de dommages-intérêts.[75]

Suite à l'affaire Clive Johnson (n° 592/1994), la Jamaïque a informé le Comité, par note du 26 mars 1999, que 'le Conseil privé jamaïcain souscrivait aux constatations du Comité et que la mise en liberté de l'auteur était imminente'.[76]

---

[72] Cf. Rapport du Comité à la 54ème session de l'Assemblée générale, supplément n° 40 (A/54/40), p. 89.

[73] in '*La protection des Droits de l'Homme...*', sous la direction de F. Sudre, *op. cit.* p. 157 et seq.

[73 bis] Affaire No. 694/1996 (*Waldman c/ Canada*), Constations adoptées le 3 novembre 1999, supplément n° 40 (A/55/40), p. 86 (CCPR/C/67/D/694/1996).

[74] Cf. M.Schmidt, *op. cit.* p. 162 et 163.

[75] Cf. Le Rapporteur du Comité à l'Assemblée générale, supplément n° 40 (A/54/40), *op. cit.* p. 96.

[76] *Ibid.* p. 97.

Tirant les conséquences de l'affaires Karttunen (n° 387/1982) la Finlande a informé le Comité qu'elle avait engagé les procédures appropriées en vue d'indemniser l'auteur et que, d'autre part, elle avait modifié avec effet à partir du 1er mai 1998 le code de procédure judiciaire qui était en jeu lors de cette affaire.[77]

Une autre illustration de suivi concluant des constatations est fournie par l'affaire, Park c/République de Corée (n° 628/1995). Le gouvernement de la République de Corée a, par note du 15 mars 1999, informé le Comité que 'la Cour suprême était saisie de la demande d'indemnisation de l'auteur' et qu'il 'envisagerait de modifier la loi sur la sécurité nationale ou de la remplacer par un nouveau texte afin de tenir compte des constatations du Comité'. Dans la note il est, en outre, souligné que 'le ministère de la justice avait traduit les constatations du Comité et les avait rendues, publiques par l'intermédiaire des médias. Les autorités judiciaires avaient, également, été informées'.[78]

Quels enseignements tirer de la procédure des communications individuelles établies par le protocole facultatif ?

D'abord, s'il est vrai que le Comité n'est qu'un comité d'experts indépendants élus par des Etats, il n'en demeure pas moins que cette condition n'est pas de nature à faire obstacle à l'observation et au développement par le Comité d'un comportement de nature juridictionnelle, notamment, au niveau de l'examen des communications individuelles.

Si le protocole facultatif ne comporte que peu de règles, fort succinctes, même lapidaires, cela n'a pas empêché le Comité d'élaborer, dans le cadre de son règlement intérieur, un important corps de principes et de règles de procédure comparable à ceux observés par des instances juridictionnelles internationales telles que, notamment, la Cour européenne des Droits de l'Homme ou la Cour interaméricaine des Droits de l'Homme. En termes de procédure, l'examen des communications se réalise dans des conditions et règles très proches des celles des organes juridictionnels.

Au niveau des règles de fond le Comité a pu préciser et développer la portée de nombreuses dispositions du pacte, établissant ainsi un corps de jurisprudence entretenu par un effort constant d'interprétation et une recherche permanente de l'adéquation entre la lettre des textes et leur esprit. Cela apparaît, notamment, au niveau de l'élaboration et de l'affinement des notions de proportionnalité, de nécessité, d'égalité, de procès équitable, de non-discrimination, de juridiction, de minorité… Un véritable travail juridictionnel est ainsi opéré dont la portée doit être appréciée non seulement au niveau du comportement du Comité lui-même et des Etats parties mais également au niveau des juridictions tant internes qu'internationales.

Relativement à l'autorité attachée aux constatations, il ne s'agit pas, bien évidement, de 'l'autorité de la chose jugée' au sens classique du terme. Mais il reste indéniable, malgré cela, que le Comité participe à l'exercice d'une fonction

---

[77] *Ibid.* p. 96.
[78] *Ibid.* p. 97.

juridictionnelle en *tranchant des contestations sur la base du droit* et c'est là l'essentiel de ce qui constitue l'acte juridictionnel. C'est parce que le Comité semble, ainsi, voir les choses, qu'il conclut systématiquement ses constatations par un rappel de l'engagement de l'Etat, notamment, à '*assurer un recours utile et exécutoire* lorsqu'une violation a été établie' et par une demande tendant à recevoir, dans les 90 jours, 'des renseignements sur les mesures prises pour donner effet' aux constatations. Le développement de la procédure du suivi vient confirmer, malgré l'hostilité ou les réserves de certains Etats, que l'obligation de respect des constatations rendues, ne relève pas, uniquement, de la sphère de la bonne volonté. Le Comité se fait une très haute idée de son rôle et de ses prises de position sur le plan du droit. Son analyse de la question des réserves ne laisse pas, à cet égard, de doute possible.

LA QUESTION DES RESERVES :

La question des réserves est l'une des questions le plus complexes du droit international.[79] Elle soulève de nombreuses interrogations, alimente de substantielles controverses et conduit à de fortes oppositions. Le débat porte, entre autres, notamment, sur l'organe habilité à apprécier les réserves[80] et sur la compatibilité des réserves avec le but et l'objet de l'instrument qui les suscite.[81]

Le Comité des Droits de l'Homme s'est vu confronté à la question des réserves. Le traitement qu'il lui a consacré mérite d'être d'autant plus souligné qu'il se caractérise par une vigoureuse démarche juridique qui, sur plus d'un plan, s'apparente à une démarche juridictionnelle.

Partant de l'idée selon laquelle 'si une déclaration, quels qu'en soient l'appellation ou l'intitulé, vise à exclure ou à modifier l'effet juridique d'un traité dans son application à l'Etat, elle constitue une réserve'[82] et que 'inversement, si ce qu'un Etat appelle une réserve ne fait que traduire l'interprétation qu'il a d'une disposition donnée, sans exclure ni modifier cette disposition dans son application au dit Etat, il ne s'agit pas en réalité d'une réserve',[83] le Comité des Droits de l'Homme constate que les réserves, par leur multiplication, leur variété, leur généralité parfois, leur teneur et leur portée peuvent compromettre l'application

[79] Voir les manuels et ouvrages de droit international, ainsi que les documents officiels de l'Assemblée générale – 39ème session, supplément n° 40 (A/39/40); 45ème session, supplément n°40 (A/45/40), etc. Consulter également les travaux de la Commission du droit international.
[80] Voir, à titre d'exemple, l'échange de lettres entre le président de la Commission du droit international et le président du Comité des Droits de l'Homme, infra.
[81] *Ibid.* Voir, également: Gérard Cohen-Jonathan: 'Conclusions', dans '*La protection des Droits de l'Homme*', sous la direction de F. Sudre, *op. cit.*, p. 186 – cf. également *infra*.
[82] Cf. observation n° 24 intitulée: Questions touchant les réserves formulées au moment de la ratification du pacte ou des protocoles facultatifs et relatifs ou de l'adhésion à ces instruments ou en rapport avec des déclarations formulées au titre de l'article 41 du pacte (1994) in *Récapitulation*, *op. cit.*, p. 47.
[83] *Ibid.*

effective du pacte. Dès lors, conclut le Comité, il importe que les Etats sachent exactement à quelles obligations ils ont souscrit et que le Comité sache également – en vue de s'acquitter de ses devoirs découlant notamment de l'article 40 et des protocoles facultatifs- si un Etat est lié par une obligation donnée et dans quelle mesure,[84] étant, par ailleurs, entendu que la non-interdiction des réserves ne signifie pas qu'un Etat peut émettre n'importe quelle réserve.

Le Comité soutient que son rôle, tant au titre de l'article 40 du pacte que des protocoles facultatifs 'suppose nécessairement l'*interprétation des dispositions du pacte et l'élaboration d'une jurisprudence*'.[85] Il en conclut que les réserves excluant ou méconnaissant la compétence interprétative du Comité, s'agissant du pacte, ne sont pas acceptables. Il ajoute que 'en raison du caractère particulier d'un instrument relatif aux Droits de l'Homme, la compatibilité d'une réserve avec l'objet et le but du pacte doit être établie *objectivement, en se référant à des principes juridiques. Le Comité est particulièrement bien placé pour s'acquitter de cette tâche'*.[86]

Cette position du Comité relativement à sa compétence, en matière de réserves portant sur un instrument relatif aux Droits de l'Homme, a été à l'origine d'une divergence d'appréciation avec la commission du droit international. Dans le paragraphe 12 des réserves aux traités multilatéraux normatifs, y compris les traités relatifs aux Droits de l'Homme,[87] il est indiqué que 'la Commission souligne que les présentes conclusions sont sans préjudice des *pratiquse et des règles mises en œuvre par les organes de* contrôle dans des contextes régionaux'.

La réaction du Comité ne s'était pas faite attendre. 'Les organes universels de contrôle, comme le Comité des Droits de l'Homme, ne jouent pas un rôle moins important dans ce processus et sont donc habilités à y participer et à y contribuer'. 'Il convient de souligner que les organes universels de contrôle, tels que le Comité des Droits de l'Homme, doivent connaître l'étendue des obligations des Etats parties pour être à même de s'acquitter des fonctions leur incombant en vertu du traité par lequel ils ont été crées'.[88]

En d'autres termes, le Comité détermine, à la lumière des réserves dont il lui revient d'apprécier la régularité et la compatibilité avec le pacte, l'étendue de sa compétence. Il est maître de sa compétence dans la limite du traité qui l'a institué. Cette maîtrise de la compétence est d'autant plus indiscutable qu'il n'existe pas d'organe juridictionnel habilité à se substituer au Comité ou à contrôler son activité juridique. Les confins de la juridiction internationale des Droits de l'Homme deviennent, ainsi, moins lointains et plus facilement déterminables.

---

[84] *Ibid.*, p. 47.
[85] *Ibid.*, p. 50.
[86] *Ibid.*, p. 53.
[87] Voir, le texte du paragraphe au document A/53/40. Annexe IX.
[88] La réaction du Comité s'est exprimée, notamment, à travers une première lettre envoyée par le président du Comité des Droits de l'Homme au président de la Commission du droit international en date du 9 avril 1998 (référence, *op. cit.*) suivie d'une seconde lettre en date du 5 novembre 1998 publiée au titre d'annexe VI, dans *Rapport du Comité des Droits de l'Homme*, volume I, supplément n°40 (A/54/40).

S'agissant de l'appréciation de la compatibilité des réserves avec le but et l'objet du pacte, le Comité a construit une analyse hardie qu'il a développée dans son observation n° 24 et qu'il a appliquée dans le cadre de sa 'fonction contentieuse'.

D'abord, pour lui, les dispositions du pacte, qui représentent des règles du droit international coutumier et *a fortiori* lorsqu'elles ont un caractère de normes impératives –(interdiction de l'esclavage, de la torture, privation arbitraire du droit à la vie, droit à la liberté de pensée, de conscience et de religion, présomption d'innocence, interdiction d'exécution des femmes enceintes et des enfants…) ne peuvent pas faire l'objet de réserves.

Ensuite, les réserves incompatibles avec l'objet et le but du pacte ne sont pas acceptables (les droits non susceptibles de dérogation ou auxquels les dérogations sont impossibles…).

Il n'est pas possible, non plus, qu'un Etat se réserve la possibilité de ne pas présenter de rapport ou de ne pas accepter que son rapport soit étudié par le Comité. 'C'est pourquoi une réserve, qui rejette la compétence qu'a le Comité d'interpréter les obligations prévues dans une disposition du pacte, serait aussi contraire à l'objet et au but de cet instrument.[89] De même, ne peuvent pas être acceptées les réserves formulées en termes généraux et qui ont, essentiellement, pour effet de rendre inopérants tous les droits énoncés dans le pacte.[90]

S'agissant du premier protocole facultatif, le Comité déclare, avec force, qu' 'une réserve touchant l'obligation d'un Etat de respecter et de garantir un droit énoncé dans le pacte, formulée au titre des droits du premier protocole facultatif, alors qu'elle n'a pas été émise auparavant au titre du pacte, ne porte pas atteinte au devoir de l'Etat de respecter ses obligations de fond'. Une réserve ne peut être émise au pacte par le biais du protocole facultatif.[91] 'La conséquence normale d'une réserve inacceptable n'est pas que le pacte restera totalement lettre morte pour l'Etat auteur de la réserve. Une telle réserve est dissociable, c'est-à-dire que *le pacte s'appliquera à l'Etat qui en est l'auteur, sans bénéficier de la réserve*'[92].

C'est à la lumière de cette analyse que l'affaire Rawle Kennedy c/Trinidad et Tobago a été examinée par le Comité des Droits de l'Homme. Rawle Kennedy, citoyen de Trinidad, condamné à mort, ayant épuisé tous les recours internes, a présenté une communication au Comité qu'il justifiait par différentes violations du pacte par Trinidad et Tobago. La communication a été présentée le 7 décembre 1998. Or le 26 mai 1998, Trinidad et Tobago avait dénoncé le premier protocole facultatif pour y adhérer de nouveau le même jour, cependant, avec la réserve suivante: '…La Trinidad et Tobago adhère, de nouveau, au protocole facultatif se rapportant au pacte international relatif aux droits civils et politiques en formulant une réserve à l'article 1er du protocole, à savoir que le Comité des Droits de

---

[89] *Ibid.*, p. 50.

[90] *Ibid.*, p. 50.

[91] Observation n° 24, *op. cit.*, p. 53.

[92] Affaire n° 845/1999 (*Kennedy c/ Trinité-et-tobago*), Décision du 4 novembre 1999, supplément 40 (A/55/40), p. 258.

l'Homme n'aura pas compétence pour recevoir et examiner des communications concernant un détenu condamné à mort pour ce qui est de toute question ayant trait aux poursuites judiciaires dont il aura fait l'objet, à sa détention, à son procès, à sa condamnation et à sa peine ou à l'exécution de la peine de mort à son encontre ou à toute question connexe'.

La question essentielle, qui s'était posée au Comité, était celle de savoir si la réserve était acceptable et si, en conséquence, la communication pouvait être déclarée recevable. Dans sa constatation du 4 novembre 1999, le Comité avait, après avoir rappelé sa compétence pour apprécier les réserves formulées à l'endroit du pacte et des protocoles facultatifs et relatifs, rejeté la réserve trinidatienne au motif qu'elle constituait une violation du principe d'égalité, qu'elle était, en réalité, une réserve au pacte et que de toute façon, par sa large portée, elle constituait une atteinte à l'objet et au but du pacte.

Au-delà de l'espèce elle-même, qui ne manquera pas de faire date dans la jurisprudence du Comité notamment, il y a lieu de souligner le contenu et la portée de l'analyse du Comité, analyse qui en fait pratiquement une juridiction dont la volonté, motivée en droit, s'impose aux Etats en particulier.

Il est peu-être prématuré de tirer toutes les conséquences de l'affaire Kennedy. Mais il est, d'ores et déjà, établi qu'une impulsion supplémentaire est, ainsi, donnée à la juridictionnalisation des fonctions du Comité des Droits de l'Homme, dans le sens d'une mise sur pied progressive d'une juridiction internationale des Droits de l'Homme. Bien évidemment celle-ci peut toujours être établie de manière conventionnelle. Mais il peut en être autrement dans la mesure où le Comité des Droits de l'Homme continuera de manière lente et progressive à développer la jurisprudence qui est la sienne et à mener l'ensemble de ses activités avec la même pondération et la même détermination, compte dûment tenu de la lettre du pacte et de son esprit. Il y a lieu de donner du temps au temps pour qu'il puisse permettre d'assimiler et d'intérioriser les progrès réalisés mais aussi provoquer, de manière volontariste, les évolutions nécessaires.

UN ZOULOU AU PALAIS WILSON

Maurice Glèlè Ahanhanzo

Un jour un Zoulou est élu membre du Comité des droits de l'Homme. Il prête serment devant le représentant du Secrétaire Général des Nations Unies, à New York, au cours d'une cérémonie très dépouillée, voire austère. Plus tard, il est convié à deux sessions successives du Comité, la même année au Palais Wilson, à Genève, siège du Haut Commissariat aux droits de l'Homme. Il s'interroge sur ce que fait le Comité dans le beau palais tranquille du bord du lac Leman.

Dix-huit personnalités de différentes formations, universitaires pour la plupart, diplomates et juristes, venant de toutes les régions et de différentes traditions et systèmes juridiques du monde, se réunissent trois fois l'an, pendant trois semaines, autour de gros dossiers. On y parle des droits de l'Homme, de rapports périodiques des Etats parties (149 en juillet 2002), de constatations et du Protocole facultatif (102 Etats parties en juillet 2002), de communications, de constatations, d'observations finales, d'observations générales et de recommandations... un vrai langage codé. Le Zoulou se prend la tête entre les deux mains: le Comité des droits de l'Homme: Qu'est-ce? Un Organe politique, une juridiction? Un Organe hybride ou sui generis ?

Petit à petit, notre Zoulou se prend à découvrir et à comprendre ce que signifient rapports périodiques, communications, constatations et recommandations, observations générales, opinions dissidentes ou séparées selon les cas, observations finales etc. Il en vient à se demander au bout d'un an si le Comité des droits de l'Homme n'est pas en réalité une juridiction internationale qui ne dirait pas son nom, par prudence ou sagesse, pour ne pas effaroucher les Etats, alors que se développe un grand mouvement de juridictionnalisation du droit international - par la création des Cours régionales des droits de l'Homme dans différentes régions du monde (Cour Européenne, Cour Interaméricaine et Cour Africaine des droits de l'Homme et des Peuples), par la création du Tribunal pénal international pour l'ex-Yougoslavie, pour le Rwanda sur le fondement du chapitre VII article 39 de la Charte des Nations Unies, et Cour Pénale Internationale (Traité de Rome-2001) -.

Notre Zoulou découvre que le Comité, par sa compétence, par ses méthodes de travail (la procédure suivie devant lui) et par ses 'Constatations, Recommandations et observations finales' constitue une juridiction puisqu'il s'agit d'un organe qui, sur le fondement d'une loi, en l'occurrence une convention internationale, lorsqu'il est saisi de faits, les constate après analyse, les confronte avec les règles de droit, et dit le droit. Il partage ici ses interrogations. C'est sa contribution à la célébration des vingt-cinq ans du Comité des droits de l'Homme.

I. UNE COMPETENCE JURIDICTIONNELLE

Le Comité des droits de l'Homme trouve son origine dans le Pacte International relatif aux droits civils et politiques qui fixe son domaine de compétence. En effet, ce dernier, en son article 28 al. 1er dispose: '*Il est institué un Comité des droits de l'Homme (ci-dessus dénommé le Comité dans le présent Pacte). Ce Comité est composé de dix-huit membres et a les fonctions ci-après:'* Curieusement, l'article 28 au lieu d'énoncer les fonctions, passe immédiatement à la Composition du Comité. De même les articles *29, 30, 31, 32, 33, 34, 35, 36, 37, 38* et *39* sont consacrés à l'organisation et au fonctionnement du comité. Les fonctions qui se dégagent de la lecture des articles 40 et suivants consistent essentiellement à protéger et à promouvoir les droits de l'Homme. Elles se déduisent des obligations des Etats parties et se présentent comme suit:

1/ examiner et étudier les rapports que 'les Etats parties s'engagent à présenter sur les mesures qu'ils auront arrêtées et qui donnent effet aux droits reconnus dans le Pacte et sur les progrès réalisés dans la jouissance de ces droits' (art 40 al. 1 et 2)

2/ adresser aux Etats parties 'ses propres rapports ainsi que toutes observations générales qu'il jugerait appropriées. Le Comité peut également transmettre au Conseil Economique et Social ses observations accompagnées de copies des rapports qu'il a reçus d'Etats parties au traité (article 40 paragraphe 4)

3/ recevoir des Etats parties 'des commentaires sur toute observation qui serait faite en vertu du paragraphe 4 du présent article'.

4/ recevoir des communications dans lesquelles un Etat partie prétend qu'un autre Etat partie ne s'acquitte pas de ses obligations au titre du Pacte.(article 41). À ce jour 47 Etats ont souscrit à cette option.

5/ recevoir et examiner les communications individuelles, émanant de particuliers qui s'estiment être victimes d'une violation de leurs droits de la part d'un Etat partie. Cette compétence qui, au bout de vingt-cinq années de vie du Comité apparaît comme la plus importante, ne peut s'exercer qu'en vertu du Protocole facultatif se rapportant au Pacte du 16 décembre 1966: 'Tout Etat partie au Pacte qui devient partie au présent Protocole reconnaît que le Comité a compétence pour recevoir et examiner des communications émanant de particuliers relevant de sa juridiction qui prétendent être victimes d'une violation, par cet Etat partie, de l'un quelconque des droits énoncés dans le Pacte. Le Comité ne reçoit aucune communication intéressant un Etat partie au Pacte qui n'est pas partie au présent Protocole' (article 1er)

Selon l'article 2 du Protocole facultatif, 'tout particulier qui prétend être victime d'une violation de l'un quelconque des droits énoncés dans le Pacte et qui épuise tous les recours internes disponibles peut présenter une communication écrite au Comité pour qu'il l'examine'.

Le Zoulou découvre ainsi le vaste et polyvalent champ d'action du Comité des droits de l'Homme:

- examiner des Rapports (initiaux et périodiques) des Etats parties au Pacte sur les mesures qu'ils ont prises pour donner effet aux droits énoncés dans le Pacte. A cette occasion le Comité, suite à un dialogue avec les Etats concernés, formule des conclusions finales à leur endroit, et le cas échéant élabore des observations générales interprétatives des dispositions du Pacte adressées à tous les Etats parties

- examiner des communications (et non des requêtes individuelles) assorties de recommandations ou observations finales (et non pas d'un dispositif).

II. DU CARACTERE OBLIGATOIRE DES OBSERVATIONS GENERALES

1) Peut-on, se demande le Zoulou, déduire du paragraphe 4 de l'article 40, le pouvoir d'interprétation du Comité? Bien que toute juridiction, en vertu d'un principe général de droit, ait compétence pour interpréter tout texte rentrant dans son domaine d'attribution ou de compétence (théorie de la compétence implicite), est-ce le cas du Comité? Notre Zoulou est d'avis que le Comité a effectivement le pouvoir de faire des observations générales qui sont des déclarations interprétatives et constituent la lecture appropriée des dispositions du Pacte. Mais quelle est la nature juridique de ces observations générales (29 depuis 1981)?

2) Celles-ci s'imposent-elles aux Etats parties, à la différence des recommandations qui accompagnent l'examen des rapports? Le Comité dans sa grande prudence, écrit avec beaucoup de doigté:

> 'Le Comité tient à réaffirmer son désir d'aider les Etats parties à s'acquitter de l'obligation qui leur incombe de présenter des rapports. Les observations générales qui suivent soulignent certains aspects de la question, sans toutefois prétendre l'embrasser complètement ni établir une priorité entre les différents aspects de l'application du Pacte. Si le temps dont dispose le Comité le permet, d'autres observations seront formulées par la suite compte tenu des nouveaux enseignements de l'expérience... Le but des présentes observations générales est de faire bénéficier tous les Etats parties de l'expérience ainsi acquise, pour les inciter à continuer à appliquer le Pacte, d'appeler leur attention sur des insuffisances que font apparaître un grand nombre de rapports, de suggérer certaines améliorations dans la procédure de présentation des rapports, et de stimuler les activités de ces Etats et des organisations internationales qui ont pour objet de promouvoir et de protéger les droits de l'Homme. Ces observations devraient aussi intéresser d'autres Etats, en particulier ceux qui envisagent d'adhérer au Pacte et de renforcer ainsi la coopération de tous les Etats en vue de la promotion et de la protection universelle des droits de l'Homme.' (HRI/GEN/1/Rev 5 du 26 avril 2001 pages 113 et 114.)

3) Le Zoulou perçoit deux catégories d'observations générales:

a) les observations générales qui apparaissent comme des suggestions pour ne pas dire des directives à l'endroit des Etats parties comme celles relatives à la présentation des rapports périodiques.

b) Les observations générales qui constituent une véritable interprétation des dispositions ou articles du Pacte. Il en est ainsi par exemple, de l'observation générale n° 5 relative à l'article 4 qui reconnaît à un Etat partie, le pouvoir, en cas de situations exceptionnelles, de déroger à ses obligations conventionnelles:

> 'Dans le cas où une situation d'urgence menace l'existence de la nation et est proclamée par un acte officiel, un Etat partie peut déroger à ses obligations en ce qui concerne un certain nombre de droits dans la stricte mesure où la situation l'exige'. Mais précise-t-il: 'Toutefois, la dérogation ne peut s'appliquer à certains droits bien déterminés, et l'Etat partie ne peut pas prendre de mesures discriminatoires sous certains prétextes. En outre, l'Etat partie est tenu de signaler aussitôt aux autres Etats parties, par l'entremise du Secrétaire Général, les dispositions auxquelles il a dérogé, ainsi que les motifs qui ont provoqué cette dérogation et la date à laquelle il y a mis fin. Aucune dérogation ne peut être apportée, même en cas d'une situation exceptionnelle, au droit à la vie (art. 6), dont la protection, ajoute le Comité, 'exige que les Etats adoptent des mesures positives... .il serait souhaitable que les Etats parties prennent toutes les mesures possibles pour diminuer la mortalité infantile et pour accroître l'espérance de vie, et en particulier des mesures permettant d'éliminer la malnutrition et les épidémies'.

On est en plein normatif. Le Zoulou retient que le Comité déclare comme droits auxquels nul ne peut déroger (par suspension, ni limitation) : le droit à la vie; l'interdiction de la torture et de traitements cruels, inhumains ou dégradants; l'interdiction de tenir un individu en esclavage ou en servitude, de l'emprisonner pour dette, le devoir pour l'Etat de garantir la non rétroactivité de la loi pénale; le droit de chacun à la reconnaissance de sa personnalité juridique; la liberté de pensée, de conscience, de religion ou de conviction.

c) Le même effort d'interprétation est déployé pour l'article 7 qui interdit la torture, les peines ou traitements cruels, inhumains ou dégradants......

Un Etat partie ne saurait au nom d'une situation d'urgence, déroger à cet article:

> 'Le Comité rappelle que, même dans le cas d'un danger public exceptionnel tel qu'envisagé dans le paragraphe 1 de l'article 4, le paragraphe 2 de l'article 4 n'autorise aucune dérogation à cette disposition, dont le but est de protéger l'intégrité et la dignité de l'individu....'.

Le Zoulou dont le pays sort d'un *système de Parti-Etat dans lequel la chasse aux sorcières* a été fortement pratiquée et où ont été arrêtées et embastillées pour 'crimes' de sorcellerie des personnes même très âgées, se réjouit en particulier que le Comité, souligne, dans l'observation générale n° 10 relative à *l'article 19* aux termes duquel

> 'Nul ne peut être inquiété pour ses opinions. Toute personne a droit à la liberté d'expression: ce droit comprend la liberté de rechercher, de recevoir et de répandre des informations et des idées de toute espèce, sans considération de frontières, sous une forme orale, écrite, imprimée ou artistique, ou par tout autre moyen de son choix...', d'aucuns estiment qu'il s'agit d'un 'droit pour lequel le Pacte n'autorise ni exception, ni limitation... ' alors que l'article 19 en son alinéa 3 prévoit expressément

> des restrictions que la loi peut imposer lorsque celles ci sont nécessaires au respect des droits ou de la réputation d'autrui ou à la sauvegarde de la sécurité nationale, de l'ordre public, de la santé ou de la moralité publiques.'

d) En 1992 à la 44ème session, soit dix ans après l'observation générale n° 7 relative à l'article 7 formulée en 1982, lors de la 16ème session, le Comité a adopté l'observation générale n° 20 relative à l'article 7; la nouvelle observation générale remplace celle de 1982. S'agit-t-il d'un changement de Jurisprudence ? Certes pas, mais l'Analyse est plus affinée. Une lecture croisée ayant été faite avec l'article 10 du Pacte. Tandis que l'article 7 interdit la torture, les peines ou traitements cruels, inhumains ou dégradants, *l'article 10* quant à lui, énonce:

> '1-Toute personne privée de sa liberté est traitée avec humanité et avec le respect de la dignité inhérente à la personne humaine. 2 a) Les prévenus sont, sauf dans des circonstances exceptionnelles, séparés des condamnés et sont soumis à un régime distinct, approprié à leur condition de personnes non condamnées; b) les jeunes prévenus sont séparés des adultes et il est décidé de leur cas aussi rapidement que possible. 3) Le régime pénitentiaire comporte un traitement des condamnés dont le but essentiel est leur amendement et leur reclassement social.. Les jeunes délinquants sont séparés des adultes et soumis à un régime approprié à leur âge et à leur statut légal'. Le Comité fait une lecture combinée des articles 7 et 10 en affirmant que 'l'interdiction faite à l'article 7 est complétée par des dispositions positives du paragraphe 1 de l'article 10 du Pacte'. Non seulement il réaffirme que le texte de l'article 7 non seulement il ne souffre aucune limitation; mais il fait également observer qu'aucune raison, y compris l'ordre d'un supérieur hiérarchique ou d'une autorité publique, ne saurait être invoquée en tant que justification ou circonstance atténuante pour excuser une violation de l'article 7. Par ailleurs, estime le Comité, "l'interdiction énoncée à l'article 7 concerne non seulement des actes qui provoquent chez la victime une douleur physique, mais aussi des actes qui infligent une souffrance mentale; .. l'interdiction doit s'étendre aux peines corporelles, y compris les châtiments excessifs infligés à titre de sanction pénale ou de mesure éducative ou disciplinaire. À cet égard, il convient de souligner que l'article 7 protège notamment les enfants, les élèves des établissements d'enseignement et les patients des institutions médicales... Le Comité note que l'emprisonnement cellulaire prolongé d'une personne détenue ou incarcérée peut-être assimilé aux actes prohibés par l'article 7".'

Par ailleurs, 'Le Comité note qu'il ne suffit pas, pour respecter l'article 7, d'interdire ces peines, ni de déclarer que leur application constitue un délit. Les Etats parties doivent faire connaître au Comité les mesures législatives, administratives, judiciaires et autres qu'ils prennent pour prévenir et réprimer les actes de torture ainsi les traitements cruels, inhumains ou dégradants dans tout territoire placé sous leur juridiction...' Ainsi, à l'occasion de l'examen et de l'étude des Rapports périodiques des Etats parties, le Comité élabore et développe un droit prétorien grâce à la technique de l'interprétation des dispositions du Pacte. Cette belle oeuvre prétorienne apparaît comme l'apport le plus appréciable du Comité à la protection et à la promotion des droits de l'Homme. Se pose alors la question de la nature juridique des observations générales, ce qui ne manque pas d'intriguer notre Zoulou qui se demande si le Comité ne joue pas le rôle d'un législateur secondaire, complétant et harmonisant les dispositions du Pacte.

e) Il arrive que ce législateur secondaire adopte des règles qui modifient sa propre interprétation, en actualisant certaines observations. Il en est ainsi de l'observation générale n° 28 (78ème session 2000) relative à l'article *3 (égalité des droits entre hommes et femmes)*. La nouvelle observation remplace l'observation générale n° 4 (13ème session 1981). Ledit article 3 énonce:

> 'Les Etats parties au présent Pacte s'engagent à assurer le droit égal des hommes et des femmes de jouir de tous les droits civils et politiques énoncés dans le présent Pacte'.

Pour le Comité, 'l'article 3 suppose que tous les êtres humains doivent jouir des droits prévus par le Pacte sur un pied d'égalité et dans leur intégralité. Cela signifie que cette disposition est violée chaque fois que la jouissance complète et sur un pied d'égalité de tout droit est refusée à une personne. De ce fait, les Etats doivent assurer aux hommes et aux femmes l'égalité dans l'exercice de tous les droits consacrés dans le Pacte.

L'obligation de garantir à tous les individus les droits reconnus dans le Pacte, énoncée aux articles 2 et 3, signifie que les Etats parties doivent prendre toutes les mesures nécessaires pour permettre l'exercice de ces droits par tous...(observation n° 4).

L'observation n° 28 (soixante-huitième session) (2000) relative à l'article 3 (*égalité entre hommes et femmes)* a particulièrement frappé l'attention de notre Zoulou qui vient d'une société où, au nom de la tradition, se pratique sans sourciller, la polygamie. Il est intrigué par l'observation qui en son *point 24* énonce: '.....Il convient de noter que la *polygamie est incompatible avec l'égalité de traitement en ce qui concerne le droit de se marier.*

La polygamie est attentatoire à la dignité de la femme. 'Elle constitue, en outre, une inadmissible discrimination à son égard. Elle doit être, en conséquence, définitivement abolie là où elle existe...' *Ne voila-t-il pas que le pays du Zoulou (Etat partie au Pacte) vient d'adopter un Code des Personnes et de la Famille qui reconnaît la polygamie comme l'un des régimes matrimoniaux, à la seule condition que les deux fiancés déclarent accepter, avant le mariage, la polygamie!* Belle communication en perspective ! Comment tranchera le Comité ? Dira-t-il qu'il n'y a pas de discrimination étant donné le libre consentement des futurs époux, et ce, dans un environnement socioculturel spécifique? Si, comme le pense le Zoulou, les déclarations interprétatives du Comité sont exécutoires, la loi admettant la polygamie, même avec le consentement des époux, ne devrait-elle pas être déclarée comme violant le Pacte? Assurément !

f) On pourrait également se demander si le Comité de par son interprétation, ne tente pas, au nom de l'égalité de l'homme et de la femme, d'imposer la monogamie, régime matrimonial dégagé par certaines civilisations et cultures religieuses, comme la norme universelle? ...Le Zoulou se garde d'aborder ce débat intéressant mais délicat et difficile. Si les déclarations interprétatives du Comité, comme il le pense, ont une valeur obligatoire (si elles sont exécutoires), la loi admettant la polygamie même avec le consentement des époux, doit être déclarée comme violant le Pacte.

Les Féministes du pays du Zoulou, assistées de militants des droits de l'Homme ne manqueront certes pas de porter cette question devant le Comité. Mais le peuvent-ils sans épuiser toutes les voies de recours internes? 'Ah ! Ah ! Ah !' se dit le Zoulou. Voilà ce qu'il en coûte aux Etats d'adhérer aux Conventions internationales: il faut les intégrer dans le droit interne et les traduire par les lois et mesures appropriées comme le prescrit expressément l'article 2 du Pacte ! Les Etats parties le savent-ils ou s'en souviennent-ils lors de l'adoption des lois et autres textes réglementaires? L'éducation aux droits de l'Homme, en l'occurrence, par des séminaires destinés aux parlementaires, aux membres de l'Exécutif et aux ONG apparaît comme la solution à la réception, dans les droits nationaux, de la législation secondaire que constituent les observations générales interprétatives du Comité des droits de l'Homme; autrement sa belle oeuvre prétorienne, si patiemment et élégamment élaborée, demeurera longtemps encore lettre morte.

III. DU CARACTERE EXECUTOIRE DES CONSTATATIONS, ET OBSERVATIONS FINALES

Le Zoulou relève que le Comité, dans l'examen des Rapports périodiques, instaure, avec les Etats parties, un dialogue qui, en dépit des précautions de forme et toute la diplomatie, se révèle comme une véritable inquisition mais toujours animée par le souci d'amener les Etats à reformuler leur législation et à prendre des mesures appropriées pour assurer sur le terrain et au quotidien l'effectivité des droits de l'Homme énoncés dans le Pacte en application de l'article 40 du Pacte, à la différence du juge qui après l'exposé des motifs ou des faits (les considérants auxquels le Zoulou est plus familier avec une pratique de dix ans à la Cour Constitutionnelle de son pays) *dit et juge* (dispositif). En fait, le Comité, en ce qui concerne les communications, (alias les requêtes, recours, plaintes) procède comme un juge en recourant à d'autres formules telles que: Recommandation – Annexe – Constatations Annexe: X session concernant la Communication n° z: 1°/ Rappel des faits – 2°/ Teneur de la plainte – 3°/ observations de l'Etat partie – 4°/ Commentaires de l'auteur et de l'Etat partie (le principe du contradictoire.) – Délibérations du Comité: a) examen de la recevabilité; b) examen quant au fond.

Le Comité conclut l'examen du rapport périodique d'un Etat par des observations finales. Ces dernières s'articulent comme suit: 1/ Introduction 2/ Aspects positifs 3/ Principaux sujets de préoccupation et recommandations. La stylistique instruirait beaucoup sur le travail du Comité, sur ses hésitations. On peut ainsi lire dans les observations finales: 'le comité accueille avec satisfaction; se félicite de...; prend note de.....;

Le Comité est préoccupé par...; note avec préoccupation; ... L'Etat-partie devrait...'veiller à ...; devrait songer à... ou faire en sorte que; devrait adopter des procédures...'.

Lorsqu'il s'avance quelque peu, il écrit: 'Le Comité estime que; le Comité regrette que; le Comité juge préoccupant...'

'Les décisions' n'en sont pas: 'L'Etat devrait fournir des renseignements supplémentaires sur la législation interne ou bien l'Etat devrait rendre public le présent examen...; il est demandé à l'Etat partie, conformément au paragraphe 5 de l'article 70 du règlement intérieur du Comité, de communiquer, dans un délai de douze (12) mois des renseignements sur l'application des recommandations figurant aux paragraphes A, C, X, Z...'

Si pour les observations finales sur les rapports périodiques des Etats parties, le Comité préfère recourir à la litote, il s'affirme davantage sur le terrain juridique, il dit et juge qu'il y a ou non violation des dispositions du Pacte même si la terminologie peut légèrement différer de celle des juridictions et même si selon l'article 5 (4) 'du Protocole facultatif se rapportant au Pacte international relatif aux droits civils et politiques, (les Communications émanant de particuliers) *le Comité fait des constatations*. 'Le Comité fait part de ses constatations à l'Etat partie intéressé et au particulier', à la différence du juge classique qui après l'exposé des motifs ou des faits décide.

> 'Le Comité des droits de l'homme, agissant en vertu du paragraphe 4 de l'article 5 du Protocole facultatif, estime que l'Etat partie a violé le paragraphe 1 de l'article 14, ainsi que les articles 26 et 2 du Pacte ou bien: en l'espèce, le Comité ne peut conclure à une violation des alinéas b et d du paragraphe 3 de l'article 14; ou bien encore; en conséquence le Comité des droits de l'homme ... estime que les faits dont il est saisi ne font apparaître de violation du Pacte international relatif aux droits civils et politiques.'

D'une manière générale, le Comité se plaît à rappeler aux Etats parties, 'qu'en adhérant au Protocole facultatif, (le pays concerné) a reconnu que le Comité avait compétence pour déterminer s'il y avait eu ou non violation du Pacte et que, conformément à l'article 2 de celui-ci, il s'est engagé à garantir à tous les individus se trouvant sur son territoire et relevant de sa juridiction les droits reconnus dans le Pacte et à assurer un *recours utile et exécutoire'* lorsqu'une violation a été établie'.

Par ailleurs, 'le Comité souhaite recevoir de l'Etat partie, dans les 90 jours suivant la transmission des présentes constatations, des informations sur les mesures qu'il aura prises pour leur donner suite . . . (cf. CCPR/WG/73/DR/747/1997 du 15 octobre 2001 Karel des Fours Walderode C. République Tchèque)'. Ainsi, le Comité, contrairement à d'autres juridictions internationales a le pouvoir de suivi de ses décisions (Décisions Choisies du Comité des droits de l'Homme 'Volumes I et II) afin de rendre celles-ci effectives. Le Comité tient cette compétence de l'article 2 du Pacte qui prescrit que les Etats parties au Pacte s'engagent à 'garantir la bonne suite donnée par les autorités compétentes à tout recours qui aura été reconnu justifié', du préambule du Protocole facultatif qui énonce 'Considérant que, pour mieux assurer l'accomplissement des fins du Pacte international relatif aux droits civils et politiques (...) et l'application de ses dispositions, il conviendrait d'habiliter le Comité des droits de l'homme à recevoir et à examiner les communications émanant de particuliers qui prétendent être victimes d'une violation d'un des droits énoncés dans le Pacte'. Le Comité tient également sa compétence de l'article 4 paragraphe 2, du Protocole facultatif ainsi que de l'article 40 paragraphe 1 du Pacte en vertu duquel: 'Les Etats parties au présent Pacte s'engagent à présenter des rapports sur les mesures qu'ils auront arrêtées et qui donnent effet aux droits reconnus dans le présent Pacte et sur les progrès réalisés dans la jouissance de ces droits'.

A cette fin, il a institué un Rapporteur spécial chargé du suivi des communications. Ce dernier organise des rencontres avec des Représentants des Etats parties qui n'ont pas répondu aux demandes de renseignements du Comité concernant les mesures prises pour donner effet aux constatations du Comité ou dont les réponses aux demandes n'ont pas été jugées satisfaisantes. Il est même prévu des missions de suivi sur le terrain mais celles-ci n'ont pu être organisées faute de moyens financiers. Ah ! heureux Comité se dit le Zoulou: si la mise en application des décisions des hautes juridictions chargées des droits de l'homme dans les pays d'Afrique pouvait être suivie, la démocratie réaliserait de grands progrès et les droits de l'homme cesseraient d'être des slogans ou de simples incantations. En améliorant ses méthodes de travail, le Comité a nommé un Rapporteur pour les nouvelles communications; ce dernier, en vertu de l'article 86 du règlement intérieur peut demander, à l'Etat partie concerné, en attendant la décision finale, des mesures provisoires de protection. Voilà une procédure qui renforcerait la démocratie en Afrique, se dit le Zoulou. Il peut ainsi garantir le droit à réparation (article 9 paragraphe 5) pour 'tout individu victime d'arrestation ou détention illégale' et fixe même le quantum de la réparation. Il est encourageant de constater que la plupart des Etats-parties, par respect du principe de la bonne foi 'pacta suunt servanda', mettent en exécution les décisions du Comité.

Le Zoulou déduit de tout ce qui précède que le Comité des droits de l'homme est bien une juridiction au sens où l'entend la doctrine puisqu'il fait des constatations, procède à l'analyse des faits qu'il confronte avec la règle de droit, en l'occurrence le Pacte et dit le droit en ces termes: 'l'Etat partie a violé telle ou telle disposition du Pacte' 'il n'y a pas violation du Pacte'. Les rédacteurs dudit Pacte n'ont pas baptisé le Comité de juridiction, mais ils ont entendu lui conférer les compétences d'une juridiction internationale. Ils lui ont donné un large pouvoir d'interprétation qui fait de lui un législateur secondaire en matière des droits de l'homme, sur le plan international. A pas feutrés, le Comité développe les notions et concepts retenus par le Pacte, en les explicitant, en leur donnant sens en fonction des progrès ou du regard contemporain sur le monde actuel.

Notre Zoulou relève avec amusement que, dans la procédure, le Comité sans rivaliser avec elles, garde l'oeil ouvert sur la Jurisprudence des Cours régionales des droits de l'homme. Par coquetterie, il habilite ses membres à exprimer des opinions dissidentes à l'instar des grandes juridictions internationales. Ainsi quand le consensus n'est pas obtenu ou qu'une majorité se dessine, on entend des membres déclarer 'j'écrirai une opinion dissidente ou séparée...'. Ces opinions dissidentes sont reproduites avec la décision dans le Rapport annuel à l'Assemblée Générale des Nations Unies...

Le Zoulou regrette que la belle oeuvre prétorienne qu'accomplit le Comité au plan normatif ne soit connue que des initiés et ne soit pas diffusée au niveau du grand public, avec le concours des Etats parties, par les technologies les plus modernes, en particulier dans les pays du sud. Il faudrait tirer le meilleur parti du vent de renouveau démocratique qui souffle à travers le monde, en développant la culture des droits de l'Homme dont le Comité apparaît comme le gardien. Et le Zoulou de rêver au jour où, de tous les continents, parviendront massivement au Comité des droits de l'Homme des Rapports des Etats parties et des communications individuelles (mille au total en 2001).

Part II

Retrospects and Prospects of the Human Rights Committee

SOLID FOUNDATIONS

Andreas Mavrommatis

There may be those who doubt whether the United Nations can claim spectacular or even many successes in so far as peace making is concerned, but nobody doubts the Organization's great contribution to human rights, especially in so far as standard setting is concerned.

Beginning with the 1948 Universal Declaration and then continuing with the two International Covenants (first universal legally binding, general as opposed to specific, international treaties) and subsequently with a series of specific instruments, whenever either the gravity or frequency of violations or the importance of the rights to be protected such as those in respect of vulnerable sectors of the population demanded, the UN set in train an ambitious programme of protection by providing the legal framework for ensuring the dignity of the human person.

With the framework in place, what had to be secured, and this was a novelty, was implementation through effective international supervision and monitoring that would bridge the gap between words and deed. The International Covenant of Civil and Political Rights (ICCPR) did provide for a mechanism, but would it prove effective, was it sufficient and would it succeed to the extent that the Covenant's text permitted? Would this be possible given the fact that this Covenant embraced all those rights that were front page news in the bitterly divided world of the sixty's and seventies?

True, there already existed at least one regional arrangement, that of Europe, which had a fair measure of success attributable to the fact that the European Convention applied to like-minded states parties, as well as the UN Convention on the Elimination of All Forms of Racial Discrimination (CERD), a treaty of global applicability which was plodding on owing to the fact that everybody paid at least lip service to non-discrimination. The convention was, then, the world's alibi for the crime of apartheid.

The success of the ICCPR's mechanism was not assured from the outset, and predictions were risky for a number of reasons, including the fact that it took the Covenant almost ten years to secure the thirty-five ratifications required for it to enter into force. This indicated that a number of signatory and other states had second thoughts about throwing open their human rights record to international, albeit expert, criticism at time when human rights were used and abused in international relations so that political points might be scored.

The policy of détente of the early seventies that led to the Helsinki Final Act with its all important third basket (which did not provide for proper monitoring) had almost completely disappeared, and the first follow-up meetings of the process had limited themselves to saving this process. The difficulties had human rights as their epicentre.

Many third world countries, which in the late sixties or early seventies (as well as in subsequent decades) had either jumped on the human rights bandwagon or were flirting with the idea of doing so, were becoming more cautious and hesitant.

These were some of the reasons why the ICCPR's monitoring mechanism had to succeed in ensuring that this new promising methodology could take deep and lasting roots. Therefore, the first years were crucial in that solid foundations had to be laid that would withstand the test of time.

During these first years the Human Rights Committee had to prove efficient and effective, knowledgeable and understanding, without being condescending, thorough and compassionate, impartial and non-politicized. Only with these attributes could it earn the trust and confidence of the international community, states parties and would-be states parties, and finally of their citizens.

It was clear to all of us during those years that the Committee had a very difficult task ahead and there were a number of intrinsic difficulties. From the start members from Eastern Block countries had come with specific 'instructions', those from West European and Others Group had been consulting on how to react and those of us from the Third World were either looking at events in a detached manner or thinking of how to make the best out of the difficulties encountered. In other words, General Assembly Third Committee practices were lurking in the corridor ready to gatecrash. Only appropriate action would prevent it.

Mark Schreiber, then the head of the Human Rights Division of the UN and a very experienced senior international civil servant, took the initiative and through a series of suggestions that included the unanimous election of the first Chair (that remained in office for five successive terms, thus ensuring continuity), guided the Committee throughout its first steps. The same applied to the first task, namely the drafting and adoption of the Rules of Procedure for which we had the assistance of another accomplished official, Enayat Houshmand.

The Rules of Procedure will be remembered because of the famous asterisk and footnote concerning the need to attempt to reach consensus (not unanimity) prior to resorting to a vote. This rule guided us through more than two decades and accounted for a lot of the prestige and good name that characterized the Committee and its work.

I believe that it is essential to trace the *modus operandi* for laying the foundation of any project as well as developments connected therewith, not only because success or failure depended on them or because of historical reasons, but also because factors and difficulties encountered permitted us to chart the road map to the future. These success factors as well as difficulties encompassed a wide range of actors including members of the Committee, members of the Secretariat, states parties and such imponderables as political climate and balance of power.

Even before the 11 September 2001 terrorist attacks, and more so thereafter, we witnessed the strains and difficulties both in maintaining the momentum to progress in applying human rights and, worse in safeguarding gains in respect of civil liberties. These strains and difficulties constituted irrefutable evidence of potential if not actual regression that would entail if we were to fail in successfully charting the road map for future development of the international protection of human rights. Such a failure would jeopardize the basic assumption for the promotion of human rights towards which the international community had been struggling so hard for since World War II.

Nobody should doubt the obligation of states and the international community to combat and eradicate terrorism, which was manifested in its worst form, in September 2001, in the attacks against the USA. However, doing so should not entail brushing aside applicable treaties and conventions altogether. There is ample provisions to ensure respect for non-derogable rights, whilst recognizing that states of emergency permit other derogations. It would appear that we are moving towards the day when all that it requires is to brand your adversary a terrorist to justify almost any action.

Certain other developments underscore the necessity for appropriate remedial action against human rights violations. These are, in the case of two treaty bodies (although this also applies to other mechanisms) denunciations of protocols and non-compliance with views, decisions, requests for interim measures and concluding observations.

Let us revert to the examination of some of the factors that have accounted for the prominent position of the Human Rights Committee as the leader in the field of treaty bodies. In the process, whenever possible, we may make a cross-reference to the present state of affairs and to whether they could provide answers to today's difficulties or problems.

The golden rules, established from the outset of operations of the Human Rights Committee, despite the difficulties of that time, were: excellent working relations, consensus decisions whenever possible, non-politicization, impartiality and devotion to duty. All these presuppose electing the best candidates.

The Human Rights Committee was fortunate in that first elections produced the calibre and qualifications of elected members that ensured success. There were and will always be a few exceptions, but through the efforts of the other members, any harm done to the process was insignificant.

In order to maintain the high credibility of the Committee's work, it is essential that states parties should provide the Committee with qualified members, and this can only be done by choosing candidates known for their impartiality and professionalism, without exchange of votes for political convenience.

As far as the Secretariat is concerned, things would have been much improved by the influx of young and devoted members, had it not been for the considerable increase in the volume of work, new demands for research and analysis. The unfortunate fact that certain of the top officials in the former Division of Human Rights and Centre for Human Rights and the Office of the High Commissioner failed to grasp the importance of treaty bodies because they do not normally generate publicity, has resulted in the shortage of necessary staff and facilities for the effective functioning of the Committee under the ICCPR (Article 36).

When we had only a few dozens of initial reports to examine and hardly any communications of significance, members could devote more time to preparatory work such as analysis, comparison, unanswered questions, outstanding issues, comparative jurisprudence, including that of other regional mechanisms. With the multiplication of states parties, things became impossible and more staff was necessary, but rarely forthcoming. Frequent transfers of officers soon after they acquired the necessary experience was also detrimental. In the case of communications, where at the beginning we were lucky to have excellent people, frequent transfers and experimentations as well as lack of staff, created a huge backlog that threatened the very credibility of the system. Recent action by the High Commissioner following urgent requests by treaty-bodies recreated the old organism and this, hopefully will improve the situation. I do believe that a certain degree of specialization and transfers that are infrequent but occur when adequate replacement is available, are called for, especially in the case of communications or petitions.

As far as NGO's are concerned, it is now conceded by all, that at least the consideration of states reports would have been difficult or inadequate, had it not been for the information provided to treaty bodies by NGO's.

On the other hand, although the days are over when we could not, as members of the Committee, divulge our sources of information, now we grant them the right to be heard, along with other privileges. Yet, sometimes NGOs do not live up to our expectations in so far as accuracy, double-checking of material, and timeliness of submissions, are concerned.

NGO's often forget that their main task is to assist in efforts, both at the local level as well as in the Committee, to ensure respect for human rights. This is something which often is not achieved by exposure – which is the last resort.

Furthermore, whilst appreciating the accurate information coming from NGO's, one has to bear in mind the sheer volume of material before the Committee, thus forcing its members to resort to executive summaries as well as consolidated reports from several NGOs. It would be helpful if international NGOs assist and sponsor local NGOs and institutionalize addresses by Committee members during their meeting with NGOs to exchange views.

The Human Rights Committee's other big secret of success was that, from the outset, it made it abundantly clear that although the consideration of the states reports (Article 40) was a lengthy affair, its primary purpose was to initiate a friendly and constructive dialogue which, through a frank exchange of views, the sharing of experiences of which the Committee is a repository, and finally through concluding observations, could lead to an improvement of the human rights situations in the country whose report was examined. It is also made clear that the cooperation of the states parties was essential to make the whole exercise a success and that the Committee in no way wished to act as an accuser but as an 'amicus'.

Yet, recently, we have observed some instances where an inadequate presentation and approach by certain treaty body members has led to the souring of relations between them and certain states parties, some of which were known for their long tradition of promotion and respect for human rights. Some have threatened to terminate their cooperation with the UN treaty bodies.

One of the reasons for the aforesaid situation is that observations, concluding or otherwise, are often repetitive, needlessly long, and sometimes sound too harsh to the states parties concerned. Of course, the treaty bodies should not lose their sharp sense of criticism. At the same time, they should not lose sight of the fact that the very purpose of considering states reports is to maintain 'constructive dialogue' with states parties.

In the case of communications or petitions, the reasons are mainly inconsistency, automaticity in requesting interim measures, incomplete or not fully read files and non-implementable recommendations in views. Most of the difficulties are a consequence of the unsatisfactory replies from certain states parties, which adopt attitudes that range from the haphazard to the cavalier.

Remedial action should include revision of methodology and approach, an in depth study and analysis and more efforts to reach consensus without exaggerating formality when it is necessary to obtain more information and clarification.

Let us not forget that it was a certain number of decisions in the first years such as those in the *Lovelace* v. *Canada* (case 24/1977), the *Anna Maroufidou* v. *Sweden* (case 58/1979) and the series of the Dutch Article 26 decisions that consecrated the reputation of the Human Rights Committee's jurisprudence.

As already stated, respect for human rights will always face problems and difficulties. Civil liberties and even the supreme right, the right to life, might be in jeopardy. Even countries with long traditions of respect for human rights, when faced with serious dangers or even difficulties such as the recent waves of economic migrants, asylum seekers, terrorism or internal disturbances (now more frequent because social justice is sacrificed on the altar of globalization) may resort to measures that are not in strict compliance with human rights standards.

Against this backdrop, I believe that treaty bodies, with the Human Rights Committee as the standard- bearer, should undertake initiatives, study the causes and decide on preventive or remedial actions that would ensure coordinated effectiveness and return to the right path.

We owe it to the fact that we are viewed as the most trusted device in the panoply of international human rights protection. We owe it to the solid foundations that the pioneer members of the Committee have laid, thus assuring success and respect for the Human Rights Committee, and by extension for all treaty bodies.

PROBLEMES PARTICULIERS RENCONTRES DANS LES PREMIERES ANNEES D'ACTIVITE DU COMITE

Nejib Bouziri

La commémoration du vingt-cinquième anniversaire du Comité devrait avoir, parmi les buts poursuivis, celui de faire le bilan des activités du Comité durant un quart de siècle.

La présente contribution tend à décrire et à analyser, aussi brièvement que possible, certaines des énormes difficultés rencontrées par le Comité durant une décennie et demie.

Ce bilan est indispensable d'une part pour satisfaire aux exigences de la vérité et d'autre part pour qu'à l'avenir certaines dérives ne se répètent plus.

Même si les accords d'Helsinki avaient détendu quelque peu l'atmosphère de guerre froide qui pesait non seulement sur les relations entre l'Ouest et l'Est mais également sur le reste du monde, la tension liée à la guerre froide était encore présente au sein du Comité des droits de l'homme lorsqu'il commença son activité en 1977 et persista presque quinze ans.

Le Comité était composé de membres provenant d'Etats parties occidentaux, communistes et du Tiers Monde. Cette composition qui comprenait trois groupes distincts correspondait à celle qui existait au sein des Nations Unies au moment où, à la fin des années 50 et début des années 60, le Pacte relatif aux droits civils et politiques était en cours d'élaboration.

Même si le Pacte avait été adopté en 1966, dix-huit ans après l'adoption de la Déclaration Universelle des droits de l'homme en 1948 et était entré en vigueur en 1976, le Comité n'avait commencé ses activités qu'en 1977. Ce long délai jusqu'à la prise en charge du Pacte par le Comité enfin constitué et en activité, prouve à quel point l'acceptation du Pacte et sa mise en œuvre ont été laborieuses et combien de méfiance et de réticence elles ont suscité.

Dès les premiers jours de son activité et pendant des années, environ quinze ans, le Comité allait connaître des tensions inhérentes, d'une part du fait que les membres des pays occidentaux et des Etats communistes étaient très marqués par la guerre froide, alors même que celle-ci s'était atténuée, d'autre part du fait que plusieurs de ces mêmes membres étaient autant juristes que politiciens. Il convient de souligner que les membres provenant des pays du Tiers Monde, ne présentaient généralement pas ces caractéristiques ou du moins pour la plupart à un degré beaucoup moindre.

Durant cette période, il y eut donc des problèmes, conséquences de la situation résumée ci-dessus, et dont seuls les plus significatifs seront succinctement analysés ici.

A- Le problème de la constitution de groupes

Il y eut, dès la naissance et le début de l'activité du Comité, la constitution de deux groupes. L'un comprenait les experts des Etats parties occidentaux, l'autre comprenait les experts des Etats parties communistes. Chaque groupe était ancré dans des certitudes politiques, philosophiques et juridiques totalement différentes, et ne partageait pas les mêmes conceptions de la démocratie et des droits de l'homme. Il va de soi que dans ces groupes, d'une part il y avait les chefs et d'autre part ceux qui faisaient du suivisme par discipline sans être toujours convaincus du bien fondé des positions des meneurs. C'était surtout vrai chez les occidentaux, parmi lesquels certains membres étaient assez réticents.

Les affrontements dans plusieurs domaines étaient inévitables, mais d'une part, le Comité, selon les termes du Pacte, n'avait pas vocation à être une arène destinée à accueillir des affrontements constants et, d'autre part, les groupes avaient à leur tête des hommes rompus à la politique, aux manœuvres et aux nécessaires compromis et qui étaient habitués à passer des accords sur des points déterminés.

Les experts des Etats parties du Tiers Monde ne constituaient pas un vrai groupe, et ils n'étaient, ni collectivement, ni individuellement, rattachés à aucun des deux groupes. De surcroît, de par leur extrême diversité d'origine, il y avait entre eux de très grandes différences. Pour des facilités de langage on peut dire que c'était un groupe mais il s'agissait plutôt d'un ensemble inorganisé.

Une partie d'entre eux appartenaient à des peuples colonisés qui étaient devenus indépendants seulement après la deuxième guerre mondiale, d'autres représentaient des peuples dont l'indépendance était beaucoup plus ancienne. Mais les uns et les autres appartenaient à des pays en développement, en lutte pour préserver leur indépendance, menacée par des néo-colonialismes et les néo-impérialismes et dont les peuples souffraient d'un déficit démocratique plus ou moins grand et de fréquentes et graves violations des droits de l 'homme dont ils étaient parfaitement conscients.

Il convient cependant de souligner trois éléments importants.

En premier lieu, si trois groupes étaient identifiables, le groupe le plus monolithique était celui des experts marxistes, avec deux chefs très politisés et manœuvriers. Le groupe occidental quant à lui, avait d'une part les meneurs qui étaient conservateurs et politiciens et d'autre part les modérés qui, bien souvent, se pliaient par esprit de solidarité à un suivisme contraint.

En second lieu, très fréquemment les positions du groupe occidental coïncidaient avec celle du groupe inorganisé. On peut dire qu'il y avait un courant Occidental – Tiers-mondiste souvent opposé au courant marxiste.

En troisième lieu, l'ensemble des éléments qui viennent d'être décrits, donnait une situation complexe, émaillée de paradoxes et souvent d'actions aboutissant à des résultats négatifs.

Ainsi était le Comité pendant les premières années de son existence, jusqu'au tournant de 1992, date à laquelle les groupes ont tout à fait cessé d'exister. Il convient de noter que la transformation du Comité et l'atténuation de ses contradictions avaient commencé en 1987 avec le départ des membres les plus marqués par la guerre froide dont les positions étaient bien souvent motivées par des considérations beaucoup plus politiques que juridiques.

Lorsque des accords avaient été conclus entre le groupe occidental et le groupe marxiste, sur des questions limitées mais importantes, cela avait entraîné des dérives.

B- La derive de la présidence du Comité

Une des plus graves dérives avait été d'avoir imposé au Comité pendant dix ans, un président qui n'avait été élu que pour deux ans.

Les deux groupes occidental et marxiste ayant conclu un accord selon lequel aucun des leurs ne serait président du Comité, ils avaient décidé de choisir un président à leur convenance, après avoir écarté un membre d'un Etat partie du Tiers Monde que d'autres experts souhaitaient voir élu président. Cela pouvait être acceptable pour la première élection, mais quand ce président fut imposé cinq fois de suite, c'est-à-dire pendant dix ans, en violation d'une règle bien établie dans tous les organes des Nations Unies qui était le principe de la rotation, on assista à la naissance d'une sorte de protectorat et d'une main mise sur le Comité, c'est-à-dire d'une véritable dérive. Celle-ci aurait pu être évitée car d'autres experts, qui étaient déjà membres du premier comité des droits de l'homme, avaient été par la suite élus à la présidence de ce comité. Il existait donc plusieurs alternatives.

Cette situation aurait pu durer plus longtemps s'il n'y avait pas eu la conjugaison de deux éléments. Tout d'abord, au fil des ans, certains membres du Comité manifestèrent de plus en plus leur mécontentement de voir une présidence de deux ans se transformer en présidence à vie.[1] Ensuite, les circonstances firent que les leaders, tant occidentaux que marxistes, quittèrent progressivement le Comité. Dès lors, le Droit reprit ses droits, le principe de la rotation retrouva sa place et les dérives du Comité dans ces domaines connurent une fin.

C- Le problème du consensus dans le règlement intérieur ou la tentation du veto

La question du consensus, au moment ou elle fut soulevée au sein du Comité, était déjà très à la mode, car tous les organes des Nations Unies, et toutes les organisations internationales utilisaient déjà le consensus, soit comme méthode de travail, soit comme une condition fréquente de la prise de décision. Il était donc inévitable que, lors de la création d'un nouvel organe supranational, la question du consensus se posât à un moment ou à un autre.

Cela se fit, lorsque le Comité élabora son règlement intérieur et la question donna lieu à un débat extrêmement intéressant mais biaisé qui se termina par un accord sur la place assignée au consensus dans le règlement.

La discussion au sein du Comité sur le consensus était née à l'occasion de l'examen du projet du Secrétariat relativement à l'article 9 qui prévoyait qu'au cours d'une session, le Comité pouvait réviser l'ordre du jour et s'il y avait lieu, ajouter, ajourner ou supprimer des points.

---

[1] Communiqué de presse du Centre des droits de l'homme du 25 mars 1985.

C'était la proposition des experts marxistes selon laquelle la décision d'ajouter des points à l'ordre du jour devait être prise à l'unanimité[2] qui avait créé le problème le plus sérieux.

Le courant Occidental Tiers-mondiste avait critiqué cette proposition en soulignant, d'une part qu'elle donnerait à certains membres le droit d'opposer un veto à l'inscription de questions additionnelles à l'ordre du jour une fois celui-ci adopté, et d'autre part que le paragraphe 2 b) de l'article 39 du Pacte disposait que les décisions du Comité devaient être prises à la majorité des membres présents. .

Se référant à la proposition selon laquelle les décisions devaient être prises par un vote majoritaire, le courant Marxiste avait rappelé que l'O.N.U. avait été créé afin d'assurer la sécurité des Etats et des relations amicales et pacifiques entre les Etats. A cette fin, il convenait de tout faire pour trouver des solutions fondées sur un consensus et non sur un vote. Le Comité venait d'ouvrir sa première session et l'efficacité du système de décision par consensus avait déjà été reconnue. Bien que le procédé d'insertion de nouvelles questions à l'ordre du jour par une décision de la majorité était acceptable sur le plan juridique, les membres du Comité devaient se rendre compte que les décisions internationales n'avaient de force que s'il y avait accord. Les experts marxistes avaient fait plusieurs tentatives pour modifier l'article 9. En premier lieu ils proposaient d'ajouter à cet article la phrase suivante:

> 'Dans ce cas, le Comité fera tout ce qui est en son pouvoir pour réaliser un consensus sur l'inscription de questions additionnelles. Cette proposition n'irait pas à l'encontre des dispositions du Pacte, mais stimulerait chez les membres une volonté de travailler dans l'harmonie.'

Il avait été objecté à cette proposition que si le Comité devait arriver au consensus en particulier sur les règles de procédure, une telle méthode devrait n'être qu'un principe de travail et non une règle de procédure qui serait incompatible avec le paragraphe 2 b) de l'article 39 du Pacte.

Mais le courant Marxiste revint à la charge et proposa de remanier l'article 9 de la manière qui suit: 'Au cours d'une session, le Comité peut réviser l'ordre du jour et, s'il y a lieu, ajouter ou supprimer des points; il peut même y ajouter des points urgents et importants si ses membres les reconnaissent comme tels par voie de consensus'. Et le courant Marxiste ajoutait que si le Comité voulait en cours de session modifier l'ordre du jour, il revenait ainsi sur sa première décision; il y aurait alors lieu, dans ce cas, d'appliquer l'article 49 qui prévoyait que le Comité devait, pour revenir sur une décision, s'appuyer sur une majorité de deux tiers de ses membres. Il proposait donc de supprimer le mot 'ajouter' de la première phrase de l'article 39 et de modifier la seconde phrase de la manière suivante: 'En cours de session, il peut être ajouté à l'ordre du jour des points urgents et importants sous réserve de l'article 49'.

---

[2] Ann. C.D.H. 1977-1978, Vol. 1, pp. 6 à 11 par. 73 et 13; par. 79,4,20 et 31; par. 74, 86, 14 et 19; par. 76 et 10; par. 78 et 11; par. 75, 84, 23 à 27; par. 5 et 28; par. 83 et 30; par. 2; par. 85; par. 32.

Cette proposition avait été fermement rejetée car il semblait y avoir incompatibilité entre la première phrase de l'article 9 selon laquelle le Comité pouvait réviser son ordre du jour et la deuxième phrase qui prévoyait que seuls des points urgents et importants pouvaient être ajoutés. Le courant Marxiste voulu contourner son échec en proposant qu'il n'y ait pas lieu d'entamer, à ce stade, un débat sur la question de la majorité simple et de la majorité des deux tiers. Il conviendrait plutôt que le Comité prenne au départ le parti de s'efforcer, toujours d'une manière générale, d'adopter ses décisions par consensus.

Le courant Occidental Tiersmondiste voulant préciser davantage sa position, estima que le Comité comme tout autre comité, devait s'efforcer d'arrêter ses décisions avec l'accord général de ses membres. Dans ce sens, il devait essayer de réaliser un consensus, mais qu'il allait de soi que ce principe étant, dès le départ, généralement admis, il ne paraissait pas nécessaire de le mentionner dans le règlement intérieur du Comité. En effet, il ne semblait pas judicieux de le lier à un article particulier de ce règlement et il ne faisait pas de doute que, dans le domaine de la procédure, il était important de faire en sorte que les décisions soient, autant que possible, prises avec l'accord général de tous les membres du Comité. Mais pour ce qui était de savoir s'il y avait lieu d'énoncer quelque part dans le règlement intérieur que le Comité devait s'efforcer de prendre ses décisions par consensus, on risquait ce faisant, d'établir une règle qui pourrait prêter à des interprétations abusives et à des malentendus. On pourrait penser qu'établir une telle règle était aller au-delà de ce que l'on pouvait normalement attendre des membres du Comité dans la recherche d'un accord, et voir là une tentative de donner à l'engagement solennel que chacun d'entre eux prenait d'agir en toute impartialité et route conscience des implications qu'il ne saurait avoir.

Cette longue discussion relative au consensus qui se déroula aux troisième et quatrième séances du Comité les 22 et 23 mars 1977, repris à la fin de la sixième séance le 23 mars, lors de l'examen de l'article 51 qui disposait que 'sauf dans le cas où le Pacte ou d'autres articles du présent règlement en disposent autrement, les décisions du Comité sont prises à la majorité des membres présents'.

Le courant Marxiste avait proposé d'ajouter, à la fin de l'article, une deuxième phrase qui se lisait comme suit: 'Le Comité fera tout son possible pour parvenir à un consensus avant de prendre une décision.' Cette phrase refléterait l'attitude des membres du Comité ainsi que leur esprit de coopération.

Mais le courant Occidental Tiers-mondiste rejeta l'idée de faire figurer une proposition aussi explicite dans le règlement intérieur. En effet, le principe du consensus, tel qu'il avait été appliqué dans le passé, signifiait plus qu'un esprit de coopération dans les travaux et impliquait plutôt une idée de compromis. Si ce principe figurait expressément dans le règlement intérieur, il courait le risque d'être interprété dans un sens qui serait incompatible avec l'indépendance et l'impartialité auxquelles s'étaient engagées les membres du Comité.

S'il était évident que le consensus devait être l'esprit dans lequel le Comité devait effectuer ses travaux, on ne pouvait toutefois faire un article de son règlement intérieur, car cela reviendrait à imposer le principe du consensus à un organe à vocation judiciaire. Or, pour un tel organe, le consensus était certes un objectif souhaitable, mais nullement une obligation.

Voulant à toute force imposer le consensus dans le règlement intérieur, le courant Marxiste insistait et constatait que les membres du Comité paraissaient pour la plupart convaincus qu'il importait au plus haut point que le Comite s'acquittât de sa tâche dans un esprit de coopération. L'activité du Comité ne pouvait pas se comparer à celle d'un tribunal - encore fallait-il noter que de nombreux tribunaux d'une certaine importance fonctionnaient selon le principe de l'unanimité du jury-mais à l'inverse d'un tribunal, le Comité n'était tenu de prononcer aucun jugement. Son rôle consistait simplement à examiner des rapports, à faire des observations à leur sujet et, en ce qui concernait les plaintes et les communications dont il était saisi, une fonction de conciliation.

Par ailleurs, on ne pouvait admettre l'argument selon lequel adopter le consensus comme mode de décision serait incompatible avec la tâche dévolue au Comité, car parmi les décisions qu'il serait appelé à prendre, nombreuses seraient celles qui auraient un caractère général et pour lesquelles il serait donc possible de réaliser un consensus.

Il était également difficile de comprendre en quoi la recherche d'une base de consensus, dans un cas donné, pourrait porter atteinte à l'indépendance des membres du Comité. Ceux-ci, en s'efforçant de réaliser ce consensus, agiraient, au contraire, conformément à leur engagement solennel de s'acquitteraient en toute conscience de leurs obligations.

Mais le courant Occidental Tiers-mondiste, décidé à ne pas accepter l'introduction du consensus dans le règlement intérieur, soulignait que s'il était tout à fait d'avis que le Comité devait s'efforcer d'aboutir à un consensus, le mode de décision devrait simplement être laissé au jugement de celui-ci. Incorporer une disposition spécifique à cet égard dans le règlement intérieur aurait inévitablement de multiples répercussions. La règle du consensus convenait parfaitement aux organes qui définissaient des politiques, mais le Comité n'était pas l'un d'eux. Il importait, en l'occurrence, au plus haut point de veiller à ce qu'aucune opinion, même si elle émanait de la minorité de ses membres, ne soit écartée à la légère. S'il est évident que le Comité devait prendre le temps de rechercher une solution communément acceptée, il n'en était pas moins certain qu'en dernier ressort les décisions devraient être prises à la majorité, conformément à l'article 39 du Pacte.

Manquant de plus en plus d'arguments, le courant Marxiste avait alors invoqué la morale en affirmant qu'on s'était depuis toujours efforcé d'introduire des principes moraux dans le droit positif. Or, l'occasion se présentait alors au Comité d'agir en ce sens, et il ne faudrait pas la laisser passer. Ce faisant, le Comité serait plus aisément amené à adopter une attitude homogène qui l'aiderait à mener à bien sa noble tâche.

Mais le courant Occidental Tiers-mondiste qui n'était pas à court d'arguments estimait que le projet de règlement intérieur contenait des dispositions suffisantes en ce qui concerne la conduite des débats lors de l'examen d'une question. Le problème que posait la proposition tendant à instituer le consensus tenait au fait qu'il serait difficile au Comité de déterminer à quel moment tous les efforts en vue de réaliser le consensus seraient épuisés. De plus, compte tenu de la durée limitée des sessions du Comité, cela ne serait pas possible dans tous les cas, surtout si d'autres pays ratifiaient le Protocole.

Le courant Marxiste ne se découragea pas pour autant et cita la pratique suivie généralement par les instances internationales: le règlement intérieur de certaines d'entre elles stipulait expressément que les décisions ne devaient être prises que par consensus. C'était le cas de la Conférence sur la Sécurité et la Coopération en Europe. Dans d'autres cas, le règlement intérieur précisait que les décisions devaient être prises par consensus et qu'il n'y avait lieu de recourir au vote qu'en cas d'absolue nécessité, en d'autres termes, à titre exceptionnel. C'est ainsi que la Troisième Conférence des Nations Unies sur le droit de la mer n'avait recouru au vote pour arrêter ses décisions qu'après avoir épuisé toutes les possibilités de réaliser un consensus. La Sixième Commission de l'Assemblée générale dont le règlement intérieur prévoyait que les décisions seraient prises à la majorité, n'avait en réalité, au cours des dix dernières années, jamais pris de décisions autrement que par consensus. Il en était de même pour la Commission de droit international et d'autres organes analogues.

Le courant Occidental Tiers-mondiste était à l'aise pour répondre que si l'on pouvait utilement considérer le règlement intérieur d'autres organes, il y avait entre le Comité et ces organes une différence très nette qu'il fallait se garder d'oublier. En effet, tous les organes mentionnés étaient des organes légiférant et devaient à ce titre rechercher l'accord général afin d'obtenir la ratification de certains traités. Le Comité lui, était régi par le Pacte et, s'il était vrai que ses membres n'étaient pas des juges, ils avaient néanmoins pour mission de faire appliquer les dispositions énoncées dans le Pacte, ce qui exigeait d'eux qu'ils se prononcent sur certains faits. Le mandat était de veiller à ce que les Etats parties s'acquittent des obligations qui leur incombaient en vertu du Pacte.

Par ailleurs, tous les membres du Comité se félicitaient des résultats qu'il avait obtenus jusque là, puisque l'on avait pu s'accorder par consensus sur quelque cinquante articles, ce à quoi l'on était arrivé sans qu'aucune référence à la notion de consensus ait été prévue dans le projet de règlement. Mais il convenait aussi de noter que si certains articles n'avaient pu être adoptés, c'était uniquement à cause de cette question de consensus.

Le Président, constatant que le Comité ne pouvait apparemment parvenir, à ce stade, à une décision unanime en ce qui concernait l'article 51, proposa de reprendre la discussion sur cette question à une séance ultérieure.[3]

A la 12è séance du Comité le 29 mars 1977, M. Suy, Secrétaire général adjoint, Conseiller juridique de l'O.N.U., répondant aux questions des membres du Comité

---

[3] *Ibid.*, pp. 21 il 24, par. 68,14,15,16 et 21; par. 70 ; par. 71 et 5; par.72; par.73; par. U 3 et 10; par.4 et 19; par.6 et 24; par. 9; par. 12; par. 17; par. 18; pp. 40 et 41; par. 5, 6 et 7.

sur la question du consensus, rappela que le paragraphe 2 b de l'article 39 du Pacte stipulait que 'les décisions du Comité sont prises à la majorité des membres présents'. Il avait été suggéré que le Comité prenne des décisions par consensus ou, pour certaines questions, à une majorité plus importante que celle prévue dans le Pacte. De l'avis du Conseiller juridique, toute disposition éliminant la possibilité d'un vote ou exigeant une majorité plus importante que la majorité des membres présents était contraire au Pacte. Rien ne s'opposait toutefois, à ce que le Comité tentât de parvenir à un consensus étant entendu que, s'il n'y parvenait pas, ses décisions seraient mises aux voix et prises à la majorité prévue à l'article 39 du Pacte.

M. Suy rappela que la Commission de la fonction publique internationale qui, comme le Comité, était un organe d'experts siégeant à titre individuel, adoptait normalement ses décisions par consensus. A défaut de consensus, il était prévu que le Président pouvait et, si un membre en faisait la demande, devait mettre les propositions aux voix. Une telle disposition n'éliminait nullement la possibilité de procéder à un vote. Le Comité pourrait donc étudier la possibilité d'incorporer un article analogue dans son règlement intérieur ce qui serait tout à fait compatible avec le Pacte.

En ce qui concernait la question de la majorité, le Conseiller juridique précisa que tout organe comme le Pacte détermine la majorité requise pour l'adoption des décisions du Comité, le paragraphe 2 de l'article 67 de la Charte des Nations Unies stipule que 'les décisions du Conseil économique et social sont prises à la majorité des membres présents et votants'. Cette disposition avait toujours été considérée comme signifiant que toutes les décisions du Conseil exigeaient la majorité prévue dans la Charte. Il convenait de noter que le règlement intérieur du Conseil contenait des dispositions relatives à un nouvel examen des propositions, mais que ces dispositions ne modifiaient pas l'article relatif à la majorité des membres présents et votants. Cette pratique était contraire à celle des autres organes des Nations Unies qui décidaient généralement de procéder à un nouvel examen à la majorité des deux tiers.

A la 13e séance, M. Suy,[4] répondant à des questions posées à la 12e séance et se referant à la question de savoir si les décisions du Comité devaient être considérées comme définitives et si, en conséquence, il convenait de faire figurer dans le règlement intérieur des dispositions concernant un nouvel examen des décisions, répondit que la pratique des organes des Nations Unies était extrêmement diverse.

Concernant la nécessité d'établir une distinction entre les organes qui avaient des fonctions législatives et ceux qui avaient un caractère judiciaire, le Conseiller juridique estima que 'le Comité des droits de l'homme, n'est ni un organe ayant des fonctions législatives ni un organe judiciaire et que tout organe d'experts est unique en son genre'. Concernant le fonctionnement du Tribunal des Nations Unies, le Conseiller juridique déclara que l'article 10 du statut de cet organe disposait qu'il devait prendre ses décisions à la majorité des voix et que, sous réserve des

---

[4] *Ibid.*, Suy, p. 43, par. 5 à 9.

dispositions des articles 11 et 12, les jugements du Tribunal étaient définitifs et sans appel.

De même, M. Suy précisa que les propositions adoptées par le Comité étaient des décisions, et en ce qui concernait la question de savoir si les fonctions de la Commission de la Fonction publique internationale étaient similaires à celles du Comité, M. Suy attira l'attention du Comité sur l'article 10 du chapitre III du statut de la Commission de l'Université des Nations Unies qui faisaient expressément état d'un consensus.

M. Suy ne pensait pas que le fait que l'acte constitutif d'un organe ne contenait pas d'allusions à un consensus faisait obstacle à l'incorporation de disposition prévoyant un consensus dans son règlement intérieur, non plus qu'à une décision de cet organe de prendre ses décisions sur cette base. Il n'était question de consensus ni dans la Charte des Nations Unies ni dans le règlement de l'Assemblée générale, toutefois, le consensus était une méthode de travail importante de l'Assemblée générale.

Egalement, le Conseiller juridique pensait personnellement que rien n'empêchait un organe de stipuler dans son règlement intérieur qu'une majorité des deux tiers était requise pour un nouvel examen des décisions.

Enfin, M. Suy termina ses explications en précisant que les décisions prises par consensus avaient la même force que les décisions prises à l'issue d'un vote.

A la 14[è] séance le 30 mars 1977, M. Lallah, coordonnateur du Groupe de travail qui avait été chargé de déterminer sous quelle forme il convenait d'exprimer la volonté du Comité de mener ses travaux dans un esprit de consensus, rappela que quatre opinions prévalaient au départ. Selon les uns, il fallait modifier l'article 51 du règlement intérieur de façon à y incorporer la notion de consensus, sans toutefois porter atteinte à l'article 39 du Pacte qui prévoyait que les décisions devaient être prises à la majorité. Selon d'autres membres, le principe du consensus devrait être mentionné dans le rapport. Pour d'autres encore, il ne devrait être évoqué ni dans le règlement intérieur ni dans le rapport, mais devrait se dégager des comptes rendus analytiques des séances. Enfin, certains membres avaient proposé d'inclure, dans le rapport ou les comptes rendus, un texte où il serait précisé que les membres – qu'il fallait distinguer du Comité lui-même – avaient reconnu qu'il était souhaitable de parvenir à un consensus avant de prendre une décision.

Un rapprochement entre ces quatre grandes tendances d'opinions s'était opéré au cours d'un échange de vues fructueux. Il semblait que les membres du Comité s'entendaient pour estimer que le Comité devait s'efforcer de travailler dans le sens d'un accord, sans porter préjudice aux dispositions de l'article 39 du Pacte. M. Lallah pensait que l'on pourrait peut-être prévoir une note en bas de page à l'article 51 du règlement intérieur, qui renverrait aux comptes rendus analytiques où seraient évoqués les débats ayant eu lieu sur la question. Le Comité devrait s'accorder un temps de réflexion avant de prendre une décision sur ce point.

A la 15[è] session, le 30 mars 1977, M. Prado Vallejo déclara qu'à la suite de consultations officieuses entre les membres du Comité il proposait d'adopter l'article 51 tel quel et d'insérer dans le règlement intérieur une note en bas de page qui se lisait ainsi:

> 'A propos de l'article 51, il y a lieu d'appeler l'attention sur le paragraphe . . . du rapport sur la première session du Comité qui se lit comme suit:
>
> "1- L'avis général des membres du Comité à été que la méthode de travail de celui-ci devrait normalement permettre d'essayer de prendre les décisions par voie de consensus avant de procéder à un vote, sous réserve que les dispositions du Pacte et du règlement intérieur soient respectées et que la recherche de ce consensus n'ait pas pour effet de retarder indûment les travaux du Comité.
>
> 2- Ayant à l'esprit le paragraphe 1 de l'article 39, le Président peut à toute séance, et à la demande de tout membre, doit mettre la proposition aux voix".'[5]

A l'issue de cette longue discussion,[6] le Comité adopta l'article 9 avec quelques modifications et sans aucune référence à une majorité spéciale. L'article 49 qui fut adopté presque sans modification immédiatement avant la discussion sur l'article 51, fut remis en cause après l'adoption de celui-ci. Le projet de cet article qui traitait précisément de la reprise en examen, au cours d'une même session, d'une proposition adoptée ou rejetée, prévoyait qu'un tel examen n'était possible qu'en cas de décision prise à la majorité des deux tiers des membres présents. Le Comité avait décidé qu'il n'y avait pas lieu de retenir cette majorité.

En premier lieu, il apparaissait clairement que le Comité avait refusé d'inclure le consensus dans le règlement intérieur sous quelque forme que ce soit, sauf une note en bas de page et reliée à l'article 51 qui disposait que les décisions du Comité sont prises à la majorité simple des membres présents.

La note, lorsqu'elle évoquait le consensus, soulignait que, s'il était normal de chercher à prendre les décisions du Comité par consensus, il convenait que les dispositions du Pacte et du règlement intérieur soient respectées et que la recherche du consensus n'ait pas pour effet de retarder indûment les travaux du Comité.

En second lieu, les experts marxistes avaient déployé le maximum d'efforts pour introduire la condition du consensus dans la prise de décisions du Comité. Mais trop d'insistance pour faire expressément sanctionner cette notion par le règlement intérieur finirait par faire douter de la sincérité du désir déclaré d'aboutir à un consensus, comme l'a fait remarquer avec malice un expert.[7]

---

[5] *Ibid.*, pp. 49 et 50 par. 1 et 2.

[6] *Ibid.*, pp. 40 à 50, y p. 40 et 41, par. 5 à 7, pp. 41 et 42, par. 16 à 18, pp. 43 et 44 par. 5 à 9 et 20; p.7 par. 8, pp. 45 et 46, par. 37 et 45, p. 47 par. 59; p. 41, par. 9, p. 46 par. 39 et par. 44; p. 4, par. 10 à 12, p. 44 par. 10, p. 46, par. 46, p. 47, par 52 et 53; p. 41, par. 13, p. 43, par. 1. p. 47 par. 2 et 3; p. 4 par. 14; p. 41, par. 15; p. 42, par 19 et 20; p. 42, par. 21, p. 44 par. 12, p. 48 par. 10; p. 44, par. 13; p. 44, par. 14.

[7] *Ibid.*, p. 24.

Il était clair qu'une fois de plus, les experts marxistes minoritaires et fidèles à la position de leurs Etats lors de l'élaboration du Pacte avaient essayé de limiter le plus possible les pouvoirs du Comité et qu'ils voulaient utiliser le consensus comme un droit de veto sur toute décision qu'ils n'agréeraient pas. Ils essuyèrent un échec cuisant.

D- Le gel des obligations du Comité découlant du paragraphe 4 de l'article 40 du Pacte et de l'article 70 du règlement intérieur

Le paragraphe 4 de l'article 40 dispose:

> 'Le Comité étudie les rapports présentés par les Etats parties au présent Pacte. Il adresse aux Etats parties ses propres rapports, ainsi que toutes observations générales qu'il jugerait appropriées. Le Comité peut également transmettre au Conseil économique et social ces observations accompagnées de copies des rapports qu'il à reçus d'Etats parties au présent Pacte.'

Par ailleurs, l'article 70 du règlement intérieur stipule:

> '1. Lorsqu'il examine un rapport présenté par un Etat partie en vertu de l'article 40 du Pacte, le Comité doit tout d'abord s'assurer que le rapport fournit tous les renseignements nécessaires conformément aux dispositions de l'article 66 du règlement intérieur.
>
> 2. Si, de l'avis du Comité, un rapport présente par un Etat partie ne contient pas de renseignements suffisants, le Comité peut demander à cet Etat de fournir les renseignements supplémentaires requis, en indiquant pour quelle date lesdits renseignements devront être présentés.
>
> 3. Si, à la suite de l'examen des rapports et des renseignements soumis par un Etat partie, le Comité décide que cet Etat partie ne s'est pas acquitté de certaines obligations qui lui incombent en vertu Pacte, il peut faire à l'Etat intéressé toutes observations générales, qu'il jugerait appropriées, conformément au paragraphe 4 de l'article 40 du Pacte.'

Le débat sur l'interprétation des dispositions de l'article 40 du Pacte et de l'article 70 du règlement intérieur avait occupé plusieurs séances du Comité et avait été d'une grande importance, car ce débat avait en réalité porté sur les obligations et sur les limites des pouvoirs du Comité. C'est-à-dire en premier lieu, sur la nature précise des fonctions qui lui incombaient en vertu notamment du paragraphe 4 de l'article 40 lequel stipule que le Comité étudie les rapports présentés par les Etats parties au Pacte et adresse aux Etats parties ses propres rapports ainsi que toutes observations générales qu'il jugerait appropriées. Et en second lieu, le débat avait porté sur la meilleure manière pour le Comité de s'acquitter de ces fonctions.

Les membres du Comité avaient estimé que la méthode de travail adoptée pour la phase initiale de l'examen des rapports des Etats parties, à savoir: présentation par les Etats de rapports conformes aux directives du Comité, questions posées aux représentants des Etats intéressés et réponses desdits représentants, avait permis de nouer un dialogue constructif avec les Etats parties et d'aider ceux-ci dans les efforts qu'ils faisaient pour promouvoir les droits de l'homme et la jouissance de ces droits.

Cependant, il était apparu à plusieurs membres que, si précieux et efficace qu'ait été le premier examen des rapports des Etats parties, et malgré toutes les possibilités que cet examen avait donné aux membres du Comité de se renseigner individuellement en posant des questions et en formulant des observations, le Comité en tant que tel, c'est-à-dire comme organe distinct des membres individuels qui le composent, devait poursuivre et achever ses travaux relatifs aux rapports des Etats parties. Le Comité devait étudier les rapports de ces derniers, c'est-à-dire faire une évaluation des rapports du point de vue de leur concordance et de leur conformité avec les dispositions du Pacte, et adresser à chaque Etat partie intéressé un rapport fondé sur son étude du rapport de l'Etat partie et les conclusions qu'il en tirait.

C'est à ce sujet que les deux grands courants s'affrontèrent une fois de plus au cours des débats. Le premier courant majoritaire, groupant les experts des Etats occidentaux et des Etats du Tiers Monde s'en tenait strictement à la lettre et à l'esprit des dispositions du Pacte et du règlement intérieur, et le courant minoritaire, composé par les experts des Etats marxistes, qui tout en proclamant un strict respect des dispositions du Pacte, les restreignait par des arguments spécieux.

La position du courant majoritaire Occidental Tiers-mondiste était fondée sur une lecture objective du paragraphe 4 de l'article 40 du Pacte et de l'article 70 du règlement intérieur, qui investissaient le Comité de deux fonctions obligatoires distinctes: d'une part étudier les rapports des Etats parties et d'autre part adresser à ces derniers ses propres rapports. Le Comité pouvait, selon l'article 40, paragraphe 4, adresser également aux Etats parties toutes observations qu'il jugerait appropriées. Il s'agissait là d'une fonction facultative.

Le Comité, après l'examen des rapports des Etats parties n'avait jamais étudié en tant qu'organe collégial ces rapports: il n'avait jamais constitué de groupe de travail pour faire une analyse et une évaluation méthodiques pour voir dans quelle mesure ces rapports étaient conformes aux dispositions du Pacte. Le Comité était pourtant tenu d'appliquer ces procédures[8] et aurait pu le faire.

Pendant l'examen par le Comité d'un rapport par un Etat partie, souvent tel ou tel de ses membres relevait que tel ou tel droit énoncé dans le Pacte ne semblait pas être l'objet de dispositions législatives ou autres le protégeant et le garantissant, ou bien que telle disposition dans la constitution ou la législation de l'Etat partie violait le Pacte. Mais il n'y avait pas là une action collective d'analyse, d'évaluation et

[8] Voir comptes rendus analytiques des 48è, 49è, 50è, 55è et 73è séances. Troisième session, 1978. Ann. C.D.H. 1977-1978, Volume I.

d'étude insérée dans un rapport propre du Comité après examen du rapport de l'Etat partie en particulier.[9]

Le Comité n'avait à aucun moment commencé cette fonction obligatoire. Il s'était contenté de présenter à l'Assemblée générale des rapports annuels dans lesquels ne se trouvait qu'un résumé des comptes rendus analytiques indiquant seulement les questions et les réponses. Le Comité aurait pu trouver, comme le dispose l'article 40 paragraphe 4, le moyen de faire la synthèse de la documentation écrite et orale qui lui avait été fournie. Lorsqu'il examinait cette documentation, le Comité devait se demander si les Etats parties avaient fait rapport comme c'était leur devoir et s'ils avaient mis en œuvre le Pacte compte tenu des facteurs et des difficultés qui affectaient cette application.[10]

Après avoir étudié et évalué le rapport de chaque Etat partie, le Comité avait l'obligation, en vertu du paragraphe 4 de l'article 40, d'adresser son propre rapport à l'Etat partie intéressé contenant des observations et des recommandations à cet Etat afin que ce dernier comble des lacunes et résolve les contradictions avec le Pacte existant dans son système législatif ou autre et le mettre en harmonie avec les dispositions du Pacte. Cette obligation ne présentait aucun doute. L'adhésion au Pacte ou sa ratification était un acte volontaire des Etats parties, et certains pays hésitaient à franchir le pas du fait des obligations spécifiques qu'il entraînait. La procédure d'établissement de rapports obligeait les Etats parties à faire la preuve qu'ils s'étaient employés à promouvoir et à protéger les droits énoncés dans le Pacte. Pour sa part, en vertu du paragraphe 4 de l'article 40, le Comité avait l'obligation d'étudier les rapports et d'adresser ses propres rapports aux Etats parties. Il devait s'acquitter de cette obligation. Que des membres du Comité aient individuellement mis en lumière des imperfections existant dans telle ou telle législation nationale, constituait un premier pas.[11] Naturellement le Comité qui n'était pas un tribunal, ne devait pas prononcer de condamnation contre l'Etat partie, même au cas où il avait constaté des violations du Pacte, mais au contraire, mettre en lumière ces violations quand elles se produisaient afin d'amener l'Etat partie concerné à modifier sa législation et le comportement fautif de son administration.[12]

Il appartenait au Comité d'essayer d'aider les Etats concernés, et les Etats eux-mêmes devaient comprendre qu'ils avaient besoin de cette aide. Si l'on faisait remarquer à l'Etat concerné qu'il n'avait pas répondu de manière adéquate, celui-ci avait la possibilité de donner des réponses plus satisfaisantes. Si, après qu'une seconde chance lui ait été accordée, l'Etat ne répondait toujours pas aux questions d'une manière satisfaisante, le Comité pouvait tirer les conclusions qui s'imposaient. L'article 70, paragraphe 3 du règlement intérieur, prévoyait bien que si le Comité

---

[9] Ann. C.D.H. 1979-1980, Vol. I pp. 405 à 410, par. 1 à 41 et pp. 410 à 416, par. 1 à 56. Dixième session 1980, 231e et 232e séances (privées) et Rapp. C.D.H. 1979, n° (A/34/40), pp. 4 et 5, par. 15 à 20.

[10] Ann. C.D.H. 1979-1980, Vol. I, p.407, par. 3 et 4; *ibid.*, p. 409, par. 25 et 27.

[11] *Ibid.*, p. 406, par.5; *ibid.*, p. 413 par. 26.

[12] *Ibid.*, p.409. par. 25 et 27.

décidait que certaines des obligations contractées par un Etat partie n'étaient pas remplies, il pouvait lui faire toutes les observations qu'il jugeait appropriées.[13]

On pouvait se demander pourquoi le Comité avait été créé, pourquoi l'article 28 du Pacte se préoccupait de préciser que ses membres devaient être des 'personnalités de haute moralité, possédant une compétence reconnue dans le domaine des droits de l'homme' et pourquoi il soulignait 'l'intérêt de la participation de quelques personnes ayant une expérience juridique'. Ce n'était pas simplement pour écouter la présentation de leurs propres rapports par les Etats parties, c'était aussi et surtout pour amener ces Etats à tenir compte des suggestions faites par le Comité dans le cadre du dialogue qui s'établissait entre eux et lui. D'ailleurs le cas du Chili en était un exemple. Dans ce cas, en effet, le Comité avait non seulement fait connaître son point de vue sur le rapport du pays, mais il avait souligné implicitement les violations du Pacte par l'Etat partie en question,[14] en demandant à cet Etat partie de présenter un nouveau rapport.

Toutefois, tout en s'associant aux membres du courant majoritaire et en partageant leur point de vue concernant les décisions du Comité, deux membres occidentaux de ce courant avaient exprimé les craintes que 'si le Comité envisage d'établir ses propres rapports après la présentation et l'examen du rapport individuel pour chaque pays, cela prendra beaucoup de temps pour un organe qui ne siège pas en permanence et exigera un surcroît d'effort qui risque d'être trop grand pour le Comité'.[15] L'autre expert occidental avait fait remarquer que la rédaction d'observations et de recommandations adressées à des Etats particuliers ouvrirait un champ d'activité beaucoup plus vaste et qu'un tel élargissement de l'article 40 pourrait exiger une profonde réorganisation du Comité et un surcroît de temps à sa disposition . . . et le premier membre occidental du Comité de conclure: 'Enfin, il n'est pas douteux que le Comité éprouverait des difficultés à arrêter d'un commun accord le contenu de ces observations sur de nombreux aspects de la situation particulière de différents Etats parties'.[16] C'était un revirement inattendu qui offrait aux experts marxistes ce qu'ils n'espéraient plus, à savoir l'imposition du consensus et du veto.

Le courant Marxiste minoritaire faisant une lecture des plus restrictives de l'article 40, paragraphe 4, prétendait que la présentation des rapports des Etats parties et leur étude par le Comité avait pour objet d'échanger des renseignements, de favoriser la coopération entre les Etats, de maintenir un dialogue régulier et d'aider les Etats à surmonter leurs difficultés.

Rien dans l'article 40 n'autorisait le Comité à faire une évaluation générale des droits de l'homme et de porter des jugements sur la manière dont les Etats parties en particulier remplissaient ou non leurs obligations, d'interpréter le Pacte et de faire des recommandations ou des suggestions à des Etats parties en particulier.

---

[13] *Ibid.*, p. 410, par.40 et 41.
[14] *Ibid.*, p. 415, par. 44, 45 et 46.
[15] *Ibid.*, p. 414, par. 41.
[16] *Ibid.*, p. 414, par. 27.

Pareille interprétation de l'article 40 allait bien au-delà des termes du Pacte. La seule obligation qui incombait aux Etats en vertu de l'article 40 était celle de présenter des rapports. Les Etats n'avaient aucune obligation, de suivre les directives du Comité, d'envoyer des représentants assister à ses délibérations, d'écouter les questions posées par ses membres et d'y répondre.

Ces procédures étaient utiles, mais elles n'étaient pas prévues par le Pacte lui-même. Le Comité avait donc déjà considérablement élargi son mandat et il ne devait pas se permettre de se transformer en un instrument d'ingérence dans les affaires intérieures des Etats.

Mais la position des experts marxistes allait beaucoup plus loin dans l'affirmation de contrevérités; c'est ainsi qu'elle prétendait que le mot 'étudie' avait apparemment été employé dans le Pacte pour faire une distinction entre les fonctions de détermination des faits et de conciliation, et la procédure d'établissement des rapports. Les articles 41 et 42 du Pacte, ainsi que le Protocole facultatif renseignaient clairement sur la procédure que le Comité devait suivre; et l'application de cette procédure faisait l'objet d'une ratification spéciale par les Etats parties; or il n'y avait pas de procédure claire de ce genre à l'article 40 et, par conséquent, le Comité n'était pas en mesure d'élaborer une procédure qui n'avait pas fait l'objet d'un accord entre les Etats parties. Si les auteurs du Pacte avaient voulu que le Comité évalue la situation en matière de droits de l'homme dans un pays donné, ils l'auraient certainement indiqué.

Le Comité devait en tout et pour tout soumettre un rapport annuel. Il n'y avait rien dans le Pacte qui autorisait le Comité à établir un rapport particulier sur chaque rapport des Etats. Le paragraphe 4 de l'article 40 faisait référence aux mêmes rapports annuels que l'article 45. Compte tenu notamment de ce dernier, de l'article 6 du Protocole facultatif ainsi que du chapitre X du règlement intérieur du Comité, il s'agissait uniquement du rapport annuel du Comité.

L'article 70 du règlement intérieur avait été fait alors que le Comité n'avait aucune expérience. En outre le règlement intérieur ne pouvait pas servir à conférer au Comité ce que le Pacte ne lui donnait pas.[17] Telle était la position du courant marxiste.

La lecture sereine et objective des dispositions de l'article 40 paragraphe 4 du Pacte et de l'article 70, paragraphe 3, du règlement intérieur, faisait apparaître la clarté des obligations que devait assumer le Comité en vertu de ces dispositions. Cette clarté ne laissait pas de place à un débat.

Pourtant ce débat eut lieu et occupa plusieurs séances du Comité au cours desquelles presque tous les membres du Comité participèrent activement. A la vérité, ce débat était la continuité de celui qui avait opposé pendant les nombreuses années de l'élaboration du Pacte, les partisans d'un véritable contrôle par un organe supranational et de la stricte application des dispositions du Pacte par les Etats

---

[17] *Ibid.*, pp. 407 et 408, par. 9a 17.

parties, et ceux opposés à ce contrôle considéré comme une ingérence dans les affaires intérieures des Etats parties.

Il était inéluctable qu'en cherchant à préciser ses obligations en vertu du Pacte, le Comité, compte tenu de sa composition par des membres venant d'Etats ayant des idéologies différentes et souvent opposées, ait vu réapparaître l'ancien clivage, même si les membres du Comité y siégeaient à titre individuel et étaient supposés être indépendants et impartiaux.

Le courant majoritaire avait une composition complexe puisqu'il comprenait les experts occidentaux, latino-américains, africains et asiatiques. Presque tous les experts occidentaux avaient une position très voisine de celle que les Etats membres occidentaux de l'O.N.U. avaient adopté dans les différents organes des Nations Unies lors de l'élaboration du Pacte. Nombre de ces Etats, à défaut d'une juridiction internationale, avaient plaidé pour la création d'un organe supranational chargé de contrôler l'application du Pacte par les Etats parties et de développer ainsi la protection internationale des droits de l'homme. D'une manière générale, les Etats membres d'Amérique Latine avaient une position similaire.

La surprise avait été créée par la position adoptée par les experts africains et asiatiques. Lors de l'élaboration du Pacte, la plupart des Etats membres d'Asie et d'Afrique avaient manifesté beaucoup de réticence, de méfiance, voire d'hostilité à l'égard d'un organe supranational aux pouvoirs de contrôle étendus qui, comme l'avait déclaré le représentant d'un Etat africain de la Troisième Commission, suspendraient une épée Damoclès au-dessus des pays dont la législation sur les droits de l'homme était encore à l'état embryonnaire.[18]

Pourtant, les trois experts africains et un expert d'un Etat du Moyen-Orient avaient plaidé pour une stricte application du pacte et défendu la seule interprétation possible de l'article 40 du Pacte et de l'article 70 du règlement intérieur. Ces experts, provenant de pays anciennement colonisés généralement encore sous-développés, avaient une attitude très claire. Ils souhaitaient et voulaient sincèrement une stricte et correcte application du Pacte pour être en accord avec le serment qu'ils avaient prêté en vertu de l'article 38 du Pacte, et pour bien manifester aux autres experts occidentaux et marxistes que le fait d'être issus de pays en voie de développement ne les empêchait pas d'être à la hauteur de leur mission et d'être sans complaisance aucune à l'égard des Etats parties du Tiers Monde, tout autant que pour les autres Etats parties.

La composition du courant minoritaire était exclusivement faite des experts des Etats parties marxistes à l'exception de l'expert yougoslave qui avait adopté une position neutre, conforme à celle adoptée généralement par son Etat.

Les experts des Etats communistes avaient adopté une position identique à celle défendue par leurs Etats lors de l'élaboration du Pacte à l'O.N.U., à savoir celle de limiter le plus possible les pouvoirs de contrôle du Comité dans l'application du Pacte par les Etats parties. Il convient de rappeler leurs efforts acharnés lors de l'élaboration du règlement intérieur du Comité, pour imposer le 'consensus' de

---

[18] (A/C.9/SR/415).

façon à empêcher toute action et bloquer toute décision qui n'aurait pas leur agrément. Ils menèrent un ultime combat d'arrière-garde afin d'essayer de réduire les fonctions du Comité en vertu de l'article 40, paragraphe 4, du Pacte et de l'article 73 du règlement intérieur, à celles d'un organe d'enregistrement. Excellents juristes, ils ne pouvaient pas ne pas avoir bien saisi le sens et la portée véritables des dispositions pertinentes déjà mentionnées. Tout autant qu'excellents juristes, ils étaient aussi des apparatchiks remarquablement disciplinés, et ils défendirent avec une parfaite mauvaise foi la thèse réductrice des fonctions du Comité utilisant sans état d'âme, une argumentation spécieuse qui n'avait de juridique que le nom.

On aurait pu penser que, forts de la justesse de leur position et de la supériorité du nombre, les experts du courant majoritaire allaient prendre les mesures adéquates pour que le Comité adoptât une procédure qui lui aurait permis de s'acquitter des obligations que lui assignait le paragraphe 4 de l'article 40, d'étudier les rapports de chaque Etat partie et de lui adresser ses propres rapports. Il n'en fut rien et le débat qui avait épuisé tous les arguments et montré la justesse de la position du courant majoritaire, tourna court faute de décision définitive. On ne fit donc rien et le Comité maintenant le *statu quo ante,* se rangea implicitement sur la position des experts des Etats marxistes, et les obligations du Comité en vertu de l'article 40, paragraphe 4, du Pacte et subsidiairement de l'article 73 du règlement intérieur, c'est-à-dire les éléments essentiels de sa fonction de contrôle à l'égard de l'application du Pacte, furent mises en veilleuse jusqu'en 1992.

Les raisons de l'impuissance du Comité d'appliquer le Pacte international des droits civils et politiques et de s'acquitter d'obligations fondamentales découlant de ses fonctions de contrôle étaient multiples et les principales étaient les suivantes:

1- L'étude, c'est-à-dire l'évaluation des rapports des Etats parties et l'élaboration des rapports du Comité autres que le rapport annuel pouvant conduire dans la plupart des cas à la constatation de violations du Pacte, auraient abouti à des tensions, voire des affrontements entre les membres du Comité, notamment entre experts des pays occidentaux et experts des pays marxistes, tous profondément attachés à des idéologies opposées et extrêmement marqués par la guerre froide.

L'absence de consensus entre les membres du Comité dans l'étude et l'évaluation d'un rapport débouchant sur un vote et la consignation d'opinions individuelles même dissidentes étaient d'autant plus possibles que dans l'application du Protocole, il arrivait que les 'constatations' auxquelles aboutissait le Comite, ne fussent pas partagées par certains de ses membres qui consignaient dans la décision du Comité leur opinion individuelle quelques fois dissidente.

Tous les membres du Comité étaient soucieux bien entendu de ne pas arriver à cette solution extrême, mais il n'était pas admissible de sacrifier l'obligation la plus importante du Comité sous prétexte que dans certains cas le consensus n'était pas possible et qu'il était inévitable de voter, comme l'article 39 alinéa 2 b) du Pacte le prévoyait.

2- Aucun Etat partie ne pouvait prétendre qu'il respectait scrupuleusement et totalement toutes les dispositions du Pacte, et les membres du Comité avaient eu amplement la possibilité de le constater dans l'examen des rapports des Etats parties, même dans les rapports des Etats parties où le Pacte était le mieux respecté.

Quand l'Etat partie, qui aurait pu faire l'objet d'un rapport critique du Comité, se trouvait dans le camp soit occidental soit marxiste, soit, à un degré infiniment moindre du Tiers Monde, les experts provenant du camp de l'Etat partie intéressé étaient, par le jeu normal de la solidarité, dans une situation des plus difficiles et souvent dans l'impossibilité de respecter l'impartialité exigée par l'article 38. Cela était inévitable pour les experts des pays marxistes, fréquent pour les experts des pays occidentaux, ne serait-ce que par réaction à la position des experts des pays marxistes, et exceptionnel, pour les experts des pays du Tiers Monde.

S'il en eut été autrement, pourquoi le Comité lors de l'examen du rapport de l'Afghanistan n'avait-il pas déclaré que ce rapport était insuffisant et demandé un autre rapport à cet Etat comme il l'avait fait pour le Chili. Pourtant, à l'instar d'un expert marxiste dans son réquisitoire contre le Chili, un expert tu Tiers Monde dont le pays était musulman et en voie de développement comme l'Afghanistan, avait prononcé contre ce dernier un réquisitoire dont bien des expressions étaient identiques et même volontairement empruntées à celles utilisées par l'expert marxiste.[19]

Si le Comité n'exigea pas un autre rapport à l'Afghanistan, ce fut uniquement parce que les experts occidentaux avaient voulu ménager les experts marxistes, dont le pays de l'un d'eux était empêtré dans la guerre d' Afghanistan, et largement responsable des violations massives des droits de l'homme qui se perpétraient dans ce pays.

3- L'étude des rapports des Etats parties par le Comité et la rédaction des rapports du Comité en conformité avec le paragraphe 4 de l'article 40 auraient sans aucun doute entraîné un surcroît de travail pour le Comité aggravé par les inévitables tensions et désaccords entre les membres du Comité. Ce dernier n'étant pas un organe siégeant en permanence et étant composé de personnes ayant ailleurs leurs activités principales, il était possible que le Comité ne trouvât pas le temps suffisant pour s'acquitter de ses obligations. Néanmoins, il aurait fallu essayer de les respecter avant de les oublier. Seule l'expérience aurait pu donner un résultat probant dans un sens ou dans un autre. Dans le cas où le résultat aurait prouvé avec certitude que le temps n'était manifestement pas suffisant pour le Comité afin de s'acquitter de ses obligations en vertu du paragraphe 4 de l'article 40, le Comité par l'intermédiaire de son Président, aurait informé les Etats parties afin qu'ils recherchent une solution lors de leur reunion ordinaire ou même lors d'une réunion extraordinaire. Or la situation depuis 1992 avait prouvé indiscutablement que le Comité aurait trouvé le temps nécessaire pour accomplir sa mission au titre de l'article 40.

4- Les constatations de violation ou de non mise en oeuvre du Pacte sans condamnation aucune et rédigée d'une manière objective par le Comité pouvaient éventuellement blesser l'amour propre d'un Etat partie qui pouvait ainsi refuser de continuer à dialoguer dans l'avenir avec le Comité. Ceci aurait pu également être

[19] Rapp C.D.H. 1985, p. 128, par. 592.

pris en considération par certains membres du Comité et constituer pour eux une autre raison de ne pas s'acquitter des obligations du paragraphe 4 de l'article 40.

Cette raison n'était pas convaincante, car il était peu vraisemblable que cela se produisît et le cas du Chili le prouvait. Il était certes peu agréable pour un Etat partie de s'entendre dire par le Comité qu'il n'avait pas respecté certaines obligations du Pacte - bien qu'au cours de l'examen du rapport certains membres du Comité ne manquassent pas individuellement de le faire - mais il était infiniment plus grave pour un Etat partie de refuser de continuer à dialoguer avec le Comité parce qu'il s'était entendu dire qu'il n'avait pas respecté le Pacte à propos de telle disposition ou de telle autre.

L'Uruguay qui avait adhéré au Protocole facultatif et que le Comité, par plusieurs constatations, avait considéré responsable de nombreuses violations notamment des articles 6 et 7 du Pacte, n'avait jamais tenté de revenir sur son adhésion au Protocole, alors même qu'il y avait au pouvoir une junte militaire.

Enfin, argument définitif depuis 1992, le Comité en tant qu'organe, n'avait cessé de souligner les violations des dispositions par les Etats parties. Ces derniers n'avaient pas pour cela cessé de dialoguer avec le Comité et de présenter leurs rapports périodiques.

5- Si l'article 40 paragraphe 4 était appliqué dans son intégralité, cela pouvait peut-être décourager certains Etats qui souhaitaient ratifier le Pacte, et par voie de conséquence freiner son universalisation et la promotion des droits de l'homme. Malgré les appels et exhortations réitérés de l'Assemblée générale, de l'O.N.U. aux Etats membres de ratifier les instruments relatifs aux droits de l'homme dont naturellement le Pacte, le nombre des Etats parties avait plafonné toutes les années précédant celle de l'implosion de l'U.R.S.S. Un contrôle plus strict par le Comité de la mise en œuvre du Pacte par les Etats parties n'aurait fait qu'aggraver cette situation.

L'argument ne manquait pas de poids à l'époque mais on peut se demander quel aurait été l'intérêt d'encourager de nouveaux Etats à ratifier le Pacte, si on les encourageait également comme c'était le cas, à ne pas en respecter les dispositions, en refusant soi-même, à savoir le Comité lui-même, de s'acquitter de la seule obligation sérieuse du Pacte c'est-à-dire le contrôle de son application. Du reste, la preuve que l'argument ne tenait pas, est que le nombre d'Etats parties n'avait cessé d'augmenter.

La méconnaissance du Comité pendant quinze ans de ses obligations au titre du paragraphe 4 de l'article 40 du Pacte, prit fin en 1992.

En effet, à sa 1123[è] séance, tenue le 24 mars 1992, 'le Comité a décidé d'adopter des observations reflétant les vues de l'ensemble de ses membres à la fin de l'examen de chacun des rapports des Etats parties. Cela s'ajouterait – sans s'y substituer – aux observations faites par les membres à la fin de l'examen de chacun des rapports des Etats parties. Un rapporteur serait choisi dans chaque cas pour rédiger un texte, en consultation avec le Président et les autres membres du Comité, texte que ce dernier adopterait. Ces observations seraient présentées sous forme écrite et envoyées à l'Etat partie concerné aussitôt que possible avant d'être rendues publiques et incluses dans le rapport annuel du Comité. Elles consisteraient en une évaluation générale du rapport de l'Etat partie et du dialogue entre le Comité et la délégation concernée et ferait ressortir l'évolution positive qui aurait été notée au cours de la période considérée, les facteurs et les difficultés qui influeraient sur la mise en œuvre du Pacte, et les problèmes particuliers que poserait l'application de ses dispositions. Dans ces observations figureraient également des suggestions et recommandations de la part du Comité à l'intention de l'Etat partie concerné.[20]

Afin de conclure cette contribution au vingt-cinquième anniversaire du Comité il n'est pas inutile de faire quelques observations et de tirer quelques conclusions.

Pendant les premières années de ses activités, le Comité avait été confronté à de graves problèmes. Mais comme on a pu le voir, il a pu résoudre, non sans difficultés du reste, le problème du consensus dans le règlement intérieur. En revanche, il n'a pas surmonté des difficultés autrement plus sérieuses que celle qui vient d'être mentionnée.

L'atmosphère de guerre froide même atténuée avait abouti à la création de deux groupes antagonistes qui avaient entraîné des résultats négatifs. D'une part, une alliance contre nature des deux groupes avait eu pour effet d'imposer, en violation des règles les plus élémentaires des Nations Unies et de l'équité, un président du Comité pendant dix ans, alors que son mandat à ce poste n'était que de deux ans. D'autre part, les deux groupes avaient gelé l'application des articles 40 paragraphe 4 du Pacte et 70 du règlement intérieur. Le groupe marxiste, parce qu'il avait constamment essayé de réduire les pouvoirs du Comité, notamment dans son rôle principal de contrôleur de l'application du Pacte par les Etats parties; le groupe occidental parce que deux de ses membres n'avaient pas eu la volonté, pour des raisons peu convaincantes, de se joindre aux autres membres occidentaux et du Tiers Monde, pour imposer à la minorité marxiste, le respect des obligations découlant du paragraphe 4 de l'article 40. Il en était résulté que le Comité en tant que tel n'avait pas respecté le Pacte en s'abstenant d'appliquer les articles 40 (4) du Pacte et 70 du règlement intérieur et par conséquent n'était pas en conformité avec les dispositions du Pacte.

Il est heureux que le gel qui avait rendu inopérants les articles 40 (4) du Pacte et 70 du règlement intérieur n'ait pas été étendu au contrôle contentieux du Comité en vertu du Protocole facultatif. Ce contrôle contentieux avait pu se faire pour la simple raison que les Etats marxistes, n'ayant pas ratifié le Protocole facultatif, leurs experts n'avaient pas de problème avec l'exercice de ce contrôle qui ne leur était pas applicable.

Quoiqu'il en soit, le Comité avait néanmoins fait un travail méritoire, surtout au niveau de nombreux experts qui avaient eu la volonté, malgré les difficultés soulignées plus haut, de faire de leur mieux pour s'acquitter en conscience de leur mission. La réussite du comité s'est manifestée d'une manière remarquable dans l'exercice de son contrôle contentieux en vertu du Protocole facultatif.

---

[20] Rapp. CD.H. 1992 (A/47/40), pp. 19–20, par. 45.

PART III

ACTIVITIES OF THE HUMAN RIGHTS COMMITTEE (1) – GENERAL ISSUES

THE HUMAN RIGHTS COMMITTEE'S PRONOUNCEMENTS ON THE RIGHT TO AN EFFECTIVE REMEDY – AN ILLUSTRATION OF THE LEGAL NATURE OF THE COMMITTEE'S WORK UNDER THE OPTIONAL PROTOCOL

Martin Scheinin

INTRODUCTION

This article discusses the development of the Committee's practice under the Optional Protocol on one specific dimension, pronouncements on the individual's right to a remedy in cases where a violation of the Covenant has been established. The discussion serves two purposes: Firstly, the aim is to illustrate the Committee's current position in the issue of the right to an effective remedy, seen against its historical development. Secondly, the article makes an effort to bring more clarity to the discussion on the legal nature of the Committee's pronouncements under the Optional Protocol by comparing three different types of such pronouncements, namely findings of a violation of the Covenant, utterances on the victim's right to an effective remedy and requests for interim measures of protection.

Already in its very first final Views under the Optional Protocol, the Human Rights Committee took an approach that has since been followed consistently: Whenever the Committee establishes a finding of a violation of one of the substantive provisions of the Covenant it also states that the state party is under an *obligation* to provide an effective remedy to the victim.

Why, then, do academic authors, governments and national judges often refer to the Committee's Views as 'recommendations'? In this article, the author takes the position that one main source for such categorizations is that the Committee's pronouncements on the right to an effective remedy in cases where a violation of the Covenant has been established, *should* be understood to include a recommendatory dimension. However, this does not mean that *all* decisions taken by the Committee under the Optional Protocol could be reduced to 'recommendations'.

EARLY AND RECENT PRONOUNCEMENTS OF THE RIGHT TO AN EFFECTIVE REMEDY

In the Committee's first set of Views, adopted in the seventh session in August 1979, the state party's obligation to provide an effective remedy was presented as a direct consequence of the actual violation.[1] Already in the eighth session, in October

[1] '... and, accordingly, is of the view that the State party is under an obligation .. to provide effective remedies to the victims', Communication No. 5/1977 (*Moriana Hernandéz Valentini*

1979, the specific remedy of *compensation* was in one case included in the Committees formulation of an obligation to afford an effective remedy.[2]

In its thirteenth session, in July 1981, the Committee formulated its position, which since then has been consistently maintained, that the obligation to provide an effective remedy flows from Article 2, paragraph 3 of the Covenant.[3] Later on, it has become customary to refer specifically to subparagraph (a) of this provision. From the perspective of a human right to an effective remedy this provision in the Covenant is a much more solid basis for legally binding obligations of states than, for instance, the reference to a remedy in Article 4, paragraph 2, of the Optional Protocol.[4]

In the more than twenty years that have followed since the adoption of the obligation to provide an effective remedy being based on Article 2, paragraph 3, of the Covenant, the position of the Committee has remained the same. While no new principles have been established as to the right to an effective remedy, there has been a gradual evolution towards more and more concrete pronouncements on what would in the Committee's view constitute an effective remedy in a concrete case. As relatively recent formulations of the right to an effective remedy, illustrating the Committee's current approach, three cases deserve to be quoted.

In a case decided in 1997 the Committee found violations of several provisions of the Covenant, including Article 14 on the right to a fair trial, in a case of an alleged terrorist leader in Peru. The paragraph on the individual's right to an effective remedy was formulated in the Committee's views as follows:

> 'In accordance with article 2, paragraph 3(a), of the Covenant, the State party is under an obligation to provide Mr. Victor Polay Campos with an effective remedy. The victim was sentenced on the basis of a trial that failed to provide the basic guarantees of a fair trial. The Committee considers that Mr. Polay Campos should be released unless Peruvian law

de Bazzano et al. v. *Uruguay*), Views adopted on 15 August 1979, Selected Decisions of the Human Rights Committee under the Optional Protocol, vol. I, 40, para. 10.

2 'The Committee, accordingly, is of the view that the State party is under an obligation… to provide effective remedies to the victim, including compensation in accordance with article 9 (5) of the Covenant', Communication No. 9/1977 (*Edgardo Dante Santullo Valcada* v. *Uruguay*), Views adopted on 26 October 1979, Selected Decisions, vol. I, 43, para. 13.

3 'The Committee, accordingly, is of the view that the State party is under an obligation, pursuant to article 2 (3) of the Covenant, to provide effective remedies to Lopéz Burgos, including immediate release, permission to leave Uruguay and compensation for the violations which he has suffered, and to take steps to ensure that similar violations do not occur in the future.' Communication No. 52/1979 (*Sergio Rubén López Burgos* v. *Uruguay*), Views adopted on 29 July 1981, Selected Decisions, vol. I, 88, para. 14; similarly, Communication No. 56/1979 (*Lilian Celiberti de Casariego* v. *Uruguay*), Selected Decisions, vol. I, 92, para. 12.

4 'Within six months, the receiving State shall submit to the Committee written explanations or statements clarifying the matter and the remedy, if any, that may have been taken by that State.'

> provides for the possibility of a fresh trial that does offer all the guarantees required by article 14 of the Covenant.'[5]

An important development towards more specific pronouncements on the remedy, by the Committee, is demonstrated by the recent (March 2000) case of *Laptsevich* v. *Belarus*.[6] In this case where a violation of Article 19 (freedom of expression) was found, the Human Rights Committee not only stated that the effective remedy includes compensation but also, for the first time, specified the amount of compensation. After establishing a violation of Article 19 in a case where the author had been punished for distributing political leaflets, the Committee continued:

> 'Under article 2, paragraph 3(a), of the Covenant, the State party is under an obligation to provide Mr. Laptsevich with an effective remedy, including compensation amounting to a sum not less than the present value of the fine and any legal costs paid by the author.'[7]

In a case decided in July 2001 the Committee found that the deportation of the foreign parents of a naturalized child would, in the circumstances of the case, violate Articles 17, 23 and 24 of the Covenant. The part related to an individual remedy read:

> 'In accordance with article 2, paragraph 3(a), of the Covenant, the State Party is under an obligation to provide the authors with an effective remedy, including refraining from removing the authors from Australia before they have had an opportunity to have their application for parent visas examined with due consideration given to the protection required by Barry Winata's status as a minor.'[8]

THE LEGAL NATURE OF THE COMMITTEE'S VIEWS

It is quite often that one finds in academic writing on the Human Rights Committee characterizations of the final Views adopted by the Committee under the Optional Protocol procedure as 'recommendations'.[9] However, a formalistic distinction

---

[5] Communication No. 577/1994 (*Polay Campos* v. *Peru*), Views adopted on 6 November 1997, UN doc. A/53/40, vol. II, 36, para 10

[6] Communication No. 780/1997 (*Vladimir Petrovich Laptsevich* v. *Belarus*), Views adopted on 20 March 2000, UN doc. A/55/40, vol. II, 178.

[7] *Ibid.*, para. 10. For another case in which the Committee has moved towards specifying the amount of compensation, *see* Communication No. 779/1997 (*Anni Äärelä and Mr. Jouni Näkkäläjärvi* v. *Finland*), Views adopted on 24 October 2001, UN doc. A/57/40, vol. II, 117, para. 8.2

[8] Communication No. 930/2000 (*Hendrick Winata et al.* v. *Australia*), Views adopted on 26 July 2001, UN doc. A/56/40, 199, para. 9.

[9] *E.g.* Davidson, S., 'Intention and Effect: The Legal Status of the Final Views of the Human Rights Committee' in Huscroft, Grant – Paul Risworth (eds.), *Litigating Rights – Perspectices*

between binding judgments and non-binding recommendations might not be the most appropriate approach to the issue. In his systematic commentary on the Covenant, Manfred Nowak rightly emphasizes that the question of formal binding force of decisions by international organs is not alone decisive as to their impact, due to the fact that the possibilities for sanctioning would in any case be limited in international law. According to Nowak the views of the Committee carry moral authority although they are not binding under international law.[10] When applying this principle to the Committee's pronouncements on an effective remedy, Nowak takes the position that although the Committee cannot 'grant' compensation by a decision that would be binding under international law, it 'points out' the obligation of states to provide an effective remedy in a way that has 'the effect of a moral appeal'.[11]

Of other authors, McGoldrick, Joseph and Ghandhi are among those who emphasize that the Committee's Views follow a judicial pattern despite the fact that the Committee is not a court and its Views are not formally binding.[12] Even those who have treated the Committee's views as non-binding recommendations recognize that the approach adopted by the Committee itself in the text of the Views is much more expansive in the issue of the legal significance of the Committee's Views.[13]

The current author shares the position of, *inter alios*, former Committee members Fausto Pocar and Elizabeth Evatt who also in their scholarly writing have emphasized the close link between the treaty obligations under Article 2, paragraph 3, of the Covenant and the consequences of a violation of the Covenant being found in and individual case.[14] The same approach is reflected also in Manfred Nowak's

---

from Domestic and International Law, Oxford and Portland, Oregon: Hart, 2002, pp. 306–307.

[10] Nowak, M., *UN Covenant on Civil and Political Rights – Commentary*, Kehl – Strasbourg – Arlington: N.P. Engel, 1993, p. 710.

[11] *Ibid.*, p. 65.

[12] McGoldrick, D., *The Human Rights Committee – Its Role in the Development of the International Covenant on Civil and Political Rights*, Oxford: Clarendon Press, 1991, pp. 150–151; Joseph, S. et al., *The International Covenant on Civil and Political Rights – Cases, Materials and Commentary*, Oxford and New York: Oxford University Press, 2000, p. 14; Ghandhi, P.R., *The Human Rights Committee and the Right of Individual Communication*, Aldershot: Ashgate, 1998, pp. 329–330.

[13] Davidson 2002, *op. cit.*, *supra* note 9, pp. 307–308.

[14] Pocar, F., 'Legal value of the Human Rights Committee's Views', *Canadian Human Rights Yearbook*, 1991–1992, p. 120; Evatt, E., 'The Impact of International Human Rights on Domestic Rights Law' in Huscroft, Grant – Paul Risworth (eds.), *Litigating Rights – Perspectices from Domestic and International Law*, Oxford and Portland, Oregon: Hart, 2002, pp. 300–301. *See also* Klein, E., 'Individual Reparation Claims under the International Covenant on Civil and Political Rights: The Practice of the Human Rights Committee', in Randelzhofer, Albrecht – Christian Tomuschat (eds.), *State Responsibility and the Individual – Reparation in Instances of Grave Violations of Human Rights*. The Hague – London – Boston: Kluwer, 1999, pp. 27–41 at pp. 35–36 where it is held that it would be against good

position referred to above. According to Henry Steiner the Committee's Views carry a normative obligation for states to provide the stated remedies, an obligation that stems from provisions of the Covenant and the Protocol.[15] In a general human rights textbook the current author has formulated a similar position in the following terms:

> 'The absence of specific provisions on the legally binding nature of the findings by the pertinent expert body in other human rights treaties does not mean that such findings are merely 'recommendations'. The treaty obligations themselves are, naturally, legally binding, and the international expert body established by the treaty is the most authoritative interpreter of the treaty in question. Therefore, a finding of a violation by a UN human rights treaty body must be understood as an indication of the State party being under a legal obligation to remedy the situation.'[16]

As reflected in Nowak's position referred to above, the relative weakness of the Optional Protocol mechanism should be attributed more to the absence of effective enforcement than the absence of a treaty provision on the formally binding force of the Committee's Views.[17] Rightly, some authors have turned from the 'theoretical' issue of formally binding force to the pragmatic question of effective follow-up mechanisms: even if the Committee's Views are not *stricto sensu* binding and the Committee cannot enforce them, it must at least have some authority to monitor the effect and implementation of its views.[18]

Although the Committee has been consistent in its actual practice under the Optional Protocol, treating the right to an effective remedy as a legal obligation

---

faith if a state party were to disregard the Committee's views. Klein also stresses the legally binding nature of Article 2, paragraph 3(a) of the Covenant.

15 Steiner, H. J., 'Individual Claims in a World of Massive Violations: What Role for the Human Rights Committee?' in Alston, Philip – James Crawford (eds.), *The Future of UN Human Rights Treaty Monitoring*, Cambridge: Cambridge University Press, 2000, pp. 15–53 at p. 30.

16 Scheinin, M., 'International Mechanisms and Procedures for Implementation' *in* Hanski, Raija – Markku Suksi (eds.), *An Introduction to the International Protection of Human Rights: A Textbook. Turku/Åbo: Institute for Human Rights*, Åbo Akademi University, 2nd revised edition, 1999, pp. 429–452, at p. 444.

17 *See also*, Kretzmer, D., 'Commentary on Complaint Processes by Human Rights Committee and Torture Committee Members: The Human Rights Committee' in Bayefsky, Anne (ed.), *The UN Human Rights Treaty System in the 21st Century*, The Hague – London – Boston: Kluwer, 2000, pp. 163–166 at p. 164 who explains the absence of an effective enforcement mechanism as a 'policy decision' by the international community of the time. Hence, the absence of a provision on the binding force of the Committee's Views should be seen as a consequence or a reflection of this policy decision.

18 Schmidt, M., 'Follow-up Procedures to Individual Complaints and Periodic State Reporting Mechanisms' in Alfredsson, G. et al. (eds.), *International Human Rights Monitoring Mechanisms*, The Hague – London – Boston: Kluwer Law International 2001, pp. 201–215 at p. 202.

whenever a violation of the Covenant has been found, it has on certain other occasions itself referred to its Views as 'non-binding recommendations'. One isolated and hardly authoritative instance is the foreword to Volume II of the publication 'Selected Decisions' under the Optional Protocol, where the Committee's views are characterized as 'non-binding recommendations'.[19]

Another isolated instance where the Committee's Views were characterized as 'recommendations' can be found in the Committee's Annual Report of 1988, specifically under the heading 'Nature of the Committee's decisions on the merits of a communication'.[20] This isolated incident and the foreword to Volume II of 'Selected Decisions' appear to deviate from the actual practice under the Optional Protocol. Hence, they should not be taken as the Committee's current position. Although the 1989 Annual Report again included an identical heading as the one in the 1988 report, no such characterization of the Views being 'recommendations' was given.[21] In later years, the Annual Report has not repeated a characterization of the Committee's Views as 'recommendations'. In the Annual Report of 2001, a new section on 'Breach of Optional Protocol obligations' was included in which it was stated, before referring to the Committee's Views in *Piandiong et al.* v. *the Philippines*, that the Committee had found that a state party that has disregarded the Committee's request for interim measures of protection in a case pending before the Committee, 'violated its obligations under the Optional Protocol'.[22]

On the basis of the discussion presented above it is submitted that the part in the Committee's Views that includes the establishment of one or more violations of the Covenant in the individual case and a reference to the victim's right to an effective remedy is *not* to be seen as a mere 'recommendation'. These parts of the Views are pronouncements by the internationally authoritative treaty monitoring body, established by the Covenant itself, on the legal obligations of the state party in question. While the persuasive force of the Views depends on the legal argumentation applied by the Committee in its Views, it is to be noted that there is no comparable alternative international authority entrusted with the regular task of issuing legal interpretations of Covenant obligations. However, it is fully possible that an issue of interpretation of the Covenant would exceptionally appear in a dispute between two states, e.g. in the International Court of Justice. Consequently, the possibility of competing international interpretations cannot be totally excluded. However, it is to be emphasized that it cannot be for one party of the original dispute, the state, to substitute the Committee's interpretation of the Covenant with its *own* interpretation after first having lost its case in an international procedure to which it has voluntarily acceded.

Certain regional human rights treaties include explicit clauses on the formally binding force of judgments issued under that treaty. However, it is to be noted that

---

[19] Selected Decisions, Vol. II, 1990, p. 1.

[20] Annual Report of the Human Rights Committee 1988, UN doc. A/43/40, para. 645.

[21] Annual Report 1989, UN doc. A/44/40, para. 623.

[22] Annual Report 2001, UN doc. A/56/40, para. 128, *see also* Final Views on Communication No. 869/1999 (*Pladiong* v. *Philippines*), adopted on 19 October 2000, UN doc. A/56/40, 181.

such formally binding force is limited to cases where the state concerned is itself involved as a party. Article 68 of the American Convention on Human Rights includes an undertaking by the states parties to comply with a judgment by the Inter-American Court of Human Rights 'in any case to which they are parties'.[23] Similarly, the binding nature of judgments by the European Court of Human Rights is, looking at explicit provisions of the European Convention on Human Rights, also restricted to cases where a particular state is involved as a party.[24] It is, however, clear that the authority and influence of regional human rights courts extends far beyond those cases in which a particular state is involved as a party. Formally speaking, the legally binding nature of the bulk of the case law by the European or American Court of Human Rights in relation to a specific state is the *same* as that of the Human Rights Committee. But through the *exception* of those cases where a state itself is involved as a party, an experience of being legally bound is developed in relation to the case law as a whole.[25]

Various domestic courts have addressed the issue of the legal effect of the Committee's Views.[26] It is quite clear that the formal status enjoyed by the Covenant in the legal order of the country concerned has a bearing on how the courts address the possible binding force of the final Views of the Committee. For instance in Finland, where the Covenant has been formally incorporated into domestic law, the domestic courts have based an order of compensation from state funds on the Committee's Views establishing a violation of the Covenant, despite the fact that the Views in question were issued at a time when the Committee simply affirmed the victim's right to an remedy, without referring to compensation .[27] In contrast, the High Court of Ireland dismissed the compensation claim that followed from the

[23] American Convention on Human Rights, O.A.S.Treaty Series No. 36, 1144 U.N.T.S. 123.
[24] European Convention on Human Rights, E.T.S. No. 5 as amended by Protocol 11 (E.T.S. No. 155), Article 46.
[25] Related to the discussion above, it should also be noted that ACHR Article 68, paragraph 2, and ECHR Article 46, paragraph 2, are provisions related to the enforcement or implementation of the rulings by the respective regional human rights courts.
[26] A wealth of information on the use of various pronouncements of the Committee and other United Nations human rights treaty bodies by domestic courts is included in the Interim Report by the Committee on International Human Rights Law and Practice within the International Law Association, prepared for the 2002 Conference of the ILA.
[27] KHO (Supreme Administrative Court) 1993 A 25, based on the Committee's Views in Communication No. 291/1988 (*Torres* v. *Finland*), Views adopted on 2 April 1990, UN doc. A/45/40, vol. II, 96; KHO 16 April 1996 No. 1069, based on the Committee's Views in Communication No. 265/1987 (*Vuolanne* v. *Finland*), Views adopted 7 April 1989, UN doc. A/44/40, vol. II, 249.

Committee's Views in *Kavanagh* v. *Ireland*,[28] related to a country in which the Covenant is not a part of domestic law.[29]

THE LEGAL NATURE OF THE COMMITTEE'S PRONOUNCEMENT ON THE REMEDY

In addition to the general clause on the right to 'an effective remedy' in Article 2, paragraph 3(a) of the Covenant, certain provisions of the Covenant specify the type of remedy that would be appropriate. Two provisions establish a specific right to *compensation* as a remedy for the violation of the respective provision. Article 9, paragraph 5, proclaims 'an enforceable right to compensation' in cases of unlawful arrest or detention. Similarly, Article 14, paragraph 6, establishes a right to compensation in certain cases of pardon or reversal of conviction where a person has already suffered criminal punishment. These provisions are applicable both in those cases where a violation has been established by the Human Rights Committee itself, when acting under the Optional Protocol allowing for individual complaints, and when a similar finding is made through domestic proceedings. Although the Human Rights Committee does not have jurisdiction to create new obligations to states parties through its decisions on remedies, it does have a mandate to interpret what are the legal obligations of a state under the provisions of the CCPR itself. The right to an effective remedy and the right to compensation for the specific violations referred to in the two Covenant provisions mentioned above are legal rights under the Covenant itself, not 'recommendations' by the Human Rights Committee.

Similar considerations apply in relation to the reference to *amnesty, pardon and commutation* of the sentence of death in Article 6, paragraph 4, and the references to *release* in Article 9, paragraphs 3 and 4. To the extent that the Committee includes in its Views a proclamation of, for instance, compensation, release or commutation being the proper effective remedy under Article 2, paragraph 3(a), for violations of above-mentioned provisions of the Covenant, one can say that the Committee is still performing its task of interpreting the state party's legal obligations under the Covenant.

As several academic authors have noted, the Committee does not restrict itself to mentioning compensation as the proper remedy only in cases that fall under Articles 9 and 14, and it frequently mentions other concrete remedies than those that have been specifically mentioned in one or more provisions of the Covenant. When a violation of, for instance, Article 14 is established, the Committee looks at the nature and effect of the breach of fair trial rights and expresses a position whether the person whose right to a fair trial has been violated should be released, whether a

---

[28] Communication No. 819/1998 (*Kavanagh* v. *Ireland*), Views adopted on 4 April 2001, UN doc. A/56/40, vol. II, 122.

[29] The dismissal was based on a number of arguments, including that the Views of the Committee were not seen as being a binding decision. See, Interim Report 2002 (*supra* footnote 26) pp. 11–12 and *Kavanagh* v. *Governor of Mountjoy Prison* [2001] IEHC 77.

fresh trial could be an alternative to release or whether the remedy should be compensation or the commutation of a death sentence.

Even in other cases than those where the violated provision itself includes a reference to a specific remedy it might be clear on the basis of the concrete violation of the Covenant that only a certain remedy would be prompt, adequate and effective.[30] Nevertheless, it is asserted that the pronouncements of the Committee on the type of the effective remedy are not merely a question of logic or legal interpretation but that this part of the Committee's work is subject to certain flexibility and discretion. For instance, there might be a dimension of policy involved when the Committee discusses what remedy to suggest in relation to the violation that has just been established. Therefore, it is submitted that it is often *correct* to refer to that specific part of the Committee's Views that deals with the effective remedy as 'recommendations'.

The Committee's pronouncements on what the effective remedy should be range from a mere repetition of the notion of effective remedy to quite complex and concrete pronouncements on judicial and non-judicial remedies, like a new trial, the reinstatement of the victim's career, medical treatment, investigations, refraining from deportation, etc.[31] In some cases the Committee has stated that the public establishment of a violation of the Covenant in the form of the Committee's Views is in itself sufficient as an effective remedy in the circumstances of the case.[32]

In one of the very few individual cases that have *returned* to the Committee in the form of a new communication after the victim was dissatisfied with the remedy provided after the Committee established a violation of the Covenant, the Committee used the notion of 'recommendation' when referring to that part in its earlier Views that dealt with the remedy. In the case of *Daniel Pinto* v. *Trinidad and Tobago* the Committee originally found a violation of the right to a fair trial in a death penalty case and stated that the remedy should entail the release of Mr. Pinto.[33] After the state party commuted the death sentence to life imprisonment Mr. Pinto submitted a new communication to the Committee, related to his prison

[30] *See* Klein, *op. cit.*, *supra* note 14, p. 38.

[31] For lists or typologizations of the Committee's statements on the remedy, *see* Boerefijn, I., 'Follow-up of the Views of the United Nations Treaty Bodies' in Barkhuysen, T. et al. (eds.), *The Execution of Strasbourg and Geneva Human Rights Decisions in the National Legal Order*, The Hague – Boston – London: Kluwer 1999, pp. 101–112 at 105–107, Klein, *op.cit.*, *supra* note 14, pp. 30–31, Shelton, D., *Remedies in International Human Rights Law*, Oxford and New York: Oxford University Press, 1999 pp. 142–144, McGoldrick, *op. cit.*, *supra* note 12, pp. 152–153, Ghandhi, *op. cit.*, *supra* note 12, p. 334.

[32] *See e.g., Frédéric Foin* v. *France*, Communication No.666/1995, para.12: '[t]he Human Rights Committee notes with satisfaction that the State party has changed the law so that similar violations will no longer occur in the future. In the circumstances of the present case, the Committee considers that the findings of a violation constitutes sufficient remedy for the author'. The Committee found a violation of article 26 due to the excessive length of alternative service, compared to the duration of military service

[33] Communication No. 232/1987 (*Pinto* v. *Trinidad and Tobago*), Views adopted on 20 July 1990, UN doc. A/45/40, vol. II, 69, para. 13.2.

conditions and the denial of release. The Committee found a violation of Article 10 and noted 'with utmost concern the non-compliance of the state party with the Committee's recommendation' of release included in the earlier views.[34]

In the preceding section of this article the conclusion was made that the Committee's pronouncements establishing a violation of the Covenant and recalling the state party's obligation to afford an effective remedy are *not* to be understood as mere recommendations. However, it is a somewhat different matter to acknowledge that the Committee's pronouncements of what the effective remedy should be in a concrete case *combine elements of legal interpretation and recommendation*. Hence, it is often justified to use the notion of 'recommendation' in that specific context.[35]

EFFECTIVE REMEDY AND PERSONS AWAITING EXECUTION

In such death penalty cases where the individual is, to the knowledge of the Committee, still subject to the penalty of death when the Committee adopts its Views, a specific problem arises in relation to the right to an effective remedy. Is there room for any other 'effective' remedy than one that would allow the individual to preserve his life?

In such cases as just described the Committee has, after finding a violation of the Covenant, often but not always specified either commutation or release as the effective remedy or an element in it. Both of these remedies make it clear that when a person has been sentenced to death in violation of the Covenant or treated contrary to the provisions of the Covenant while awaiting execution, the remedy should include an irreversible decision not to implement the death penalty. The Committee has been particularly clear and consistent on this point when the requirements of a fair trial under Article 14 have been violated.[36]

In cases involving a violation of Articles 7 and/or 10 of the Covenant in relation to the treatment of persons awaiting execution the Committee has not been consistent in formulating its specific pronouncements as to the remedy. This cannot, of course, alter the main rule that the victim is entitled to an effective remedy under Article 2, paragraph 3, of the Covenant. In the final paragraph of the Views in one of its most important cases related to the death penalty, the case *of Earl Pratt and Ivan Morgan* v. *Jamaica*,[37] the Committee gave a clear and convincing answer to the question what constitutes 'effective remedy' to a person awaiting execution:

---

[34] Communication No. 512/1992 (*Pinto* v. *Trinidad and Tobago*), Views adopted on 16 July 1996, UN doc. A/51/40, vol. II, 61, paras. 9 and 8.2.

[35] *See also* Boerefijn, *op. cit.*, *supra* note 31, p. 103.

[36] This approach can be based on the text of Article 6 itself: as one of the limitations under paragraph 2 of that provision is that capital punishment may not be imposed 'contrary to the provisions of the present Covenant', a violation of the right to a fair trial in a procedure leading to a sentence of death constitutes not only a violation of Article 14 (fair trial) but also of article 6 (right to life).

[37] Communications Nos. 210/1986 and 225/1987 (*Pratt and Morgan* v. *Jamaica*), views adopted on 6 April 1989, UN doc. A/44/40, vol. II, 222.

> 'Although in this case article 6 is not directly at issue, in that capital punishment is not *per se* unlawful under the Covenant, it should not be imposed in circumstances where there have been violations by the State party of any of its obligations under the Covenant. The Committee is of the view that the victims of the violations of articles 14, paragraph 3(c), and 7 are entitled to a remedy; the necessary prerequisite in the particular circumstances is the commutation of the sentence.'[38]

However, in one case decided in 1998, the Committee restricted itself to calling for an 'effective remedy including compensation' for a person who, at least in the light of the submissions made to the Committee, was still under the risk of execution.[39] This was a result of the simultaneous consideration of two Jamaican cases and the fact that as in one of the two cases 'only' a violation of Articles 7 and 10 was found, the majority of Committee members felt that this was the proper way to formulate the remedy.[40] Therefore and relying on the *Pratt and Morgan* rationale, the current author submitted a partly dissenting individual opinion in order to present and substantiate the position that in a case where a violation of the Covenant is found in respect of a person subject to the penalty of death the remedy must include, first and foremost, absolute protection of the victim against execution.

THE LEGAL NATURE OF THE COMMITTEE'S REQUESTS FOR INTERIM MEASURES OF PROTECTION

As a third type of the Committee's positions taken under the Optional Protocol, a brief look must be taken at the Committee's requests for interim measures of protection, issued pursuant to Rule 86 of the Committee's Rules of Procedure.[41] As the legal basis of such requests appears to be in an instrument adopted by the Committee itself in accordance with Article 39 of the Covenant and not in the Covenant or its Optional Protocol, one could be tempted to draw the conclusion that the legal authority of such requests is probably lower than that of the Committee's actual Views.[42]

---

[38] *Ibid.*, para. 15.

[39] Communication No. 749/1997 (*McTaggart* v. *Jamaica*), views adopted on 31 March 1998, UN doc. A/53/40, vol. II, 221.

[40] Compare with the Views in Communication No. 734/1997 (*McLeod* v. *Jamaica*), adopted on 31 March 1998, A/53/40, vol. II, 213.

[41] UN doc. CCPR/C/3/Rev.6. According to the text of Rule 86, the Committee 'may', prior to adopting its Views, inform the State 'of its views as to whether interim measures may be desirable to avoid irreparable damage to the victim of the alleged violation'.

[42] Such a position was taken by the European Court of Human Rights in respect of a request for interim measures of protection issued by the then existing European Commission of Human Rights on the basis of its own rules of procedure. *See Cruz Varas* v. *Sweden*, Judgment of the European Court of Human Rights, 20 March 1991, para. 98. However, in the case of *Mamatkulov and Abdurasulovic* v. *Turkey,* Judgment of 6 February 2003, the European Court changed its earlier position, making explicit reference to the approach taken by the Human Rights Committee.

In certain cases decided in the 1990s and involving the extradition or deportation of a person from Canada to the United States under the risk of capital punishment the Committee appeared to follow the approach of not treating the duty to afford interim protection as a legal obligation.[43]

In 2000, the execution by the Philippines of three individuals who had submitted a case under the Optional Protocol and in respect of whom the Committee had issued a request for interim measures of protection, necessitated the Committee to take a fresh look at the compatibility of such conduct with state obligations under the Covenant and the Optional Protocol. Certainly, there cannot be a clearer case of irreparable damage to the alleged victim than his execution before the Committee has had an opportunity to examine the admissibility and merits of the case.

In the case of *Dante Piandiong et al.* v. *the Philippines* the Committee concluded that by ratifying the Optional Protocol on the procedure for individual communications a state undertakes to cooperate with the Committee in good faith so as to permit and enable it to consider the communication and that a state party commits a 'grave breach' of its obligations under the Optional if it acts to prevent or frustrate consideration by the Committee of a communication. Specifically, a state party breaches its obligations under the Protocol if it, having been notified of the communication, proceeds to execute the alleged victim.[44]

In light of the Committee's Views in *Piandiong,* the approach of dealing with the possible duty to afford interim measures of protection as emanating from the Committee and, hence, to be subject to the same or even greater limitations as to its legally binding nature as what is perceived in relation to the final Views issued by the Committee, is clearly mistaken. When the obligation to afford interim protection in order to avoid irreparable damage is derived directly from the ratification of the Optional Protocol, it is fully justified to state that such an obligation has a *stronger* legally binding force than the Committee's final Views or its specific pronouncements on the right to an effective remedy therein. Under this approach, a request under Rule 86 is of a declaratory nature, and not constitutive of any new obligations than the obligations that follow directly from the Optional Protocol.

As a recent example of an erroneous approach to interim measures of protection reference can be made to the case of *Ahani* v. *H.M. the Queen, the Attorney General of Canada and the Minister of Citizenship and Immigration*, decided by the Court of Appeal for Ontario (Canada), on 8 February 2002. A recognized Iranian refugee who was considered a terrorist and a danger to the security of Canada was facing

[43] In its Views in Communication No. 470/1991 (*Kindler* v. *Canada*), adopted on 30 July 1993, UN doc. A/48/40, vol. II, 138, the Committee 'expresses its regret' for the fact that the alleged victim was extradited to the United States despite the Committee's request for interim measures of protection (paragraph 17). Similarly, in Communication No. 469/1991 (*Charles Chitat Ng* v. *Canada*) the Committee, in its admissibility decision, 'expressed its regret that the State party had not acceded to the Committee's request under Rule 86 to stay extradition of the author', *see* Views of 5 November 1993, UN doc. A/49/40, vol. II 208, para. 7.

[44] Communication No. 869/1999 (*Piandiong* v. *Philippines*), Views adopted on 19 October 2000, UN doc. A/56/40, vol. II, 181, paras. 5.1 and 5.2.

deportation to Iran after the Canadian Supreme Court had considered that there was no real risk of torture involved. After the Committee issued a request for interim measures of protection, counsel sought an injunction against the implementation of the deportation order. By two votes against one the Court of Appeal for Ontario decided not to grant the injunction.[45] From the perspective of the theme of the current article it is interesting to note that the decision includes some discussion on the legal nature of the final Views of the Committee[46] but takes it for granted that the same arguments would apply in respect of interim measures of protection, completely disregarding the *Piandiong* case.[47]

It is submitted that the reported case illustrates the need for distinguishing between the legal nature of the Committee's various types of pronouncements under the Optional Protocol.

CONCLUSIONS

In its Views under the Optional Protocol the Human Rights Committee has consistently retained its position that in a case where a violation of the Covenant has been established through the Optional Protocol procedure, the state party in question has a legal obligation to provide an effective remedy. This approach is an elegant and solid way to emphasize the legally binding nature of the treaty obligations despite the absence of a specific provision that would give the Human Rights Committee the power to issue judgments that *per se* would be binding in international law.

Despite this general approach to the legal nature of the Committee's Views it is submitted that the part of the Views that relates to the remedy to be afforded as a consequence of a violation established by the Committee often includes not only an authoritative legal interpretation of the state party's treaty obligations but also a dimension of recommendation. This is, for instance, often the case when the Committee refers to compensation in other cases than those where a violation of Article 9 or 14 has been established.

Over its 25 years of existence the Committee has gradually moved towards more and more concrete pronouncements on the remedy to be afforded. It is to be expected that this evolution will continue. It should, for instance, be welcomed by the Committee that authors or counsel specify, when sending submissions to the Committee, the amount of compensation they consider appropriate for the violation suffered, and that state parties present their observations on such claims when answering to communications. This would enable the Committee to take the next logical step in addressing the issue of remedies, namely, to specify the amount, currency and interest rate of compensation in those cases where compensation is seen by the Committee to be an appropriate remedy. This would strengthen both the

[45] Docket C37565 M28156. On 15 May 2002, the Supreme Court of Canada refused leave to appeal against the decision, also by two votes against one.
[46] *Op. cit.*, *supra* note 44, paras. 37–40.
[47] *Op. cit.*, *supra* note 44, paras. 35–36.

nature of the Optional Protocol procedure as an international recourse to justice and the Committee's role as the internationally authoritative interpreter of the Covenant.[48]

When comparing the Committee's final Views with binding judgments by regional human rights courts it should be remembered that even where such binding jurisdiction exists, it is only in relation to the state that is a party to the case in question that the judgment is binding under international law. In relation to the general relevance of the jurisprudence for all states, the force of the Views by the Committee or of judgments by regional human rights courts depends primarily on the strength of argumentation, not the issue whether the conclusions in a particular case are formally binding in respect of one specific state.

In the opinion of the author, the main weakness of the Optional Protocol is not the lack of formally recognized binding force of the Committee's Views but the underdeveloped state of effective follow-up and implementation by the political organs of the United Nations.

REFERENCES

Boerefijn, Ineke, 'Follow-up of the Views of the United Nations Treaty Bodies', pp. 101–112 in Barkhuysen, Tom et al. (eds.), *The Execution of Strasbourg and Geneva Human Rights Decisions in the National Legal Order*, The Hague – Boston – London: Kluwer 1999

Evatt, Elizabeth, 'The Impact of International Human Rights on Domestic Law', pp. 305–321 in Huscroft, Grant – Paul Risworth (eds.), *Litigating Rights – Perspectives from Domestic and International Law*. Oxford and Portland, Oregon: Hart 2002

Davidson, Scott, 'Intention and Effect: The Legal Status of the Final Views of the Human Rights Committee', pp. 323–343 in Huscroft, Grant – Paul Risworth (eds.), *Litigating Rights – Perspectivces from Domestic and International Law*. Oxford and Portland, Oregon: Hart 2002

Ghandhi, P.R., *The Human Rights Committee and the Right of Individual Communication*. Aldershot: Ashgate 1998

Interim Report on the Impact of the Work of the United Nations Human Rights Treaty Bodies on National Courts and Tribunals, Committee on International Human Rights Law and Practice of the International Law Association, 2002. <www.ila-hq.org/html/layout_committee.htm>.

Joseph, Sarah et al., *The International Covenant on Civil and Political Rights – Cases, Materials and Commentary*. Oxford and New York 2000: Oxford University Press.

Klein, Eckart, 'Individual Reparation Claims under the International Covenant on Civil and Political Rights: The Practice of the Human Rights Committee', pp. 27–41 in Randelzhofer, Albrecht – Christian Tomuschat (eds.), *State Responsibility and the Individual – Reparation in Instances of Grave Violations of Human Rights*. The Hague – London – Boston: Kluwer 1999.

[48] It might be that when submissions on the amount of compensation are made by the parties and the Committee concludes that there was a violation of the Covenant and that compensation should be the remedy, the Committee would leave in its Views to its Special Rapporteur on Follow-up under the Optional Protocol to decide about the particulars of compensation.

Kretzmer, David, 'Commentary on Complaint Processes by Human Rights Committee and Torture Committee Members: The Human Rights Committee', pp. 163–166 in Bayefsky, Anne (ed.), *The UN Human Rights Treaty System in the 21st Century*. The Hague – London – Boston: Kluwer 2000

McGoldrick, Dominic, *The Human Rights Committee – Its Role in the Development if the International Covenant on Civil and Political Rights*. Oxford: Clarendon Press 1991

Nowak, Manfred, *UN Covenant on Civil and Political Rights; CCPR Commentary*. Kehl – Strasbourg – Arlington: N.P.Engel 1993

Pocar, Fausto, 'Legal Value of the Human Rights Committee's Views', *Canadian Human Rights Yearbook 1991–1992* pp. 119–123

Scheinin, Martin, 'International Mechanisms and Procedures for Implementation', pp. 429–452 in Hanski, Raija – Markku Suksi (eds.), *An Introduction to the International Protection of Human Rights: A Textbook*. Turku/Åbo: Institute for Human Rights, Åbo Akademi University, 2nd revised edition, 1999.

Selected Decisions of the Human Rights Committee under the Optional Protocol, Volume II. New York: United Nations 1990.

Shelton, Dinah, *Remedies in International Human Rights Law*. Oxford and New York: Oxford University Press 1999

Steiner, Henry J., 'Individual Claims in a World of Massive Violations: What Role for the Human Rights Committee?', pp. 15–53 in Alston, Philip – James Crawford (eds.), *The Future of UN Human Rights Treaty Monitoring*. Cambridge 2000: Cambridge University Press.

Tomuschat, Christian, 'Individual Reparation Claims in Instances of Grave Human Rights Violations', pp. 1–25 in Randelzhofer, Albrecht – Christian Tomuschat (eds.), *State Responsibility and the Individual – Reparation in Instances of Grave Violations of Human Rights*. The Hague – London – Boston: Kluwer 1999.

LOS ESTADOS DE EXCEPCIÓN Y LA PROTECCIÓN DE LOS DERECHOS HUMANOS

Rafael Rivas Posada

Quizás en ningún otro campo del derecho internacional se efectuaron progresos tan notables en la segunda mitad del siglo XX como en el de la promoción y protección de los derechos humanos. En realidad, progresos en materia legislativa y doctrinaria, tanto en el plano doméstico como multilateral, pero no, desafortunadamente, en la práctica de las sociedades modernas. Nada más desalentador que dirigir una mirada retrospectiva para ver las violaciones constantes que caracterizaron la mayor parte del siglo que pasó, y no sólo las ocurridas durante las dos grandes conflagraciones mundiales, sino como resultado de las guerras regionales, los conflictos internos, la inestabilidad política de múltiples Estados y los enfrentamientos étnicos y religiosos que han ensangrentado la historia universal de los últimos decenios. Esta contradicción entre el desarrollo teórico y normativo de los derechos humanos y la realidad que vive el mundo constituye una de las características mas inquietantes de la vida internacional contemporánea.

La definición conceptual de los derechos que se le deben reconocer al individuo y de las libertades fundamentales de los ciudadanos tienen su base en la Declaración Universal de 1948, sin que esto implique negar la importancia de varios antecedentes históricos que sirvieron para inspirar el pensamiento libertario de las sociedades modernas. Es a partir de la Declaración Universal, fruto de la aspiración por crear un mundo distinto después de la hecatombe de la Segunda Guerra, alrededor de una comunidad internacional solidaria, pacífica y progresista, que se inicia el proceso de perfeccionamiento normativo de los derechos humanos. Pocos meses antes de la aprobación de este texto por la Asamblea General de las Naciones Unidas, la Novena Conferencia Internacional Americana había aprobado la Declaración Americana de los Derechos y Deberes del Hombre, y, en 1950, el Consejo de Europa aprobó in Roma la Convención para la Protección de los Derechos Humanos y de las Libertades Fundamentales, instrumentos que señalaron el camino para avanzar en la empecinada labor de crear una cultura universal de respeto a la dignidad del hombre.

Este proceso tuvo su punto culminante en 1966, cuando la Asamblea General de las Naciones Unidas adoptó el Pacto Internacional de Derechos Civiles y Políticos que, con su Protocolo Facultativo, constituye el fundamento del sistema de defensa universal de los derechos humanos. Por primera vez se establecieron obligaciones claras para los Estados Partes y se creó un sistema de vigilancia y supervisión a través del Comité de Derechos Humanos, encargado no sólo de esa vigilancia sino, también, de ir creando una jurisprudencia que permita la adopción de criterios interpretativos para la correcta aplicación de las normas establecidas por el Pacto y su Protocolo Facultativo.

La experiencia histórica, y la necesidad de obtener el más amplio consenso para la aprobación de un instrumento tan ambicioso como el Pacto de Derechos Civiles y Políticos, llevaron a la conclusión de que, en ciertas circunstancias, era indispensable aceptar limitaciones a la plena vigencia de los derechos reconocidos en el tratado. De allí el reconocimiento de los estados de excepción a los que hace referencia el artículo 4 del Pacto. Ya en la Convención de Roma de 1950 se había aceptado, en su artículo 15, la posibilidad de suspensión transitoria de las obligaciones previstas en ese instrumento, 'en caso de guerra o en caso de otro peligro público que amenace la vida de la Nación'. El lenguaje utilizado en el Pacto es más amplio, en el sentido de que no limita al estado de guerra la facultad de suspender las obligaciones contraídas, sino que la extiende a 'situaciones excepcionales que pongan en peligro la vida de la Nación', añadiendo el requisito de que la existencia de esas situaciones excepcionales 'haya sido proclamada oficialmente'. El párrafo 1 del mismo artículo 4 impone la restricción de que las disposiciones que limitan la plena vigencia de los derechos del Pacto deben responder estrictamente a las exigencias de la situación excepcional y no ser incompatibles con las demás obligaciones que impone el derecho internacional.

No obstante el avance que significa el lenguaje consignado en el Pacto, es indudable que la formulación del artículo 4 en su párrafo 1 es demasiado general e imprecisa, no sólo en lo que respecta a las distintas situaciones excepcionales que pueden justificar la suspensión de las obligaciones, sino también en lo relativo a la diferenciación que debe hacerse entre la proclamación del estado de excepción y las medidas que se toman para limitar derechos específicos, en desarrollo de la declaratoria de emergencia. La Convención Americana sobre Derechos Humanos de 1972, o Pacto de San José de Costa Rica, fue más explícita en su artículo 27, al hablar de casos de guerra, de peligro público y de otras emergencias que amenacen la independencia o seguridad del Estado como situaciones que justifican la suspensión transitoria de las obligaciones contraídas. Pero no hay duda de que hubiera sido deseable una mayor claridad para distinguir las circunstancias excepcionales. En defecto de esta precisión, es responsabilidad de quienes tienen la facultad de interpretar las disposiciones del Pacto la tarea de distinguir las diferentes situaciones a que se refiere el artículo 4, con el propósito de definir las consecuencias de los regímenes de excepción.

El Comité de Derechos Humanos ha venido cumpliendo una encomiable labor en materia de interpretación de la obligación impuesta por el Pacto a los Estados Partes de presentar informes periódicos sobre las medidas que adopten para garantizar la protección de los derechos humanos. Por medio de los comentarios generales a que se refiere el párrafo 4 del artículo 41 del Pacto, ha precisado los requisitos que deben cumplir estos informes y, al hacerlo, ha interpretado muy variados aspectos de las obligaciones que han aceptado los Estados. En el tema que nos ocupa, es de destacar la importancia de la Observación General No. 29, aprobado por el Comité en 2001, sobre la aplicación del artículo 4 del Pacto, que ha venido a reemplazar a la Observación General No. 5 de 1981 sobre la misma materia. Sin embargo, quedan todavía varios aspectos de las relaciones entre los estados de emergencia y la debida protección de los derechos reconocidos por el Pacto que plantean la necesidad de esfuerzos adicionales de clarificación.

Una de las mayores dificultades para el tratamiento de los estados de excepción por parte del Comité es el carácter tan restrictivo impuesto por el lenguaje del artículo 4, párrafo 1, del Pacto. Según esta formulación, sólo está autorizada la suspensión de las obligaciones contraídas en virtud del instrumento cuando las situaciones excepcionales 'pongan en peligro la vida de la Nación'. En la práctica, los estados de excepción, llámense de emergencia, de sitio o distinguidos con una de tantas expresiones utilizadas para este fin, son declarados por los Estados por razones diferentes al peligro que puede correr 'la Nación', en el sentido habitual de este término. En general, sólo en casos de guerra internacional sería aplicable esta definición, y aún así es dudoso que las naciones, como tales, tengan el riesgo de desaparecer. Casi siempre los Estados recurren a los estados de excepción por motivos diferentes a la defensa de la Nación. Sería importante establecer una clara distinción entre las situaciones que pueden generar el peligro a que se refiere el artículo 4, aquellas que pueden poner en peligro el desarrollo normal de las actividades sociales, como son los desastres naturales, y las que se refieren a las amenazas al orden público o a la estabilidad de las instituciones. Estas últimas, que incluyen los intentos de golpes de Estado, las luchas internas contra el orden político establecido y el desorden social grave, son en realidad situaciones que ponen en peligro la vida de los gobiernos, y sólo raramente la vida de las naciones. Por ser precisamente actos amenazantes contra el poder político, con frecuencia se prestan a toda clase de abusos en el campo de los derechos humanos.

Debería establecerse una gradación que permitiera diferenciar las distintas circunstancias que llevan a los Estados a limitar el disfrute de los derechos individuales y colectivos, escudándose en el carácter excepcional de los acontecimientos a los cuales deben enfrentarse. Tanto la declaratoria de emergencia, que contemplan las constituciones o leyes de la gran mayoría de las naciones, si no de todas, como las medidas específicas que suspenden o limitan la aplicación de las normas que les imponen obligaciones, tendrían que ser sometidas a requisitos claros y definidos, que permitan el debido control de esas medidas y los correspondientes recursos a la disposición de los ciudadanos. En el caso del acto que proclama el estado de emergencia, el artículo 4 hace referencia a esa declaratoria y, aunque no en forma contundente, parece exigir que debe siempre existir previamente a la adopción de las medidas concretas de suspensión, o al menos simultáneamente con éstas. Así lo contempla la mayor parte de las constituciones del mundo, si bien las modalidades de estos actos de proclamación varían enormemente y, por razón de esta variedad, el tratamiento que se debe dar a sus implicaciones ofrece dificultades muy serias. Unas veces la declaratoria de emergencia corresponde a los órganos legislativos y otras a la rama ejecutiva del poder, por lo general al Jefe del Ejecutivo, pero los controles internos sobre su legalidad o conveniencia son tratados de manera diferente en los distintos sistemas políticos. Por esta razón, no sería fácil que el Comité fuese mas allá de exigir, como claramente lo hace en el párrafo 5 de la

Observación General No. 29, que no sólo las medidas específicas de suspensión sean cuidadosamente justificadas por la naturaleza de la situación excepcional, sino, también, que la proclamación misma del estado de emergencia, base jurídica constitucional de las facultades que se arroga el Estado, responda a las circunstancias y cumpla con los requisitos de la legislación interna.

No todos los disturbios del orden público o catástrofes naturales pueden calificarse como situaciones de emergencia aceptadas por el Pacto, como correctamente lo ha dicho el Comité en su Observación General No. 29. Así como en casos de grave conflicto internacional aparece claro el peligro para la supervivencia nacional, esto no ocurre normalmente cuando se trata de catástrofes naturales o de alteraciones del orden público debidas a intentos desestabilizadores de las instituciones políticas. Por ello es importante que los Estados Partes hagan el mayor esfuerzo para justificar la declaratoria de los estados de excepción, y de igual manera las distintas medidas que, con base en esa declaratoria, tienen por resultado limitar, restringir o suspender los derechos reconocidos por el Pacto.

Pero, además de este requisito, sería de desear, aunque esta exigencia no es explícitamente mencionada en el instrumento, que tanto la proclamación de la emergencia como las disposiciones que se tomen en desarrollo de la misma sean susceptibles de recursos a la disposición de los ciudadanos, para controlar los excesos que se puedan presentar. En algunos Estados la declaratoria de emergencia da lugar a un control político ejercido por el parlamento; en otros, existe un control constitucional, a veces ejercido por los tribunales superiores ordinarios, en otros casos por tribunales constitucionales especializados. Lo importante es que los individuos que corren el riesgo de ver conculcados o violados sus derechos puedan acudir a la justicia para obtener la protección de sus derechos fundamentales. Con mayor razón, debe exigirse de los Estados que en sus disposiciones constitucionales o legales ofrezcan los recursos indispensables para que las medidas concretas que se dicten con base en el estado de excepción, y que suspendan derechos específicos, puedan ser revisadas por órganos judiciales independientes que certifiquen sobre su legalidad.

No deben existir dudas sobre dos condiciones fundamentales para poder invocar el artículo 4 del Pacto. La primera es la declaratoria previa del estado de emergencia, y la segunda la gravedad de la situación. Esta gravedad, según el lenguaje empleado por el Pacto, debe ser de tal magnitud que los acontecimientos ocurridos pongan en peligro la vida de la Nación, pero, como ya se ha dicho, en la práctica la justificación para la proclamación de la emergencia no requiere una amenaza de tan dramático carácter. La causa más frecuente del régimen de excepción a que acuden los Estados es la turbación del orden público que pone en peligro la vida, o al menos la tranquilidad, del gobierno en el poder. O sea, una situación definida más con criterio político que jurídico y, por esta razón, más difícil de justificar con las luces que brindan los instrumentos internacionales. De igual manera, las medidas restrictivas de los derechos humanos que por lo general dictan las autoridades cuando se presentan situaciones amenazantes contra las mismas, contienen, por lo general, elementos de claro alcance político que pueden ser aprovechados para suspender obligaciones del Estado, como es el caso del respeto a las libertades de opinión, de reunión y de asociación, y las garantías de los derechos referentes a la integridad personal, a la participación política y a ser juzgado de conformidad con las prescripciones del artículo 14 del Pacto.

Debe quedar claramente establecido que, al acudir a los estados de excepción, los Estados deben conformarse a las exigencias de su legislación interna, tanto en lo que se refiere a la declaratoria de emergencia como a las disposiciones que dicte con base en la declaratoria. El respeto a los principios que rigen al Estado de Derecho así lo exige. No puede aceptarse la discrecionalidad absoluta en materia tan delicada, cuando se trata de circunstancias que pueden llevar a la violación de derechos fundamentales del ser humano. La jurisprudencia del Comité ha sido consecuente en este punto, y así está consignada en la Observación General No. 29.

Fuera de las normas contenidas en el artículo 4 del Pacto, existen obligaciones por parte de los Estados que sirven para prevenir los abusos que podrían cometerse en la aplicación de los estados de excepción. Las prescripciones del derecho internacional humanitario deben ser respetadas en el caso de guerra internacional o interna, cualquiera que sea la gravedad o la extensión del conflicto o las características del enfrentamiento. Pero esta limitación a las facultades de los Estados durante los estados de emergencia no se extiende, como es obvio, a los casos de desastres naturales y, con enormes dificultades, puede aplicarse en la práctica a las situaciones de amenazas a las instituciones o a los gobiernos en el poder. El problema en relación con el respeto al derecho internacional humanitario es su carácter simplemente declarativo, sin respaldo compulsivo alguno, y el hecho de que, en principio, sólo los Estados Partes de las Convenciones de Ginebra y sus Protocolos Adicionales están obligados a respetarlo, dejando por fuera de su cobertura a las partes que, en los conflictos internos o aún internacionales, actúan irregularmente, no responden a la autoridad de los Estados Partes y no han declarado que se acogen a sus disposiciones. Un problema surge cuando la situación de emergencia es proclamada con base en disturbios políticos que no pueden calificarse como guerras o conflictos internos, como ocurre comúnmente con los intentos de derrocar un gobierno o producir cambios importantes en el funcionamiento de las instituciones. En estos casos, por definición, no son aplicables las disposiciones del Protocolo II de Ginebra y, sin embargo, son la causa más común de la utilización de los estados de excepción. Si para ellos no es aplicable el Protocolo II, sólo los principios consignados en el Pacto y 'las demás obligaciones que les impone el derecho internacional', según el lenguaje del párrafo 1 del artículo 4 del mismo instrumento, servirían para limitar las facultades de los Estados Partes en el manejo de los estados de emergencia.

En relación con las demás obligaciones que impone el derecho internacional, distintas a las establecidas por el Pacto, se presenta la duda sobre el alcance exacto de esta expresión usada en el artículo 4. Mas concretamente, ¿debe el Comité, al ejercer el mandato que le ha sido otorgado para examinar los informes que presentan los Estados Partes, tener en cuenta obligaciones contraídas por los mismos Estados en instrumentos internacionales distintos del Pacto? Si la respuesta es negativa, la conclusión a la que habría que llegar es que sólo los principios generales del derecho internacional deberían ser tenidos en cuenta por el Comité, sin entrar a estudiar las obligaciones contractuales contraídas, es decir, como lo dice la Observación General No. 29, que los Estados deben únicamente 'tener en cuenta los desarrollos del derecho internacional en relación con los estándares de los derechos humanos aplicables en situaciones de emergencia'. Si, por contrario la respuesta es positiva, el Comité vería considerablemente ensanchado su campo de acción, a no ser que sólo exija información sobre las demás obligaciones internacionales del Estado que utiliza el estado de excepción, sin pretender analizar su justificación o vigilar su cumplimiento.

El Comité, en la Observación General tantas veces citada, sigue una vía intermedia en este punto, que puede calificarse como cautelosa. Expresa que, además del necesario respeto a las normas del derecho internacional humanitario en casos de guerra internacional o interna, el Estado Parte debe siempre informar sobre las obligaciones contraídas en otros instrumentos de protección de los derechos humanos, dando a entender que esa información es importante para ayudar a analizar la justificación del estado de excepción, sin llegar a afirmar que entra dentro de su mandato la facultad de juzgar la actitud del Estado como violatoria de normas que no están consignadas en el Pacto. Esto quiere decir que, por el momento, el Comité considera que no es su función la supervisión de la conducta del Estado que limita o suspende derechos contemplados en tratados diferentes al Pacto, pero que las restricciones que llegue a imponer a dichos derechos deben ser conocidas por el Comité, que debe tener presente el marco legal dentro del cual se mueve el Estado informante.

El aspecto referente al alcance de las funciones del Comité para vigilar el cumplimiento de obligaciones impuestas por los distintos instrumentos que los Estados deben respetar es importante en la práctica, porque dichos instrumentos varían en la enumeración de los derechos que no son susceptibles de suspensión. Por ejemplo, en la Convención de Roma de 1950, sólo se exceptúan de la posibilidad de suspensión los artículos 2 (derecho a la vida, salvo en las situaciones enumeradas en el mismo); 3 (derecho a no ser sometido a tortura ni a penas o tratamientos inhumanos o degradantes); 4, párrafo 1 (derecho a no ser mantenido en esclavitud o servidumbre) y 7 (derecho a no ser condenado por acciones u omisiones cometidas antes de ser calificadas como infracciones). El Pacto de San José de Costa Rica, por su parte, es mucho más restrictivo que el tratado europeo y que el mismo Pacto de Derechos Civiles y Políticos, ya que en su artículo 27, párrafo 2, excluye de la suspensión por razón de emergencia a los artículos 3 (derecho al reconocimiento de la personalidad jurídica); 4 (derecho a la vida); 5 (derecho a la integridad personal); 6 (prohibición de la esclavitud o la servidumbre); 9 (principio de legalidad y de retroactividad); 12 (libertad de conciencia y de religión); 17 (protección a la familia); 18 (derecho al nombre); 19 (derechos del niño); 20 (derecho a la nacionalidad) y 23 (derechos políticos), además de las garantías judiciales indispensables para la protección de tales derechos.

Volviendo al texto del Pacto, no hay duda de que un requisito fundamental que deben satisfacer las medidas adoptadas en situaciones de emergencia, tendientes a limitar derechos individuales reconocidos, es que dichas medidas estén directamente relacionadas con la naturaleza de la emergencia y que sean limitadas en su duración. En algunos países no existen disposiciones que le impongan a las autoridades limitaciones en la duración del estado de emergencia o, en el mejor de los casos, permiten que, con el cumplimiento de ciertos requisitos de poca importancia, el régimen de excepción se prolongue por largos períodos, si no indefinidamente. Son numerosos los ejemplos en la historia reciente de naciones que han vivido decenios enteros en estado de sitio, alegando la persistencia de las condiciones de perturbación que, en su concepto, justifica la suspensión de derechos y garantías ciudadanas.

No sólo la duración del estado de excepción debe estar limitada a las estrictas necesidades de la situación, sino que es imprescindible aplicar el principio de relación directa entre el propósito de las disposiciones dictadas y los hechos que deben ser superados. Debe respetarse, también el principio de proporcionalidad de la respuesta del Estado, ya que serían inaceptables medidas excesivamente drásticas para neutralizar débiles amenazas contra el orden público o la estabilidad de las instituciones. El mismo Pacto acepta estos principios de pertinencia y de proporcionalidad en su artículo 4, párrafo 1, y para ser más explícito descarta tajantemente, en el párrafo 2 del mismo artículo, la posibilidad de suspender durante los estados de emergencia los artículos allí enumerados. El sentido implícito de esta norma es que la suspensión de los derechos que no están sujetos a limitaciones violaría el principio de proporcionalidad, ya que ninguna amenaza o peligro para la normalidad institucional tiene la gravedad suficiente para justificar su desconocimiento.

Además del carácter transitorio de las medidas de emergencia, y de su relación con la situación que se pretende superar, el aspecto de la extensión geográfica del estado de excepción constituye un elemento importante para ser tenido en cuenta por el Comité. Así lo reconoce la Observación General No. 29, que es consecuente con el criterio restrictivo con el que deben interpretarse las implicaciones de los estados de emergencia. No sería aceptable que para combatir supuestas amenazas generadas por acontecimientos claramente localizados en el territorio nacional, que no tienen capacidad de extenderse a todas sus regiones, se apliquen medidas limitativas de los derechos de todos los habitantes del país. Los límites geográficos de la emergencia es, en estos casos, otra aplicación del principio de relación directa entre los actos perturbadores y las soluciones que pretenden superarlos. Esta limitación en el espacio es común cuando se trata de estados de emergencia provocados por desastres naturales, pero menos frecuente en caso de perturbaciones de carácter político o de conmoción interior. Es precisamente en esta última categoría de acontecimientos que el Comité debe prestar la mayor atención, para analizar la justificación de una declaratoria de excepción en todo el territorio nacional, cuando la naturaleza de la situación de anormalidad está limitada a una zona específica.

La aplicación del párrafo 2 del artículo 4 del Pacto ha sido siempre problemática para el Comité. La dificultad que plantea reside fundamentalmente en saber hasta qué punto la enumeración de los artículos que no pueden ser materia de suspensión o limitación es exhaustiva, y si no existen otras restricciones para los Estados para la utilización de los estados de emergencia. La respuesta, en parte, ha sido dada por medio de los criterios expuestos en la Observación General No. 29, aunque aún subsisten dudas al respecto. No hay duda de que las disposiciones mencionadas en el párrafo 2 no pueden ser materia de suspensión, pero en el caso del artículo 18 (libertad de pensamiento, de conciencia y de religión) su párrafo 3 permite limitaciones 'prescritas por la ley que sean necesarias para proteger la seguridad, el orden, la salud o la moral públicos, o los derechos y libertades fundamentales de los demás'. Este párrafo no deja de ser inquietante, porque abre la posibilidad de ser interpretado como un recurso disponible para la aprobación de medidas atentatorias de las libertades que el mismo artículo trata de proteger.

En primer lugar, no es claro a qué ley se refiere el mencionado párrafo 3 del artículo 18. ¿Acaso a la ley o norma con fuerza de ley dictada por el Estado en uso de las facultades que le confiere el estado de emergencia? Si es así, el Estado podría hacer un uso amplio de sus facultades para coartar las libertades de pensamiento, conciencia y religión, con sólo justificarlo como necesario para superar las circunstancias excepcionales a que se ve enfrentado. Otra posible interpretación de este párrafo es que la ley a que se refiere es la norma que, en el derecho interno, limita las facultades del Estado en regímenes de emergencia o, al menos, impone requisitos tanto para la proclamación del estado de excepción como para la aprobación de las medidas específicas que suspenden determinadas obligaciones. Ante la imposibilidad práctica de cambiar la formulación del artículo 18, sería importante que el Comité aclarara su alcance para evitar posibles abusos en materia tan fundamental como es el respeto a las libertades de religión y de opinión.

El Comité, en su Observación General No. 29, hizo un valioso esfuerzo para elucidar el interrogante relativo al posible carácter exhaustivo de la enumeración de los artículos no susceptibles de suspensión en el artículo 4, párrafo 2. En él se refiere a la aplicación de las normas que ha venido desarrollando la comunidad internacional sobre los crímenes contra la humanidad, en caso de que la conducta de los individuos que actúan bajo la autoridad del Estado sea violatoria de principios fundamentales que protegen la dignidad humana. El desarrollo legislativo de los crímenes contra la humanidad todavía es incipiente, como lo demuestran las dificultades que ha tenido la aceptación de la codificación de los mismos en el Estatuto de la Corte Penal Internacional. Pero no queda duda de que, en la medida en que aumente la aprobación de los principios contenidos en dicho Estatuto, como seguramente ocurrirá, el Comité los tendrá muy en cuenta al estudiar el comportamiento de los Estados Partes del Pacto.

Los ejemplos que propone la mencionada Observación General en el párrafo 13, de obligaciones que no pueden ser materia de suspensión, adicionales a las mencionadas en el párrafo 2 del artículo 4, cubren aspectos importantes, como son el respeto a la inherente dignidad de la persona humana cuando los individuos se hallan privados de su libertad, la prohibición de la toma de rehenes, la protección a los derechos de los individuos pertenecientes a las minorías, el desplazamiento forzado de poblaciones y la prohibición de la apología de la guerra o la defensa del odio nacional, racial o religioso. Esta última prohibición entra dentro de las limitaciones impuestas por razón de la necesidad de combatir la discriminación basada en motivos de raza, color, sexo, idioma, religión u origen social. No es de descartar la posibilidad de que en el futuro se pueda extender el número de obligaciones de los Estados Partes del Pacto que no son susceptibles de suspensión o limitación en situaciones de emergencia, si se acepta con un criterio amplio la aplicabilidad de normas generales del derecho internacional, no consignadas explícitamente en el Pacto.

El interés creciente de la comunidad internacional por la promoción y protección de los derechos humanos está en relación directa con las amenazas cada vez más frecuentes que surgen en todas las regiones del globo. Hasta el momento, no parece que el siglo que comienza vaya a ser diferente de lo que el mundo vivió en la centuria que pasó. A las causas conocidas de perturbaciones sociales que han servido de fundamento a los estados de emergencia, con sus dramáticas consecuencias para la vigencia de los derechos y libertades teóricamente aceptados por la enorme mayoría de las naciones, se ha venido a añadir el fenómeno del terrorismo a escala universal. Sin negar la gravedad del hecho, no es menos cierto que se corre el riesgo de convertir la lucha contra el terrorismo en la justificación de conductas que contrarían abiertamente el propósito de asegurar la dignidad del hombre. La definición misma de terrorismo adolece de deficiencias conceptuales que están llevando a muchos Estados a ensayar medios de defensa que, en la práctica, alejan a las sociedades contemporáneas de las metas de justicia y de solidaridad que en un momento se creyeron accesibles. El estado de guerra ya no tiene la acepción a que estábamos acostumbrados, en vista de que cualquiera acción de los poderes públicos puede denominarse 'guerra': guerra contra el terrorismo, guerra contra el narcotráfico, guerra contra la corrupción, guerra contra la enfermedad, guerra contra la pobreza. Cada una de estas 'guerras', al lado de su carácter aparentemente noble, y quizás necesario, genera acciones que pueden poner en serio peligro la vigencia de los derechos de todos, y no solamente de los presuntos culpables.

El reconocimiento de la necesidad de apelar a medidas de excepción, cuando se presentan situaciones excepcionales en la vida de las naciones, no puede convertirse en una patente de corso para la violación sistemática de las obligaciones impuestas por el Pacto de Derechos Civiles y Políticos y demás garantías aceptadas por el derecho internacional. Por ello es que se justifica la permanente vigilancia del Comité y su función de ir desarrollando una jurisprudencia que evite, en lo posible, la tendencia de los poderes públicos a desconocer sus compromisos.

REFLECTIONS ON ARTICLE 5 OF THE INTERNATIONAL COVENANT ON CIVIL AND POLITICAL RIGHTS

Eckart Klein

I. ARTICLE 5 CCPR – A FORGOTTEN PROVISION?

Looking through the relevant documents one will swiftly notice that Article 5 of the International Covenant on Civil and Political Rights (CCPR) does not attract much attention in practice – to say the least.[1] With one exception, states parties apparently had no problems with accommodating to this provision; only the United States of America, upon ratification, made a declaration clarifying its understanding.[2] States reports, submitted to the Human Rights Committee (HRC) under Article 40 CCPR, which comment, article by article, on the legal situation in their country against the background of the Covenant, are rather silent on Article 5. Periodic reports usually merely refer back to earlier reports, especially initial reports.[3] In most cases reports are confined to describe the status of international law, and more specifically the Covenant, within the national legal order, whether the provisions of the Covenant may be invoked by individuals and – of course! – how domestic law and the jurisprudence of the courts are in full compliance with the requirements of the Covenant[4].

Only in rare cases does one find some more substantial comments. Ecuador, e.g., in its fourth periodic report (1999), concedes that, while most Covenant provisions have been incorporated into domestic law, the courts sometimes fail

[1] With regard to Article 17, the equivalent provision of the European Convention on Human Rights (ECHR) to Article 5, paragraph 1, CCPR, Jean-François Flauss, *L'abus de droit dans le cadre de la Convention européenne des droits de l'homme*, 4 Revue universelle des droits de l'homme (RUDH), p. 461 (1992) has similarly observed that this Article would only play a secondary role ('role secondaire').

[2] The declaration reads: 'That it is the view of the United States that States Party to the Covenant should wherever possible refrain from imposing any restrictions or limitations on the exercise of the rights recognized and protected by the Covenant, even when such restrictions and limitations are permissible under the terms of the Covenant. For the United States, article 5, paragraph 2, . . . has particular relevance to article 19, paragraph 3, which would permit certain restrictions on the freedom of expression. The United States declares that it will continue to adhere to the requirements and constraints of its Constitution in respect to all such restrictions and limitations'; cf. UN Doc. CCPR/C/2/Rev. 4, p. 42.

[3] *See e.g.*, the 2nd periodic report of Switzerland (1998), UN Doc. CCPR/C/CH/98/2, para. 80.

[4] *See e.g.*, the initial report of the Czech Republic (2000), UN Doc. CCPR/C/CZE/2000/1, para. 111; 2nd periodic report of Georgia (2000), CCPR/C/GEO/2000/2, paras. 74–78; 4th report of Morocco (1998), CCPR/C/115/Add. 1, paras. 48–49.

> 'to identify those provisions within the domestic legal system and consequently apply them in a restrictive manner or not at all. The cause of the problem lies in the fact that the majority of judges interpret written provisions in an almost literal fashion without resorting to other mechanisms of legal interpretation which would permit application of the provisions of the Covenant . . .'[5].

The Federal Republic of Germany, in its second periodic report (1985), outlines its 'particularly vulnerable position' as a divided country during the Cold War and, referring to Article 5, paragraph 1, describes its efforts 'to counteract the growth of totalitarian ideologies'.[6] Of particular interest are the remarks contained in the third periodic reports of the Libyan Arab Jamahiriya (1995) and of Yemen (2001). Libya notes, that regarding Article 5, paragraph 1, the Committee's comments 'accord precedence to the provisions of the Covenant over any domestic legislation in force. We believe this is a matter that cannot fail to give rise to questions . . .': Regarding Article 5, paragraph 2,

> 'the Committee seeks to affirm the rights that are already recognized under other legislation while, at the same time, expanding the scope of application of the provisions of the Covenant. Hence, the Covenant implicitly gives retroactive effect to its provisions. However, given the existence of religious and cultural diversity, potential areas of conflict will remain and, in such cases, the principles embodied in the Covenant will enjoy high status as an authoritative source. In our view, the question in this respect is one of mutual interaction between domestic legislation, with all its particularities and elements constituting the rule of law, and international conventions which, as a binding source of law are governed by the common values of the international community which are evolving and developing with a certain amount of difficulty.'[7]

The government of Yemen affirms that it does not seek to apply the Covenant in the narrowest sense, and continues:

> 'On the contrary, it liberally accords to the individual rights which are above and beyond those recognized in the Covenant, being an Islamic state which treats human beings in accordance with the expectations that the Islamic Sharia has of them. The constitution and other laws also accord extensive rights to citizens. Yemen regards those rights recognized in the Covenant as complementing the substance of Yemeni legislative enactments.'[8]

---

[5] UN-Doc. CCPR/C/84/Add. 8, para. 65.
[6] UN-Doc. CCPR/C/28/Add. 6, paras. 36–37.
[7] UN-Doc. CCPR/C/102/Add. 1, paras. 116–117.
[8] UN-Doc. CCPR/C/YEM/2001/3, para. 28.

As far as can be seen, the Concluding Observations of the HRC that draw conclusions from the dialogue with the state party, have not yet specifically referred to Article 5 CCPR.

Concerning individual communications received under the Optional Protocol the picture is more or less the same. Only in very few instances has Article 5 been invoked by an author or has the Committee, on its own initiative, found it necessary to include this provision in its reasoning.[9] In fact, the Article was substantially dealt with only in two cases, and then in individual opinions of Committee members.[10]

On the other hand, during the last five years, Article 5 has received some more favourable attention in the General Comments of the Human Rights Committee.[11] It is true that no specific General Comment has yet been devoted to this provision. However, the General Comments dealing with Articles 25, 12 and 3 CCPR explicitly refer to Article 5 applying the interpretative rule contained in paragraph 1 to the respective human right.[12] General Comment No. 29 (2001) on states of emergency takes into account both parts of Article 5 in developing its understanding of Article 4 CCPR.[13]

As will be shown, Article 5 CCPR deserves more attention, by the states parties as well the HRC. In fact, it is an important provision, shedding some light on the interpretation of the other articles of the Covenant, presenting, however, at the same time considerable difficulties for its correct understanding.

II. A FIRST RAPPROCHEMENT

1. Content

Article 5 CCPR contains two separate safeguarding or saving clauses that pursue very different purposes. Paragraph 1 of Article 5, based on Article 30 of the Universal Declaration (UDHR), grants protection against abuse of the Covenant provisions by states parties, groups or persons. It prevents use of the Covenant as a justification for any attempt to militate against the aims of the Covenant.[14]

---

[9] *See* Communications Nos. 117/1981, 268/1987, 398/1990; *infra* notes 64, 101, 103.

[10] *See* Communications Nos. 52/1979 (*de Lopez Burgos* v. *Uruguay*), Views of 29 July 1981,(CCPR/C/13/D/52/1979) and 470/91 (*Kindler* v. *Canada*),Views adopted of 30 July 1993, UN Doc. A/48/40, 138 (CCPR/C/48/D/470/1991); *infra* note 43.

[11] For a general assessment of General Comments *see* Torkel Opsahl, *The General Comments of the Human Rights Committee,* in: Festschrift K. J. Partsch, pp. 273 *et seq*. (1989); Eckart Klein, *General Comments,* in: Festschrift D. Rauschning, pp. 301 *et seq*. (2001).

[12] General Comments No. 25 (12 July 1996), at para. 27; No. 27, UN Doc. CCPR/C/21/Rev.1/Add.9 (2 November 1999), at paras. 13–14; No. 28, UN Doc. CCPR/C/21/Rev.1/Add.10 (29 March 2000),at para. 9.

[13] General Comment No. 29, UN Doc. CCPR/C/21/Rev.1/Add.11 (31 August 2001),at paras. 3, 9 and 10.

[14] Dominic McGoldrick, *The Human Rights Committee,* p. 19 (1994); Nehemiah Robinson, *The Universal Declaration of Human Rights,* p. 143 (1958).

Addressed as a warning against states it means that they must not use the Covenant, in particular its limitation or derogation clauses, 'as a sword' to restrict the rights and freedoms beyond what the Covenant allows[15] or even to destroy the very essence of the rights.[16] Addressed as a warning to groups and persons, Article 5, paragraph 1, aims to prevent them from invoking Covenant rights when their goal is the destruction of all the Covenant stands for.[17] It is meant to be a 'straightforward prohibition of subversive activities'[18]; the provisions of the Covenant must not be used 'as a shield' for activities that will undermine the order of liberty and freedom established by the Covenant.[19] States are entitled to defend this order against the enemies of freedom. In doing so, however, they must be aware that they are likewise addressed by Article 5, paragraph 1.

Paragraph 2 of Article 5 enunciates the idea that the Covenant does not intend to reduce the protection granted by any other legal norm, be it national or international, which is more favourable for the individual than the respective Covenant provision. Any possible legal conflict between relevant norms should be solved in favour of the person concerned.[20]

By giving instructions for the interpretation of Covenant rights, Article 5 has some systematic links to other interpretative clauses, such as Articles 44, 46 and 47 of the Covenant. While these provisions are of a procedural nature, Article 5 is a major material provision with an essential impact on the understanding of the scope and the restriction possibilities of the rights in question.

2. HISTORY

Article 5, paragraph 1, CCPR is founded on Article 30 UDHR.[21] The only change in the text was made as early as 1949 at the very beginning of the discussions on the Covenant. The change concerned the last part of paragraph 1 ('or at their limitation to a greater extent than is provided for in the present Covenant'). Hereby not destruction of the Covenant rights alone but also their unnecessary limitation is covered.[22] This wording emphasizes the principle of proportionality more strongly. Another important development had already taken place during the negotiations on

---

[15] Erica-Irene A. Daes, *Freedom of the Individual under Law. A Study on the Individual's Duties to the Community and the Limitations on Human Rights and Freedoms under Article 29 of the Universal Declaration of Human Rights,* UN Doc. E/CN. 4/Supp. 2/432/Rev. 2, p. 175 (reprint 1990).

[16] Ralph Beddard, *Human Rights and Europe*, p. 186 (1993) regarding Article 17 ECHR.

[17] Beddard *supra* note 16.

[18] Helle Kanger, *Human Rights in the U. N. Declaration,* p. 159 (1984).

[19] Daes, *supra* note 15, p. 175.

[20] McGoldrick, *supra* note 14, p. 19; Manfred Nowak, *CCPR Commentary,* p. 95 (1993).

[21] Another protection clause against the abuse of rights is contained in Article 29, para. 3, UDHR.

[22] *See* Marc J. Bossuyt, *Guide to the 'Travaux Préparatoires' of the International Covenant on Civil and Political Rights,* pp. 103–112 (1987); UN Doc. A/2929, pp. 26–28 (July 1955).

Article 30 UDHR.[23] The first proposal, made by the Lebanese delegate in the Human Rights Commission, was directed only against 'individuals'; it purported to prevent any resurrection of Nazism and fascism and to give states the possibility to take action against any such resurrection. Later on 'groups' were included as well. On the proposal of the Australian delegate, who pointed out that in the past it was states which had usually violated human rights, states were also mentioned as addressees of Article 5.

Article 5, paragraph 2, had no predecessor provision in the Universal Declaration.

3. Parallel Provisions

Interestingly enough, the provisions of Article 5 CCPR – identical with Article 5 of the International Covenant on Economic, Social and Cultural Rights – are reflected in most of the major human rights conventions.[24] This indicates that the ideas embodied in Article 5 are generally accepted, on the universal and regional level.

Parallel provisions to Article 5, paragraph 1, CCPR can be found in Article 29(a) and 30 of the American Convention on Human Rights/ACHR (1969), Article 17 and 18 of the European Convention on Human Rights ECHR (1950), and Article 54 of the Charter of Fundamental Rights of the European Union (CEU), solemnly proclaimed at the meeting of the European Council held in Nice in December 2000.[25]

Article 5, paragraph 2, CCPR for its part is paralleled by Article 29(b) ACHR[26], Article 53 ECHR[27] and Article 53 CEU.[28]

---

[23] Albert Verdoot, *Naissance et signification de la Déclaration Universelle des Droits de l'Homme,* pp. 272–274 (1964).

[24] *See generally* Paul Sieghart, *The International Law of Human Rights,* pp. 104–109 (1983, reprint 1995). An important exception is the African Charter on Human and Peoples' Rights (Banjul Charter) of 1981 which does not contain analogous clauses; only Articles 60 and 61 may be held to be similar to Article 5, para. 2, CCPR.

[25] Article 54 reads: 'Nothing in this Charter shall be interpreted as implying any right to engage in any activity or to perform any act aimed at the destruction of any of the rights and freedoms recognised in this Charter or at their limitation to a greater extent than is provided for herein'. The Charter, not yet being included in the text of the European treaties is, as such, not legally binding. For a general assessment of the Charter *see* Koen Lenaerts/Eddy de Smijter, *A 'bill of rights' for the European Union,* 38 Common Market Law Review, pp. 273 *et. seq*. (2001).

[26] Article 29(c) and (d) ACHR are not paralleled by other provisions and seem to be 'exclusively American'; *see* Cecilia Medina Quiroga, *The Battle of Human Rights. Gross, Systematic Violations and the Inter-American System,* p. 109 (1988); Héctor Gros Espiell, *La Convention Américaine et la Convention Européenne des droits de l'homme, Analyse Comparative,* 218 Recueil des Cours 1989 VI, p. 378 (1991); *see also* Scott Davidson, *The Inter-American Human Rights System,* p. 37 (1997) who finds some similarity of Article 29 (d) ACHR with Article 5, para. 2, CCPR.

III. ARTICLE 5, PARAGRAPH 1, CCPR: PROTECTION AGAINST ABUSE

1. States as Addressees

In the context of human rights conventions there is nothing astonishing when states become obliged. By the power they hold, states may rather easily interfere with the rights of individuals who, exactly for this reason, need protection. By directing itself to states, Article 5, paragraph 1, makes it clear that the powers they may use under the Covenant in order to restrict[29] or even derogate from[30] the rights enshrined in the Covenant, are limited themselves.[31] This purpose of Article 5, paragraph 1, makes this provision an integral part of all restriction and derogation clauses and must always be taken into account in the assessment of actions taken by a state party in this respect.[32]

The restriction or limitation clauses of the Covenant usually form a sufficient yardstick to judge the compliance of a state action (or omission) with the Covenant. But some of the provisions of the Covenant, though open for restrictions, do not expressly invoke the necessity of restrictions[33] (while others do), and some provisions do not provide for restrictions at all.[34] Not in all these cases can the rights concerned be held absolute, i.e. immune against any limitation.[35] In these circumstances when restrictions are not excluded but not sufficiently governed by specific Covenant provisions, Article 5, paragraph 1, gives the decisive hint. It orders the application and strict respect of the principle of proportionality. Any unreasonably broad interpretation of the limits of human rights is prohibited[36] as well as the deprivation of these rights of their true content.[37] It is in this sense, that

---

27 Before the entry into force of the 11th Protocol to the ECHR in 1998, Article 53 was numbered Article 60.

28 Article 53 CEU reads: 'Nothing in this Charter shall be interpreted as restricting or adversely affecting human rights and fundamental freedoms as recognised, in their respective fields of application, by Union law and international law and by international agreements to which the Union, the Community or all the Member States are party, including the European Convention for the Protection of Human Rights and Fundamental Freedoms, and by the Member States' constitutions'.

29 *Cf., e.g.*, Articles 12, 19, 21, 22 CCPR.

30 *See* Article 4 CCPR; *cf.* General Comment No. 29 (2001) para. 3: '. . . to prevent the abuse of a State's emergency powers'.

31 P. van Dijk/G. J. H. van Hoof, *Theory and Practise of the European Convention on Human Rights,* p. 751 (1998), with regard to Article 17 ECHR.

32 Thomas Buergenthal, *To Respect and to Ensure: State Obligations and Permissible Derogations, in:* L. Henkin (ed.), The International Bill of Rights. The Covenant on Civil and Political Rights, pp. 72, 87 (1981).

33 *E.g.*, Article 9, para. 1, cl. 3, CCPR.

34 *E.g.*, Article 7, 26, 27 CCPR.

35 While Article 7 is absolute, Articles 26 and 27 are not; *see* with further references Nowak, *supra* note 20, pp. 426 *et seq.*, 504 *et seq.*

36 Daes, *supra* note 15, p. 174.

37 Davidson, *supra* note 26, pp. 70–71.

General Comment No. 27 (1999) on 'Freedom of movement' says: '. . . States should always be guided by the principle that the restrictions must not impair the essence of the right (cf. Article 5, para. 1); the relation between right and restriction, between norm and exception, must not be reversed'.[38] The possible limitations of the right to liberty of movement (Article 12, para. 3) were often used in such an extreme manner, particularly by communist states, so that the right to move within the country or, still more, to leave the country had completely faded away. Article 5, paragraph 1, points to an immanent limitation of the limitation clauses, which was evidently ignored by those states.[39]

If a state makes use of its powers under the Covenant to restrict the rights enshrined therein, literally applying the relevant limitation clause, although its real intention is not to pursue the legitimate aims of that clause, but to use the powers for other illegitimate purposes, then this conduct is likewise covered by Article 5, paragraph 1. This provision embodies the principle of '*détournement de pouvoir*' [40], which is also clearly expressed in some other conventions.[41] However, the application of this principle may turn out to be rather cumbersome, because the illegitimate motivation of the state cannot easily be maintained.[42] In an early case, the Committee took Article 5, paragraph 1, as a supportive argument that Article 2, paragraph 1, of the Covenant – despite its wording – 'does not imply that a state party cannot be held accountable for violations of rights under the Covenant which its agents commit upon the territory of another state'.[43] What really counts is the fact that the state is exercising its jurisdiction; this is also in line with the general principle of public international law.[44] In an individual opinion, Mr. Christian Tomuschat dissociated himself from the reasoning of this finding, though not from the result. 'In principle, the scope of application of the Covenant is not susceptible to being extended by reference to Article 5, a provision designed to cover instances where formal rules under the Covenant seem to legitimize actions which

---

[38] General Comment No. 27 (1999), para. 13.

[39] *See* Georg Brunner, *Freedom of Movement,* in: G. Brunner et al., Before Reforms. Human Rights in the Warsaw Pact States 1971–1988, pp. 187 *et. seq*. (1990).

[40] *See* Buergenthal, *supra* note 32, p. 87; D. J. Harris/M. O'Boyle/C. Warbrick, *Law of the European Convention on Human Rights,* p. 512 (1995). For the principle of 'détournement de pouvoir' as applied in French administrative law *see* Jean Rivero/Jean Waline, *Droit administratif,* 18th ed., p. 247 *et seq.* (2000).

[41] *E.g.,* Article 18 ECHR and 30 ACHR; *see also* van Dijk/van Hoof, *supra* note 31, p. 756, and R. A. Lawson/H. G. Schermers, *Leading Cases of the European Court of Human Rights,* pp. 32 *et seq*. (1997), both with references to case law under Article 18 ECHR.

[42] *See* Nowak, *supra* note 20, p. 97.

[43] Communication No. 52/1979 (*de Lopez Burgos* v. *Uruguay*), Views of 29 July 1981, Selected Decisions of the HRC under the Optional Protocol, vol. I, 89 (CCPR/C/13/D/52/1979) at para. 12.3.

[44] *Cf.* Article 1 of the Draft Articles on responsibility of States for internationally wrongful acts, adopted by the International Law Commission at its 53rd Session (2001).

substantially run counter to its purposes and general spirit'.[45] In fact, the correct result concerning the interpretation of Article 2, paragraph 1, has to be found without reference to Article 5, paragraph 1, of the Covenant.

2. Groups and Persons as Addressees

By addressing 'groups and persons' Article 5, paragraph 1, intends to prevent the danger that the Covenant rights might be nullified by using them to impair or even destroy the freedom of others.[46] Groups and persons should not be allowed to exploit the provisions of the Covenant for this purpose.[47] The (former) European Commission of Human Rights, dealing with the application of the Federal Republic of Germany's Communist Party (KPD), which had been prohibited under Article 21 of the German Basic Law[48], determined the object of Article 17 ECHR, the homologue of Article 5, paragraph 1, CCPR, as follows:

> 'Considérant que cette disposition fondamentale de la Convention a pour objectif la sauvegarde des droits que cette Convention énumère, par la protection du libre fonctionnement des institutions démocratiques (voir Travaux Préparatoires, Comptes Rendus de l'Assemblée Consultative, Année 1949, 1ère session, pages 1235, 1237 et 1239: 'Il s'agit d'empêcher que les courants totalitaires puissent exploiter en leur faveur les principes posés par la Convention, c'est-à-dire invoquer les droits de liberté pour supprimer les Droits de l'Homme').'[49]

One cannot deny that at least some rights are open for abuse, be they of a procedural or substantive nature.[50] Persons may abuse their right to assemble or to express opinions in a way that threatens the democratic process. A terrorist may try to justify his or her criminal acts by invoking human rights.[51]

The idea embodied in Article 5, paragraph 1, as far as groups or persons are concerned, has its origin in the Jacobinian motto 'no freedom for the enemies of

---

[45] The opinion is appended to the Views of the HRC, *supra* note 43.

[46] Robinson, *supra* note 14, p. 143; van Dijk/van Hoof, *supra* note 31, p. 750 (regarding Article 17 ECHR).

[47] *See* Beddard, *supra* note 16, pp. 186–7.

[48] Judgement of the Federal Constitutional Court of 17 August 1956, 5 BVerfGE (Official collection of judgements) pp. 85 *et seq.*

[49] Decision of 20 July 1957, European Commission of Human Rights, Documents and Decisions (1955–58) pp. 222, 224 (1959).

[50] *See e.g.,* Article 3 Optional Protocol; *cf.* also HRC, Views of 16 July 2001 on Communication No. 787/1997 (*Gobin* v. *Mauritius*),UN Doc. A/56/40, vol. II, 222(CCPR/C/72/D/787/1997), at para. 6.3, and the appended individual opinions of six Committee members.

[51] Torkel Opsahl/Voijin Dimitrijevic, in: G. Alfredsson/A. Eide (eds.), *The Universal Declaration of Human Rights. A Common Standard of Achievement,* p. 649 (1999).

freedom'.[52] Though it would go too far to characterize Article 5, paragraph 1, CCPR as well as Article 30 UDHR as a 'vicious circle'[53], it is true that in dealing with the issue of abuse of rights by individuals and drawing legal consequences from such behaviour one walks on a tight rope[54]: On the one hand, a free democracy should have the means to defend itself against those who purport to undermine this free order, but, on the other, it may swiftly push to its limits and betray the very idea it is defending if it reacts too harshly.[55] Prohibition of political parties or other associations and the forfeiture of rights are the most prominent examples in this respect.[56]

In such situations, prudent restraint is to be recommended.[57] This restraint should involve a clearly regulated procedure, identifying the authorities allowed to act or, better, react and, in accordance with Article 2, paragraph 3, CCPR provide for judicial remedies if the whole procedure is not assigned to the (constitutional) courts, as it is partly the case in Germany.[58]

Article 5, paragraph 1, gives some more indications. By saying that the Covenant may not be interpreted as implying 'any right to engage in any activity or perform any act aimed at the destruction' etc., it has been made clear that the expression of opinions as such, even if most critical of the government, does not authorize the government to rely on this provision in order to curtail human rights. Further, the distinction between 'expression of opinion' and 'action' must not be interpreted so that any step from mere holding or expressing opinions to engaging in activities or performing acts would give a state party the opportunity to invoke Article 5, paragraph 1. Not being able to strive for the realization of one's plans and designs and opinions would leave but a shadow of freedom.[59] Therefore the 'activities' and 'acts' mentioned in the provision must be 'aimed at the destruction of any of the rights and freedoms recognized (in the Covenant) or at their limitation to a greater extent than is provided for in the present Covenant'. 'Activities' and 'acts' must have a certain intensity[60] and they must aim at the undermining of the

---

[52] Opsahl/Dimitrijevic, *supra* note 51, p. 648; related to Article 17 ECHR *see* Flauss, *supra* note 1, p. 403; Jochen Abr. Frowein/Wolfgang Peukert, *Europäische Menschenrechts-konvention. EMRK-Kommentar,* p. 491 (2nd ed. 1996).

[53] Opsahl/Dimitrijevic, *supra* note 51, p. 648.

[54] An in-depth study on this issue has been published by Helmut Steinberger, *Konzeption und Grenzen freiheitlicher Demokratie* (1974).

[55] Here the first part of Article 5, paragraph 1, directed to states must be recalled.

[56] *Cf. e.g.*, Articles 18 and 21 of the German Basic Law.

[57] The first part of the US-Declaration (note 2) relates to this point.

[58] Regarding the prohibition of political parties and the decision on a forfeiture of basic rights only the Federal Constitutional Court has the relevant competences.

[59] *See* Steinberger, *supra* note 54, p. 591.

[60] The German Federal Constitutional Court has held in its judgement on the prohibition of the Communist Party that it is not sufficient that the party does not recognize the free and democratic order. Rather the party must show an actively struggling, aggressive attitude

enjoyment of rights by others.[61] It would be wrong, however, to grant a state the possibility to react only to activities or acts that would be just short of forceful revolution. Express support for use of non-democratic means to effect political changes would be sufficient for the state to react.[62]

The legal possibility for the state to react – within the limits Article 5, paragraph 1, provides for the state itself[63] - does not put the individuals concerned out of the scope of protection of the Covenant. I would not agree with the view of the Committee, in the case *M. A.* v. *Italy*, 'that the acts of which M. A. was convicted (reorganizing the dissolved fascist party) were of a kind which are removed from the protection of the Covenant by Article 5 thereof' and that therefore the communication was declared 'inadmissible under Article 3 of the Optional Protocol as incompatible with the provisions of the Covenant, *ratione materiae*'.[64] In the same way, the European Commission of Human Rights in the case of the *German Communist Party* v. *Federal Republic of Germany*, declared the application, on the basis of Article 17 ECHR, inadmissible as incompatible with the provisions of the Convention.[65] Though it is certainly correct to state that a person may not use a Covenant right aiming at the destruction of the ideas of liberty and freedom enshrined in the Covenant, it is highly problematic to exclude this person *a priori* from the scope of protection of any Covenant right. It is more consistent with modern understanding of freedom not to deny, without further scrutiny, the applicability of those Covenant rights which were allegedly violated by the state. Therefore, the criticism of this approach taken by the Committee and the European Commission is unanimous. The question of a violation complained of by an author should be examined on the merits if Article 5 is involved.[66] It was a step in the right direction in the *Kühnen* case, where the applicant had been convicted by German courts for aggressively advocating the reinstitution of the NSDAP and of national socialism, when the European Commission referring, i.a., to Article 17 ECHR, held

---

against the existing order; it must deliberately strive to impair the functioning of the order with the intent to abolish it in the future; *see supra* note 48, p. 141.

[61] *See* Sarah Joseph/Jenny Schultz/Melissa Castan, *The International Covenant on Civil and Political Rights. Cases, Materials, and Commentary*, p. 8 (2000).

[62] In the case No. 550/1993 (*Faurisson* v. *France*) the HRC in its Views of 8 November 1996,UN Doc. A/52/40,84 (CCPR/C/58/D/550/1993) did not apply Article 5. The provision was also not quoted in the numerous individual opinions. The reason is simple: Mr. Faurisson's non-acceptable statements on the holocaust were not aimed at the destruction of the rights of others in the sense of Article 5, paragraph 1.

[63] *See* above III. 1.

[64] Decision of 10 April 1984, Selected Decision of the HRC under the Optional Protocol, Vol. 2, 17th to 32nd sessions (October 1982–April 1988), UN Doc. CCPR/C/OP/2, pp. 31, 33 (1990).

[65] *Supra* note 49, p. 225. In an identical way the European Commission decided in the Glimmerveen and Hagenbeek case, 18 DR pp. 187, 194–197 (1980).

[66] *See e.g.*, van Dijk/van Hoof, *supra* note 31, p. 753; Frowein/Peukert, *supra* note 52, p. 492; Oliver Klein, *Parteiverbotsverfahren vor dem Europäischen Gerichtshof für Menschenrechte,* 34 Zeitschrift für Rechtspolitik, pp. 397, 399–400 (2001).

that the application was 'manifestly ill-founded' and therefore inadmissible under Article 27, paragraph 2, (now Article 35, para. 3) of the Convention.[67] This reason for inadmissibility includes actually, a prior examination of the case on its merits. Article 5, paragraph 1, CCPR as well as Article 17 ECHR should not have an '*effet guillotine*'.[68]

The effect of any legitimate application of Article 5, paragraph 1, does not 'outlaw' the individual concerned. He or she cannot successfully rely on a certain Covenant right, if it is used in the way described by the provision. But the person is not stripped of other rights. This has been stressed very clearly by the European Court of Human Rights in the famous *Lawless* case in relation to Article 17 ECHR.[69] According to the European Commission, quoted in approval by the Court, 'Article 17 covers essentially those rights which, if invoked, would facilitate the attempt to derive there from a right to engage personally in activities aimed at the destruction of 'any of the rights and freedoms set forth in the Convention'.[70] Not all rights are liable to abuse in the sense of Article 17 ECHR or Article 5, paragraph 1, CCPR. The right to hold an opinion and the right to have a religion are, as such, hardly open to abuse. It may be different with the rights to move, to assemble, to associate, to express opinions or to manifest religion. Article 7 can also be abused by an individual.

In cases where the infringement of human rights (e.g., Articles 19, 21, 22) is justified under Article 5, paragraph 1, the person still enjoys all the procedural guarantees embodied in the Covenant. A person who aims at the destruction of any of the rights and freedoms recognized in the Covenant is not stripped of the right to a fair trial[71] or of any of those rights that are absolute, i.e., if no limitation exists (not even inherent limitations) or if they are of a non-derogable nature.[72] Thus, the Jacobinian slogan must be changed accordingly: 'No *absolute* freedom for the enemies of freedom'.[73]

---

[67] Kühnen v. Germany, case No. 12194/96, decision of 12 May 1988, 56 DR pp. 205, 210 (1988).

[68] Flauss, *supra* note 1, p. 464.

[69] Judgement of 1 July 1961, Series A, vol. 3, pp. 27, 45–46.

[70] Kühnen case, *supra* note 67, p. 209.

[71] *See* the Lawless case, *supra* note 69, p. 45, referring to Articles 5 and 6 ECHR.

[72] Article 4, para. 2, CCPR – *See also* van Dijk/van Hoof, *supra* note 31, pp. 761–763.

[73] In this sense the German Federal Constitutional Court used the phrase 'Keine unbedingte Freiheit für die Feinde der Freiheit', *supra* note 48, p. 138. Of course, there can never be completely unlimited freedom.

IV. ARTICLE 5, PARAGRAPH 2, CCPR – PREVENTION OF LOWER PROTECTION

1. Meaning

Article 5, paragraph 2, intends to prevent another kind of abusive interpretation. The Covenant shall not be used as a pretext for denying or restricting other more favourable or more extensive human rights that individuals may enjoy or are entitled to on the basis of domestic or international law or practice.[74] In other words, Article 5, paragraph 2, is an expression of the idea that the Covenant, like other human rights conventions[75] protects a minimum standard, which may always be surpassed.[76] If such more favourable human rights provisions or custom exist in a state party, it is this level of protection that counts, and it would a violation of the Covenant itself if in an individual case the protection would fall short of this level. Article 5, paragraph 2, has aptly been characterized as the 'most-favourable-to-individual clause'.[77] If, e.g., a derogation from a Covenant provision is admissible under Article 4, but not allowed under another international obligation or under domestic law, then Article 4 must not be used as a basis for derogation from this provision.[78] If property is protected in a state party on the ground of an international (e.g., Article 1 of the 1st Additional Protocol of 1952 to the ECHR) or a national obligation, then the fact that the right to property as such is not protected under the Covenant would not present any justification for the violation of this right.[79]

2. Difficulties

While at first sight this interpretative clause seems to be rather clear, a further look reveals some difficulties. What does it actually mean that the Covenant must not be misused to lower protection? Lower protection may be granted either by a less broad scope of protection regarding a certain human right or by wider restriction or derogation clauses assigned to this right.[80] However, one has to take into account that restriction – and, as the case may be, even derogation – clauses serve not only to

---

[74] Buergenthal, *supra* note 32, p. 89; Marc-André Eissen, *Convention européenne des Droits de l'Homme et Pacte des Nations Unies relatif aux droits civils et politiques: problème de 'coexistence',* 30 Zeitschrift für ausländisches öffentliches Recht und Völkerrecht, p. 237, 257 (1970).
[75] *Cf.* the references in section II. 3, above.
[76] Nowak, *supra* note 20, p. 95.
[77] Louis B. Sohn, *The Human Rights Law of the Charter,* 12 Texas International Law Journal, p. 129, 137 (1977); similarly Karel Vasak, *Vers un droit international spécifique des droits de l'homme,* in: UNESCO (éd.), Les dimensions internationales des droits de l'homme, pp. 707, 710 (1978).
[78] HRC, General Comment no. 29, UN Doc. CCPR/C/21/Rev.1/Add.11 (31 August 2001), para. 9.
[79] Nowak, *supra* note 20, p. 101.
[80] Sohn, *supra* note 77, pp. 137 *et seq.*

enlarge the power of the state vis-à-vis individuals to the detriment of their freedom, but they may also serve the protection of one individual vis-à-vis another, thus enabling the former to enjoy his or her rights. Restriction of human rights is not only a means to protect social values and public interests but also to balance conflicting private interests and rights and, used in this sense, has a very protective function. The duty to protect and to ensure human rights, may, according to the concrete situation, not only require states to restrain themselves from making use of restriction clauses, but also to use them.[81] Effective guarantee of freedom for one will often mean effective restriction of freedom for others. The *Faurisson* case is just one example.[82] What would be in such circumstances the higher or lower protection? The right to freedom of expression must be balanced against the rights or reputations of others. Does a legal order as that of the United States with its strong protection of First Amendment rights (i.e. freedom of speech and the press) grant more or less protection than the Covenant, and how can the French (or German) domestic law be assessed which allows for more protection of the reputation of others by lowering the protection of the freedom of speech?[83] One cannot assess this question only from the point of view of the individual who claims a violation, because it depends completely on the circumstances of the case whether the plaintiff (or author of a communication under the Optional Protocol) is the one who feels restricted in his freedom of expression or the one who feels violated in his or her rights or reputation. The declaration of the United States to Article 5, paragraph 2[84], and the relevant comments of Libya in its third periodic report reflect the inherent problem.[85]

Another question is whether in cases where the discrimination clauses (Articles 3, 26) have been violated, Article 5, paragraph 2, excludes a remedy that would have the effect of 'equalizing down', i.e. would put an end to the discrimination by creating equality through opting for the lower level.[86] The answer depends on whether a right to the higher level of protection exists under domestic or international law, and, if so, whether this right can be modified by the state party.[87]

---

[81] *See* Eckart Klein (ed.), *The Duty to Protect and to Ensure Human Rights* (2000); Buergenthal, *supra* note 32, pp. 72 *et seq*.

[82] *See supra* note 62. Another relevant case, see Nackenheim v. France, Communication No.854/1999, UN Doc. CCPR/C751/D/854/1999, UN Doc. A/57/40 at 228 (2002). Here is an issue whether a person may be restricted in his freedom in order to protect him against himself.

[83] *Cf.* to this issue David Kretzmer/Francine Kershman Hazan (eds.), *Freedom of Speech and Incitement Against Democracy,* passim (2000).

[84] *Cf. supra* note 2.

[85] *Cf. supra* note 7.

[86] *See* Joseph/Schultz/Castan, *supra* note 61, p. 570. Similar questions arise under the jurisprudence of the German Federal Constitutional Court; *see* for further details Ernst Benda/Eckart Klein, *Verfassungsprozeßrecht,* pp. 210, 524 *et seq*. (2nd ed. 2001).

[87] *See* the HRC Views of 3 November 1999 in the case No. 694/1996 (*Waldman v. Canada*, UN Doc. A/55/40, 86(CCPR/C/67/D/694/1996) at para. 10.6.

Where the right is granted under domestic law this can be more easily assumed than where it is protected by international commitments.

3. Relationship of the Covenant to the Rights Referred to by Article 5, Paragraph 2

The rights which are protected under domestic or international law and to which Article 5, paragraph 2, is referring do not lose their nature as non-Covenant rights; they do not become part of the Covenant.[88] For this reason, it is not acceptable to conclude from the reference made in this provision that they cannot or must not be modified.[89] Having not lost their original legal nature, the respective procedures for amendments according to domestic or international law fully apply. The more favourable protection granted by domestic law compared with the protection of the Covenant may therefore get lost with the result that, at the end of the day, it would be the Covenant which guarantees higher protection.

However, where a legal norm or custom referred to in Article 5, paragraph 2, presents a more favourable protection, any measure of a state party, complying only with the lower protection granted by the Covenant, would not be in conformity with the Covenant. Everything else would not do justice to the binding force of the interpretative order contained in Article 5, paragraph 2. The Committee, therefore, stated correctly in its General Comment No. 29 on states of emergency that '(a) although it is not the function of the Human Rights Committee to review the conduct of a state party under other treaties, in exercising its functions under the Covenant the Committee has the competence to take a state party's other international obligations into account when it considers whether the Covenant allows the state party to derogate from specific provisions of the Covenant'.[90] In an analogous way the jurisprudence of the European Court of Human Rights quite clearly indicates that the Court identifies and scrutinizes other international obligations incumbent on a state party (e.g. Article 4 of the Covenant) when it has to decide on the compatibility of the state's actions with Articles 15 and 53 (ex. Article 60) ECHR.[91] Generally there will be some reluctance to push this examination too far, since the Committee or the Court will move on a terrain that is not exactly their own.[92] On the other hand, the Committee cannot disclaim a responsibility openly assigned to it by the

---

[88] Buergenthal, *supra* note 32, p. 90; Nowak, *supra* note 20, p. 101; Eissen, *supra* note 74, p. 258.

[89] Buergenthal, *ibid.*; Vasak, *supra* note 77, pp. 710 *et seq.*

[90] *See* HRC, General Comment No. 29 (31 August 2001),UN Doc. CCPR/C/21/Rev.1/Add.11, at para. 10.

[91] *See e.g.*, *Lawless* v. *Ireland* (*supra* note 69), para. 41; *Ireland* v. *United Kingdom*, judgement of 18 January 1978, Series A 25, para. 222; *Brannigan and McBride* v. *United Kingdom*, judgement of 26 May 1993, Series A 258-B, para. 68. – *Cf. also* Davidson, *supra* note 26, p. 37 regarding Article 29(d) ACHR.

[92] Harris/O'Boyle/Warbrick, *supra* note 40, pp. 502 *et seq.*, therefore think that Article 53 (ex Article 60) ECHR, corresponding with Article 5, paragraph 2, CCPR 'has been of little significance'.

references in Article 5, paragraph 2, namely the responsibility to ensure protection on the highest level available.

In an interesting case – *Kindler* v. *Canada*[93] -, Article 5, paragraph 2 was used by two dissenting Committee members to show that by extraditing Mr. Kindler to the United States where he probably would face execution, Canada, having abolished the death penalty, had fallen short of its obligation to apply the higher level of protection.[94] It is true that in this situation, where only the bilateral relationship between a state and an individual is at stake, the kind of difficulties do not exist that arise when rights or interests of other individuals are involved.[95] But this fact alone does not necessarily bring Article 5, paragraph 2, into play. The right question would be whether the prohibition of capital punishment and, in particular execution, within Canada also covers any Canadian act that makes execution possible outside Canada. This understanding, however, is certainly not the meaning of the domestic law, according to the interpretation by the Canadian Courts. It would not be easy for the Committee to push this interpretation aside as completely unreasonable and therefore arbitrary. The Committee might perhaps have found a violation of Article 6 on the basis of the argument that, by this provision alone, a state party that has abolished the death penalty is prevented from engaging in any activity that may lead to a death sentence or execution outside its borders.[96] But the Committee could not rely on Article 5, paragraph 2, because there did not exist, in this respect, a higher protection through the domestic law than through the Covenant (Article 6). The majority decision therefore rightly abstained from applying this provision.[97]

V. ENFORCEMENT POSSIBILITIES

As there is no doubt that Article 5 CCPR as a whole is binding on the states parties (and the Committee) in applying Covenant rights, the question arises how the interpretative orders of Article 5 can be enforced.

On the domestic level, as far as the Covenant rights are directly applicable[98] and can be relied upon by individuals or, as the case may be, by the state party justifying its measures taken against an 'enemy of freedom'[99], Article 5 may be invoked

[93] Communication No. 470/1991 (*Kindler* v. *Canada*), Views of 30 July 1993, UN Doc. A/48/40, 138 (CCPR/C/48/D/470/1991).
[94] *See* the individual opinions of Mr. Lallah (para. 6) and Mr. Aguilar Urbina (para. 21), appended to the Committee's Views, *supra* note 93.
[95] *See* above in the text at notes 80 et seq.
[96] This issue was discussed by the Committee (*supra* note 93), paras. 14.1–14.6.
[97] In fact, it did not mention it at all.
[98] *Cf.* the declaration of the US, made upon ratification, 'that the provisions of Articles 1 through 27 of the Covenant are not self-executing'.
[99] *See supra* note 52.

together with a specific right protected under the Covenant.[100] In applying the rights concerned, the courts must take Article 5 into account as an integral part of the restriction and derogation clauses provided for in the Covenant.

On the international level, the states parties have to report on the measures they have adopted which give effect to the rights recognized in the Covenant and on the progress made in enjoyment of those rights (Article 40, para. 1). This includes a report about how far a state has made use of restriction or derogation possibilities and whether the provisions of Article 5 have been respected.

Under the Optional Protocol (individual communications) the jurisprudence of the Committee has been that Article 5, like Article 2 CCPR, belongs to those provisions, which contain general undertakings and cannot be invoked by individuals. Respective communications have therefore been held inadmissible.[101] It is by no means certain that this jurisprudence will prevail in the long run, at least as far as Article 2 is concerned.[102] With regard to Article 5 a change may also occur where a fundamental human right is recognized or exists in a state party on which legal ground whatsoever but is not recognized by the Covenant or only to a lesser extent, a violation of this right might be contrary to Article 5, paragraph 2. Thus the purpose of this provision would support the view that there is good reason to invoke Article 5 on its own. At any rate, this provision can be invoked in conjunction with specific Covenant rights. In cases where the author only claims a violation of Article 5, the Committee *ex officio* examines whether the facts submitted raise an issue under other articles of the Covenant.[103]

It should be noted further that states parties have not only a right but also a duty to monitor compliance of other states parties with the provisions of the Covenant.[104] They may therefore address themselves directly to the state concerned and claim fulfilment of its international obligations or use other mechanisms at their disposal according to international law, including Article 41 CCPR.[105]

---

[100] *Cf.*, regarding Article 17 ECHR, van Dijk/van Hoof, *supra* note 31, p. 751; Heinz Guradze, *Die Europäische Menschenrechtskonvention,* p. 203 (1968).

[101] *Cf.* Communications No. 268/1987 (*M. G. B. and S. P.* v. *Trinidad and Tobago*), decision of 3 November 1989, A/45/40, 157 (CCPR/C/37/D/268/1987) and No. 398/1990 (*A. M.* v. *Finland*), decision of 23 July 1992, UN Doc. A/47/40, 399 (CCPR/C/45/D/398/1990).

[102] *See* the dissenting opinion by Mmes. Evatt, Medina Quiroga, and Chanet in the case No. 552/1993 (*Kall* v. *Poland*), appended to the Views of the HRC of 14 July 1997, UN Doc. A/52/40, 105 (CCPR/C/60/D/552/1993). In more recent Views a more lenient language has been used, *cf.* cases No. 767/1997 (*Jensen* v. *Australia*), Views of 22 March 2001,UN Doc. A/56/40,vol.II, 213 at para. 6.6, and No. 779/1997 (*Äärelä* v. *Finland*), Views of 24 October 2001,A/57/40,vol. II, 117 (CCPR/C/73/D/779/1997) at para. 7.7. *See also* Joseph/Schulz/Castan, *supra* note 61, pp. 8–10.

[103] Communication No. 268/1987 (*H.G.B. and S.P.* v. *Trinidad and Tobago*),Decision adopted on 3 November 1989, UN Doc. A/45/40, vol. II, 157 (CCPR/C/37/D/268/1987) at para. 6.2.

[104] *See* General Comment No. 29, CCPR/C/21/Rev.1/Add.11, CCPR (2001), at para. 17.

[105] Generally for this question *see* Eckart Klein, *Die Verantwortung der Vertragsparteien, Überlegungen zu einer effektiveren Durchsetzung menschenrechtlicher Verpflichtungen,* in:

VI. FINAL REMARKS

Article 5 is a very important provision from a systemic point of view. However, it is doubtful whether it will play a more prominent role in practice than in the past, because its message is not so lucid. Nevertheless, all actors in the human rights field, including the Committee, should bear it in mind as it helps to understand what human rights, and of course in particular the Covenant, are all about.[106] To be sure, Article 5 needs a lot of reflection, but it presents a key for a holistic perception of an order that strives to establish a framework where it is possible to live together in peace. Human rights is not a minimalistic concept. Human rights are evolving and expanding, but they do not mildly close their eyes on those who lay the axe on the roots of this growing tree.

H.-J. Cremer/T. Giegerich/D. Richter/A. Zimmermann (eds.), Tradition und Weltoffenheit des Rechts, Festschrift H. Steinberger, pp. 243 *et seq*. (2002).
[106] Likewise Buergenthal, *supra* note 32, p. 87.

Part IV

Activities of the Human Rights Committee (2) – Specific Issues

LA PEINE DE MORT ET LE PACTE INTERNATIONAL SUR LES DROITS CIVILS ET POLITIQUES

Christine Chanet

INTRODUCTION

Seul instrument à *valeur normative*, de portée universelle, le Pacte international sur les droits civils et politiques traite à la fois directement et indirectement de la question de la peine capitale comme châtiment suprême. Le Protocole *facultatif* relatif à l'abolition de la peine de mort n'a, jusqu'à ce jour fait l'objet d'aucune communication devant le Comité des droits de l'homme. Les Etats Parties au Pacte, lorsqu'ils soumettent leur rapport au Comité en vertu de l'article 40 du Pacte se bornent à énoncer, spontanément ou sur demande des membres du Comité, s'ils entendent ou non souscrire à cet engagement.

Pour aborder ces différents textes et problématiques, il conviendra d'examiner dans une première partie l'approche de la peine capitale adoptée dans le Pacte lui-même et dans la jurisprudence du Comité au titre du Protocole facultatif relatif aux communications individuelles. En effet, plusieurs articles du Pacte concernent plus ou moins directement la peine capitale. Il s'agit plus particulièrement des articles 6, 7, 4, 2, 14, 15, 26. Nous étudierons ensuite, dans une deuxième partie, la peine capitale dans la jurisprudence de Comité des droits de l'homme. La jurisprudence du Comité dans ce domaine concerne plus particulièrement:

- l'extradition
- la notion de crimes les plus graves
- la question du juge compétent
- la règle 86 du règlement interne du Comité
- la question du couloir de la mort
- la question des méthodes de l'exécution capitale

I. L'APPROCHE DE LA PEINE CAPITALE DANS LE PACTE

Seul l'article 6 vise directement la peine capitale:

a) Article 6:

> 'Le droit à la vie est inhérent à la personne humaine. Ce droit doit être protégé par la loi. Nul ne peut être arbitrairement privé de la vie.
>
> Dans les pays où la peine de mort n'a pas été abolie, une sentence de mort ne peut être prononcée que pour les crimes les plus graves, conformément à la législation en vigueur au moment où le crime a été commis et qui ne doit pas être en contradiction avec les dispositions du présent Pacte ni

avec la Convention pour la prévention et la répression du crime de génocide. Cette peine ne peut être appliquée qu'en vertu d'un jugement définitif rendu par un tribunal compétent.

Lorsque la privation de la vie constitue le crime de génocide, il est entendu qu'aucune disposition du présent article n'autorise un Etat partie au présent Pacte à déroger d'aucune manière à une obligation quelconque assumée en vertu des dispositions de la Convention pour la prévention et la répression du crime de génocide.

Tout condamné à mort a le droit de solliciter la grâce ou la commutation de la peine. L'amnistie, la grâce ou la commutation de la peine de mort peuvent dans tous les cas être accordées.

Une sentence de mort ne peut être imposée pour des crimes commis par des personnes âgées de moins de 18 ans et ne peut être exécutée contre des femmes enceintes.

Aucune disposition du présent article ne peut être invoquée pour retarder ou empêcher l'abolition de la peine capitale par un Etat partie au présent Pacte'.

Toutefois elle est aussi implicitement visée par plusieurs autres articles du Pacte.

b) d'autres dispositions du Pacte visent indirectement la peine de mort:

1) Ainsi en est-il de l'article 2. En effet la peine capitale, lorsqu'elle est prononcée, doit pouvoir être mise en échec par un recours au titre de l'article 2 du Pacte. Celui-ci est sans préjudice aux recours en grâce et en commutation de peine prévu au *§ 4 de l'article 6.*

2) D'autre part, aucune des garanties prévues par le prononcé de la peine capitale ne peut compter de dérogation au titre de *l'article 4 du Pacte (v.al 4 § 2).* Le Comité des droits de l'homme l'a expressément rappelé dans l'observation générale n° 29.

3) Selon le § 2 de l'article 6, la peine de mort ne peut être appliquée qu'en vertu d'un jugement définitif *rendu par un tribunal compétent.* Le même texte précise que la peine de mort ne peut être prononcée que pour 'les crimes les plus graves' conformément à la législation en vigueur au *moment* où le crime a été commis, c'est-à-dire en conformité avec les dispositions de *l'article 15 du Pacte.*

En outre cette législation ne doit pas être en contradiction avec les dispositions du Pacte. Ce qui signifie, notamment, que le tribunal compétent doit satisfaire à l'ensemble des exigences requises par *l'article 14* dans toutes ses dispositions.[1]

4) Conformément à *l'article 26* du Pacte, la peine de mort ne saurait être imposée de manière discriminatoire comme le Comité des droits de l'homme l'a

---

[1] Communications 482/1991 et 464/1991 (*Peart et Peart* v. *Jamaïque*), Constatations du 19 juillet 1995, U.N. document A/50/40, vol. II.

rappelé lors de l'examen du cas *Kennedy* contre *Trinite-et-Tobago* en novembre 1999.[2] En effet, à l'occasion de cette communication, le Comité a critiqué la réserve de l'Etat partie sur le fondement de l'article 26 du Pacte en reprochant à l'Etat d'exclure la compétence du Comité pour connaître des recours d'une catégorie de personnes, en l'espèce les *condamnés à mort.*

5) La peine capitale est également implicitement visée par *l'article 5 § 2* en vertu duquel le Pacte n'admet aucune restriction ou dérogation aux droits énoncés sous prétexte que le Pacte ne les reconnaît qu'à un moindre degré. Ce dernier élément trouve toute son importance lorsque le droit à la vie est protégé de manière plus extensive dans un Etat: cet Etat partie ne pourrait subitement déroger à sa loi en prétextant que le Pacte ne va pas aussi loin. (Voir l'opinion séparée de M. Lallah dans le cas Kindler.)[3]

6) Enfin, l'application de la peine capitale ne saurait être imposée en violation des *articles 7 et 10* du Pacte.

Une question fondamentale agite la doctrine au sujet d'un éventuel paradoxe dans le texte même du Pacte.

Seul l'article 6 évoque directement la question de la peine capitale. Il l'aborde dans son § 2 pour énoncer: '*Dans les pays où la peine de mort n'a pas été abolie* ...'.

Certains auteurs et plusieurs membres du Comité des droits de l'homme estiment que ce texte 'autorise' la peine capitale et déroge en quelque sorte à l'article 7 qui interdit les peines cruelles, inhumaines ou dégradantes. L'existence d'un protocole spécifique relatif à l'abolition de la peine de mort et qui se définit lui-même comme *facultatif*, conforte dans leur position les adeptes de cette thèse.

D'autres, dont fait partie l'auteur de ce texte, considèrent que l'article 6 du Pacte se borne à tenir compte d'une situation de fait existant dans certains Etats qui n'ont pas aboli la peine de mort pour édicter des garanties minimales. Le dernier alinéa renforce cette interprétation. Le second paragraphe commence par '*Dans les pays qui n'ont pas aboli la peine de mort* ... La formule négative du texte témoigne de l'exigence d'interprétation restrictive alors que le dernier alinéa traduit le but à atteindre: l'abolition.

Tenir compte d'une situation, c'est prendre en compte une réalité, ce n'est pas donner une autorisation, ce n'est pas non plus, selon nous, reconnaître que la peine de mort ne constitue pas en soi une violation du Pacte. Cela signifie simplement que le non respect des prescriptions des articles 6 §2, §4 et §1 constituent une violation du Pacte.

Le choix entre ces deux approches n'est pas sans conséquence. Ainsi en matière d'extradition vers un Etat qui maintient la peine capitale, la solution ne sera pas la même selon que l'Etat ait aboli ou non la peine de mort.

---

[2] Communication 845/1999 (*Kennedy* c. *Trinité-et-Tobago*), Constatations du 26 mars 2002, U.N. document A/57/40, vol. II, p.161.

[3] Communication 470/1991 (*Kindler* c. *Canada*), Constatations du 30 juillet 1993, U.N. document A/48/40, vol. II, p. 138 (Appendix, p.160).

Qu'en est-il de la *jurisprudence* du Comité des droits de l'homme?

II. APPROCHE DE LA PEINE CAPITALE DANS LA JURISPRUDENCE DU COMITE DES DROITS DE L'HOMME

a) au regard de l'extradition:

Dans le cas *Kindler*,[4] le Comité a adopté l'approche de l'autorisation' et a considéré qu'un Etat ayant aboli la peine de mort pouvait, sans violer l'article 6, extrader une personne vers un Etat qui n'a pas aboli la peine de mort et que la personne extradée encourait celle-ci ou même avait été condamnée à la peine capitale dès lors que les autres exigences de l'article 6 étaient respectées par l'Etat en cause (v.Kindler §14.3). Le Comité relève que M. Kindler a été condamné pour meurtre, crime grave au sens de l'article 6 §2 du Pacte. Il s'agit là d'une analyse qui ne tient pas compte du fait que l'article 6 §2 du Pacte ne concerne que les Etats parties n'ayant pas aboli la peine capitale, ce qui n'est pas le cas du Canada.

Cette affaire a fait l'objet de plusieurs opinions dissidentes.

M. Lallah pour sa part a considéré que le Canada, ayant aboli la peine de mort, n'était pas concerné par l'article 6, étant donné que le § 2 visait seulement les pays ne l'ayant pas abolie.

Notre avis est que le Comité a fait fausse route en consacrant de longs développements au respect par le Canada des garanties minimales requises par l'article 6 du Pacte au regard du prononcé et de l'exécution de la peine capitale. En effet, *dans la mesure* où, comme cela est précisé au dernier alinéa du texte, le but poursuivi par le Pacte est l'abolition, une interprétation extensive de l'article 6 aux Etats qui ont aboli la peine de mort les plaçant dans la *situation d'Etats qui ont* rétabli cette peine, constitue une erreur.

L'application distributive de l'article 6 effectué par le Canada, selon qu'il s'agit d'un ressortissant étranger ou d'un national constitue également selon nous et aux yeux des membres dissidents du Comité, une violation des articles 2 et 26 du Pacte.

Les opinions dissidentes ont eu une influence certaine sur les juges de la Cour suprême du Canada qui ont, depuis, effectué un revirement de jurisprudence dans ce domaine en 2001.

b) s'agissant de la *notion des crimes les plus graves,* notion peu précise permettant des interprétations différentes, il convient de noter que, lorsque le Comité examine les rapports périodiques des Etats, il note souvent que les crimes assimilables à des délits d'opinion ou les infractions autres que les crimes de sang ne sont pas considérés par lui comme entrant dans la catégorie des crimes les plus grâves. (Voir notamment Observation finale du Comité des droits de l'homme sur la Corée du Nord).

Dans le cas *Lubuto contre la Zambie*,[5] le Comité a constaté une violation de l'article 6 considérant qu'un crime qui n'avait pas été suivi de blessures ou de mort

---

[4] Communication 470/1991 (*Kindler* c. *Canada*), *ibid.*

[5] Communication 390/1990 (*Lubuto* c. *Zambie*), Constatations du 31 octobre 1995, U.N. document A/51/40, vol. II, p.11.

de la victime n'entrait pas dans la catégorie des crimes les plus graves. Cette décision est très discutable, comme l'a souligné M. Ando dans son opinion dissidente. En effet on ne peut prendre en compte le résultat pour évoluer la gravité d'un crime.

Une autre question à propos de la peine capitale et de la notion de 'crimes les plus graves' s'est posée à l'occasion de l'affaire *Thompson* c. *St. Vincent et les Grenadines*[6] qui mettait en cause le caractère *obligatoire du prononcé* de la peine dès lors qu'une infraction de meurtre était commise.

Le Comité dénonce le système d'imposition obligatoire de la peine de mort 'qui prive l'individu de son droit le plus fondamental, le droit à la vie sans considérer si cette forme exceptionnelle de châtiment est appliquée dans les circonstances particulières de l'affaire'.

Plusieurs membres du Comité ont contesté cette approche, considérant que le Pacte n'exige pas que les tribunaux disposent d'une forme d'appréciation et que la seule exigence du Pacte est que les crimes les plus graves, tels que définis par la loi, soient passible de la peine de mort.

Toutefois le Pacte évoque les crimes les plus graves sans énoncer ce qu'il faut entendre par cette notion. Or, c'est une notion subjective. A *Madagascar*, le vol d'un animal de ferme est considéré comme l'un des crimes les plus graves, tandis que, dans la plupart des pays européens, un vol sans violence n'est pas considéré comme tel.

En outre, le texte ne prévoit pas qui, de la loi ou du juge, détermine ce qu'il faut entendre par '*crimes les plus graves*'.

Les auteurs de l'opinion séparée ont, selon nous, *déplacé* le problème en plaçant le pouvoir d'appréciation au centre du débat.

Le Comité, dans sa majorité, a seulement considéré que la notion de 'crimes les plus graves' ne pouvait être définie par une sorte de *tarification légale*. L'étiquette 'meurtre' ne suffit pas à elle seule à faire entrer le crime dans la catégorie des crimes les plus graves au sens du Pacte; il faut d'abord que le crime ait été jugé comme tel.

c) Au regard de l'exigence du juge compétent et du respect des autres droits garantis par le Pacte tels que définis par l'article 6 § 2 du Pacte, le Comité témoigne d'une particulière exigence en ce qui concerne les garanties fixées par l'article 14.

Ainsi, à chaque fois que, dans une affaire où la peine de mort est prononcée ou encourue, une disposition de l'article 14 relative au procès équitable a été violée, le Comité considère qu'il y a une violation de l'article 6, conjointement avec une violation de l'article 14.

Les cas de ce genre sont très nombreux, car systématiques, et non contestés au sein du Comité.

En vertu son *règlement intérieur - règle 86* - le Comité peut demander à un Etat partie de prendre, à titre provisoire, une mesure de suspension, lorsque l'acte que cet

[6] Communication 806/1998 (*Thompson* c. *St. Vincent et les Grenadines*), Constatations du 18 octobre 2000, U.N. document A/56/40, vol. II, p. 93.

Etat se propose d'accomplir, est susceptible d'avoir des conséquences irréparables à l'égard de l'auteur de la communication.

Dans 95 % des cas, le Comité a été entendu. Malheureusement, à plusieurs reprises, en matière de peine capitale, l'Etat n'a pas respecté la décision du Comité et a procédé à l'exécution capitale.

Ainsi dans l'affaire *Piandiong et autres contre Philippines*, le Comité a dénoncé l'inobservation par l'Etat partie de la décision de suspendre l'exécution de la peine capitale et a rappelé que la règle 86 était une application de l'article 39 du Pacte et qu'elle était essentielle conformément au rôle confié au Comité en vertu du Protocole Facultatif.

Le non respect de cet article *sape* la protection des droits concernés par le Pacte assurée par le Protocole Facultatif.

e) En ce qui concerne la question du couloir de la mort, celle-ci a donné lieu à de nombreux débats et controverses au sein du Comité. La question s'est posée de savoir si une détention prolongée dans le couloir de la mort en attendant une exécution capitale constituait une violation de l'article 7 du Pacte, c'est-à-dire une torture ou un traitement cruel inhumain ou dégradant.

Le Comité a répondu par la négative à cette question dès 1989 v. *Pratt et Morgan* c. *Jamaïque*.[7]

L'approche du Comité est en opposition avec la position de la Cour Européenne des Droits de l'Homme dans l'affaire *Soering contre Royaume-Uni*.

En 1992 la même question s'est à nouveau présentée devant le Comité dans le cas *Barrett and Sutcliffe contre Jamaïque*.[8]

Le Comité n'a pas été suivi dans son approche par plusieurs juridictions nationales telles que la Cour Suprême du Zimbabwe dans le cas *Commission catholique pour la justice contre l'attorney général* de 1993 et la section judiciaire du Conseil privé à Londres dans le cas *Pratt contre l'attorney général de la Jamaïque* qui à limité à 5 ans la durée au-delà de laquelle une personne dans le couloir de la mort devient victime d'un traitement cruel inhumain ou dégradant.

Ebranlé par ces dernières décisions, le Comité, tout en maintenant sa jurisprudence, à atténué légèrement sa formule en précisant que l'article 7 n'était pas violé en soi par une détention prolongée dans le couloir de la mort, en dehors de circonstances exceptionnelle qui viendraient caractériser un traitement inhumain ou dégradant.[9]

Cette modification rédactionnelle n'a pas d'incidence sur la position du Comité dès lors que toute circonstance exceptionnelle, qui est dénoncée, constitue par elle-même une violation distincte du Pacte.

f) Au regard des méthodes d'exécution de la peine de mort:

---

[7] Communications 210/1986 et 225/1987 (*Pratt et Morgan* c. *Jamaïque*), Constatations du 6 avril 1989, U.N. document A/44/40, p.222.

[8] Communications 270/1988 et 271/1998 (*Barrett et Sutcliffe* c. *Jamaïque*), Constatations du 30 mars 1992, U.N. document A/47/40, p. 244.

[9] Communication 588/1994 (*Johnson* c. *Jamaïque*), Constatations du 22 mars 1996, U.N. document A/51/40, vol. II, p. 174.

Dans le cas *Ng*[10] c. *Canada*, le Comité a noté que toute méthode d'exécution de la peine capitale pouvait constituer un traitement cruel et inhumain. L'intéressé redoutait une extradition vers la Californie qui lui aurait fait encourir la peine de mort infligée par gaz asphyxiant.

Le Comité considérait que dans la mesure où le § 2 de l'article 6 du Pacte 'autorisait' la peine de mort, la peine de mort ne pouvait pas ne pas être imposée pour échapper à une violation de l'article 7 mais l'imposition devait faire le moins de dégâts physiques ou mentaux possible. Selon le Comité tel était le cas de l'exécution par gaz asphyxiant en Californie dès lors que la mort intervenait dans les dix minutes suivant la diffusion du gaz.

Cette décision, contestée par plusieurs membres dissidents du Comité, n'a pas manqué de provoquer de nombreux commentaires. Face à cette question, le Comité s'est heurté de plein fouet à la contradiction de son interprétation de 'l'autorisation' de la peine de mort selon le Pacte (article 6 § 2).

Existe-il une méthode permettant d'exécuter une personne sans douleur, physique ou mentale? Comment exécuter une personne humaine sans encourir les foudres de l'article 7 du Pacte?

La solution adoptée par le Comité dans le cas Ng ne résout pas cette question car elle n'apporte pas de réponse à la compatibilité de l'article 7 avec une interprétation littérale et isolée de l'article 6 § 2 qui ne serait rapprochée, ni du paragraphe premier ni du dernier paragraphe de ce même article 6.

EN CONCLUSION

Le Comité connaît en son sein, au regard de la peine capitale, des divergences qui ne se sont pas estompées au fil du temps. Les abolitionnistes ne manquent pas une occasion pour interpréter le Pacte aux fins de réduire au maximum les cas d'imposition de la peine capitale; tandis que ceux qui sont de sensibilité différente penchent pour une interprétation du Pacte qui repose sur la conception d'autorisation' étudiée plus haut et qui est ouverte par l'article 6 § 2 du Pacte aux Etats qui ont recours à la peine capitale. Néanmoins la communauté internationale évolue assez rapidement sur cette question.

Le mouvement initié aux Etats-Unis, avec les récentes interventions de deux juges de la Cour Suprême, notamment le juge O'Connor, fut très prometteur à cet égard, du moins jusqu'au 11 septembre 2001.

[10] Communication 469/1991 (*Ng* c. *Canada*), Constatations du 5 novembre 1993, U.N.document A/49/40, vol. II, p. 189.

Nous regrettons que le Comité ne se montre pas plus audacieux en prenant des initiatives dans ce sens, mais il faut conserver l'optimisme et suivre la méthode de Ghandi:

Au début on nous ignore

Ensuite on se moque de nous

Après on nous combat

et enfin nous gagnons

EL COMITE DE DERECHOS HUMANOS Y LA OBJECION DE CONCIENCIA AL SERVICIO MILITAR

Hipólito Solari-Yrigoyen[*]

I. PARTE GENERAL

Concepto y características

La objeción de conciencia es el derecho fundamental que tiene toda persona para no efectuar el servicio militar cuando es obligatorio si sus creencias no se lo permiten. Este derecho se basa en el libre ejercicio de la libertad de pensamiento, de conciencia, de religión o, en general, de las creencias de cada persona y no puede ser menoscabado con medidas coercitivas.

La naturaleza jurídica de la objeción de conciencia es la de ser un derecho humano fundamental y, como tal, integra el grupo de derechos que los seres humanos adquieren por el solo hecho de nacer y sin los cuales no pueden vivir con la dignidad que se identifica con su naturaleza, independientemente de la condición política, jurídica o internacional del país o territorio de cuya jurisdicción dependan. Estos derechos no son creados por las autoridades nacionales o por los organismos internacionales, son simplemente reconocidos por estos.

Desde el punto de vista de la cronología de su reconocimiento, la objeción de conciencia al servicio militar es uno de los nuevos derechos humanos, entendiendo por tales a los que se han ido incorporando con posterioridad a la aprobación de la Declaración Universal de 1948, basados en sus principios generales y en los de los Pactos posteriores, y que no están explícitamente reconocidos en estos instrumentos internacionales.

Este derecho es individual ya que su sujeto es una persona y no un grupo de personas, como pasa con los derechos que tienen una dimensión colectiva, como, por ejemplo, los derechos que protegen a la familia. El sujeto es la persona que está obligada en virtud de una ley a cumplir con el servicio militar. La persona tiene que ser física, ya que no puede atribuirse este derecho en ningún caso a personas jurídicas por tratarse de un derecho humano, y puede ser, por lo tanto, hombre o mujer, aunque en la práctica, salvo escasas excepciones, son los hombres los obligados a cumplir con el servicio militar. Este servicio es conocido también con el nombre de conscripción. Quien invoca la objeción de conciencia se llama objetor.

La objeción debe fundarse en la religión o en las creencias del objetor que le prohíben o le crean un problema de conciencia que le impide asumir la obligación del servicio impuesto por la ley. No es lo mismo religión que creencia. La creencia puede basarse en convicciones que tiene la persona, las que pueden no ser religiosas

[*] El autor es miembro del Comité de Derechos Humanos de las Naciones Unidas desde 1999 y fue vicepresidente del mismo.

y, en tal sentido, la objeción de conciencia puede ser invocada por un agnóstico. Hay religiones que proclaman la abstención militar y hay muchas otras que no crean tal oposición a sus fieles. Una persona puede profesar una religión que no está en pugna con el servicio militar obligatorio pero puede, no obstante, ser objetor por otras creencias no religiosas igualmente sólidas y auténticas.

Las convicciones profundas en favor del pacifismo y la no violencia se encuentran entre las razones filosóficas o morales que respaldan la objeción de conciencia al servicio militar. Pero existen otras razones válidas, como por ejemplo las convicciones constitucionales que impiden cumplir con el servicio militar en fuerzas armadas que han usado su poder para derrocar un gobierno constitucional legítimo e instaurar una dictadura de facto. Esta causa difícilmente podría ser invocada en el propio país, pero sí ante un tercero para obtener el asilo o el refugio. Otra razón para ejercer este derecho que fue reconocida por la Asamblea General de las Naciones Unidas en 1978 (Resolución 33/165), es la de negarse a integrar fuerzas militares o policiales que se empleasen para imponer el *apartheid*. Esta razón se refiere a la oportunidad o al motivo del empleo de la fuerza y no al rechazo de la misma. En todos los casos para invocar este derecho tiene que haber una razón de conciencia y no meras especulaciones de oportunismo o comodidad.

En cuanto al servicio que se puede objetar, de acuerdo al alcance del presente trabajo, tiene que tener el carácter de militar, es decir relativo a la milicia o a la guerra. La interpretación del servicio objetable está restringida a tal característica y no es susceptible de ampliarse a otros servicios de diferentes modalidades. En cambio puede decirse que, sin excepción alguna, comprende a todas las formas de servicio militar, cualquiera sea el arma en que se realice, sea de tierra, mar o aire e, incluso, alcanza al servicio en las fuerzas de seguridad o policiales en aquellos países que extienden a estas el servicio militar. Lo militar se opone al concepto civil.

El servicio militar tiene que ser obligatorio. No obstante, en los países en que el servicio militar es voluntario, puede darse el caso que la persona después de alistarse y de comprometer sus servicios por un lapso determinado, en el transcurso del mismo se convierta en objetor de conciencia. Debe tenerse en cuenta que en estos casos por el compromiso adquirido, el servicio militar también es obligatorio y el objetor estará en condiciones de ejercer su derecho basado en sus convicciones, sin perjuicio de las responsabilidades civiles que se hubieran pactado en forma voluntaria en el compromiso de incorporación por el posible abandono del servicio.

Los Estados que no admiten la objeción de conciencia al servicio militar aplican medidas coercitivas a los objetores, algunas veces muy severas, especialmente en tiempos de guerra. En estos casos no debieran ser los tribunales militares los encargados del juzgamiento de los objetores pues sus integrantes carecen de la formación necesaria para garantizar decisiones independientes y objetivas. Los Estados debieran eliminar las penas de prisión de sus legislaciones para los objetores que no cumplen con el servicio militar obligatorio. Cuando se impone la pena de prisión, las víctimas son presos de conciencia ya que el castigo aplicado es la consecuencia de sus creencias y convicciones profundas no respetadas por el Estado.

La lucha por la liberación de estos presos está comprendida en la causa universal por la vigencia de los derechos humanos.

La libertad de pensamiento, de conciencia y de religión que respalda la objeción de conciencia al servicio militar es uno de los derechos humanos que no puede ser objeto de suspensión alguna en las situaciones excepcionales que pongan en peligro la vida de una nación y que permiten la declaración de los estados de emergencia, conforme lo especificado en el artículo 4.2 del Pacto Internacional de Derechos Civiles y Políticos.

El servicio civil sustitutivo

Hay países que aceptan la objeción de conciencia sin necesidad de probarla. Basta en estos casos exponer con claridad y sin contradicciones los motivos por los que se invoca la objeción para que se la acepte, pero hay otros que exigen pruebas de que la convicción es seria y profunda. La manera de probarlo depende de los procedimientos que impone cada Estado. Sin embargo, dado la complejidad que demanda esta prueba, los Estados están obligados a facilitarla para no transformarla en una exigencia de cumplimiento casi imposible. La autoridad administrativa que toma la decisión de si se acepta o no el derecho invocado tiene que ser civil y no sujeta a la autoridad militar, para otorgar seguridades de un análisis justo. La imparcialidad de quienes toman la decisión debe ser absoluta. El objetor debe tener también la posibilidad de interponer un recurso judicial contra la decisión denegatoria. Hasta que no se haya agotado el procedimiento no se podrá incorporar al objetor al servicio militar.

El Estado que ha reconocido a una persona el carácter de objetor de conciencia puede no imponerle ninguna obligación adicional, pero la mayoría prescribe la obligación de cumplir con un servicio civil sustituto, llamado también servicio alternativo o servicio social. La designación de alternativo no es precisa porque el servicio civil no constituye una alternativa al servicio militar ya que no puede ser elegido libremente. Los que ejercen el derecho de la objeción de conciencia para no hacer el servicio militar, no pueden, en principio, oponerse a hacer un servicio civil cuando la ley del país así lo dispone. La excepción es cuando el servicio sustitutivo tiene un carácter punitivo hacia quien ha ejercido el derecho a la objeción de conciencia. El servicio civil no puede ser una simple alternativa a hacer un servicio militar sin armas o en funciones de no combatiente. Tiene que ser un servicio totalmente ajeno al ámbito militar y a sus características y al control de las autoridades militares. El servicio sustitutivo puede revestir muchas formas diferentes pero tiene que ser netamente civil y estar dirigido por autoridades civiles. Debe tratarse también de un servicio útil a la comunidad que se encuadre en el respeto a los derechos humanos.

El carácter punitivo del servicio puede residir en las tareas del mismo o en el plazo de la duración. Las tareas tienen que respetar la dignidad de la persona. Si consistieran en trabajos forzados o deshonrosos tendrían un carácter punitivo. La mayor extensión del servicio civil con respecto al militar por sí sola no implica un castigo al ejercicio de la objeción de conciencia pero puede ser una presunción sobre la intención punitiva del plazo mayor. En general, la duración de ambos servicios debería ser igual pero se puede justificar que el plazo del servicio civil exceda en algo al del militar si se basa en criterios razonables y objetivos, como puede ser, por ejemplo, la formación especial que debe tener quien lo presta, o la naturaleza del servicio sustitutivo. No solo en su duración ambos servicios deben estar equiparados, sino también en el tratamiento de otros aspectos, como la carga de trabajo y salarios. La equiparación debe hacerse entre el servicio militar y el servicio sustitutivo y no entre este y otras actividades civiles.

El carácter punitivo del servicio civil surge de su modalidad cualquiera sea la opinión o la calificación que haga el Estado Parte sobre el mismo. Cada caso debe ser estudiado en particular para comprender si tiene o no ese carácter. Si bien el artículo 26 del Pacto prohíbe toda discriminación, permite diferencias de trato que deben basarse en los criterios razonables y objetivos ya mencionados y que deben también ser analizadas siempre con carácter restrictivo.

El reconocimiento de los Estados a la objeción de conciencia al servicio militar puede hacerse a través de la ley o de la práctica. Quienes se oponen tanto al servicio militar como al civil sustitutivo se llaman 'objetores totales'. Ni el servicio militar ni el servicio civil, por tener un carácter obligatorio, pueden ser confundidos con la esclavitud, la servidumbre o los trabajos forzosos, los que con algunas excepciones taxativas han sido abolidos por estar en oposición a la esencia misma de la dignidad humana.

Fuentes internacionales

La Carta Internacional de Derechos Humanos está integrada por los tres instrumentos fundamentales de las Naciones Unidas en la materia: la Declaración Universal de Derechos Humanos, el Pacto Internacional de Derechos Civiles y Políticos y el Pacto Internacional de Derechos Económicos, Sociales y Culturales. La Carta contiene dos fuentes que respaldan el derecho a la objeción de conciencia al servicio militar obligatorio o compulsivo. La primera es la misma Declaración Universal y la segunda el Pacto Internacional de Derechos Civiles y Políticos. Ambos instrumentos reconocen el derecho a la libertad de pensamiento, de conciencia y de religión. La Declaración le dedica el artículo 18, norma que con ligeras variantes ha sido recogida por el primer párrafo del artículo 18 del Pacto citado.

El Pacto menciona expresamente a la objeción de conciencia al servicio militar en el artículo 8 que prohíbe la esclavitud y la trata de esclavos y establece también que nadie estará sometido a servidumbre y que nadie será constreñido a ejecutar un trabajo forzoso u obligatorio. Sobre este último punto aclara que la prohibición de trabajos forzosos no puede ser interpretada como que excluye las condenas penales de trabajos forzados impuestas por tribunales competentes y, asimismo, especifica cuatro casos que no quedan incluidos entre los trabajos forzosos prohibidos. Uno de ellos es el servicio militar.

El artículo 8 del Pacto señala que se excluye de la prohibición del trabajo forzoso al 'servicio de carácter militar y, en los países donde se admite la exención por razones de conciencia, el servicio nacional que deben prestar conforme a la ley quienes se opongan al servicio militar por razones de conciencia'. De este artículo surge entonces con claridad que ni el servicio militar ni el servicio civil, al que el Pacto menciona como 'servicio nacional', pueden considerarse trabajos forzosos, pero de su simple lectura se desprende que la norma no ha abordado la objeción de conciencia al servicio militar sino que solo se propuso sustraer a este servicio y al civil alternativo de los trabajos forzosos prohibidos. La conclusión que se puede sacar de este artículo es que no se puede invocar como eximente del servicio militar y de su sustituto el derecho a la libertad que garantiza a cada individuo el artículo 9 del Pacto.

Algunos pensaron sin razón que esta referencia específica a la objeción de conciencia al servicio militar que hace el artículo 8 del Pacto admitía la facultad de los Estados para reconocer o no la objeción de conciencia al servicio militar sin considerar que tal mención no abordaba el fondo del asunto y que, además, el artículo 8 no podía interferir con los deberes que surgen de otros artículos del Pacto, en particular del artículo 18 párrafo 1 que garantiza el derecho a la libertad de pensamiento, de conciencia y de religión.

Una de las características de los derechos humanos fundamentales es su interdependencia. 'Todos los derechos humanos son universales, indivisibles e interdependientes y están relacionados entre sí', afirma la Declaración y el Programa de Acción aprobados en 1993 en la Conferencia Mundial de Derechos Humanos de Viena. Por lo tanto, todos los derechos deben interpretarse globalmente, cada uno en armonía con los demás y de una manera justa y equitativa. En tal sentido la norma sobre la libertad de religión y creencias debe examinarse en forma conjunta con otros derechos. Por ejemplo, con el derecho a no ser objeto de discriminación que consagra la Declaración Universal en su artículo 2º y que legisla el Pacto de Derechos Civiles y Políticos en varias disposiciones, especialmente en los artículos 2 y 26. Estas normas contra la discriminación del Pacto avalan también el derecho a la objeción de conciencia al servicio militar como lo hacen igualmente otros artículos, como el 3, 4, 5, 14, 17, 19, 20, 22 y 27.

Así como la Declaración Universal y el Pacto Internacional de Derechos Civiles y Políticos consagran en el plano mundial el derecho a la libertad de pensamiento, de conciencia y de religión, en el que se basa el derecho a la objeción de conciencia al servicio militar, las declaraciones y convenciones regionales han hecho lo mismo para América, Europa y Africa. La Declaración Americana de Derechos y Deberes del Hombre, que precedió a la Universal, lo hace en el artículo III y la Convención Americana sobre Derechos Humanos en el artículo 12; en Europa la Convención para la Protección de los Derechos Humanos y de las Libertades Fundamentales, en el artículo 9, y la Carta Africana sobre Derechos Humanos y de los Pueblos, en el artículo 8.

La interpretación del Comité

El Pacto Internacional de Derechos Civiles y Políticos, en su Parte IV creó el Comité de Derechos Humanos, integrado por dieciocho personas, preferentemente juristas, de gran integridad moral y con reconocida competencia en materia de derechos humanos. Estas características de los miembros del Comité, unido a que los mismos son elegidos teniendo en cuenta una distribución geográfica equitativa y que son representantes de las diferentes formas de civilización y de los principales sistemas jurídicos del mundo, han permitido que el Comité sea quien interprete las normas del Pacto en sus Observaciones Generales, basándose en las facultades que le otorga el artículo 40.4 del Pacto. Es esta una función muy importante porque permite fijar el significado y el alcance de cada uno de los artículos de dicho instrumento internacional, lo que sirve para orientar a los Estados Partes en la aplicación del mismo.

El Comité dedicó la Observación General 22 al Derecho a la libertad de pensamiento, de conciencia y de religión al que hace referencia el artículo 18 del Pacto. En este documento se admitió que el derecho a la objeción de conciencia al servicio militar no está explícitamente mencionado, pero se afirmó que 'el Comité cree que ese derecho puede derivarse del artículo 18, en la medida en que la obligación de utilizar la fuerza mortífera puede entrar en grave conflicto con la libertad de conciencia y el derecho a manifestar y expresar creencias religiosas u otras creencias'. La Observación General citada expresa, además, que 'cuando este derecho se reconozca en la ley o en la práctica no habrá diferenciación entre los objetores de conciencia sobre la base del carácter de sus creencias particulares, del mismo modo (que) no habrá discriminación contra los objetores de conciencia porque no hayan realizado el servicio militar'.

Esta interpretación, aprobada en 1993, significó un paso decisivo en el reconocimiento práctico del derecho, aunque la redacción potencial, y hasta podría decirse algo débil, al afirmar que 'el Comité cree que puede derivarse del artículo 18', no ha sido la más acertada y merecería ser corregida en una futura Observación General que se dedique al tema. El Comité debió afirmar con seguridad que la objeción de conciencia al servicio militar está comprendida en la norma del artículo 18 del Pacto que ampara la libertad de pensamiento, de conciencia y de religión, derecho que incluye la libertad de tener o de adoptar tanto la religión como las creencias de su elección.

Pese a la observación expresada, el Comité interpretó correctamente el artículo 18.1 del Pacto admitiendo como derecho humano fundamental la objeción de conciencia al servicio militar obligatorio. En el introito de la Observación General 22 se afirma que el derecho a la libertad de pensamiento, de conciencia y de religión 'es profundo y de largo alcance' y que 'la libertad de pensamiento y la libertad de conciencia se protegen de igual modo que la libertad de religión y de creencias'.

También debe destacarse el párrafo dedicado a garantizar la no discriminación entre los objetores de conciencia sobre la base de sus creencias particulares y la de los objetores que no hayan realizado el servicio militar. El Comité ha señalado, en la Observación General 18 dedicada a la no discriminación, que el término 'discriminación', tal como se emplea en el Pacto debe entenderse referido a toda distinción, exclusión, restricción o preferencia que se base en determinados motivos, como la religión o las opiniones del objetor en el caso que nos ocupa.

Reconocimiento de las Naciones Unidas

El Pacto Internacional de Derechos Civiles y Políticos con su mención a la objeción de conciencia en el artículo 8 reflejó el reconocimiento de la existencia del tema en el ámbito de las Naciones Unidas. Debe recordarse que el Pacto fue aprobado en 1966 y que entró en vigor el 23 de marzo de 1976. La Comisión de Derechos Humanos ya en 1971 había pedido al Secretario General que pusiera a su disposición la información existente sobre la objeción al servicio militar por razones de conciencia (Resolución 11 B-XXVII). La Asamblea General, en 1978 aprobó la resolución ya mencionada 33/165 relativa al ejercicio del derecho en caso de *apartheid* y en 1981 la Comisión solicitó a la Subcomisión de Prevención de Discriminaciones y Protección de Minorías que estudiara la cuestión de la objeción de conciencia al servicio militar.

Esta subcomisión aprobó una resolución ese mismo año para seguir examinando la cuestión y encargó a dos de sus miembros, los señores Asbjorn Eide y Chama Mubanga-Chipoya, que hicieran un análisis de los distintos aspectos de la objeción de conciencia al servicio militar y de sus interrelaciones con la promoción y la protección de los derechos humanos (Resolución 14-XXXIV). Una vez redactado el informe definitivo de estos autores, el Consejo Económico y Social decidió en 1984 imprimir y distribuir el mismo (E/RES/1984/27) La obra se editó en 1985 y fue entregada para recibir comentarios entre los gobiernos, organizaciones y agencias especializadas de las Naciones Unidas, organizaciones intergubernamentales y no gubernamentales. El ECOSOC pidió también en la resolución citada a la Comisión de Derechos Humanos el estudio del informe y de sus recomendaciones, como así también de los comentarios recogidos al respecto por el Secretario General.

La Comisión de Derechos Humanos ha contribuido con su acción a profundizar el debate sobre la objeción de conciencia al servicio militar y al reconocimiento del derecho. En una decisión (Resolución 34/2000) exhortó a todos los Estados a que 'reconsideren su legislación y sus prácticas actuales en relación con la objeción de conciencia al servicio militar a la luz de la resolución 77/1998', del 22 de abril de 1998. En esta resolución la Comisión, siguiendo lo resuelto en decisiones anteriores tomadas a partir de 1987 (Resolución 46/1987), reconoce el derecho de toda persona a la objeción de conciencia al servicio militar como forma legítima de ejercer el derecho a la libertad de pensamiento de conciencia y de religión, según lo establecido por la Declaración Universal de Derechos Humanos, por el artículo 18 del Pacto Internacional de Derechos Civiles y Políticos y por el Comentario General 22 aprobado por el Comité de Derechos Humanos en su 48 período de sesiones, en 1993.

La UNESCO en 1980 convocó al Congreso Mundial de Educación para el Desarme, en el que se aprobó un documento final que en uno de sus párrafos recomendó que en los programas de educación relativos al desarme se prestara debida atención al derecho a la objeción de conciencia y al derecho a negarse a matar. Las ONG, tanto las de derechos humanos, como las que luchan por este derecho específico, tuvieron una participación activa y valiosa en el debate que precedió al reconocimiento de la objeción de conciencia al servicio militar, como la tienen ahora resguardando el ejercicio de este derecho. Debe señalarse que en los últimos años se ha editado en varias lenguas una valiosa bibliografía dedicada al tema.

Los análisis del Comité

El Comité de Derechos Humanos trata la Objeción de Conciencia al Servicio Militar en ocasión de dos de sus funciones específicas. En primer lugar, cuando analiza los informes presentados por los Estados Partes del Pacto, conforme al artículo 40 del mismo. En esta instancia en algunas ocasiones interroga en su lista de cuestiones presentadas por anticipado al Estado sobre la aplicación y el respeto de los derechos garantizados en el mismo, sobre si se admite o no la objeción de conciencia al servicio militar y, si ello no ocurre, suele emitir una recomendación para su cumplimiento en las Observaciones Finales a cada informe.

La jurisprudencia reclamando a los Estados Partes el respeto a la objeción de conciencia al servicio militar en las Observaciones Finales es numerosa. A título de ejemplo se pueden citar dos casos de interés. En el primero, en las Observaciones Finales del Comité sobre el tercer informe de Venezuela, estudiado en marzo del 2001, se dice en el punto 26: 'El Comité toma nota de que la ley venezolana no contempla la condición de objetor de conciencia al servicio militar, en el legítimo ejercicio del artículo 18 del Pacto. El Estado Parte debe asegurar que las personas obligadas al servicio militar pueden invocar la eximente de objeción de conciencia y beneficiarse de un servicio sustitutivo no discriminatorio'.

El segundo caso fue el de Ucrania, cuyo informe se estudió en octubre de 2001. Este país admitió reconocer sólo la objeción de conciencia por razones religiosas y limitada a una lista autorizada de credos. En sus Observaciones Finales el Comité señaló que el Estado Parte debía incorporar la objeción de conciencia en la ley, aplicándola sin discriminación a todas las creencias religiosas y a otras convicciones y que, asimismo, debía velar porque el servicio alternativo de los objetores de conciencia se realizase en forma no discriminatoria. Esta última referencia al servicio sustitutivo se refiere a su duración.

Debe admitirse, sin embargo, que el Comité no siempre incluye en su lista de cuestiones escritas preguntas sobre el respeto al derecho a la objeción de conciencia. Sería conveniente que el Comité no siguiera un camino errático en este aspecto y que a los países que tienen el servicio militar obligatorio se les interrogase, en todo los casos, sobre el respeto al derecho a la objeción de conciencia. Cuando el Comité no lo hace puede algún miembro preguntarlo en forma oral a título particular, lo que generalmente ocurre.

En segundo lugar, el Comité aborda la objeción de conciencia cuando se le presentan comunicaciones sobre el tema conforme al Protocolo Facultativo del Pacto Internacional de Derechos Civiles y Políticos. La opinión del Comité en este sentido ha seguido una evolución favorable. En su seno ha habido múltiples debates, que han ido desde la negación del derecho hasta llegar al reconocimiento oficial en la Observación General 22 ya citada. Tal reconocimiento, sin embargo, no agotó la discusión ni logró un consenso sobre el alcance de la aplicación del derecho en el análisis de las comunicaciones. En tal sentido puede decirse, conforme se desprende de los fundamentos de los votos, que en el Comité existen dos corrientes. La primera se inclina por la admisión del derecho del objetor en forma amplia y tiene, en consecuencia, un criterio más restrictivo para analizar las diferencias de trato que puede establecer el servicio sustitutivo. La segunda corriente es más restrictiva para reconocer el carácter de objetor y al mismo tiempo es más permisiva para analizar si las diferencias de trato del servicio civil pueden llegar a ser discriminatorias.

La objeción de conciencia al servicio militar pretende ser extendida por algunos al derecho a negarse a pagar impuestos que se destinen a gastos militares. Sostienen que si se puede ser objetor para no participar en matanzas también se debería reconocer que no se debe pagar para que sean otros los que maten. No desconocen el derecho del Estado a imponer tributos sino a que los mismos se dediquen a la guerra o a su preparación. Reclaman, entonces, el reconocimiento al derecho de objeción de conciencia a los impuestos militares como una legítima expresión o manifestación de la libertad de pensamiento, conciencia y religión. Esta posición no ha sido aceptada por el Comité de Derechos Humanos. 'El rechazo del pago de impuestos por razones de conciencia claramente no corresponde al ámbito de protección del artículo 18 del Pacto', ha afirmado el Comité en el caso 'K.V. y C.V. c/ Alemania' (Comunicación 568/1993), como lo hizo en otras comunicaciones anteriores presentadas sobre este tema, todas las cuales fueron declaradas inadmisibles.

En la segunda parte del presente trabajo se hará un análisis crítico de algunas de las comunicaciones vinculadas al tema de la Objeción de Conciencia al Servicio Militar resueltas por el Comité de Derechos Humanos en los últimos años, antes y después de que el mismo aprobase la Observación General 22 sobre la libertad de pensamiento, de conciencia y de religión, derecho que incluye la libertad de tener o de adoptar la religión o las creencias que cada persona elija, así como la libertad de manifestarlas sin ser objeto de medidas coercitivas.

II. JURISPRUDENCIA DEL COMITÉ: ANÁLISIS CRÍTICO

L.T.K. c/Finlandia. Comunicación 185/ 1984

El autor se consideró víctima de la violación de los artículos 18 y 19 del Pacto Internacional de Derechos Civiles y Políticos por cuánto el gobierno de su país, Finlandia, no había reconocido su objeción de conciencia al servicio militar, con armas o sin armas, fundada en sus creencias pacifistas. En lugar del servicio militar, con armas o sin ellas, el autor ofreció cumplir un servicio de otro tipo. La Junta Examinadora del Servicio Militar consideró que no había probado sus convicciones. El autor interpuso una apelación ante el ministerio de Justicia el cuál le ordenó que cumpliera un servicio militar sin armas, pero él se negó a cumplir ningún tipo de servicio militar. A raíz de ello se le inició un proceso judicial y se lo condenó a nueve meses de prisión. La apelación confirmó la resolución anterior.

El Comité observó que al autor no se lo procesó ni condenó a causa de sus creencias u opiniones sino porque se negó a cumplir su servicio militar. El Pacto, agregó la decisión, no se pronuncia respecto del derecho a objetar por razones de conciencia y tampoco puede considerarse que ese derecho esté establecido en el artículo 18 ni en el artículo 19, sobre todo si se tiene en cuenta lo dicho en el artículo 8.3 (inciso ii del apartado c). En consecuencia el Comité decidió que la queja era incompatible con las disposiciones del Pacto.

Crítica: Es cierto como lo afirma el Comité que al autor se lo condenó por negarse a cumplir con el servicio militar, pero no se puede omitir en el análisis que esta actitud se debió a sus creencias pacifistas y a su carácter de objetor de conciencia. La decisión del Comité fue errónea al pretender desvincular estos dos hechos y tratarlos en forma independiente cuando el primero –la negativa- fue la consecuencia del segundo, es decir, de sus creencias.

La decisión del Comité negando el derecho a la objeción de conciencia al servicio militar, alegando que el Pacto no se pronuncia sobre tal derecho y afirmando que no puede considerarse que el derecho a la objeción esté establecido en el artículo 18 del mismo, fue francamente desafortunada. El Comité se pronunció de tal manera por la negativa del derecho humano a la objeción de conciencia. Tal decisión fue desautorizada por el mismo Comité al aprobar su Observación General 22.

JÄRVINEN Aapo c/ Finlandia. Comunicación 295/ 1988

El autor de la comunicación, ciudadano finlandés, consideró que en su caso se había violado el artículo 26 del Pacto por cuanto el servicio militar tenía una duración de 8 meses y el servicio civil por el que él optó duplicaba esa duración. Hasta fines de 1986 el servicio civil era de 12 meses, pero el interesado debía probar sus convicciones religiosas o éticas que lo convertían en objetor ante una junta examinadora especial. En la fecha indicada se cambió la legislación teniéndose por probada la objeción de conciencia con la propia declaración del interesado, pero se extendió a l6 meses la duración del servicio, lo que el autor consideró un elemento punitivo. Si bien el autor manifestó su objeción antes de la reforma legal, la misma no fue considerada y debió reiterar su declaración con la vigencia de la reforma.

Debe tenerse en cuenta también que el Comité resolvió esta comunicación con anterioridad a la aprobación de su Observación General 22. El Comité en forma correcta decidió en su resolución que si bien el Pacto no establece expresamente la objeción de conciencia, lo mismo debe analizarse si ha habido una discriminación, ya que el artículo 26 no solo prohíbe la discriminación de los derechos garantizados en el Pacto. El artículo 26 'declara que todas las personas son iguales ante la ley y tienen derecho sin discriminación a igual protección de la ley'. Sin embargo, el Comité señaló que la extensión del plazo del servicio sustitutivo se basaba en criterios razonables y objetivos ya que tendían a facilitar la administración de este último servicio y que la reforma legal no tenía ningún propósito discriminatorio. La decisión contó con el voto en disidencia de tres miembros que entendieron que la diferencia de trato no se basaba en criterios razonables y objetivos y era discriminatoria.

Crítica: En materia de discriminación más que el propósito del legislador deben tenerse en cuenta los efectos de la ley y esta, al duplicar el tiempo del servicio militar, tiene un efecto punitivo ya que castiga a los objetores de conciencia al servicio militar con un servicio de doble duración, lo que resulta irrazonable y viola, por lo tanto, el artículo 26 al discriminar a los objetores en forma inequívoca con respecto a la duración del servicio militar. Esta circunstancia conduce a alentar a que los objetores dejen de lado sus creencias o, en caso contrario, a sufrir las consecuencias de la duplicación del plazo del servicio alternativo.

El Estado Parte no ha demostrado que la diferencia de trato, en este caso la duplicación del tiempo del servicio sustitutivo, se deba a criterios razonables y objetivos. Es cierto que la reforma estableció que bastaba la declaración del interesado para tener en cuenta la objeción, lo que allanó las dificultades que tenía el trámite anterior tanto para el Estado Parte como para el objetor. Pero la forma del reconocimiento de la objeción no tiene una relación directa con las condiciones que se imponen al servicio civil. El argumento del Comité de encontrar razonable y objetiva la duplicación del servicio no ha sido fundado debidamente y tampoco es correcto que al estudiarse la diferencia de trato, en lugar de hacerlo en forma restrictiva, se lo haya hecho con enorme amplitud.

H.A.E. de J. c / Países Bajos. Comunicación 297/1988

El autor de esta comunicación, que había sido reconocido como objetor de conciencia y que cumplía un servicio civil sustitutivo, consideró que había sido discriminado por los Países Bajos por haber recibido un pago de la ley de Asistencia General de un diez por ciento menos del nivel mínimo de subsistencia aplicable en todo el país a las personas de 23 años o más que tenían a su cargo el sustento del hogar. Al estar el autor en esas condiciones había solicitado un subsidio suplementario que le fue denegado. La discriminación invocada por el autor no era entre los objetores de conciencia y los que hacían el servicio militar, sino entre los objetores que cumplían un servicio civil frente a otros civiles. El Estado Parte señaló que las normas que se le aplicaron al autor no eran distintas a las que regían para todos los objetores de conciencia y que no era procedente comparar su situación con las que contempla la ley de Asistencia General.

El Comité consideró que ni en el caso del servicio militar ni en el del servicio sustitutivo existe el derecho a una remuneración como la que percibiría un civil y que no existe prueba alguna de que la ley de Asistencia General no se aplique de manera igual a todos los que cumplen con el servicio sustitutivo, motivo por el cuál declaró la comunicación inadmisible.

Crítica: La decisión del Comité fue correcta. El presente caso tiene una importancia secundaria para nuestro estudio pues en él no se planteó el desconocimiento de la objeción de conciencia que le había sido reconocida expresamente al autor. Tampoco se alegó que existiera una discriminación entre el servicio sustitutivo que cumplía el autor con respecto al servicio militar, ya que en ambos el trato era igual. Si bien la remuneración no es un derecho, los objetores de conciencia y los conscriptos no eran discriminados porque ambos percibían la misma remuneración. Esta comunicación también fue anterior a la Observación General 22.

BRINKHOF Enricus Antonius Godefredus c/ Países Bajos. Comunicación 402/1990

El autor de la comunicación, al presentarse a la convocatoria para cumplir con el servicio militar declaró, en virtud de sus creencias pacifistas, que se oponía al servicio militar y al servicio público sustitutivo, negándose a obedecer las órdenes de que aceptase un uniforme y equipo militar. Fue condenado por el Tribunal Militar de Arnhem a seis meses de prisión y a la expulsión del servicio militar. El Tribunal Militar Supremo, en la apelación, elevó la pena a 12 meses y mantuvo la expulsión como culpable de violar el Código de Justicia Militar. El interesado interpretó que este código no se le podía aplicar por ser objetor de conciencia. El Tribunal Supremo sostuvo que el Código de Justicia Militar no hace distingos entre objeciones al servicio militar y otras objeciones y que, por lo tanto, le era aplicable.

El autor alegó que se ha violado el artículo 26 del Pacto, que prohíbe la discriminación, porque se puede procesar a los objetores de conciencia pero no se puede hacerlo con los Testigos de Jehová, que se encuentran exentos del servicio militar en virtud de una ley dictada en 1974. El Comité rechazó algunas de las alegaciones del autor pero decidió pronunciarse sobre si existían diferencias de trato entre los Testigos de Jehová y los objetores de conciencia al servicio militar y al servicio civil sustitutivo. El Estado Parte admitió las diferencias pero señaló que ellas se basaban en criterios objetivos y razonables, mientras que el autor insistió en su carácter discriminatorio.

El Comité consideró que la exención a un sólo grupo de objetores de conciencia sin aplicarla a todos los demás no se puede considerar razonable y que la Observación General sobre el artículo 18 señala que, cuando un Estado Parte reconoce el derecho a la objeción de conciencia al servicio militar, no puede establecer diferencias entre unos objetores de conciencia y otros, sobre la base de la naturaleza de sus creencias particulares. Sin embargo, el Comité entendió que el autor no había demostrado que sus convicciones como pacifista eran incompatibles con el sistema de servicio sustitutivo de los Países Bajos ni que el trato privilegiado concedido a los Testigos de Jehová afectase negativamente a sus derechos como objetor. Por consiguiente, el Comité no lo consideró víctima de discriminación. No obstante, aconsejó al Estado Parte que debería dar el mismo trato a todas las personas que tengan objeciones firmes contra el servicio militar y le recomendó que examinase las disposiciones aplicables para eliminar cualquier matiz de discriminación.

Crítica: La decisión del Comité fue acertada en cuanto al fondo del asunto al no admitir discriminaciones entre los diferentes grupos de objetores y también lo fue en cuanto señaló que el autor no demostró que sus convicciones pacifistas le impedían hacer el servicio civil alternativo. No ha acertado, sin embargo, al decidir que el trato diferente otorgado a los Testigos de Jehová no ha afectado al autor de la comunicación como objetor de conciencia al servicio militar. La condena a prisión y la pena impuesta al mismo contradicen este argumento. En igual sentido la última recomendación que se dirige al Estado Parte para evitar discriminaciones entre los objetores al servicio militar no se compagina con la decisión de no haber considerado al autor como víctima de la violación del artículo 26 del Pacto.

En la Observación General 18 que se refiere a la no discriminación el Comité ha considerado que el término 'discriminación', tal como se emplea en el Pacto, debe entenderse como toda distinción, exclusión, restricción o preferencia que se base en determinados motivos, entre los que figuran la religión y las opiniones políticas o de otra índole. La distinción que hace la legislación de los Países Bajos a favor de una religión para el reconocimiento de la objeción de conciencia al servicio militar constituye una discriminación y el autor de la presente comunicación ha sido, una víctima de la misma.

WESTERMAN Paul c/ Países Bajos. Comunicación 682/1996.

El autor de la comunicación alega haber sido víctima de la violación de los derechos 15 y 18 del Pacto, al haberse rechazado su solicitud de ser reconocido como objetor de conciencia al servicio militar y al haber sido condenado por el Tribunal del Distrito de Arnhem, en virtud de las normas del Código Penal Militar, a nueve meses de prisión por haberse negado a realizar tal servicio, pena que fue luego confirmada por el Tribunal Supremo y ejecutada.

El Comité desestimó la violación del artículo 15 del Pacto por cuanto la pena impuesta fue menor a la que habría correspondido con la legislación anterior a la que se aplicó. Esta decisión fue unánime, aunque con fundamentos diferentes a los de la decisión tomada, dados por uno de los miembros.

Finalmente el Comité determinó que la cuestión a decidir consistía en determinar si la sanción para hacer cumplir el servicio militar violó el derecho a la libertad de conciencia del autor. Conforme a lo expuesto, en un fallo dividido, el Comité resolvió que no habiendo convencido el autor a las autoridades del Estado Parte de que su objeción de conciencia al servicio militar a causa de la utilización de medios violentos tenía un carácter insalvable, concluyó que no hubo violación de ninguno de los artículos del Pacto. Siete miembros del Comité aprobaron esta decisión y seis se pronunciaron por la violación del artículo 18, cinco de ellos con iguales fundamentos y el sexto con los propios.

Crítica: La decisión recaída en esta comunicación, definida por un voto de diferencia, refleja la interpretación más restrictiva tomada por el Comité sobre el alcance de la institución de la objeción de conciencia al servicio militar. Los fundamentos dados en los votos minoritarios avalan las críticas que se hicieron a la decisión de la mayoría que rechazó la objeción consagrada por el artículo 18 del Pacto basándose en que se habían cumplido las normas del derecho interno del Estado. El voto de los cinco miembros disidentes que lo hicieron en conjunto entiende que la objeción del autor constituyó una legítima manifestación de su libertad de pensamiento, de conciencia o de religión, conforme al artículo 18 del Pacto y que los argumentos del Estado Parte para justificar su denegación pueden bastar sólo para explicar la negativa con arreglo al derecho interno pero no para justificar su decisión de menoscabar la condición de objetor de conciencia y la imposición de una pena de prisión al autor.

Por su parte el voto disidente restante insiste en que la reiterada negativa del Estado Parte a admitir la objeción invocada por el autor se basa en el reconocimiento limitado que el mismo otorga en su legislación a la objeción de conciencia al servicio militar, y que la pena que se le impuso es la consecuencia directa del rechazo de la objeción basado en dicha legislación que está en contradicción con el Pacto. Aunque los métodos violentos invocados por el autor no se empleen en tiempos de paz, no se puede negar que el servicio militar, incluso en tiempos de paz, está relacionado con la guerra. Por lo tanto, se ha violado el artículo 18 del Pacto Internacional de Derechos Civiles y Políticos que ampara la objeción de conciencia como una manifestación inequívoca de la libertad de pensamiento, de conciencia y de religión.

FOIN Frédéric c/ Francia. Comunicación 666/1995.

El autor, al que se le había reconocido la condición de objetor de conciencia, hizo el servicio civil correspondiente hasta cumplir un año y después abandonó el mismo por considerar discriminatoria la legislación que asignaba dos años para este servicio en lugar de un año para el militar. Fue acusado de desertor y un tribunal Correccional de Marsella lo condenó a ocho meses de prisión y ordenó quitarle la condición de objetor. La apelación bajó la condena a seis meses en suspenso. El Tribunal de Casación confirmó el fallo. Frente a la denuncia del autor ante el Comité por sentirse discriminado, el Estado Parte señaló que el doble plazo del servicio civil servía para comprobar la seriedad de las objeciones de una persona.

El Comité resolvió que la cuestión a resolver consistía en decidir si las condiciones concretas en que el autor debió cumplir su servicio sustitutivo violaban el Pacto. Si bien el Comité reiteró que el artículo 26 no prohíbe las diferencias de trato, recordó que esas diferencias debían basarse en criterios razonables y objetivos. A juicio del Comité el criterio del Estado Parte de que la duplicación de la duración del servicio es la única forma de poner a prueba la sinceridad de las convicciones del individuo, no tiene las características señaladas. Por lo tanto, se ha violado el artículo 26 por cuanto el autor ha sido objeto de discriminación en razón de su convicción de conciencia.

Tres miembros del Comité votaron en disidencia por entender que un Estado debe establecer mecanismos para poder distinguir a los objetores de conciencia de los que desean evitar el servicio militar por otros motivos inaceptables. Consideraron estos miembros que establecer un órgano de decisión crea muchos problemas porque el mismo podría llegar a intervenir en la vida privada y en la conciencia de la persona. Por el contrario, la exigencia de un servicio algo más prolongado sería un mecanismo razonable para evitar que se invoquen falsamente motivos de conciencia.

Crítica: La decisión del Comité ha sido correcta. La exigencia de un plazo más largo para el servicio civil con respecto al militar, sólo puede aceptarse si se basa en criterios razonables y objetivos y estos deben ser analizados con sentido restrictivo, porque de lo contrario se incursionaría en el campo de la discriminación. En el presente caso el argumento dado por el Estado Parte no se ajusta a dichas condiciones. La duplicación sin fundamento tiene un carácter punitivo.

En cuánto al voto en disidencia debe señalarse que es válido el argumento de que el tener que decidir si existen o no los fundamentos de la objeción de conciencia que invoca el objetor no es tarea fácil. Precisamente es por eso que muchos Estados han concluido por aceptar la declaración del interesado sin obligarle a probarla. Pero ello no justifica que un plazo más largo sea la solución porque esta alternativa estaría lesionando el principio de la igualdad ante la ley y el derecho a no ser discriminado y a obtener la igual protección de la ley. En el presente caso no parece justo hablar de un servicio 'algo más prolongado', como lo hacen los votos disidentes, cuando se trata de una duplicación del tiempo del servicio.

El Estado Parte informó al Comité que en octubre de 1997 aprobó una ley de reforma del servicio nacional, en virtud de la cuál todos los varones y mujeres serían llamados entre los 16 y 18 años a participar de una jornada para la defensa y que podría prestarse un servicio voluntario facultativo de 12 meses renovables hasta 60 meses. El Comité tomó nota con satisfacción de dicha reforma legislativa que evitará que puedan producirse violaciones análogas en el futuro El Comité consideró que la comprobación de la violación constituía una reparación suficiente para el autor.

VENIER Marc y NICOLAS Paul c/ Francia. Comunicaciones 690/1996 y 691/1996

Los autores, a los que se les había reconocido la condición de objetores de conciencia, hicieron el servicio civil hasta cumplir aproximadamente un año y después notificaron a las autoridades que hacían abandono del mismo, por considerar discriminatoria la legislación que asignaba dos años para este servicio en lugar de un año para el militar. Ambos fueron acusados de desertores en tiempos de paz y a uno de ellos, Paul Nicolas, un Tribunal Correccional de París lo condenó a un año de prisión, mientras que el Tribunal Correccional de Orleans condenó a Venier a diez meses de prisión. El Tribunal de Apelación de París redujo la pena de Nicolas a dos meses de prisión en libertad condicional, mientras que el Tribunal de Apelación de Orleans redujo la condena de Venier a ocho meses de prisión, seis de los cuales en libertad condicional. El Tribunal de Casación confirmó ambos fallos.

Frente a la denuncia de los autores ante el Comité por sentirse discriminados el Estado Parte señaló que el doble plazo del servicio civil servía para comprobar la seriedad de las objeciones, tal como lo había hecho en la comunicación de Frédéric Foin c/ Francia, examinada con anterioridad. Entre los argumentos esgrimidos por el Estado Parte para oponerse a la denuncia de los autores se indica que la situación de quienes prestan un servicio civil sustitutivo y la de los que prestan el servicio militar es diferente, sobre todo en lo que se refiere a las condiciones más duras de servir en el ejército.

El Comité resolvió que la cuestión a resolver consistía en decidir si las condiciones concretas en que los autores debieron prestar un servicio sustitutivo violaban el Pacto. Si bien el Comité reiteró que el artículo 26 no prohíbe las diferencias de trato, recordó que esas diferencias debían basarse en criterios razonables y objetivos. Y que las razones aducidas por el Estado Parte no mencionan ningún criterio de este tipo, o sólo mencionan criterios generales sin referirse concretamente a los casos de los autores. A juicio del Comité el criterio del Estado Parte de que la duplicación de la duración del servicio es la única forma de poner a prueba la sinceridad de las convicciones del individuo, no tiene las características señaladas. Por lo tanto se ha violado el artículo 26 por cuanto los autores han sido objeto de discriminación en razón de sus convicciones de conciencia.

Cuatro miembros del Comité votaron en disidencia remitiéndose a las razones dadas en Foin c/Francia.

Crítica: La decisión del Comité ha sido correcta. La exigencia de un plazo más largo para el servicio civil con respecto al militar, sólo puede aceptarse si se basa en criterios razonables y objetivos y estos deben ser analizados con sentido restrictivo, porque, de lo contrario, se incursionaría en el campo de la discriminación. En el presente caso el argumento dado por el Estado Parte no se ajusta a dichas condiciones. La duplicación sin fundamento tiene un carácter punitivo. Ha acertado también el Comité al rechazar, como lo hizo en la comunicación Foin c/Francia, las razones del Estado Parte que sólo mencionan criterios generales sin referirse concretamente al caso de los autores, como es señalar que la situación de quienes prestan un servicio civil sustitutivo y la de los que prestan el servicio militar es diferente sobre todo en lo que se refiere a las condiciones más duras de servir en el ejército. Esta es sólo una presunción que puede ser cierta o no según los casos que se examinen y que en la materia que nos ocupa no constituye un argumento razonable para justificar la ampliación del plazo de duración del servicio civil. La objeción de conciencia al servicio militar en razón de las creencias del objetor es extraña a las características de mayor o menor rigor que pueda tener uno u otro servicio.

En esta comunicación también el Estado Parte informó sobre la reforma legislativa y el Comité tomó nota con satisfacción de la misma y consideró que la comprobación de la violación constituía reparación suficiente para el autor.

MAILLE Richard c/ Francia. Comunicación 689/1996

Este caso es similar a las dos comunicaciones anteriores seguidas contra Francia que se acaban de examinar. El autor, al que se le había reconocido la condición de objetor de conciencia, hizo el servicio civil correspondiente hasta cumplir un año y después abandonó el mismo, por considerar discriminatoria la legislación que asignaba dos años para este servicio en lugar de un año para el militar. Fue acusado de insubordinación en tiempo de paz y el Tribunal Correccional de Montpellier lo condenó a 15 días de prisión y le exigió que reanudara su servicio, lo que no hizo el autor. En consecuencia el mismo Tribunal lo condenó, fallo que fue confirmado en el Tribunal de Apelación. No interpuso recurso de Casación, atento que ya habían sido rechazados recursos similares.

Frente a la denuncia del autor ante el Comité por sentirse discriminado, el Estado Parte señaló que el doble plazo del servicio civil servía para comprobar la seriedad de las objeciones de una persona. Como en los casos anteriores el Comité rechazó este argumento por no basarse en criterios razonables y objetivos y consideró que se había violado el artículo 26 por cuanto el autor había sido objeto de discriminación en razón de su convicción de conciencia.

Crítica: El mérito de esta decisión, similar a las dos anteriores que se han analizado es haber afianzado una jurisprudencia que, además de admitir la objeción de conciencia, ha rechazado el argumento del Estado Parte para duplicar el tiempo del Servicio Civil basándose en criterios que no son razonables y objetivos.

III. EPILOGO

Pese a tratarse de un derecho humano fundamental, la Objeción de Conciencia al Servicio Militar, no ha sido universalmente aceptada. Muchos Estados Partes niegan este derecho y otros lo aceptan con carácter restrictivo. No obstante, se debe reconocer que en los últimos años muchos países han suprimido el servicio militar obligatorio y, en consecuencia, la negación del derecho se ha restringido. De todas maneras se impone la obligación de continuar la lucha por el reconocimiento del derecho a la objeción de conciencia al servicio militar para hacer avanzar el mismo.

La acción del Comité de Derechos Humanos de las Naciones Unidas es fundamental para lograr tal objetivo. En primer lugar, cabría redactar una nueva

Observación General del artículo 18 del Pacto Internacional de Derechos Civiles y Políticos afirmando en su plenitud y de manera más casuística el principio que ya hemos comentado, consagrado en la Observación General 22. En segundo lugar, en el análisis de los informes del artículo 40 del Pacto, debería examinarse en todos los casos en que exista el servicio militar obligatorio si los Estados Partes reconocen y respetan el derecho a la objeción de conciencia. Finalmente, debería profundizarse la jurisprudencia en las comunicaciones que el Comité resuelva sobre el tema conforme al Protocolo Facultativo, analizando siempre con sentido restrictivo los criterios sobre las diferencias de trato entre el servicio militar y el sustitutivo.

DEMOCRACY AND LIBERTY AS HUMAN RIGHTS

Louis Henkin

From the middle of the Twentieth Century, 'democracy' has been the universally avowed political ideology, and one commonly identified with respect for human rights. Yet the word 'democracy' does not appear in the Universal Declaration of Human Rights, and a human right to live in a democratic society does not appear among the rights, which states parties to the International Covenant on Civil and Political Rights (ICCPR) undertake to respect and to ensure. (Article 2(1)).

'Liberty', too was a foundational element of the human rights idea, yet 'liberty', as an over-arching independent right, without explicit qualification as a particular freedom – such as, 'freedom of expression' (ICCPR Article 19(2)), or liberty of movement and freedom to choose one's residence (Article 12(1)) – can be found among those rights only once, ambiguously, (Article 9)[1] and there, too, in a context that might seem to limit its scope and content, so as to protect only 'liberty of the person' from incarceration and from physical restraint.

In my view, both democracy and liberty, both broadly conceived, are essential elements of the human rights ideology, are fundamentals of the international law of human rights, and are properly to be sought, and found, in the Covenant, as essential to 'human dignity'.

DEMOCRACY

'Democracy,' undefined, appears in numerous international instruments of the second half of the 20th Century, as a value intimately related to human rights, perhaps, indeed, as a concept embracing all the values reflected in the ideology of human rights. 'Democracy' was prominent in the rhetoric of the Cold War (on both sides in the conflict), and was explicitly enshrined in the ideology of the new international order, which resulted with the end of the Cold War. 'Democracy' appears also as itself a major human right, as well as a foundation for other human rights, in documents emanating from the Copenhagen and Moscow Conferences in 1990 and 1991.[2]

And yet, 'democracy' is a word not to be found in the Universal Declaration of Human Rights or in the Covenants which derived from the Declaration.

---

[1] Article 9 provides: 'Everyone has the right to liberty and security of person. No one shall be deprived of his liberty except on such grounds and in accordance with such procedures as are established by law'.

[2] The Organization for Security and Cooperation in Europe (OSCE), which emerged from the post-Helsinki conferences, established an Office for Democratic Institutions and Human Rights.

Both the Declaration and the Covenant on Civil and Political Rights do declare rights commonly associated with democracy. Article 25 of the Covenant provides:

> Every citizen shall have the right and the opportunity, without [discrimination] . . . and without unreasonable restrictions:
>
> (a) To take part in the conduct of public affairs, directly or through freely chosen representatives;
>
> (b) To vote and to be elected at genuine periodic elections, which shall be by universal and equal suffrage and shall be held by secret ballot, guaranteeing the free expression of the will of the electors;
>
> (c) To have access, on general terms of equality, to public service in his country.[3]

It may be that Article 25 of the Covenant was intended to define democracy, but while the requirements of that Article may be necessary for democracy, it is less obvious that they are sufficient to constitute authentic 'democracy' as now understood. A number of states parties to the Covenant can properly be described as 'totalitarian' – by many definitions, perhaps, the antithesis of 'democratic' – states which by their constitutions and in practice have held occasional elections, referenda, or plebiscites. During the Cold War, Communist countries ratified the Covenant and claimed to be adhering to its provisions, yet few outside the Communist World (and not all inside that world) would accept that the Communist states were democracies.[4] Non-communist countries, too, could be faulted for imperfect systems of representation, for gender and racial discrimination in respect of the right to vote, or for other derogations from authentic popular sovereignty.[5] In the United States, – a country generally characterized and recognized as a democracy – the President is elected by an archaic 'electoral college,' not by direct vote of the citizenry (and sometimes, as in the year 2000, resulting in a 'minority' President).[6] And the bicameral legislative system, giving residents of states with

---

[3] Similar provisions are found in Article 21 of the Universal Declaration: 'Everyone has the right to take part in the government of his country, directly or through freely chosen representatives. ... The will of the people shall be the basis of the authority of government; this will shall be expressed in periodic and genuine elections which shall be by universal and equal suffrage and shall be held by secret vote or by equivalent free voting procedures.' This text differs from that of Article 25 of the Covenant in some respects, most notably in its explicit recognition of the idea of popular sovereignty.

[4] *See for example*, exchanges between members of the Human Rights Committee and representatives of the Ukrainian SSR at UN Doc. A/34/40 (1979) paras. 252 and 267.

[5] *See for example*, Human Rights Committee observations concerning equality of voting rights in Chile (CCPR/C/79/Add.104 para. 8), Paraguay (CCPR/C/79/Add.48;A/50/40 para. 214), Morocco (CCPR/C/79/Add.44 para. 16), and Kuwait (CCPR/CO/69/KWT paras. 9 and 10).

[6] *See* U.S. Constitution, Article II, sec.1.

small populations representation in the U.S. Senate equal to that of heavily populated states, is not obviously in conformity with Article 25 of the Covenant.

Some explanation of the differences between the terms of Article 25, and the assumptions of authentic democracy, may lie in the import of the adjectives in Article 25 defining the required elections -– 'genuine,' 'periodic,' and indeed in the term 'elections' itself; in the import and implications of 'universal and equal suffrage,' of 'secret ballot,' and of 'free expression of the will of the people.' Much may lie also in the meaning and implications of 'representatives,' and of 'freely chosen.' Neither the Declaration nor the Covenant identifies the political institutions in which 'the people' is to be represented, the offices for which elections are required to be held, and the authority and powers of these bodies.

Article 25 of the Covenant appears to commit states parties to respect democracy, as implying popular sovereignty, 'government by the people,' and representative government.[7] But the Covenant clearly reflects also a broader conception of democracy, a conception with legal significance. Although the word 'democracy' does not appear in the Covenant, there are several references to 'a democratic society' that may imply legal obligation. Articles 21 and 22 of the Covenant permit restrictions on the right of peaceful assembly, on the freedom of association, 'which are necessary in a democratic society'.[8] Article 14 provides that

---

[7] The Human Rights Committee interpreted Article 25 in its general comment, issued during July 1996. The Committee emphasizes that representatives exercising governmental power must be accountable through the electoral process for their exercise of power, which is predicated on 'the free expression of the will of electors' as the basis for governmental authority. The Committee did not assert that Article 25 requires a particular electoral system – although it does declare the principle of 'one person, one vote,' subject to only objective and reasonable restrictions. But the Committee affords Article 25 a broader role, beyond electoral systems. This is evident in the Committee's view that the freedoms of expression, assembly and association are all pre-requisites to the exercise of Article 25 rights. The Committee considers that 'Article 25 lies at the core of democratic government.'

[8]Article 21:

'The right of peaceful assembly shall be recognized. No restrictions may be placed on the exercise of thus right other than those imposed in conformity with the law and which are necessary in a democatic society in the interests of national security or public safety, public order (ordre public), the protection of public health or morals or the protection of the right and freedoms of others'.

Article 22:

'1. Everyone shall have the right to freedom of association with others, including the right to form and join trade unions for the protection of his interests.

2. No restrictions may be placed on the exercise of this right other than those which are prescribed by law and which are necessary in a democratic society in the interests of national security or public safety, public order (ordre public), the protection of public health or morals or the protection of the rights and freedoms of others. This article shall not prevent the imposition of lawful restrictions on members of the armed forces and of the police in their exercise of this right.

3. Nothing in this article shall authorize States Parties to the International Labour Organisation Convention of 1948 concerning Freedom of Association and Protection of the

the Press and the public may be excluded from a criminal trial for reasons of morals, public order (*ordre public*) or national security 'in a democratic society'. Do these allusions to 'a democratic society' imply, perhaps, an obligation on state parties to the Covenant to establish and to maintain 'a democratic society' generally, for purposes going beyond the articles containing those references?

What is a democratic society? In my view, references in the Covenant to 'a democratic society' imply a society committed to 'constitutional democracy,' to a society governed by a constitution established by the people, and respectful of the elements of 'constitutionalism.' Beyond popular sovereignty, universal suffrage and representative government, a democratic society, as contemplated by the Covenant, is one committed also to the 'rule of law,' to 'due process of law,' and to respect for principles of 'justice.' A democratic society includes commitment to limited government; to civilian control of the armed forces; to respect for individual rights; to an independent judiciary; to government in accordance with the constitution of the country, and to authentic monitoring by judicial or other form of 'constitutional review'.

The Covenant on Civil and Political Rights is punctuated with implications of such elements of constitutional democracy. Article 14, for example, refers repeatedly to the obligation of state parties to act in accordance with the law, and to respect 'the protections of the law.' Article 14(1) requires a tribunal 'established by law.' Article 14(2) requires that everyone charged with a criminal offence shall have the right to be presumed innocent until proved guilty 'according to law.'[9] Numerous other articles in the Covenant invoke commitment to 'the rule of law.' Article 26 implies commitment to both the rule of law and to the equal protection of the laws. Several provisions of the Covenant prohibit actions that are 'arbitrary,' incorporating recognized principles of reasonableness and of justice in the application of the laws.[10]

The human rights ideology and the law of human rights represented in the International Covenant, include, I believe, a right to democracy in the sense of constitutionalist democracy and its elements – authentic popular sovereignty, respect for individual rights, the rule of law, due process of law, and commitment to principles of justice. I think that these principles were what those who drafted the Covenant contemplated and what states that became parties to the Covenant committed themselves to abide by.

Right to Organize to take legislative measures which would prejudice, or to apply the law in such a manner as to prejudice, the guarantees provided for in that Convention'.

[9] *See also* Articles 9(2), 14(3)(a), 14(3)(b), 14(3)(c), 14(3)(d), and 14(3)(f).

[10] *For example*, Article 17:

'1. No one shall be subjected to arbitrary or unlawful interference with his privacy, family, home or correspondence, nor to unlawful attacks on his honour and reputation.

2. Everyone has the right to the protection of the law against such interference or attacks.'

See also Articles 6(1), 9(1), and 12(4).

Liberty

Human rights are commonly conceived and expressed as human freedoms. There is frequent mention of 'liberty' (or 'freedom') in the Covenant on Civil and Political Rights. There are references to 'liberty of movement and freedom to choose [one's] residence' (Article 12(1)); the 'liberty of parents . . . to ensure the . . . education of their children in conformity with their own convictions' (Article 18(3)). A right to a specific liberty or freedom is implied in other articles, for example, in provisions outlawing slavery, or those guaranteeing freedom of thought, conscience and religion. Indeed, a right is sometimes expressed in terms of freedom from interference with the enjoyment of that right.

But the Covenant nowhere expresses a right to individual 'liberty' or individual autonomy generally.[11] That omission begs for explanation. In the history of the idea of human rights, individual liberty was a foundational concept. The ancestors of the idea of human rights in the West – notably, John Locke, Immanuel Kant, the authors of the American Declaration of Independence and of the French Declaration of the Rights of Man and of the Citizen – assumed that rights were 'natural'; that man was endowed with certain inalienable rights, notably, prominently, 'liberty'. Liberty was not defined but it clearly assumed individual autonomy, and on that conception was built the idea of 'social contract' and popular sovereignty: free, autonomous human beings, possessing moral authority, exercised their autonomy to join with others, to form societies and establish governments, in order to secure their natural rights and liberties.

All the liberties particularized in the Covenant derive, I believe, from commitment to a fundamental individual autonomy and liberty, subject, of course, to the Police Power of the state, to which all rights and liberties are subject in some measure. But a right to essential individual autonomy, a right to 'liberty' generally, was not expressly included in the International Bill of Rights, probably because it reflects a theory of government and of its origins on which there was not likely to be

[11] Only once, in Article 9, does the Covenant on Civil and Political Rights refer to 'liberty' without immediate reference to a particular freedom. 'Everyone has the right to liberty and security of the person.' But that sentence too may in fact refer, not to 'liberty' generally but to a particular freedom, to freedom from incarceration, since it is followed immediately by: 'No one shall be subjected to arbitrary arrest or detention.'
It has been suggested that the reference to 'security' in the same article establishes a right to security of a person generally, beyond security from arrest, trial, and incarceration. *See* the views of the Human Rights Committee concerning communications under the Optional Protocol: Communications No. 195/1985 (*Delgado* v. *Columbia*), Views adopted on 12 July 1990, UN doc. A/45/40 vol. II, p. 43, No. 314/1988 (*Bwalya* v. *Zambia*), Views adopted on 14 July 1993, UN doc. A/48/40 vol. II, p. 52, No. 468/1991 (*Olo Bahamonde* v. *Equatorial Guinea*), Views adopted on 20 October 1993, UN doc. A/49/40 vol. II, p. 183 and No. 711/1996 (*Dias* v. *Angola*), Views adopted on 18 April 2000, UN doc. A/55/40 vol. II, p. 111. There is no similar interpretation by the Committee of 'liberty' in the same clause as an independent right.

agreement in international instruments drafted and concluded during an ideological Cold War.

In this regard, the history of the development of a right to individual autonomy in national constitutional jurisprudence is instructive. Notably, the U.S. Bill of Rights guarantees a number of particular 'freedoms' – for example, the free exercise of religion, and the freedom of expression and of the Press. But there is no express, constitutional enshrinement, or even mention, of 'liberty,' of 'natural' individual autonomy, as had been articulated earlier by the thinkers of the Enlightenment, expressly, prominently, in the American Declaration of Independence and in the constitutions of the new American states, and in the French Declaration of the Rights of Man and of the Citizen.

The only reference to 'liberty,' without more, in the U.S. Constitution is to be found in the U.S. Bill of Rights added to the Constitution by Constitutional Amendment shortly after the Constitution came into effect. The Fifth Amendment to the U.S. Constitution provides, inter alia, that no person shall be deprived of life, liberty, or property without due process of law. In that provision, too, in its terms and context, liberty plausibly referred to freedom from physical restraint except as punishment for crime and only pursuant to fair trial.

Towards the end of the 19th Century, however, in what may have been the most far-reaching 'amendment' of the U.S. Constitution by judicial interpretation, the Supreme Court of the United States interpreted 'liberty' as well as 'due process of law' broadly. The Supreme Court wrote:

> 'The liberty mentioned in that Amendment meant not only the right of the citizen to be free from the mere physical restraint of his person, as by incarceration, but the term is deemed to embrace the right of the citizen to be free in the enjoyment of all his faculties, to be free to use them in all lawful ways; to live and work where he will; to earn his livelihood by any lawful calling; to pursue any livelihood or avocation, and for that purpose to enter into all contracts which may be proper, necessary and essential to his carrying out to a successful conclusion the purposes above mentioned.'[12]

In that and other cases of the time, the Court also interpreted 'due process of law' to require not only a basis in law, and lawful, fair procedures, but conformity of legislation to 'substantive due process' to principles of 'ordered liberty,' requiring rationality, fairness, and justice.

Since that time, more than a hundred years ago, the U.S. Supreme Court has applied that conception of liberty and the Court's interpretation of due process of law, in monitoring the constitutionality of legislation. The Court recognized the authority of government under its 'police power' to limit individual autonomy and liberty by laws necessary to protect health, safety, morals, or the general welfare.

Originally, the police power was narrowly conceived, and the Amendment recognized *prima facie* individual autonomy as requiring economic *laissez faire*. In

[12] *Allgeyer* v. *Louisiana*, 165 U.S. 578 (1897).

time, however, legislatures in the United States, reflecting 'the will of the people,' moved away from commitment to 'the liberal state' towards a significant commitment to 'the welfare state,' as also within the Police Power, as also being for the general welfare.[13]

The broad interpretation of liberty and the requirement that law must conform to substantive as well as procedural requirements remained, and remains, essential constitutional jurisprudence in the United States. Later, this jurisprudence was reflected in broadened conceptions of liberty to include protection for 'privacy,' and a more limited view of the scope of the Police Power so as to protect individual autonomy in intimate matters, such as the right to marry, or a woman's liberty to resort to an abortion.[14]

Liberty as autonomy, with heightened protection in intimate matters, is the constitutional jurisprudence of the United States in the 21st Century. But there has been reluctance to find that conception of liberty in international human rights jurisprudence as reflected in 'the International Bill of Rights,' in the Universal Declaration and the Covenants. Suggestion that such autonomy be located in the 'liberty' mentioned in Article 9 of the Covenant or in the 'privacy' protected by Article 17 have not persuaded sceptical, resisting governments, and have not encouraged the Human Rights Committee and other 'treaty bodies' to dare creative interpretation. Yet this particular interpretation is surely in the spirit of the natural right to liberty from which the international law of human rights derives.

Human Dignity

One might consider instead – or in addition – support for a broad conception of a human right to liberty, to autonomy, in the concept that is the foundation of the human rights ideology at the end of the 20th Century, 'human dignity.' Derived essentially from the writings of Immanuel Kant, it was brought into international human rights in the preambles of the Universal Declaration and of each of two international covenants.

The text of the Covenant, as concluded in 1966, was designed to encourage universal participation, and contained, therefore, purposeful omissions and ambiguities. The world was divided into two, and a 'Third World' was emerging. The Covenant's various allusions to democracy – to 'a democratic society' as implying constitutionalism – were opaque, and shrouded in euphemism, but these were the only terms on which the negotiating parties could agree.

Political circumstances discouraged being explicit about the scope of the liberty and of the democracy to which many aspired. There could have been no agreement on a 'natural' right to 'liberty.' But all apparently were prepared to commit to 'human dignity' as the foundation of and the justification for, human rights. Now, 50 years later, with totalitarian socialism discredited, and the 'Third World' increasingly aspiring to liberal democratic values, the interpretation of the Covenant

---

[13] *E.g., Nebbia* v. *New York,* 291 U.S. 502 (1934).
[14] *E.g., Roe* v. *Wade*, 410 U.S. 113 (1973).

in the 21st Century should reflect the aspirations as well as the reluctance and the compromises. Commitment to human dignity is an authentic foundation for interpretation of the Universal Declaration and of the Covenants.

The history of the idea of human rights, then, plausibly supports interpretation of 'liberty' to include *prima facie* individual autonomy. One might recall the natural right to liberty, and the exercise of that liberty by 'the social contract,' to support interpretations of the Covenant to justify a human right to 'democracy,' understood as comprising the elements of constitutionalism, an interpretation that follows readily from the specifics of Article 25 and from the Covenant's references to a democratic society. In my view, interpreting those references in their authentic spirit should produce no other result.

Some might find allusions to democracy also in other values that underlie human rights – in the commitment to 'justice' and to 'human dignity.'[15] Resort to underlying values has indeed been available to adjudicative bodies that have earned respect and acceptance, such as the growing number of national constitutional courts. Multinational and international courts, commissions and committees in Europe and the Americas have also earned respect and acceptance, and analogous bodies in other regions may be in the process of achieving it.

Over its 25 years, the Human Rights Committee appears to have earned a significant measure of such acceptance. The original hesitant euphemisms in the Covenant which were all that states were then thought willing to accept, have in fact been converted by the Committee into established interpretations of the Covenant. Perhaps the Committee, and other 'treaty bodies', might invoke other authentic if yet inchoate elements of democracy, of constitutionalism, and of the rule of law, as implications of 'human dignity' justifying interpretations of the Covenant that would provide additional protections for human rights. For such daring interpretations they will require the support of the states parties, the ultimate masters of the covenants and those ultimately responsible for compliance with its provisions.

---

[15] *See* preambles to ICCPR and ICESCR.

THE HUMAN RIGHTS COMMITTEE'S GENERAL COMMENT ON ARTICLE 25

Elizabeth Evatt

INTRODUCTION

This paper discusses some of the issues confronted by the Human Rights Committee in preparing its General Comment on Article 25 of the International Covenant on Civil and Political Rights (the Covenant).[1] It draws from the Committee's summary records, and from its communications, concluding observations on state party reports and annual reports.

When the Committee decided in 1981 to prepare General Comments on the application of particular provisions of the Covenant, its stated intention was to make its experience available for the benefit of all states parties, and to draw their attention to insufficiencies disclosed by a large number of reports. Over the next 12 years General Comments were adopted on several provisions. However, the Committee had been unable to prepare a General Comment on Article 25, because of fundamental differences about the implementation of that provision.

ARTICLE 25 IN THE COMMITTEE'S EARLY YEARS

Article 25 provides that

> Every citizen shall have the right and the opportunity, without any of the distinctions mentioned in article 2 and without unreasonable restrictions:
>
> (a) To take part in the conduct of public affairs, directly or through freely chosen representatives;
>
> (b) To vote and to be elected at genuine periodic elections which shall be by universal and equal suffrage and shall be held by secret ballot, guaranteeing the free expression of the will of the electors;
>
> (c) To have access, on general terms of equality, to public service in his country.

Among the first states to ratify the Covenant were Eastern bloc countries which could only be described as 'one party states', totalitarian regimes, where resort to the ballot box did not enable citizens to exercise free choice or to participate effectively in the conduct of public affairs. Those states made no reservations in respect of Article 25.[2] Apparently, their governments were able to satisfy themselves that their

---

[1] General Comment No. 25, Article 25, 57th Session, 12 July 1996.

[2] States which entered reservations to Article 25 included the UK, Switzerland and Australia.

own systems met the requirements of Article 25 by taking a minimalist view of that provision.[3]

Some members of the Committee were less than satisfied with that approach. It is clear from their questions and comments that they had grave doubts whether Article 25 rights were in fact enjoyed by citizens in states where there was no political freedom of choice.[4] However, the Committee was not unanimous in this view; members from the eastern bloc countries accepted that their own systems met the required standards. These differences meant that there was little prospect that the Committee could reach consensus on the proper application of Article 25. Nevertheless, despite the differences between members on some issues, the Committee agreed that Uruguay had violated Article 25 rights when it arbitrarily deprived certain members of the communist party of their political rights.[5]

The situation began to change in the mid-1980s, when Mikhail Gorbachev began a process of reform in the Soviet Union, which would lead to greater political freedom. When the USSR reported to the Committee in October 1989, it announced that genuinely democratic elections were being introduced which would enable citizens to elect candidates who would protect their rights and interests.[6]

From that time onwards, former Eastern bloc states reported to the Committee on their transition to democracy and to multi-party elections.[7] Poland, which had elected its first non-communist government in 1989, was particularly frank about the repression of the past, informing the Committee that previously it had been virtually impossible actually to exercise such essential rights as freedom of speech, association and participation in the conduct of public affairs.[8]

In the same period, a number of Latin American and other states were re-engaging with or strengthening political pluralism and democratic institutions.[9]

These factors opened the way for the Committee to prepare a General Comment on Article 25. The proposal for the General Comment was first mentioned on the

---

[3] For drafting issues *see* Marc J Bossuyt, *Guide to the 'travaux preparatoires' of the International Covenant on Civil and Political Rights*, Martinus Nijhoff, 1987, p. 469 *et seq* ('Bossuyt'); Manfred Nowak, *UN. Covenant on Civil and Political Rights, CCPR Commentary*, Engel, 1993, p. 435 *et seq* ('Nowak').

[4] *E.g.,* Evans, SR.65, 27 Jan 1978, at para. 39 (Czechoslovakia); Tomuschat 30 Jan 1978, at SR 67.66 (GDR); Tarnopolsky, at SR.99.25, 27.7.78 (Yugoslavia); Lallah SR.136, 17 April 1979, at para. 2, (Romania);

[5] *E.g.,* Case No. 28/1978 (*Luciano Weinberger Weisz* v. *Uruguay*), views adopted on 29 October 1980, *Human Rights Committee, Selected Decisions*, vol 1, 1985, p. 57; Case No. 44/1979 (*Pietraroia Zapala* v. *Uruguay*), views adopted on 27 March 1981, *Selected Decisions*, Vol. 1 p. 76 (discussed below).

[6] HRC Report for 1990, UN doc. A/45/40, para. 73.

[7] Yugoslavia, Belarus, Mongolia, HRC Report for 1992, UN doc. A/47/40; Hungary, Bulgaria, HRC Report for 1993, UN doc. A/48/40; Romania, HRC Report for 1994, UN doc. A/49/40.

[8] Poland, HRC Report for 1992, UN doc. A/47/40, para. 126.

[9] Uruguay, 1989; Chile, 1990; Nicaragua, 1990; Panama 1991; El Salvador 1994; Paraguay, 1995; Zambia, 1996 (year is that of the Committee's annual report).

record in November 1991.[10] The preliminary work of preparing a draft for a pre-session working group was assigned to Mr Myullerson. After his term on the Committee ended in 1992, the draft Comment was reassigned to the author in July 1993. After a delay, caused by the Committee's work on other General Comments, detailed discussions on the draft began at the 53rd Session in March 1995 and continued at the next four Sessions. General Comment No 25 on Article 25 was adopted at the 57th Session, in July 1996.

ARTICLE 25 AND DEMOCRATIC IDEALS

On the face of it, Article 25 supports 'democracy', though it makes no reference to that concept. The Covenant refers to 'democracy' in the context of permitted limitations on the right of peaceful assembly and the right of freedom of association, and in Article 14.[11] But the Covenant does not define 'democracy'. Nor does it expressly affirm, as does the UDHR, that 'the will of the people shall be the basis of the authority of government'.[12]

The experience in some countries has been that while Article 25 rights exist on paper, the exercise of those rights does not deliver 'democracy' in its broadest sense, and has little or no influence on the actual exercise of power. The right to freely choose representatives and the right to vote in genuine elections are rendered worthless if there are unacceptable limits on who can stand for election, or if elections do not give citizens an opportunity to elect representatives who would exercise actual government power. If the bodies that citizens elect have no more than a semblance of government power, and if that power, or asubstantial part of that power remains in the hands of un-elected persons, not accountable to the electors, the rights which Article 25 guarantees would have little real meaning.

A challenge for the Committee in drafting the General Comment was whether it could spell out from Article 25, considered as a whole, minimum standards of democratic government, minimum requirements about the way in which government powers are defined, allocated and exercised, and about the accountability of government for the exercise of power.

In early discussions on the General Comment, Mr Ban asked the Committee to make the General Comment more than a mere guide to reporting or a procedural guarantee of voting rights. He contended that, despite the lack of jurisprudence, the Committee should emphasise that Article 25 ensured to citizens, as a minimum standard of substantive democracy, the right to participate in bodies exercising real power.[13] The aim of Article 25 was to ensure that the exercise of government power is based on sovereignty of the people, and that government is answerable for the exercise of power to citizens who could remove it from office.

---

[10] 43rd Session, SR.1109, 31 October 1991 paras. 1–119.

[11] Articles 21 and 22.

[12] The drafters of the Covenant discarded the term 'government' in favour of the 'conduct of public affairs'Bossuyt, pp. 469, 471.

[13] 52nd session, SR.1385, 3 November 1994, para. 66.

Questions relating to the powers exercised by elected bodies had not been directly considered by the Committee up to that time. A communication had complained that much of an elected local council's power had been transferred to a government appointed governor in violation of Article 25; however, the communication was found inadmissible.[14]

The Committee took up the issue raised by Mr Ban, and agreed that Article 25 should be seen as giving substantive rights and that the Comment should deal with issues such as whether elected bodies exercised effective government power, whether electors had a real choice and whether there was a potential for government power to change hands. Very few members expressed a preference to focus on the procedural aspects of Article 25.

Although the Committee did not agree to incorporate in the General Comment the words of Article 21(3) of the UDHR, it made clear that democratic government is the objective of Article 25:

> 'Article 25 lies at the core of democratic government based on the consent of the people and in conformity with the principles of the Covenant'. (para. 1)

The Committee further agreed that Article 25 requires democratic government in which citizens possess, through the forms of direct or indirect participation protected by that provision, a real opportunity to determine and/or to influence the conduct of public affairs, and where the elected representatives are accountable for the exercise of government power.

> 'Where citizens participate in the conduct of public affairs through freely chosen representatives, it is implicit in article 25 that those representatives do in fact exercise governmental power and that they are accountable through the electoral process for their exercise of that power. It is also implicit that the representatives exercise only those powers which are allocated to them in accordance with constitutional provisions.' (para. 7)

The Committee's approach to Article 25 is that it requires a chain of accountability for the exercise of power, under which the representatives elected by the citizens are responsible for monitoring the executive. This concept proved difficult to express in absolute terms, bearing in mind that some states with strong democratic systems maintain anomalies, such as the UK House of Lords, the appointed Senate in Canada or the exercise of certain powers by hereditary, constitutional monarchs.[15] While these anomalies can be distinguished from the clearly undemocratic exercise of power by unaccountable totalitarian governments and military juntas, the boundary

---

[14] Case No. 318/88 (*EP* v. *Colombia*), decision adopted on 15 July 1990, HRC Report for 1990, UN doc. A/45/40, Vol. II, p. 184: non-exhaustion of domestic remedies, OP Article 5.2.b.

[15] Bossuyt, p. 474, an early draft of Article 25 had provided that there must be elections to all organs of authority, but this was later removed

could not be drawn with precision; it would have to be assessed in each case whether the state had met its obligations under Article 25.

PARTICIPATION IN THE CONDUCT OF PUBLIC AFFAIRS

Article 25 guarantees to citizens the right to take part in the conduct of public affairs directly or through freely chosen representatives. The General Comment describes the 'conduct of public affairs' as:

> 'a broad concept which relates to the exercise of political power, in particular the exercise of legislative, executive and administrative powers. It covers all aspects of public administration, and the formulation and implementation of policy at international, national, regional and local levels.' (para. 5)

Referenda and popular assemblies are common forms of direct participation mentioned in the Comment (para. 6). The Comment also contemplates other possibilities of direct participation, though the scope of the right to participate was limited by the *Miqmak* case, decided in 1991.[16]

Mikmaq case

In the *Mikmaq* case, several constitutional conferences were held to identify Canadian aboriginal and treaty rights. The participants in these conferences were the elected leaders of the federal and provincial governments. Representatives of four national associations of aboriginal people were invited to attend. The authors, members of an indigenous tribal group, claimed that their exclusion from the conferences was an unreasonable restriction of their right to participate, and that their interests were not properly represented.

The Committee found that Constitutional conferences constituted 'the conduct of public affairs'.[17] The fact that aboriginal representatives were invited in addition to elected representatives did not alter this. However, the failure to invite representatives of the Mikmaq tribal society did not infringe their Article 25 rights nor restrict them unreasonably.

The Committee's view was that the conduct of public affairs in a democratic state is the task of representatives of the people, elected for that purpose, and of public officials appointed in accordance with the law. The legal and constitutional system of the state party provides for the modalities of such participation, but it is not for individual citizens to determine whether to participate directly or through their freely chosen representatives. To give a directly affected group the unconditional right to choose the modalities of participation in the conduct of public

---

[16] Case No. 205/1986 (*Mikmaq people* v. *Canada*), views adopted on 4 November 1991, HRC Report for 1992, UN doc. A/47/40, p. 213, paras. 5.4 and 5.5.
[17] Ibid.

affairs 'would extend the right to direct participation by the citizens, far beyond the scope of art 25 (a)'.[18]

The General Comment follows the *Mikmaq* case up to a point, by stating that 'the allocation of powers and the means by which individual citizens exercise the right to participate in the conduct of public affairs protected by Article 25 should be established by the constitution and other laws' (para. 5). It further recognises that citizens have a role in setting the modalities of participation in the conduct of public affairs, such as by taking part in constitutional referenda or by electing representatives to a constitutional convention or to the legislature (para. 6).

The Comment also envisages direct participation by citizens as members of bodies established to represent citizens in consultation with government. Where such a mode of direct participation by citizens is established, the Comment states that no distinction should be made between citizens as regards their participation on the grounds mentioned in Article 2, paragraph 1, and no unreasonable restrictions should be imposed (para. 6). This could imply that where the government establishes a formal process of consultation with citizens on particular issues, it might be called on to show that the selection of particular interest groups for representation or participation was based on reasonable and objective factors. The basis on which the participants had been selected was not dealt with in *Mikmaq*.

The Committee's General Comment on Article 27, on the rights of members of minorities, adds another dimension to the issues of participation and consultation. It asserts that the effective enjoyment of rights under Article 27, particularly in the case of indigenous people 'may require positive legal measures of protection and measures to ensure the effective participation of members of minority communities in decisions which affect them'.[19]

The extent of the state's obligation to consult indigenous minorities under Article 27 was considered in the case of *Ilmari Lansman et al* v. *Finland*,[20] where the Committee took into account that the authors had been consulted and their interests considered when quarrying permits were granted, in finding that there had been no denial of Article 27 rights. A comparable issue arose in the Maori fisheries claims.[21] A complex consultation process had been undertaken by New Zealand in order to secure broad Maori support for a national settlement of the claims. The Committee concluded that the state party had, by engaging in that process before legislating and by paying specific attention to the sustainability of Maori fishing

[18] Ibid.

[19] Human Rights Committee, General Comment No. 23, Article 27 (Fiftieth session, 8 April 1994), Compilation of General Comments and General Recommendations Adopted by Human Rights Treaty Bodies, U.N. Doc. HRI\GEN\1\Rev.3 at 39 (1997), para 7.

[20] Case No. 511/1992 (*Ilmari Länsman et al* v. *Finland*), views adopted 26 October 1994, HRC Report for 1995, UN doc. A/50/40, Vol. II, p. 66, 74. A similar conclusion was reached in Case No. 671/1995 (J. E. *Länsman* v. *Finland*), views adopted on 30 October 1996, HRC Report for 1997, UN doc. A/52/40, vol. II, p 191.

[21] Case No. 547/1993 (*Apirana Mahuika et al* v. *New Zealand*), views adopted on 27 October 2000, HRC Report for 2001, UN doc. A/56/40, vol. II, p. 11 *et seq*, para 9.6.

activities, taken the necessary steps to ensure that the Fisheries Settlement was compatible with Article 27, and that there was reasonable and objective justification to apply the agreement to all Maori, including those who claimed that it infringed their rights under Article 27. The obligation to consult, which can be derived from these decisions, supports the view that indigenous minorities are entitled to participate in certain decisions affecting their interests.

The General Comment strengthens the links between Article 25 and Article 1 by making it clear that the right to choose the form of constitution or government is covered by both provisions, and that this particular aspect of the right of peoples to self-determination depends on the effective enjoyment by individual citizens of the rights protected by Article 25 (para. 2). In a recent decision the Committee expressed the view that Article 1 could be relevant to the interpretation of Article 25 and other articles.[22] The implications of this view have not yet been explored.

THE RIGHT TO VOTE AND TO STAND FOR ELECTION

Unlike most other Covenant rights, the rights protected by Article 25 are to be enjoyed by 'citizens' and not by all individuals in the state. Nationality and citizenship are often equated. But in some countries (e.g., Latin America), the term 'citizenship' has a more limited connotation, and applies only to those nationals who are adults and meet the requirements for exercising political rights, including the right to vote. This concept of 'political citizenship' led to some difficulties in discussing the permissible conditions and restrictions on the exercise of Article 25 rights by citizens.[23] To avoid ambiguity, the General Comment asks states to outline the legal provisions defining citizenship for the purposes of Article 25.

The rights under Article 25 are to be guaranteed without any distinctions on Article 2(1) grounds, and without unreasonable restrictions. The General Comment accepts that it is reasonable to set a minimum age for the right to vote (para. 10), and to deny that right to persons lacking mental capacity (para. 4). It affirms, however, that physical disability, literacy, educational or property requirements are not permissible grounds for excluding or restricting the right to vote (para. 10).

In practice, however, some states make distinctions, which are incompatible with Articles 2(1) and 25, or impose restrictions which are unreasonable and which erode the principle of universal suffrage.

Distinctions on ground of sex

With rare exceptions, the right of women to vote and to stand for election is recognised by states parties, at least on paper. Kuwait is an exception. Its legislation denies political rights to women, despite constitutional provisions on equality. The

[22] Case No. 760/1997 (*J.G.A. Diergaardt, Captain of the Rehoboth Baster Community* v. *Namibia*), views adopted on 25 July 2000, HRC Report for 2000, UN doc. A/55/40, vol. II, p. 140.

[23] For discussions, *see* SR.1399, 28 March 1995, and later meetings.

General Comment did not deal expressly with this unique example of discrimination. Kuwait ratified the Covenant only in 1996; when the Committee considered its initial report in 2000 it was unanimous in its condemnation of the exclusion of women.[24]

For women in most states, however, the issue is not legal exclusion, but denial of equal opportunity in the exercise of political rights. This is discussed below.

Distinctions based on birth and naturalisation

Another impermissible distinction, under Articles 25(1) and 2(1) of the Covenant, is between those who are citizens by birth and those who are naturalised. In accordance with the Committee's views on equality and non-discrimination, states should be called on to show that any such distinction is reasonable and objective and that its aim is to achieve a legitimate purpose. However, some states make naturalised citizens wait for a period before being entitled to vote, sometimes up to 10 years. Other states preclude naturalised citizens from standing for certain offices. Some Latin American states go further, requiring presidential candidates to be born of parents who were themselves citizens by birth. The justification for these distinctions is not apparent.

The Committee was ambivalent about distinctions restricting the political rights of naturalised citizens. Most thought that restrictions on the right to vote were not permissible, but some members accepted that restrictions in regard to elective office might be reasonable; the example of the US presidency was cited. Various approaches to drafting were tried, such as to say that 'in principle' there should be no distinction in regard to Article 25 rights between citizenship by birth or by naturalisation. This was later softened to say that the distinction 'may raise questions of compatibility' (para. 3), leaving the issue to be dealt with on a case by case basis. The exclusion of candidates on the ground of 'descent' was, however, considered as prima facie unreasonable and discriminatory (para. 15).

At the July 1996 Session, during which the General Comment was adopted, the Committee considered a provision in the Brazilian constitution that only persons born in Brazil could run for the offices of President or Vice-President, or serve as justices of the Supreme Court, as members of diplomatic corps or as officers of the armed forces. The Committee's opinion was that these distinctions were incompatible with Articles 2 and 25 of the Covenant.[25]

Distinctions and restrictions on the ground of political or other opinion

Effective democracy requires that citizens be free to present and to have access to a wide range of political views, popular or unpopular. Regrettably, the Committee has

---

[24] Kuwait, initial report, HRC Report for 2000, UN doc. A/55/40, at paras. 452 *et seq*, 460, 461.

[25] Brazil, initial report, SR.1508 paras 37, 56, 82, 11 July, 1996, HRC Report for 1996, UN doc. A/51/40 at para. 306 *et seq.*

encountered states whose governments have prevented their opponents from participating in the conduct of public affairs, by imposing legislative restrictions or by arbitrary action. In several communications the Committee found that Uruguayan laws depriving citizens, who as members of certain political groups had been candidates in the elections of 1966 and 1971, of any political rights for a period as long as 15 years was an unreasonable restriction of the political rights protected by Article 25[26] In other cases, governments resorted to arbitrary detention to prevent their opponents from campaigning for office.[27]

The General Comment expressly affirms that states may not discriminate or restrict the exercise of Article 25 rights on the ground of political opinion or political affiliation (paras. 10, 15, 17). However, there remains a danger that persons or groups might seek to use the rights protected by Article 25 to destroy or subvert those or other rights. It is implicit in Article 5(1) that states may impose limitations or restrictions strictly necessary to prevent activities of this kind.[28] The General Comment affirms this principle, though its parameters are far from clear.

Party membership

The question whether states can insist that persons standing for office be members of a political party proved to be surprisingly controversial, especially to those who are accustomed to independent candidates. The original draft of the General Comment proposed that any requirement that candidates belong to a party should be considered unreasonable. However, some members thought that as parties play such a significant role in politics, the Committee should accept that states may require candidates to belong to a party, unless that requirement was in the circumstances unreasonable or discriminatory. Others thought that it would not be unreasonable to require party membership in a proportional system, where voting is by party list. Another view was that the requirement to belong to a party would help to restrain rich and powerful individuals who might 'manipulate public opinion and secure election'.[29]

A different perspective was put by Mr Ndiaye, who argued that to require party membership would unreasonably preclude many people from seeking office, whereas permitting individuals outside party machines to participate in public affairs

---

[26] *E.g.*, Case No. 28/1978 (*Luciano Weinberger Weisz* v. *Uruguay*), views adopted on 29 October 1980, *Human Rights Committee, Selected Decisions*, vol. 1, 1985, p. 57; Case No. 44/1979 (*Pietraroia Zapala* v. *Uruguay*), views adopted on 27 March 1981, *Selected Decisions*, Vol. 1 p 76.

[27] Case No. 138/1983 (*Ngalula Mpandanjila* v. *Zaire*), views adopted on 26 March 1986, HRC Report for 1986, UN doc. A/41/40, p. 121; Case No. 157/1983 (*Mpaka-Nsusu* v. *Zaire*), views adopted on 26 March 1986, HRC Report for 1986, UN doc. A/41/40, vol. II, p. 142. Case No. 314 1988 (*Bwalya* v. *Zambia*), views adopted on 14 July 1993, HRC Report for 1993, UN doc. A/48/40, vol. II, p. 52.

[28] Case No. 117/1981 (*MA* v. *Italy*), views adopted on 10 April 1984, *Selected Decisions* Vol. 2, p. 31.

[29] *See* 55th Session, SR.1448, 17 October 1995.

would raise the level of debate. Ms Medina argued that proportional representation did not depend solely on party lists and that as the party system became more élitist, the candidacy of (independent) individuals who had wide support was being encouraged in some countries.

In the outcome, the Committee agreed to uphold the rights of independent candidates, and to assert that party membership, as a condition of candidacy was prima facie unreasonable. It was also agreed, by way of compromise, that a minimum level of support could be a condition of candidacy, provided that this was reasonable and not a barrier to the candidacy of an individual (para. 17). In this, the Committee has recognised that there may be a need to balance the goal of enabling individuals to participate in the political process with that of preventing over-fragmentation of the political spectrum.

Other restrictions

The General Comment acknowledges that certain public positions, including military service, are likely to be incompatible with elective office (paras. 16, 18). This incompatibility might justify restricting the holders of those positions from standing for election.[30]

Some states preclude ministers of religion or bankrupts from exercising political rights, and in particular the right to stand for election. The Committee's preference was not to mention these disqualifications expressly, but to leave the question whether any such grounds of exclusion are reasonable to be considered on a case-by-case basis.

The General Comment puts the onus on the state party to justify any restrictions on the right to vote (para. 14). It seems highly probable that the Committee would consider it incompatible with Article 25 to exclude any of the above-mentioned groups from exercising the right to vote.[31] The Committee had no difficulty in agreeing that persons not convicted of any offence should not have their right to vote suspended (para. 14).[32]

Depriving convicted persons of the right to vote

A more contentious issue for the Committee was whether it is compatible with the Covenant to deprive persons convicted of offences of the right to vote. A reservation had been entered to Article 25 by Australia, in regard to the right to vote of persons

---

[30] Case No. 500/1992 (*Debreczeny* v. *The Netherlands*), views adopted on 3 April 1995, HRC Report for 1995, UN doc. A/50/40, vol. II, p. 59.

[31] Paraguay, HRC Report for 1995, UN doc. A/50/40, at paras. 195, 196 (restrictions on voting by students of military schools considered unreasonable).

[32] 54th Session SR.1422, 13 July 1995; 55th Session, SR.1447, 17 Oct 1995.

convicted of serious criminal offences.[33] Other states parties preclude persons convicted of certain offences from exercising political and civil rights, though without any such reservation or declaration. This is not a universal practice; in some states, convicted persons do not lose their right to vote, even if they may not be able to exercise it in practice while in detention.[34]

In 1980, the Committee observed, in the context of a communication, that many countries deprive criminal offenders of certain political rights and that Article 25 prohibits only 'unreasonable' restrictions.[35] It appeared to contemplate, at that time, that such deprivations may sometimes be reasonable, or at least that the question was open. By 1993, the Committee seemed less willing to accept such restrictions as reasonable. In 1993 it suggested to Luxembourg that it should abolish the deprivation of the right to vote as part of legitimate punishment.[36] In 1995, while the General Comment was under consideration, the Committee concluded that Hong Kong laws which deprived convicted persons of their voting rights for periods of up to 10 years may be a disproportionate restriction of the rights protected by Article 25.[37]

In discussing this issue, some members put the view that it would always be unreasonable to deprive a person convicted of an offence of the right to vote (or to stand for office). Others thought that some deprivations might be considered reasonable, for example, depriving persons convicted of electoral offences of the right to vote. The Committee could not reach consensus on the limits of reasonable restriction of political rights on the basis of criminal conviction.[38] It was finally agreed that if conviction for an offence is a basis for suspending the right to vote, the period of such suspension should be proportionate to the offence and the sentence (para. 14), thus leaving the issue for case-by-case consideration.

In October 2001 the Committee appeared to take firmer line on the issue, when it recommended to the United Kingdom that it should reconsider its law depriving convicted prisoners of the right to vote, saying that it failed to discern the justification for such a practice in modern times, considering that it amounts to an additional punishment and that it does not contribute towards the prisoner's reformation and social rehabilitation, contrary to Article 10, paragraph 3, in conjunction with Article 25 of the Covenant.[39] This broad statement goes beyond the view expressed in the General Comment.

---

[33] Reservations, Declarations etc relating to the ICCPR and the Optional Protocols, CCPR/C/2/Rev.4, 1994, p 13. The reservation was withdrawn in 1984; some convicted persons are still disqualified from voting: Australia, third report, paras. 1260–1262.

[34] In *CF* v. *Canada* 113/1981, views adopted 12.4.85, HRC Report for 1985 p 217.

[35] Case No. 28/1978 (*Weinberger Weisz* v. *Uruguay*), *supra* note 26.

[36] Luxembourg, Report of HRC to July 1993, UN doc. A/48/40, at paras. 136 *et seq*, 143.

[37] Hong Kong, UK 4th Report, HRC Report for 1996, UN doc. A/51/40, at paras 47 *et seq*, 65, 71.

[38] For discussions, *see* 54th session, July 1995, SR.1422, at paras. 44, 47, 51, 63, 78.

[39] UK, 5th report, Oct 2001, 73rd session, concluding observations, at para. 10.

The question whether persons serving sentences of detention could, in practice, exercise the right to vote is a separate issue.[40] The Committee did not agree to include in the General Comment a proposal calling on states to enable overseas residents and prisoners to make use of absentee, postal voting systems, where such systems are available. However, states parties are obliged under Article 2(1) and (2) to give effect to rights on a non-discriminatory basis.

Compulsory voting

Some states parties make voting compulsory for all eligible voters, with penalties for failure to comply.[41] The Committee's views on this issue were divided. Several members argued that compulsory voting was precluded by the Covenant. On the other hand there was some support for mandatory voting, on the ground that it is an obligation of citizenship, and that it ensures that voting is not just exercised by a minority. The General Comment is silent on the issue.

RIGHTS IN REGARD TO ELECTIONS

For the vast majority of citizens, participation in the conduct of public affairs is effected by voting for candidates for election to parliaments or other elected bodies, at a national, regional or local level. The essence of genuine elections, as required under paragraph (b) of Article 25, is that they should give citizens the opportunity to choose freely their representatives to exercise government power. Article 25 implies 'a plurality of choice among candidates expressing alternative political views'.[42]

The General Comment deals with the practical requirements for the conduct of genuine periodic elections (paras. 11, 12, 19–22). It covers the periodicity of elections, their fair conduct, the need for an independent electoral authority to supervise the process, the security of the ballot, and the opportunity for candidates to monitor the counting of votes. States must act to prevent fraud or undue pressure directed against electors, and ensure that elections are free from violence. Electors must be free to vote for or against government, and the results of genuine elections must be respected, with the possibility of peaceful change if that is the will of the electors. In addition, there are positive duties on the State to facilitate registration and to make voting rights effective for the illiterate, homeless and disabled. These issues were not controversial in discussion.

The Comment makes it clear that in accordance with 'universal and equal suffrage', the principle of one person, one vote should be respected, and each person's vote should have equal weight 'within the framework of each state's

[40] In Case No. 113/1981 (*CF* v. *Canada*), views adopted on 12 April 1985, HRC Report for 1985, UN doc. A/40/40, p. 217; the authors, who were federal prisoners, claimed that arrangements should be made to enable them to exercise their continuing right to vote. The case was found inadmissible for non-exhaustion of domestic remedies.
[41] *E.g.*, Australia, Ecuador; discussions at 55th Session, SR.1447, 17 October 1995.
[42] Mrs. Higgins 53rd Session, 28 March 1995, SR.1399 para. 30.

electoral system' (para. 21). Systems, which give some individuals additional voting rights, are clearly incompatible with the principle of equal suffrage. For example, in Morocco and Hong Kong, some seats in the legislature are elected by electoral colleges or functional constituencies. These were considered by the Committee to be incompatible with equal suffrage.[43]

Other issues related to equal suffrage are harder to resolve. Does the Covenant require that electoral systems should ensure a reasonably equal distribution of voters between electoral districts? In the more blatant forms of 'gerrymandering', the distribution of voters is carried out by governments in such a manner as to concentrate large numbers of opposition voters or racial groups into certain districts, thereby ensuring that their representation is disproportionately reduced. Such distributions have been the subject of constitutional challenge in a number of countries, with varied outcomes, but they have not been directly confronted by the Committee.[44]

The Committee was cautious in its approach to this question, avoiding a definitive statement.[45] It did not consider that Article 25 required any particular electoral system. It agreed, however, that 'the drawing of electoral boundaries and the method of allocating votes should not distort the distribution of voters or discriminate against any group' (para. 21). This could be taken as an indication that there should not be an unreasonable differentiation between the numbers of voters in different electoral districts.[46] If the rights of citizens to participate in public affairs were restricted in a totally disproportionate manner by such a distribution, the Committee might be willing to consider whether this was incompatible with Articles 25, 2(1) and 26.

A much more difficult issue is whether the objective of universal and equal suffrage under Article 25 is to ensure that members of different political groupings and viewpoints in the community have a fair and reasonable opportunity to be represented in elected bodies. A state party could, for example, ensure the representation of minority groups, by adopting a system of proportional voting or reserved seats. But governments and major parties are often unwilling to contemplate the reduction in the number of their elected members by such means. The question for the Committee is whether there is an obligation under the Covenant to ensure such representation.

---

[43] Morocco, HRC Report for 1995, UN doc. A/50/40; Hong Kong, UK 4th report, HRC Report for 1996, UN doc. A/51/40, at paras. 47 *et seq*, paras. 65, 71.

[44] *E.g.*, USA: *Baker* v. *Carr, USSC* 1962; *Reynolds* v. *Sims* 1964; *Wesberry* v. *Saunders* 376 US 1 (1964). Australia: *AG* v. *Commonwealth, ex rel McKinlay* (1975) 135 CLR 1 at 36; *McGinty* v. *Western Australia,* (1996) 70 ALJR 200.

[45] For discussion, *see* 55 Session, SR.1460, 25 October 1995.

[46] Sarah Joseph, Jenny Schultz, and Melissa Castan, *The International Covenant on Civil and Political Rights, Cases, materials and Commentary*, Oxford UP, p. 504, at paras. 22.22, 22.24, citing the Committee's request to Zimbabwe for a breakdown in the size of constituencies, Zimbabwe, initial Report, March 1998, 62nd Session, HRC Report for 1998, UN doc. A/53/40, at paras. 203 *et seq*, 225.

The Committee might, in a particular case, be concerned at the exclusion of certain groups from elected bodies. But in drafting the General Comment, it was not ready to resolve the question whether the failure by a state party to ensure that individuals who are part of a minority group are able to participate by electing representatives of their own group to elected bodies would violate Article 25 rights. The Comment leaves this question open for the future, probably the distant future. It does, however, tentatively ask states to 'explain how the different political views in the community are represented in elected bodies' (para. 22).

PARTICIPATION BY WOMEN AND MINORITIES (PARA 2, [23])

The extent of the obligation of states parties to ensure the equal participation of women in the conduct of public affairs was the subject of considerable debate. As mentioned earlier, in most states parties, the issue for women is not legal exclusion from the political process, but de facto exclusion. In many states, women are seriously under-represented in public offices and in elected bodies as a result of long standing discrimination, direct and indirect. Does Article 25 require, or permit, positive measures to overcome this exclusion?

Articles 2(1) and 3 of the Covenant call for the equal enjoyment of Covenant rights by women, without discrimination. In conjunction with those provisions, Article 25 requires that the principles of equality and non-discrimination apply to elective office, to appointed positions involving the exercise of government power, to consultative bodies established by government, and to public service appointments.

Some states parties have adopted positive measures to increase the representation of women in elected and other public bodies. India, for example, reported to the Committee on constitutional measures to reserve one third of the seats in elected local bodies for women and on a bill to reserve one third of the seats for women in the federal parliament and in state legislatures. Some of the Nordic states have introduced measures aimed at the equal representation of both sexes on public committees and boards.

The issue for the Committee was whether and to what extent Article 25 *requires* states to take affirmative action to ensure the equal participation of women in the conduct of public affairs. The Committee's earlier General Comment on equality and discrimination made it clear that the obligation to ensure Covenant rights on the basis of equality sometimes requires affirmative measures to be taken to overcome discrimination, and that such action may involve granting, for a time to the part of the population concerned, preferential treatment in specific matters.[47] The Committee had recommended to more than one state party that it should take

[47] General Comment No. 18 on Articles 2(1) and 26 (37th Session, 10 November 1989).

positive measures or affirmative measures to improve the participation by women in the conduct of public affairs.[48]

An early draft of the General Comment on Article 25 proposed that affirmative measures might be justified for the purpose of ensuring the equal participation of women in the conduct of public affairs, provided the measures were compatible with Article 25 and the principle of equal suffrage.[49] The proposal extended to the representation of minorities, though most members thought that minorities raised different issues.[50] Mr Pocar suggested that affirmative measures to ensure the equal participation of women in the conduct of public affairs were not incompatible with the principle of equal suffrage; they could take the form of stipulating that a certain percentage of candidates must be women or reserving a certain number of seats for women candidates.[51] Others agreed that affirmative action for women would be consistent with equality as a legitimate goal. Mr Francis thought that the participation of women should be a matter for political parties to deal with. Others were reluctant to accept the concept of quotas.

After considerable discussion at the 55th Session,[52] the Committee could not agree that the General Comment should refer to any general obligation of states parties under Article 25 to take affirmative action to ensure the equal participation of women in the conduct of public affairs. A different outcome resulted in regard to access to public service (below).

In the three years following the adoption of the General Comment in July 1996, the Committee recommended to no less than nine states parties that they take measures to promote the full and equal participation by women in political life.[53] By 1999, when the Committee was working on its General Comment on Article 3, its reluctance to recommend affirmative action in regard to women's participation in the conduct of public affairs had been overcome. The new General Comment calls on states to

> 'ensure that the law guarantees to women article 25 rights on equal terms with men and take effective and positive measures to promote and ensure

---

[48] Hungary, HRC Report for 1993, UN doc. A/48/40, at paras. 617 *et seq*, 665; Romania, Slovenia, Italy, Report of HRC to July 1994, UN doc. A/49/40; Paraguay, Ukraine, HRC Report for 1995, UN doc. A/50/40.

[49] Discussions at 55th Session, SR.1460, 25 October 1995.

[50] Minorities include both political and ethnic (Article 27) minorities; the goal of numerical equality is missing, though the concept of equal opportunity applies.

[51] SR.1460, 25 October 1995, para. 13.

[52] SR.1460.

[53] India, HRC Report for 1997, UN doc. A/52/40; Iraq, Lithuania, Israel, Italy, HRC Report for 1998, UN doc. A/53/40; Chile, Lesotho, Romania, HRC Report for 1999, UN doc. A/54/40; Guyana, HRC Report for 2000, UN doc. A/55/40.

> women's participation in the conduct of public affairs and in public office, including appropriate affirmative action.'[54]

This exhortation to states covers all aspects of participation in the conduct of public affairs, including the right to vote and to be elected, as well as the appointment of women to public positions.

The Committee has continued to recommend to states that they take measures to improve generally the participation of women in the conduct of public affairs, in parliament or other political institutions.[55] In doing so, the Committee appears to acknowledge that the obligations of states parties under Articles 25, 3 and 2(1) include the implementation of affirmative action measures. It has not yet articulated the kind of affirmative measures, which might be appropriate for this purpose in a particular state. In doing so, it might be useful to refer to the general recommendation of CEDAW on Political and Public life, adopted in 1997, which sets out examples of strategies which have been developed effectively by states to achieve equality of participation by women.[56] While the obligation to take affirmative action now seems clear, it could be difficult for an individual woman to establish in a particular case that failure to take such measures was a violation of individual rights. Here, too, the Optional Protocol to the Women's Convention may offer the possibility of an inquiry into a 'systematic violation' under Article 8.

In its General Comment on Article 25, the Committee did not expressly deal with the question of participation by and representation of members of minorities. Although some members supported the proposal that states should take affirmative measures to ensure that members of ethnic, religious and linguistic minorities had equal opportunities to participate in the conduct of public affairs, there was no consensus on how to incorporate this in the draft. The issue was deferred for consideration in a specific context.[57] The Committee has since recommended that FYR Macedonia and Croatia take affirmative measures in this regard.[58]

---

[54] General Comment No. 28 on Article 3, 68th Session, 29 March 2000, UN doc. CCPR/C/21/Rev.1/Add.10, at para. 29.

[55] *E.g.,* Kuwait, Kyrgyzstan, Ireland, HRC Report for 2000, UN doc. A/55/40; Guatemala, Gabon, Uzbekistan, Czech Republic, HRC Report for 2001, UN doc. A/56/40; Azerbaijan, Ukraine, UK, Oct 2001, 73rd session, HRC Report for 2002, A/57/40

[56] CEDAW, General Recommendation No 23 (16th Session, 1997) Political and Public Life, para. 15.

[57] For discussion, *see* 55th Session, October 1995 SR.1460 paras 5–41.

[58] FYR Macedonia, initial Report, HRC Report for 1998, UN doc. A/53/40, at paras. 368 *et seq*, 383. Croatia, initial Report, HRC Report for 2001, UN doc. A/56/40, para. 80.22. In Case No. 760/1997 (*J.G.A. Diergaardt, Captain of the Rehoboth Baster Community* v. *Namibia*), views adopted on 25 July 2000, HRC Report for 2000, UN doc. A/55/40, vol. II, p. 140, the Committee found that the Article 25 rights of members of a minority had not been adversely affected by merging their community into other regions,.

FREEDOM OF EXPRESSION, ASSOCIATION AND POLITICAL PARTIES

Weak democracies are often associated with restrictions on freedom of expression, association and assembly; a recent example of this is Zimbabwe, which imposed severe restrictions on the media and on political meetings in the lead up to the election early in 2002.

The General Comment recognises that the rights recognised in Article 25 would be little more than paper rights if citizens were not able to debate freely the conduct of public affairs, to organise politically, to criticise and to protest against the actions of governments (para. 25). It emphasises that freedom of expression supports the right of citizens to influence political action through public debate and dialogue with their representatives and the free exercise of the right to votes (paras. 8, 12). These issues were not contentious in discussion, and the details are not discussed in this paper.

An issue which attracted considerable attention in discussions was the role of political parties and their influence on the exercise of Article 25 rights. Most candidates for election are members of parties, and are selected for candidacy by the party organisation. In parliamentary systems, the leadership of the government is usually determined by the dominant party or by party allegiances.

The General Comment acknowledges that the right to form and to join associations concerned with political and public affairs plays an essential role in the democratic process (para. 26). On the other hand, it also makes clear, as mentioned earlier, that membership of a party or particular party should not be a condition of standing for election (para. 17).[59]

Although the General Comment has been criticised for not expressly declaring that one party systems are incompatible with Article 25, the Committee has made it quite clear that states must not obstruct the formation of opposition parties or prevent them from pursuing political activity.[60] In a communication from Zambia, the Committee determined that restrictions on political activity outside the only recognised political party were an unreasonable restriction on the right to participate in the conduct of public affairs.[61] It has, at least since the end of the cold war, consistently expressed the view that states which do not permit the formation of alternative political parties, or which try to suppress their activities, are thereby restricting the enjoyment of Article 25 rights.[62]

---

[59] For discussion, *see* 52nd Session, SR.1385, 3 November 1994.

[60] Roland Rich, 'Bringing Democracy into International Law' (2001) 12 *Journal of Democracy*, p. 20, criticised the general comment for not dealing expressly with the issue of multi-party elections.

[61] Case No. 314/1988 (*Bwalya* v. *Zambia*), views adopted on 14 July 1993, HRC Report for 1993, UN doc. A/48/40, vol. II, p. 52. The Committee found violations of Article 9, 12 and 25.

[62] Zimbabwe, HRC Report for 1998, UN doc. A/53/40, at paras. 203 *et seq*, 211; Kuwait, HRC Report for 2000, UN doc. A/55/40, at paras. 452 *et seq*, 489, 493; DPR Korea, HRC Report for 2001, UN doc. A/56/40, at paras. 86 and 25.

Some interesting questions about the internal management of political parties were raised by Mr Bruni-Celli. In view of their considerable power and influence in choosing candidates and thus determining the choices open to electors, he wanted the Committee to include in the Comment a proposal that parties to be required to operate on democratic lines.[63] This was supported by some members. However, others did not want to encourage state intervention in the affairs of political parties. To allay their concerns about undue interference by government, it was agreed that the Comment should state that '[s]tates should ensure that, in their internal management, political parties respect the applicable provisions of Article 25' (para. 26).

The reluctance of the Committee to support any form of state control over political parties also prevented the Committee from agreeing to call on states to ensure that registration requirements for political parties are compatible with Article 25,[64] even though it had frequently been critical of stringent registration requirements which unnecessarily restricted rights.[65]

Since adopting the General Comment the Committee has continued to be critical of restrictions imposed by states on political parties,[66] and of strict registration requirements, which inhibit their participation in the electoral process.[67] The Committee may need to consider in detail what, if any, registration requirements or restrictions are justifiable in terms of Articles 22 and 25.

ACCESS TO PUBLIC SERVICE AND DISCRIMINATION

Paragraph (c) of Article 25 protects the right of citizens to have access to public service on general terms of equality. The General Comment deals with a number of issues relating to the terms and conditions of appointment to public service positions, and with promotion, suspension and dismissal. It calls for general principles of merit to apply, and for secure tenure (paras. 23, 24).[68] These issues were not contentious.

The Committee debated at some length whether political factors could ever be relevant to the employment of public service officials. This arose from a proposal in an early draft of the Comment that states should ensure that no-one have preference or suffer disadvantage in regard to access to public service on unreasonable or discriminatory grounds, *'such as political opinion'*. The reason for singling out 'political opinion' for express mention, rather than any of the other potential

---

[63] 56th Session, SR.1493, 29 March 1996, para. 27; discussions continued at 57th Session, SR.1509.

[64] For discussion *see* 56th Session, March 1996SR.1493.

[65] *E.g.,* Tunisia, HRC Report for 1995, UN doc. A/50/40, at paras. 12, 20.

[66] *E.g.,* Algeria, 2nd Report, HRC Report for 1998, UN doc. A/53/40, at paras. 349 *et seq*, 365.

[67] *E.g.*, Uzbekistan, initial Report, HRC Report for 2001, UN doc. A/56/40, at paras. 79, 23.

[68] The discussion of these provisions were mainly at 55th session, SR.1460, 25 October 1995, and 56th session, SR.1492, 29 March 1996.

grounds of discrimination, was that the public service is especially vulnerable to this form of discrimination. The Committee had, in fact, found a violation of Article 25(c) on this ground only a few days before adopting the General Comment.[69] It had observed that '[a]ccess to public service on general terms of equality encompasses a duty for the state to ensure that there is no discrimination on the ground of political opinion or expression. This applies a fortiori to those who hold positions in the public service.'

Nevertheless, some members were unwilling to make an express reference to discrimination on the ground of political opinion. Their view was that differentiation on political grounds is inevitable at the highest levels of public service, in order to further the political objectives of government. Others agreed that there are overtly political posts in many systems and that not all jobs could be exempt from political considerations. To meet these objections a suggestion was made to exclude 'clear political appointments' from the prohibition of discrimination on political opinion. This was not accepted; instead the specific reference to 'political opinion' was deleted. The Comment emphasises, however, the importance of ensuring that persons holding public service positions are free from political interference or pressures (para. 23).

Although, as mentioned, the Committee did not support affirmative action to improve the level of participation in public life by women or members of minorities, the General Comment accepts that some degree of affirmative action might be called for in the context of access to public service.[70] The draft proposed that states should adopt affirmative action measures to overcome under representation of certain groups and to give effect to the 'right and the opportunity' to have access to public service on general terms of equality. Some members were concerned that giving emphasis to affirmative action might detract from the merit principle or lead to quotas. Others thought that the express reference to 'women, minorities and indigenous people' was too sweeping and that the need for affirmative action for any particular group should be considered in its own particular context. The final text includes a modest statement allowing for affirmative action 'in appropriate cases' (para. 23).

Following the adoption of the General Comment, no less than 18 of the Committee's concluding observations have included recommendations to states parties to take positive action to ensure the greater representation of women in public service, the judiciary or in other political or public bodies. The increase in support for affirmative action for women may be partly due to the effect on members of the Committee's work on the later General Comment on Article 3.

---

[69] Cases Nos. 422-424/1990 (*Adimayo M Aduayom and others* v. *Togo*), views adopted on 12 July 1996, HRC Report for 1996, UN doc, A/51/40, vol. II, p.17; violations of Article 9 and 25 (c).

[70] For discussions, 56th session, SR.1492, 29 March 1996.

THE JUDICIAL PROCESS

The Committee discussed briefly whether the judiciary and the exercise of judicial functions should be included in the General Comment as part of the conduct of public affairs, or in relation to public service. The participation by citizens in juries and as lay judges in some countries was noted, but there was no support for regarding this form of participation as a right protected by Article 25. The Committee had earlier expressed its view that the election of judges was not compatible with the independence of the judiciary.[71] The Committee agreed to include the judiciary among the positions which might be considered incompatible with elective office (para. 16). But no agreement was reached on the inclusion of judicial power either as part of the conduct of public affairs or as part of public service. Questions relating to the judiciary and to the exercise of judicial functions were left to be dealt with under Article 14, should a new General Comment be prepared on that provision.

'CONCLUDING COMMENTS'

As explained, some of the views set out in the General Comment are based on the Committee's prior jurisprudence. The General Comment also developed new jurisprudence in relation to several issues, which had not previously been discussed in depth by the Committee, such as the obligation implicit in Article 25 to ensure that the elected representatives of citizens are accountable for the exercise of real government power.

Some of the views expressed by the Committee in the General Comment have since been applied in the reporting process. For example, the Committee has made many recommendations for affirmative action in regard to the participation by women in public life. More generally, the Committee has asked states parties to have regard to its General Comment in taking steps to ensure full compliance with Article 25.[72]

The General Comment has also been directly quoted in a communication, which related to the denial of access by a journalist to the parliamentary press gallery.[73] The quotation makes the point that the free communication of ideas about public and political issues between citizens, candidates and elected representatives is essential to ensure the full enjoyment of rights protected by Article 25.

But those looking for a definitive and detailed interpretation of how Article 25 should be applied in practice will not be entirely satisfied. The General Comment

---

[71] The Committee asked the United States to reconsider the system of election of judges, HRC Report for 1995, UN doc. A/50/40, at paras. 288, 301.

[72] DPR Korea, 2nd Report , July 2001, 72nd Session, HRC Report for 2001, UN doc. A/56/40, at paras. 86, 25; Kyrgyzstan, initial, HRC Report for 2000, UN doc. A/55/40, at paras. 382 *et seq*, 419, 420.

[73] Case No. 633/1995 (*Gauthier* v. *Canada*), views adopted on 7 April 1999, HRC Report for 1999, UN doc. A/54/40, p. 93, at para. 13.4.

leaves many questions unanswered. This is inevitable when, as in the case of Article 25, there was limited jurisprudence to draw from.

The Committee had originally decided to prepare General Comments partly as an alternative to issuing comments reflecting on how individual states had implemented their Covenant obligations. Instead of assessing state compliance on the basis of their individual reports, the Committee would 'make generalized comments based on information gathered from many reports.'[74]

When the cold war tensions eased, General Comments became more detailed, and there was a greater willingness to include views about matters which had not previously been the subject of a jurisprudential view, either in the communications procedure or in the Committee's concluding observations.

During the discussion of the draft on Article 25, Mr Lallah stressed the need for the Committee to ground its General Comments firmly in its jurisprudence.[75] Soon after the Committee adopted that General Comment, in July 1996, it both asserted the jurisprudential nature of General Comments, while at the same time adopting a relatively cautious approach to drafting future General Comments:

> 'The Committee acknowledge that General Comments constitute a jurisprudential commitment, making it difficult for the Committee to take a different view later. The Committee should be prudent in taking up and dealing with a matter for a General Comment when the jurisprudence of the area is not highly developed.'[76]

A factor influencing this note of caution was the negative reaction of certain states parties to its earlier General Comment on Reservations.[77]

In relation to Article 25, there was strong support in the Committee for developing the General Comment, even though the absence of jurisprudence made it difficult for the Committee to commit itself to a definitive interpretation of all aspects of the provision. Other difficulties arose from the fact that Article 25 is expressed in general terms, and may be implemented by many diverse constitutional and legal measures and arrangements for elections.

Another difficulty faced by the Committee in applying Article 25 is that legal and practical measures to implement that provision, however good they may appear to be on paper, are not always a sufficient guarantee of effective democracy. Although the Comment attempts to make the link between the election process and

---

[74] Lallah, SR.1399, 28 March 1995, para. 15; For history *see* Ineke Boerefijn, The Reporting Procedure under the Covenant on Civil and Political Rights: Practice and Procedures of the Human Rights Committee, School of Human Rights Research Series Vol 2, Intersentia – Hart, Antwerpen, Gronigen, Oxford, 1999, chapter XIV, p. 285 *et seq.*

[75] SR.1460, 25 Oct 1995, para. 41 (in relation to affirmative action).

[76] Report of informal meeting of the members of the U.N. Human Rights Committee to discuss reform of the procedures of the Committee, 27–28 July 1996, CCPR/C/133 (on web site), at para. 54.

[77] *See* the responses of the US, the UK (HRC Report for 1995, Annex) and France (HRC Report for 1996, Annex).

accountability for the exercise of power, there are many intangible factors, which determine where the real power resides in a particular state party and whether participation by citizens in the conduct of public affairs is real or illusory. Those factors are hard to identify or to fit within the framework of obligations, which the Covenant imposes on states parties.

While it may not be too difficult to identify laws or practices in a particular state that are incompatible with Covenant rights, it is much harder to assert confidently that if particular measures were adopted by such state parties, governments would be more democratic, more accountable and more willing to tolerate dissent and to accept the transfer of power to others. It is also difficult to assert that a state's failure to adopt certain measures would be incompatible with its obligations under Article 25, or that individual rights would be violated by that failure.

In the outcome, the General Comment on Article 25 has left some important issues to be resolved in later communications or in the Reporting process. These include:

- The nature and scope of affirmative action to ensure that women enjoy the right to participate in the conduct of public affairs on an equal basis.
- The extent to which government powers may be exercised by non-elected bodies compatibly with article 25.
- Whether and in what circumstances it is compatible with article 25 to exclude military personnel, ministers of religion and bankrupts from the right to stand for elective office or to hold public office; and whether any of these groups can reasonably be excluded from the right to vote.
- Whether and to what extent persons convicted of offences may be deprived of the right to vote.
- Whether compulsory voting is compatible with the Covenant.
- Whether and if so to what extent States may regulate the formation and activities of political parties.

Unfortunately, the current pressures on the Committee and its lack of time and resources leave it little time in its examination of state parties' reports to pursue in detail all issues relevant to the implementation of the Covenant. Inevitably, some significant issues are excluded from consideration. The constraints mentioned also mean that the Committee's concluding observations are often rather general in nature, and do not give clear guidance as to the measures which states are expected to take to fulfil their obligations.

There is a continuing need for the Committee to develop precise conclusions and recommendations about the laws and practices which states should adopt to ensure the proper functioning of the democratic process in accordance with Article 25 and associated provisions of Articles 19, 21 and 22. In this regard, a positive step was taken in October 2001, when the Committee requested Azerbaijan to report back within 12 months under its new follow up procedure.[78] The issues that the Committee identified were the implementation of the Committee's recommendations regarding restrictions on freedom of expression, and measures taken to ensure that general elections adequately reflect popular choice.[79]

In its General Comment and in it subsequent work, the Committee has recognised that the rights protected by Article 25 are important to the overall implementation of the Covenant, and that democratic government plays a critical role in securing the protection of rights under the Covenant. It has also recognised that Article 25 imposes positive obligations on state parties to take the measures necessary to give effect to the rights and opportunities it protects (para. 1). Taking into account that state deficiencies in this area are frequently associated with other human rights failings, it is hoped that the Committee will continue to emphasise Article 25 issues in its concluding observations and requests for follow-up action.

[78] This procedure, pursuant to rule 70, paragraph 5, of the Committee's rules of procedure, was first implemented at that Session.
[79] Azerbaijan, 2nd Report, 73rd session, October 2001, at paras. 22, 24, 27.

THE EVOLUTION AND PROBLEMS OF THE JURISPRUDENCE OF THE HUMAN RIGHTS COMMITTEE'S VIEWS CONCERNING ARTICLE 26

Nisuke Ando

I. INTRODUCTION

The purpose of the present article is to examine the evolution of the Human Rights Committee's jurisprudence on Article 26 of the International Covenant on Civil and Political Rights as well as to clarify the problems, which have arisen in the process of that evolution.

The International Covenant on Civil and Political Rights is one of the achievements of the United Nations' efforts to codify the Universal Declaration of Human Rights.[1] A state party to both the Covenant and its Optional Protocol allows individuals subject to its jurisdiction to submit to the Human Rights Committee[2] a communication that he/she is a victim of a violation by that state party of any of the rights set forth in the Covenant. The state party also recognizes the competence of the Committee to examine such a communication in the light of all written information made available to it by the claimant and the state party itself.

Article 26 of the Covenant provides:

> 'All persons are equal before the law and are entitled without any discrimination to the equal protection of the law. In this respect, the law shall prohibit any discrimination and guarantee to all persons equal and effective protection against discrimination on any ground such as race, colour, sex, language, religion, political or other opinion, national or social origin, property, birth or other status.'

---

[1] The Universal Declaration of Human Rights adopted by the General Assembly of the United Nations in 1948 indicated 'a common standard of achievement for all peoples and all nations'. The declaration itself had no legally binding force, and the subsequent efforts of the United Nations to codify the declaration culminated in the adoption in 1966 by the General Assembly of two international treaties: the International Covenant on Economic, Social and Cultural Rights and the International Covenant on Civil and Political Rights. With the ratification by 35 states both the Covenants came into force in 1976. At the time of writing the number of states parties to each of the two covenants is nearly 150.

[2] The organ established under the International Covenant on Civil and Political Rights to monitor the domestic implementation of the Covenant provisions by states parties. The Human Rights Committee consists of 18 members elected at the conference of all the states parties to the Covenant, who serve 'in their personal capacity'. The Committee also considers individual communications submitted to it under the Optional Protocol attached to the Covenant.

This is based on the so-called principles of equality and non-discrimination, but the Covenant also contains a similar provision in Article 2(1):

> 'Each State Party to the present Covenant undertakes to respect and to ensure to all individuals within its territory and subject to its jurisdiction *the rights recognized in the present Covenant*, without discrimination of any kind, such as race, colour, sex, language, religion, political or other opinion, national or social origin, property, birth or other status.' (*emphasis supplied*)

An obvious difference between the provisions of Article 26 and of Article 2(1) is that, while the latter limits the scope of its application to 'the rights recognized in the present Covenant', the former has no such limitation.[3] Consequently, since the Human Rights Committee started its work in 1977,[4] a question has been asked if the provisions of Article 26 merely repeat those of Article 2(1) and, if not, what is the scope of their application.

The Committee gave an answer to the question in 1987 when it adopted its views in the cases of the Dutch Unemployment Benefits Act, and in subsequent years, basing itself on these views, the Committee has developed its jurisprudence with regard to the application of the principles of equality and non-discrimination as provided in Article 26.[5] However, in the process of that development or evolution, it appears that a few problems have arisen in applying Article 26 to concrete cases. For the purpose of examining the evolution and analyzing the problems, it is convenient to divide the period of evolution into the following three stages: (1) The years prior to 1987 during which the Committee maintained a cautious approach in applying Article 26; (2) The years during which the Committee adopted its views on the *Dutch Unemployment Benefits Act* cases and then elaborated its jurisprudence through the adoption of the General Comment on Non-Discrimination[6]; and (3) The subsequent years during which the Committee developed its jurisprudence on the basis of the General Comment, when a few problems have arisen in the process of that development.

---

[3] A similar provision to limit the scope of application is stipulated in Article 1 of the European Convention on Human Rights as well as in Article 1 of the American Convention on Human Rights.

[4] Both the International Covenant on Economic, Social and Cultural Rights and the International Covenant on Civil and Political Rights came into force in 1976, and the Human Rights Committee started its work in 1977.

[5] Article 5(4) of the Optional Protocol provides that: 'The Committee shall forward its *views* to the State Party concerned and to the individual' (*emphasis supplied*). When the Committee receives a communication, it first decides on the admissibility of the communication under the relevant provisions of the Optional Protocol. After deciding the communication as admissible, the Committee proceeds to examine its merits. In the practice of the Committee the term 'views' usually means its final decision on the merits of a communication.

[6] A General Comment is a commentary on various issues and articles of the Covenant, which is adopted by the Human Rights Committee to clarify understanding of them.

II. EARLY JURISPRUDENCE PRIOR TO 1987

During the first ten years of its activities the Human Rights Committee maintained a cautious approach in applying the provisions of Article 26 to concrete cases of communications, which were submitted to it under the Optional Protocol. The two well-known cases in this period that involved the application of the principles of equality and non-discrimination were the case of the Mauritian women and the case of Sandra Lovelace, but the Committee's views on both the cases were based not so much on Article 26 as on Article 2(1) or other related Articles of the Covenant.

In the case of the Mauritian women,[7] the issue was whether the provisions of the Immigration (Amendment) Act, 1977, and the Deportation (Amendment) Act, 1977, constituted discrimination based on sex against Mauritian women in violation of Articles 2, 3, 17, 23, 25 and 26 of the International Covenant on Civil and Political Rights. The amendments of 1977 were adopted following certain events in connection with which some alien spouses of Mauritian women had been suspected of subversive activities. Prior to the amendments both alien husbands and wives, who married Mauritian nationals, enjoyed the same residence status; that is, alien spouses of both sexes had the right, protected by law, to reside in the country with their Mauritian wives or husbands. Under the amended acts, however, husbands of Mauritian women lost their residence status and they had to apply anew for a 'residence permit', which might be refused or removed at any time by the Mauritian Minister of Interior. Contrary to this, the amendments did not affect alien wives of Mauritian men and the wives retained their right to reside in the country. According to the claimants, twenty Mauritian women, not only were the amendments discriminatory on the basis of sex in violation of Articles 2(1), 3 and 26 of the Covenant but also they constituted 'an arbitrary interference with family' in violation of Article 17 as well as 'lack of protection of the family by the state' in violation of Article 23.[8]

In its views adopted on 9 April 1981 the Human Rights Committee excluded the communications of the seventeen unmarried women because there could be no question of actual interference with, or lack of protection of, any family. Of the communications of the three married women, however, the Committee found that there had been a violation of Articles 2(1), 3 and 26 in conjunction with Articles 17 and 23. Considered as a whole, the views emphasized a violation of Articles 17 and 23 and thus should be regarded as relying more on Articles 2(1) and 3 than on Article 26.

At issue in the case of Sandra Lovelace was whether the claimant, who by marrying a non-Indian lost her Indian status as well as her right to return to the

---

[7] Communication No. (hereinafter Comm. No.) 35/1978 (*Aumeeruddy-Czifra and 19 other Mauritian women*), Views adopted on 9 April 1981, United Nations, International Covenant on Civil and Political Rights (hereinafter UN, ICCPR), *Human Rights Committee Selected Decisions under the Optional Protocol* Second to sixteenth Sessions (UN document number: ICCPR/C/OP/1), pp. 67–71.
[8] *Ibid.*

reserve after divorce, was a victim of a violation by Canada of Articles 2(1), 3, 23, 26 and 27 of the International Covenant on Civil and Political Rights.[9] The claimant pointed out that, since an Indian man who married a non-Indian did not lose his Indian status and retain his right to reside in the reserve, her situation under the Indian Act of Canada constituted discrimination on the ground of sex. The views adopted by the Human Rights Committee on 30 July 1981 were based mainly on Article 27, which concerns the rights of minorities. The Committee noted that the claimant's right to access to her native culture and language 'in community with other members' of her group had been interfered with, particularly after the dissolution of marriage, by applicable Canadian law. In the opinion of the Committee Article 27 must be construed and applied in the light of other related Articles of the Covenant, such as Article 12 (the right to choose one's own residence), 17 and 23 (the protection of family), together with Articles 2(1), 3 and 26 (non-discrimination). For that reason, the Committee concluded that the statutory denial of her recognition as belonging to an Indian band was not justifiable under Article 27. On the other hand the Committee found it not necessary to examine indirect issues under Articles 17 and 23 or the general issue of discrimination under Articles 2(1), 3 and 26. Apparently, in this case, the Committee did not deal squarely with the principles of equality and non-discrimination as provided under Article 26 of the Covenant.

Besides these two cases, there were several other communications during the first ten years, which involved possible application of Article 26. For example, in the case of K.B., a Norwegian woman invoked 'the right to dispose of one's property' in order to prevent her former husband from moving into a flat owned by her.[10] After the domestic courts of Norway rejected her claim, she submitted a communication to the Human Rights Committee, asserting that the decisions of the domestic courts were in violation of Articles 2(1), 3 and 26 of the Covenant. In its views adopted on 14 August 1979 the Committee noted that the right to dispose of property, as such, was not protected by any provision of the International Covenant on Civil and Political Rights and concluded that the facts submitted by the claimant did not substantiate her claim, thus making the communication inadmissible under the Optional Protocol.[11] Similarly, in the case of I.M., a naturalized Norwegian citizen who had been born in South Africa, complained that he was a victim of a violation of racial discrimination in matters of tax assessment and housing allocation by the

[9] Comm. No. 24/1977 (*Lovelace* v. *Canada*), Views adopted on 29 December 1977, *ibid.*, pp. 83–87. Subsequently the Canadian government informed the Committee that with revisions of the relevant domestic law it became possible for Sandra Lovelace to recover her Indian status. United Nations, General Assembly, Official Records, 38th Session, Supplement No.40 Report of the Human Rights Committee (A/38/40. Hereinafter cited as *Report of HRC* (A/38/40)), p. 249 *et seq.*; *Report of HRC* (A/40/40), p. 145 §704.

[10] Comm. No. 53/1979 (*K.B.* v. *Norway*), Decision adopted on 14 August 1979, UN, ICCPR, *Human Rights Committee Selected Decisions under the Optional Protocol*, ICCPR/C/OP/1. see *supra* note 7 p. 24.

[11] For 'a decision on the admissibility of a communication', *see supra* note 5.

Norwegian authorities.[12] According to the views adopted by the Human Rights Committee on 25 October 1982, the tax assessment and the housing allocation were not in themselves matters to which the Covenant applies. In any event the Committee declared the communication inadmissible because there was no evidence to substantiate the claim of racial discrimination.

Furthermore, in the case of J.B.D., a TV-radio repairman in the Netherlands, who had been prosecuted and fined because he had been engaged in the work without a license, claimed before the Committee that he was discriminated against by the Dutch legislation requiring him to have a license, which in his opinion violated Article 26 of the Covenant.[13] He also invoked Article 6 of the International Covenant on Economic, Social and Cultural Rights that provided the right to work. In its views adopted on 26 March 1984 the Human Rights Committee did not refer to Article 6 of the International Covenant on Economic, Social and Cultural Rights, simply declaring the communication inadmissible due to lack of substantiation. A few other communications in which a violation of Article 26 was claimed were all declared inadmissible by the Committee on the same ground of non-substantiation of the claims.[14] Thus, during the first ten-years of its activities, the Human Rights Committee did have opportunities to pronounce on the applicability of Article 26 to rights, such as the right to dispose of property, the right to work or the right to tax assessment and housing allocation, which were not recognized in the International Covenant on Civil and Political Rights. However, the Committee did not proceed to examine the merits of the communications in question because it declared all of them inadmissible.

III. THE DUTCH UNEMPLOYMENT BENEFITS ACT CASES AND THE ADOPTION OF GENERAL COMMENT 18 ON NON-DISCRIMINATION

The cautious approach maintained by the Human Rights Committee concerning the application of the principles of equality and non-discrimination as provided in Article 26 of the International Covenant on Civil and Political Rights was drastically changed on 9 April 1987 when the Committee adopted its views in the two cases of communications in regard to the Dutch Unemployment Benefits Act. They were Comm.No.172/1984 (*S.W.M.Broeks* v. *The Netherlands*)[15] and Comm.No.182/1984

---

[12] Comm. No. 129/1982 (*I.M.* v. *Norway*), Decision adopted on 6 April 1983, UN, ICCPR, *Selected Decisions of the Human Rights Committee under the Optional Protocol*, Vol.2 Seventeenth to thirty-second Sessions(CCPR/C/OP/2), p. 41.

[13] Comm. No. 178/1984 (*J.D.B.* v. *The Netherlands*), *ibid.*, p. 55.

[14] *See for example*, Comm. No. 163/1984 (*C et al.* v. *Italy*), Decision adopted on 10 April 1984, *ibid.*, pp. 47–48, on discrimination in employment against handicapped persons under the Italian law, and Comm.No.183/1984 (*D. F. et al.* v. Sweden) on discrimination against Arabs and Moslems in Sweden, *ibid.* pp. 55–56.

[15] Comm. No. 172/1984 (*Broeks* v. *The Netherlands*), Views adopted on 9 April 1987, *ibid.*, pp. 196–201.

(*F.H.Zwaan-de Vries* v. *The Netherlands*),[16] in both of which the claim was based on exactly the same ground. For the sake of convenience, the latter case alone will be examined below.

1. The Zwaan-de Vries Case

The claimant, F.H.Zwaan-de Vries, was a married Dutch woman. In 1979 she applied for unemployment benefits under the Unemployment Benefits Act. Her claim was rejected by the Dutch authorities on the ground that she did not meet the condition of the Act that she be a breadwinner of the family. In her communication to the Human Rights Committee she argued that the Act did not require the same condition for a married man to be eligible for the benefits and that the Act in question had elements of discrimination based on sex and marital status in violation of Article 26 of the Covenant.

Responding to her argument the Dutch government stated as follows: (1) In Dutch society around 1979 it was generally conceived that the roles of men and women in marriage differed, men being breadwinners of the family, and that women were required to have a certain level of income in order to be considered as breadwinners; (2) The right to social security, as such, was provided in Article 9 of the International Covenant on Economic, Social and Cultural Rights and was to be realized only progressively; (3) The fact that the Universal Declaration on Human Rights had to be divided into two International Covenants, one on Economic, Social and Cultural Rights and the other on Civil and Political Rights, each with different regimes for implementation, implied that the latter's Optional Protocol should cover only civil and political rights and that it was incompatible with the aim of both the regimes to extend the application of the Optional Protocol to the rights set forth in the International Covenant on Economic, Social and Cultural Rights; and (4) Even if the Human Rights Committee should decide that Article 26 was applicable to the field of economic, social and cultural rights, a state party to the International Covenant on Civil and Political Rights was merely obliged to remove discriminatory elements from its domestic legislation to the maximum extent possible with available resources.

In its final views adopted on 9 April 1987 the Human Rights Committee welcomed that the Dutch authorities had amended the Unemployment Benefits Act in 1985 to eliminate the disputed condition, taking into account the change of social situations under which many married women had come to earn their living. At the same time, the Committee noted that the rejection in 1979 by the Dutch authorities of unemployment benefits to the claimant continued to have its effect. In the opinion of the Committee, the inter-related drafting history of the two Covenants did not prevent the Committee from fully applying provisions of the International Covenant on Civil and Political Rights. The Committee considered that Article 26 did not merely duplicate the guarantee already contained in Article 2(1). Rather, Article 26,

[16] Comm. No. 182/1984 (*Zwaan-de Vries* v. *The Netherlands*), Views adopted on 9 April 1987, *ibid.*, pp. 209–214.

which derived from the principle of equal protection of the law without discrimination embodied in Article 7 of the Universal Declaration of Human Rights, prohibited discrimination in law and in fact in any field regulated and protected by public authorities. In other words, Article 26 did not require a state party to enact legislation to provide social security, but were such legislation enacted in the exercise of the state party's authority, then Article 26 would require that the legislation should comply with the principles of equality and non-discrimination. The principles of equality and non-discrimination did not make all differences of treatment discriminatory if the differentiation was based on reasonable and objective criteria. However, the elimination by the 1985 amendment of the condition that a married woman had to be a breadwinner in order to be eligible for unemployment benefits under the act indicated that the condition, which was not applicable to a man, was not reasonable. Under the circumstances, the Committee concluded that the claimant was a victim of a violation of Article 26 and that the state party should offer her an appropriate remedy.

Thus, in its views on the *Dutch Unemployment Benefits Act* cases, the Committee made clear that the provisions of Article 26 did not merely repeat those of Article 2(1) and that Article 26 applied to any field regulated and protected by public authorities of a state party, including not only civil and political rights but economic, social or cultural rights as well.

2. The Adoption of General Comment 18 on Non-Discrimination

After the adoption of its views on the *Dutch Unemployment Benefits Act* cases, the Human Rights Committee proceeded to prepare a General Comment on Non-Discrimination. The prepared draft elaborated the views but it was essentially based on the jurisprudence of the *Dutch Unemployment Benefits Act* cases. With minor modifications the Committee adopted it as the General Comment 18 on Non-Discrimination at its thirty-seventh session in 1989.[17] The main features of the General Comment were as follows:

Non-discrimination, together with equality before the law and equal protection of the law without discrimination, constitutes a basic and general principle relating to the protection of human rights, as provided in Articles 2(1) and 26. (General Comment, paragraph 1)

Because of its basic and general character the principle of non-discrimination is reflected in the provisions of some other Articles of the Covenant. Thus, Article 3 obligates a state party to ensure the equal rights of men and women to the enjoyment of the rights set forth in the Covenant. While Article 4(1) allows a state party to take measures derogating from certain obligations under the Covenant in time of public emergency, the same Article requires, *inter alia*, that those measures should not involve discrimination solely on the ground of race, colour, sex, language, religious

[17] *See for example*, United Nations, International Human Rights Instruments, *Compilation of General Comments and General Recommendations Adopted by Human Rights Treaty Bodies* (HRI/GEN/1/Rev.5), pp. 134–137.

or social origin. Furthermore, Article 20(2) obligates a state party to prohibit, by law, any advocacy of national, racial or religious hatred which constitutes incitement to discrimination.(Ibid., paragraph 2)

In addition, the principle of non-discrimination is reflected in some provisions of the Covenant relating to particular categories of human rights. For example, Article 14(1) provides that all persons shall be equal before courts and tribunals, and Article 14(3) provides that, in the determination of any criminal charge against a person, everyone shall be entitled, in full equality, to the minimum guarantees enumerated therein. Article 23(4) provides that a state party shall take appropriate steps to ensure equality of rights as well as responsibilities of spouses as to marriage, during marriage and at its dissolution. Article 24 provides that children, without any discrimination as to race, colour, sex, language, religion, national or social origin, property or birth, have the right to such measures of protection as are required by their status as minors on the part of their family, society and the state (*ibid.*, paragraphs 3 and 5).

However, the principle of non-discrimination does not mean identical treatment in every instance. For example, Article 6(5) of the Covenant prohibits the death sentence both from being imposed on persons below 18 years of age and from being carried out on pregnant women. Similarly, Article 10(3) requires the segregation of juvenile offenders from adults, and Article 25 guarantees certain political rights, differentiating on grounds of citizenship. Thus, the Committee observes that not every differentiation of treatment constitutes discrimination, if the criteria for such differentiation are reasonable and objective and if the aim is to achieve a purpose which is legitimate under the Covenant (*ibid.,* paragraphs 8 and 13).

As to the relationship between Article 2(1) and Article 26, it is obvious that, while Article 2(1) limits the scope of the rights to be protected against discrimination to those recognized in the Covenant, Article 26 does not specify such limitations. In the view of the Committee Article 26 does not merely duplicate the guarantee already provided in Article 2(1) but provides in itself an autonomous right. It prohibits discrimination in law and in fact in any field regulated and protected by public authorities. Article 26 is therefore concerned with the obligation imposed on a state party in regard to its legislation and the application thereof (*ibid.,* paragraph 12).

IV. THE SUBSEQUENT DEVELOPMENT AND SOME ACCOMPANYING PROBLEMS

Through the adoption in 1987 of the afore-mentioned views on the *Dutch Unemployment Benefits Act* cases and the elaboration of the views in 1989 by General Comment 18 on Non-Discrimination, the Human Rights Committee clarified and confirmed its jurisprudence that Article 26 provided for an autonomous right which prohibited discrimination in law or in fact in any field regulated and protected by public authorities and was applicable to rights not recognized in the International Covenant on Civil and Political Rights. Thereafter, the Committee has received a number of communications from individuals, mostly of developed states parties, who claimed to be victims of a violation of Article 26 in one field or another. Many of the views adopted by the Committee in response to these communications witness several problems in the application of the principles of equality and non-discrimination to concrete cases. Below are examined some of such views divided into four different categories: (1) The views demonstrating a cautious and restrictive application of Article 26; (2) The views revealing the existence of *de jure* or *de facto* difficulties in their implementation by the state party concerned; (3) The views indicating inconsistency of the Human Rights Committee's jurisprudence in its application of Article 26; and (4) The views showing inappropriate application of Article 26 by the Committee.

(1) The Views Demonstrating a Cautious and Restrictive Application of Article 26 by the Human Rights Committee

Already in the years preceding the *Dutch Unemployment Benefits Act* cases, there were submissions of communications in which individual claimants alleged that they were victims of a violation of Article 26 with respect to rights not recognized in the International Covenant on Civil and Political Rights. All these communications were declared inadmissible by the Human Rights Committee for lack of substantiation.[18] Likewise, in the years following the cases, a number of communications have been declared inadmissible on similar grounds.

For example, in the case of H.v.d.P., a Dutch industrial engineer employed by the European Patent Office submitted a communication to the Human Rights Committee, alleging that he had been denied equal treatment in promotion due to discriminatory practices in the patent office and that, since five European states including the Netherlands were both members of the European Patent Office and states parties to the International Covenant on Civil and Political Rights, he was a victim of a violation by the Netherlands of Articles 2(1), 14, 25 and 26 of the Covenant.[19] The Committee decided that the communication was inadmissible because the recruitment policy of an international organization could not come within the jurisdiction of the Netherlands or any other states parties to the Covenant and the Optional Protocol. Similarly, in the case of R.T.Z. and that of M.J.G., two Dutch youths in military service submitted a communication to the Human Rights Committee, alleging that they were victims of a violation by the Netherlands because, while ordinary Dutch citizens could appeal against a summons before the courts, they were denied the possibility of appeal under military penal procedure.[20]

---

[18] *See ibid.*, pp. 3–4 and *supra* note 14.

[19] Comm. No. 217/1986 (*H.v.d.P.* v. *The Netherlands*), Decision adopted on 8 April 1987, UN, ICCPR, *Selected Decisions of the Human Rights Committee under the Optional Protocol*, Vol.2 (CCPR/C/OP/2. *supra* note 12), pp. 71–72.

[20] Comm. No. 245/1987 (*R.T.Z.* v. *The Netherlands*), Decision adopted on 5 November 1987, *ibid.*, pp. 73–74; Comm. No. 267/1987 (*M.J.G.* v. *The Netherlands*), Decision adopted on 24 March 1988, *ibid.*, pp. 74–75.

The Committee decided, in both the cases, that the communications were inadmissible on the ground that the Covenant did not preclude the institution of compulsory military service and that some rights of individuals might be legitimately restricted within the exigencies of such service. The views of the Committee on these cases testify that the Committee has maintained a cautious approach with respect to the principles of equality and non-discrimination and has applied Article 26 in a careful and restrictive manner.

In addition, there have been communications, which the Committee declared admissible and, in deciding on their merits, it also interpreted and applied Article 26 in a careful and restrictive manner. For example, in its views on the *Danning* case, which was adopted on the same day as the views on the cases of Broeks and Zwaan-de Vries, the Human Rights Committee dealt with the claim of a Dutch citizen who had become disabled by an automobile accident and had been receiving payments from an insurance program.[21] However, unlike Ms.Broeks and Ms.Zwaan-de Vries, Mr. Danning had been cohabiting with his girl friend. According to him, the insurance program provided higher payments to a married beneficiary as compared with a beneficiary like him who was treated as a single person, which he claimed constituted discrimination in violation of Article 26. In its views adopted on 9 April 1987 the Committee noted the explanation of the Dutch government that under the domestic law of the Netherlands a married person was subject to greater legal regulation and resulting obligations than an unmarried person in terms of maintenance, common property, housing, divorce, etc. By choosing not to enter into marriage, the claimant and his cohabitant had not legally assumed the full extent of the duties and responsibilities incumbent on a married couple. Therefore, the Committee concluded that he did not receive the full benefits of the insurance program provided for a married man, and that the difference of treatment was based on reasonable and objective criteria and did not constitute discrimination under Article 26.

Furthermore, in its views on the *Blom* case of 4 April 1988,[22] the Human Rights Committee dealt with a communication from a Swedish student concerning the denial of an educational allowance to him. The claimant was a pupil at a private school and his application for a public educational allowance for the school year 1981/82 was rejected. He argued that this denial constituted a violation of Article 26 of the Covenant, since a pupil going to a public school was entitled to the allowance. The Committee noted, in its views, that in Sweden a public school was subject to state supervision whereas a private school was not, but that a pupil at a private school was also entitled to apply for a public educational allowance to the extent that the school's curricula were subjected to state supervision. Although the private school, which the claimant was attending, had submitted an application for state supervision in regard to certain parts of curricula, the authorities' evaluation of the

---

[21] Comm. No. 180/1984 (*Danning* v. *The Netherlands*), Views adopted on 9 April 1987, *ibid.*, pp. 205–209.

[22] Comm. No. 191/1985 (*Blom* v. *Sweden*), Views adopted on 4 April 1988, *ibid.*, pp. 216–219.

application took some time and its final decision was not made in time to cover the school year 1981/82. Under the circumstance, the Committee concluded that the relevant facts did not sustain a claim of a violation of Article 26.

(2) The Views Revealing the Existence of de jure or de facto Difficulties in their Implementation by the State Party Concerned

Some of the views adopted by the Human Rights Committee in application of Article 26 suggest or reveal that *de jure* or *de facto* difficulties do, or appear to, exist in their implementation by the state party concerned. For instance, in the case of Waldman at issue was whether the provision of public funding only to Roman Catholic schools, but not to other non-secular schools, in the Canadian province of Ontario amounted to discrimination in violation of Article 26.[23] In the opinion of the Canadian government, this system of funding originated in the 1867 Constitution of the Confederation of Canada in order to prevent the Protestant majority, then occupying 82 per cent of the province's population, from depriving the right to education of the Catholic minority representing 17 per cent, education being under the exclusive jurisdiction of provinces. Since that time, however, the religious composition of the population has gradually changed, and a 1991 census showed that 44 per cent of the Ontario inhabitants were Protestant, 36 per cent Catholic, and 8 per cent other religious affiliations. Yet, even after the inclusion of a Charter of Rights and Freedoms in Canada's Constitution of 1982, the Supreme Court of Canada has continued to hold that the funding of Roman Catholic schools could not give rise to an infringement of the Charter because the province of Ontario was constitutionally obliged to provide such funding. In its views adopted on 3 November 1999 the Human Rights Committee observed that members of the Roman Catholic community were not in a disadvantageous position compared to members of other religious denominations. Accordingly, the Committee rejected Canada's argument that the preferential treatment of Roman Catholic schools was non-discriminatory because it was a constitutional obligation. Instead, the Committee concluded that such treatment could not be considered reasonable and objective, thus constituting a violation of Article 26.

Nevertheless, by note of 3 February 2000, the government of Canada informed the Committee that because matters of education fell under the exclusive jurisdiction of the Provinces the government of Ontario had no plan to change the existing funding system.[24] While it is not the purpose of the present Article to discuss the issue of implementation or follow-up of views adopted by the Human Rights

[23] Comm. No. 694/1996 (*Waldman* v. *Canada*), Views adopted on 3 November 1999, *Report of HRC* (A/55/40), Vol. II, pp. 86–99.
[24] *Report of HRC* (A/55/40), Vol. I, p. 98 §608.

Committee,[25] this Canadian case reveals that the *de jure* domestic situation of a state party may cause difficulties in implementing the Committee's views on Article 26.

In contrast to *de jure* difficulties as illustrated by the Canadian case, there has been a case where a *de facto* situation of a state party appears to cause difficulties for that state party to implement the Committee's views. As observed earlier, in the *Dutch Unemployment Benefits Act* cases, the Human Rights Committee found a violation of Article 26 and recommended that the state party should offer the victims an appropriate remedy. The government of the Netherlands responded that, while it was unable to share the Committee's views on the merits of the cases, it would implement the recommendation 'out of respect for the Committee'.[26] Necessarily, such implementation would put considerable financial burden on the state party concerned but the government of the Netherlands would, and could, bear the burden. However, it might not always be the case with every state party.

In this respect, of interest are the cases, which concern the former Czechoslovakia's attempt to rectify the loss of private property confiscated during the communist regime. After the collapse of the communist regimes in Eastern European countries around 1990, various attempts were made by their new governments to eradicate injustices committed under the former regimes. In the former Czechoslovakia this line of attempts led to the adoption of Act 87/1991, which provided restitution of, or compensation for, private property confiscated during the communist regime on conditions that the original owners of the property were citizens of Czechoslovakia and were permanent residents in its territory. However, in the case of the communication from Simunek and others, the claimant argued that those conditions would exclude their claims because they had been forced to leave Czechoslovakia by political persecution of the former regime and had sometimes had to acquire nationality of a newly settled state.[27] They alleged, further, that the Act would in reality legalize the former regime's practices since more than 80 per cent of the confiscated property belonged to persons who did not meet those conditions.

Although Czechoslovakia ceased to exist at the end of 1992, both the Czech Republic and Slovakia succeeded to the International Covenant on Civil and Political Rights as well as its Optional Protocol and continued to apply Act 87/1991. In regard to the case of Simunek and others, the Czech Republic contended that Act 87/1991 was not discriminatory and that the conditions in question were not intended to violate human rights. The Czech Republic emphasized that restitution of confiscated property would involve very complicated and *de facto* unprecedented measures and that it could not be expected to rectify all the damage suffered and to

[25] *See for example*, Nisuke Ando, 'The Follow-Up Procedure of the Human Rights Committee's Views', p. 1437 *et seq*., N.Ando et al (Eds.), *Liber Amicorum Judge Shigeru Oda* (Kluwer Law International, 2002).

[26] *See* in this connection, *Report of HRC* (A/46/40), p. 174 §708. *See also Official Records of the Human Rights Committee* 1988/89 (CCPR/8), Vol.I, p. 90 §§55–57 & p.95 §§29–30.

[27] Comm. No. 516/1992 (*Simunek* v. *The Czech Republic*), Views adopted on 19 July 1995, *Report of HRC* (A/50/40), Vol.II, pp. 89–97.

satisfy all the people affected during the communist regime. Notwithstanding, in its views adopted on 19 July 1995, the Human Rights Committee noted that the requirements of citizenship and permanent residence were unreasonable because, for one thing, the claimants' original entitlement to the property had not been predicated on either of the two conditions and, for another, the state party itself had been responsible for forcing the claimants to leave the country and seek citizenship in other states. For that reason, the Committee decided that the disputed act contravened Article 26, and recommended that the state party provide claimants with an effective remedy. On 23 July 1996 the Committee adopted similar views with respect to the communication of Adam.[28]

Subsequently, on 27 October 1997, the Committee's Special Rapporteur for the Follow-Up of Views met with the Representative of the Czech Republic in Geneva, who explained that Czech domestic courts had proceeded slowly in handling the restitution claims under Act 87/1991 because of the sheer number of complaints and of difficulties in establishing title to the property.[29] The representative also explained that the claimants in the cases of Simunek and others and of Adam would be required to pursue their claims before Czech courts within the statutory time-limit, and that the constitutional court was not expected, in the near future, to address the issue whether the conditions of citizenship were discriminatory since no formal claim on that point had been filed.[30] Furthermore, on 17 July 1999, the Committee's Special Rapporteur for the Follow-Up of Views met again with the Czech Representative in Geneva, who referred to political problems which the state party was facing in implementing the Committee's views in the two cases.[31] All these seem to suggest that the state party has been experiencing not only *de jure* but also *de facto* difficulties in complying with the Committee's views.

Another communication on Czech restitution claim submitted by Des Fours Walderode clearly demonstrates the existence of such difficulties.[32] The claimant was born in the Austro-Hungarian Empire and after World War I became a citizen of the newly-established Czechoslovakia. In 1941 he succeeded to real estate of his father, but during the reign of post-World War II communist regime the property was confiscated by the government and he had to leave Czechoslovakia. Following the collapse of the communist regime in Czechoslovakia the claimant returned to Prague and in 1992 the Czech Ministry of Interior conferred Czech citizenship on him. In the same year Act 243/1992 came into force, under which he became eligible for restitution of the property in question. In fact, in 1993, he took

---

[28] Comm. No. 586/1994 (*Adam* v. *The Czech Republic*), Views adopted on 23 July 1996, *Report of HRC* (A/51/40), Vol.II, pp. 165–173.

[29] In order to monitor the compliance by states parties with views adopted by the Human Rights Committee, the Committee decided in July 1990 to nominate, among its members, a Special Rapporteur for the Follow-Up of Views. *Report of HRC* (A/45/40), Vol.II, pp. 205–206.

[30] *Report of HRC* (A/53/40), Vol. I, pp. 76–77 §492.

[31] *Report of HRC* (A/54/40), Vol. I, p. 96 §465.

[32] *Report of HRC* (A/57/40), Vol. II, pp. 88–95, Comm. No. 747/1997.

possession of his lands. However, political pressure against the claimant gradually built up, and in 1995 a group called 'Citizens' Initiative' petitioned the revision of the restitution arrangements. Finally, in 1996, Law 243/1992 was amended to add a new condition which required of any claimant for restitution 'uninterrupted Czechoslovakia/Czech citizenship from the end of World War II until 1 January 1990'. As a result, the restitution arrangements concerning the claimant's property were invalidated.

In its views adopted on 30 October 2001, the Human Rights Committee referred to its views on the communication of Simunek and others and concluded that the addition of a new condition requiring uninterrupted citizenship as well as the retroactive application of that condition was arbitrary, constituting a violation of Article 26 of the International Covenant on Civil and Political Rights. However, irrespective of the propriety of these specific views, the following factors need to be taken into account:

First, Article 1, which is common to both the International Covenant on Civil and Political Rights and the International Covenant on Economic, Social and Cultural Rights, provides the right to self-determination by which each state party is entitled to choose freely its political and economic system. As a matter of fact, in 1966 when the two Covenants were adopted by the United Nations General Assembly, many member states of the United Nations maintained socialist or centrally-planned economies. Even today some states exclude foreigners from the ownership of real estate in their territories. *Second*, there exists no principle of international law which protects an absolute right to inherit private property, and the issue of such inheritance is left to regulations of relevant rules of private international law of the states concerned. *Third*, the Human Rights Committee itself makes it clear, in its General Comment 18 on Non-Discrimination, that the principle of equality and non-discrimination allows different treatment if the criteria of differentiation are reasonable and objective and if the aim is to achieve a legitimate purpose under the Covenant. Considering the *de facto* financial burden that the restitution of confiscated property can impose on the Czech Republic, it is not impossible to argue that the requirements of citizenship and residence may well constitute such criteria and that the different treatment of original owners of the confiscated property does not necessarily violate the principle of equality and non-discrimination as provided by Article 26 of the International Covenant on Civil and Political Rights.

(3) The Views Indicating Inconsistency of the Human Rights Committee's Jurisprudence in its Application of Article 26

Some of the views adopted by the Human Rights Committee appear to reveal inconsistency of its jurisprudence in applying Article 26 to similar cases. For example, in its views adopted on 25 July 1990, the Committee dealt with a communication concerning conscientious objectors.[33] According to the communication, the Finish Act on Unarmed and Civil Service was amended in 1986 and the duration of civilian service, which had been 12 months before the amendment, was extended to 16 months, whereas the duration of military service remained eight months. The claimant argued that the previous term of 12 months had not necessarily been discriminatory within the meaning of Article 26 of the Covenant, but that a prolongation from 12 to 16 months was disproportionately long, indicative of the government's intention to introduce a punitive element against alternative service of a civil nature. The government of Finland contended that the amendment, under which applicants for civil service were merely required to make their own declarations, did not indicate any intention of, or actual, discrimination vis-à-vis conscientious objectors. The *ratio legis* for the amendment was to ascertain the conscientious conviction of conscripts in a manner so as not to encourage conscripts to escape military service purely for personal benefit or convenience.

The Committee noted, in its views, that the amended procedure was designed to facilitate the administration of alternative service and had no discriminatory purpose. The Committee, while being aware that the impact of the legislative differentiation might work to the detriment of genuine conscientious objectors, concluded that the new arrangements removed from them the often difficult task of proving the genuineness of their convictions and that the extended period of alternative service was neither unreasonable nor punitive. Thus, the Committee found that the relevant facts did not disclose a violation of Article 26 of the Covenant.

Nevertheless, in its views adopted on 3 November 1999, the Committee reached a completely opposite conclusion with respect to a similar communication submitted by a conscientious objector in France.[34] In this communication the claimant, who had been criminally punished for deserting his alternative service after one year, alleged that the relevant French law prescribed a period of 24 months for civil service in comparison with a period of 12 months for military service, and that the length of alternative service twice as long as that of military service amounted to a punitive element, not based on any reasonable and objective criterion. The French government contended that the domestic law in question allowed individuals to opt freely by a mere request for alternative service according to their beliefs, that the different period for the services reflected heavier constraints of service in the army, that the difference in length of the services was said to be the only way to verify the seriousness of objections, that conscientious objectors had a wide choice of posts including service within their professional interest, and that the punishment of the claimant was not based on his beliefs but on his refusal to respect the conditions of the service of his own choosing.

---

33 Comm. No. 295/1988 (*Järvinen* v. *Finland*), Views adopted on 25 July 1990, *Report of HRC* (A/45/40), Vol. II, pp. 101–107.

34 Comm. No. 666/1995 (*Foin* v. *France*), Views adopted on 3 November 1999, *Report of HRC* (A/55/40), Vol. II, pp. 30–40.

The Committee recognized, in its views, that a difference between military service and alternative service might justify a longer period for the latter if the differentiation was based on reasonable and objective criteria. In this particular case, however, the Committee considered that the reasons forwarded by the French government referred to criteria for differentiation in general terms without specific reference to the claimant's communication. In the opinion of the Committee, since the government appeared to argue that doubling the length of service was the only way to test the sincerity of individuals' beliefs, such argument did not satisfy the requirement that the difference in treatment in this particular case was based on reasonable and objective criteria, thus making it a violation of Article 26.

As a matter of fact, in the Finish case, three members of the Committee appended a dissenting opinion to the effect that the amended procedure was for the sake of administrative convenience to replace the earlier method of testing the sincerity of applicants' objection and it did constitute a sanction against genuine conscientious objectors. Therefore, it may be observed that, as a result of subsequent development, the majority of the Committee members have changed their positions. But, at the same time, it must not be overlooked that three other members appended a dissenting opinion in the French case, in which they pointed out that the testing of sincerity of conscientious objectors was likely to involve intrusion into matters of privacy and conscience, that the French law allowed a wide range of choice for alternative service including service in fields of individuals' professional interest, and that military service was accompanied by various burdens and risks not attached to alternative service. Considering all these elements, the dissenting opinion emphasized that the differentiation between the two categories of service under the French law was based on reasonable and objective criteria and did not constitute a violation of Article 26. Whichever views might prevail in the Committee, this difference of opinion among its members certainly testified to the difficulty in applying the principle of equality and non-discrimination to concrete cases, and the Committee's jurisprudence in these two cases suffered from inconsistency.

The same holds true with the Committee's jurisprudence on the Czech restitution cases. As noted earlier, after the collapse of communism, Czechoslovakia attempted to eradicate injustices committed during the former regime and adopted Act 87/1991 which provided restitution of, or compensation for, private property confiscated by that regime.[35] The restitution Act was succeeded to by both the Czech Republic and Slovakia after the dissolution of Czechoslovakia. In 1993 one of the original owners of such property in Slovakia tried to avail himself of the Act, but his claim was rejected by domestic courts because the property in question was confiscated in 1945 whereas the law was applicable to confiscations which took place in the period from 1948 to 1989. Subsequently, he submitted a communication to the Human Rights Committee based on a similar claim. In its views adopted on 14 July 1997[36] the Committee noted that the claimant was not alleging discriminatory

---

[35] *See supra* note 27.

[36] *Report of HRC* (A/52/40), Vol.II, pp. 300–303, Comm. No. 643/1994.

treatment with respect to property confiscated after 1948 but that he was alleging Act 87/1991 was discriminatory because it did not compensate victims of confiscation which took place earlier in 1945. However, in the opinion of the Committee the fact that the Act did not apply to property confiscated in 1945 by the pre-communist regime did not appear to be *prima facie* discriminatory within the meaning of Article 26. Thus, the Committee declared the communication inadmissible on the ground that the claimant failed to substantiate his claim under Article 26. The Committee reached the same conclusion on two similar communications against the Czech Republic.[37]

Nevertheless, in its views adopted on 31 October 2001, the Human Rights Committee chose an entirely different approach in another communication concerning the Czech restitution Act.[38] The claimant was to inherit his parents' house in Prague, which was confiscated in 1940 and 1941 by the German occupation authorities and was sold to a private company in 1942. In 1946, after the defeat of Germany, the Czech Ministry of the Interior decided to reinstate the parents as the rightful owners of the house pursuant to Decree No.5/1945, but the private company, which had been nationalized with all its possessions in 1945, appealed against this decision and the Czech courts annulled the Ministry's decision because Decree No.5/1945 excluded national property from its application. After the collapse of the communist regime the claimant sought to recover the house under Act 87/1991 as amended by Act 116/1994. The amended Act referred to restitution or compensation to victims of racial persecution during World War II, on the basis of which the claimant argued that the amendment should allow restitution of property confiscated during the German occupation. The Czech courts rejected the claimant's argument on the ground that even the amended Act was applicable only to property confiscated during the communist regime, i.e. in the period between 25 February 1948 and 1 January 1990.

However, the Human Rights Committee considered that the Act in question or its application by the Czech courts disclosed discriminatory treatment of the claimant in the following way: On the one hand, the original owners of the private property, which had been confiscated by the German occupation authorities during World War II but had not been nationalized in 1945, could claim restitution or compensation under Act 87/1991 as amended by Act 116/1994 if that property was confiscated during the relevant period. On the other hand, the claimant, whose private property had been similarly confiscated by the German occupation authorities and was nationalized in 1945, was excluded from raising such a claim. Thus, in the opinion of the Committee, the claimant was denied his right to equal protection of the law in violation of Article 26 of the International Covenant on Civil and Political Rights.

---

[37] *Report of HRC* (A/54/40), Vol.II, pp. 291–297, Comm.No.669/1995; *ibid.*, pp. 298–304, Comm. No. 670/1995.

[38] Comm. No. 774/1997 (*Brok* v. *The Czech Republic*), Views adopted on 31 October 2001, *Report of HRC* (A/57/40), Vol. II, pp. 110–116.

In general it is doubtful whether and to what extent the Human Rights Committee could and should question the interpretation and application of domestic laws by domestic courts, but in this particular case the Committee appeared to have gone far beyond the limit to which it usually keeps.[39] In any event it is obvious that the Committee's views on this communication contradicted its earlier jurisprudence in similar cases.

(4) The Views Showing Inappropriate Application of Article 26 by the Human Rights Committee

At least in one communication the Human Rights Committee adopted views, which seem to show inappropriate application of Article 26. It was the communication of Rehoboth Baster Community et al, in which the claimants alleged that the denial of their self-determination and the expropriation of their communal land under the Namibian Constitution constituted a violation by Namibia of Articles 1, 14, 17, 25, 26 and 27 of the Covenant.[40] In its views adopted on 25 July 2000, as far as their claim under Article 1 was concerned, the Committee recalled its jurisprudence that it would not address the issue whether the claimant belonged to a 'people' as stipulated by Article 1 because the Optional Protocol provided a procedure for 'individuals' to claim a violation of their rights protected in Chapter III (Articles 6–27) of the Covenant. The Committee also found no violation of the other Articles invoked by the claimants except Article 26. As for Article 26 the Committee noted that the constitution made English the official language of Namibia and that the government instructed civil servants not to reply in the Afrikaans language to the claimants' written or oral communications with the authorities. Considering the claimants' allegation that the instruction intentionally targeted the use of Afrikaans in dealing with public authorities, the Committee concluded that the claimants, as Afrikaans speakers, were victims of a violation of Article 26 of the Covenant.

Six members of the Committee appended dissenting opinions, pointing out that a state party with numerous tribes and languages had a legitimate concern to choose an official language for the purpose of promoting national integration, that the government circular in which the disputed instruction was given specifically stated that Afrikaans which once enjoyed the status of an official language was now granted the same status as other tribal languages, and that consequently the issue of discrimination did not arise. As the dissenting opinion indicated, the Human Rights Committee in its views in this particular case unfortunately applied Article 26 in such a far-fetched way that it ignored the clear language of the circular in question, and the Committee was to blame for this inappropriate application of the principle of equality and non-discrimination.

---

[39] The present writer submitted his dissenting opinion in this case. However, for unknown reasons, it did not appear in the relevant Annual Report (A/57/40, Vol. II at p. 116).

[40] Comm. No. 760/1997 (*Diergaardt* v. *Namibia*), Views adopted on 25 July 2000, *Report of HRC* (A/55/40), Vol. II, pp. 140–160.

V. CONCLUDING REMARKS

The examination in the present Article has clarified an interesting evolution of the jurisprudence of the Human Rights Committee concerning the application of Article 26 of the International Covenant on Civil and Political Rights. At the initial stage of its activities the Committee maintained a cautious approach in applying the provisions of Article 26 to concrete cases of communications submitted to it under the Optional Protocol. In 1987, however, with the adoption of its views on the *Dutch Unemployment Act* cases, the Committee decided that Article 26 provided an autonomous right to equality before the law and the equal protection of the law without discrimination, and that the principle of equality and non-discrimination prohibited discrimination in law and in fact in any field regulated and protected by public authorities. As such Article 26 was applicable not only to the rights set forth in the Covenant but also to any other right including, in particular, rights of an economic and social nature.

This meant that the Human Rights Committee had to decide on communications involving such issues as social security and/or pension rights, and that the adoption of its views might impose heavy financial burdens on states parties concerned. Probably because of that consideration, the Committee has generally exercised due caution in applying Article 26 to concrete cases of communications. However, as the examination above indicates, the Committee's jurisprudence on Article 26 revealed inconsistency in a few cases and the Committee applied Article 26 inappropriately at least in one case.

Perhaps, the Human Rights Committee has been correct in extending the scope of application of Article 26 to any field regulated and protected by public authorities of states parties. The Committee has also been correct in exercising due care in its application of Article 26 to concrete cases of various communications. For example, in the case of *Gauthier* v. *Canada* the Committee dealt with the claim of a publisher that his freedom of expression was unduly limited in violation of Article 19 of the Covenant.[41] According to the claimant, access to the precincts of Parliament was available only to members of the Parliamentary Press Gallery Association and the state party allowed the association to exercise exclusive control over the qualifications for its membership, which had been denied him. He also alleged that his repeated requests for equal access on the same terms as reporters who belonged to the association had been constantly rejected by the Speaker of the House. In its views adopted on 7 April 1999, the Committee admitted the publisher's claim, finding a violation of Article 19 by Canada. However, in their separate opinions, several Committee members argued that the facts as presented by the claimant disclosed a violation of Article 26 in addition to a violation of Article 19. Against this argument, another member of the Committee warned in his individual opinion in the following words, which are set out below in place of Concluding Remarks in the present Article:

---

[41] Comm. No. 633/1995 (*Gauthier* v. *Canada*), Views adopted on 7 April 1999, *Report of HRC* (A/54/40), Vol. II, pp. 93–110.

In my mind, it is not sufficient, in order to substantiate a violation of [A]rticle 26, merely to state that no reason[s] were given for a decision [to reject the claimant's request for access to the precincts of Parliament]. Furthermore, it seems to me that the author's [the claimant's] claim under [A]rticle 26 is in essence a restatement of his claim under [A]rticle 19. It amounts to the argument that while others were allowed access to the Press Gallery, the author was denied access. Accepting that this constitutes a violation of [A]rticle 26 would seem to imply that in almost every case in which one individual's rights under other Articles of the Covenant are violated, there will also be a violation of [A]rticle 26.

THE HUMAN RIGHTS COMMITTEE'S JURISPRUDENCE ON ARTICLE 26 – A PYRRHIC VICTORY?

Christian Tomuschat

I. INTRODUCTION

In 1987, the Human Rights Committee (hereinafter: the Committee) took a bold decision by giving a wide interpretation to Article 26 of the International Covenant on Civil and Political Rights (hereinafter: the Covenant).[1] In two final views under Article 5(4) of the (First) Optional Protocol (hereinafter: Optional Protocol), the cases of *Broeks* and *Zwaan-de Vries*, it held that Article 26 sets forth an autonomous guarantee the applicability of which, by contrast to Article 2(1), is not confined to the rights listed elsewhere in the Covenant.[2] Textually, it said that on a par with Article 7 of the Universal Declaration of Human Rights Article 26 applies 'in any field regulated and protected by public authorities'.[3] Two years later, the new doctrine was consolidated in a general comment under Article 40(4).[4] By so opining, the Committee extended its area of jurisdiction beyond the realm of civil and political rights to all the activities, which states, to whom the obligations arising from the Covenant are addressed, may undertake at any given point in time. Through the concept of equality and non-discrimination, states parties to the Covenant are henceforth placed under comprehensive supervision. In political terms, one might say that the Committee has thereby attained for itself the first place among all the treaty bodies called upon to monitor compliance with one of the treaty instruments for the protection of human rights. All the other treaty bodies have a limited field of competence. Only the Committee is able to pass judgment on the conduct of states parties irrespective of the subject-matter concerned, provided that an applicant raises complaints under Article 26.

---

[1] In the following, all the articles referred to without any more specific identification will be articles of the Covenant.

[2] At the end of this article, the reader will find in chronological order a list of all the decisions deemed relevant for a proper understanding of the case law of the Committee.

[3] Case No. 172/1984 (*Broeks* v. *The Netherlands)* and Case No. 182/1984 (*Zwaan-de Vries* v. *The Netherlands*), Views adopted on 9 April 1987, UN doc. A/42/40, 139 (CCPR/C/29/D/172/1984) and p. 160 at para. 12.3. *See* our comment 'Der Gleichheitssatz nach dem Internationalen Pakt über bürgerliche und politische Rechte', *Europäische Grundrechte Zeitschrift* 1989, p. 37 *et seq*.

[4] General Comment 18 (37), adopted on 10 November 1989, Official Records of the Human Rights Committee 1989/90 (ORHRC 1989/90), Vol. II, p. 377, at p. 378 para. 12.

II. THE CONTROVERSY SURROUNDING THE *BROEKS – ZWAAN-DE VRIES* JURISPRUDENCE

Even today, the rationale with which the Committee attempted to justify its construction of Article 26 does not seem to be entirely convincing. In *Broeks* and *Zwaan-de Vries* the Committee proceeds in three steps. In the first step (para. 12.1), it emphasizes the autonomy of the International Covenant on Civil and Political Rights vis-à-vis the parallel Covenant on Economic, Social and Cultural Rights (ICESCR). To be sure, both treaties are independent from one another. Yet it can hardly be contested that the drafters intended to entrust the protection of economic, social and cultural rights to ECOSOC[5] and not to the Committee.[6] Secondly, the Committee examines the *travaux préparatoires*, calling its scrutiny 'inconclusive' (para. 12.2). The present author has also attempted to clarify the complex drafting history and has come to a different result,[7] but there is no doubt that one may in good faith appraise the tortuous discussions in the Commission on Human Rights and the General Assembly in a different light, given the fact, in particular, that many delegates in the two bodies lost their road map and were not fully aware of what was really at stake.[8] Lastly, the Committee invokes the 'ordinary meaning' of the provision in its context and in the light of its object and purpose (para. 12.3). It is at this point that the arguments put forward by the Committee fall short of what could have been expected from a careful analysis of the legal position. It rightly states that 'Article 26 does not merely duplicate the guarantees already provided for in Article 2'. In fact, it is precisely the relationship between Article 2(1) and Article 26 which

---

[5] It is a matter of common knowledge that today the functions entrusted to ECOSOC are discharged by an expert body, the Committee on Economic, Social and Cultural Rights.

[6] Article 16 ICESCR. Hardly understandable is the assertion by Syméon Karagiannis, 'Considérations sur l'article 26 du Pacte des Nations Unies relatif aux droits civils et politiques', in: *Les droits de l'homme au seuil du troisième millénaire. Mélanges en hommage à Pierre Lambert, Bruxelles* 2000, p. 467 *et seq*., at p. 476, that, proceeding from the premise of complementarity of the two Covenants, 'une disposition, comme celle de l'article 26, reconnaissant l'égalité devant la loi de manière générale et inconditionnelle, devrait pouvoir régir tous les droits de l'homme, que ceux-ci soient consignés dans le Pacte sur les droits civils et politiques ou dans le Pacte sur les droits économiques, sociaux et culturels'.

[7] 'Equality and non-Discrimination under the International Covenant on Civil and Political Rights', in: Ingo von Münch (ed.), *Staatsrecht – Völkerrecht – Europarecht. Festschrift für Hans-Jürgen Schlochauer*, Berlin / New York 1981, p. 691 *et seq*. Although studying the drafting history, Warwick McKean, *Equality and Discrimination under International Law*, Oxford 1983, p. 137–141, does not touch upon the decisive issues.

[8] Rightly, Karagiannis, *supra* note 6, at p. 487, writes that the real problem was never clearly raised in debates which he characterizes as 'touffus, longs et peut-être lassants'.

needed to be clarified.[9] General comment 18(37) did not provide any fresh reasons to buttress the interpretation chosen and to dispel the remaining doubts.[10]

Both provisions must have a real meaning. Since both are integral elements of the Covenant, none of them can be interpreted away. It is clear also that they define their scope of application differently. Whereas Article 2(1) sets forth a non-discrimination clause which like Article 14 of the European Convention on Human Rights is confined to 'the rights recognized in the present Covenant', Article 26 speaks of equality and non-discrimination in a general way, without specifying any limitation *ratione materiae*. Undoubtedly, to reconcile these two seemingly contradictory propositions is not easy. But there was – and still is – a way out of this dilemma. Equality before the law and equal protection of the law could be taken to mean that, after it has been enacted, the law – i.e. any legal rule – must be applied and enforced in full respect for its terms, without differentiating in the process of implementation between men and women, rich and poor etc. according to considerations of political expediency.[11]

Such interpretation would at the same time do justice to the general mandate of the Committee, which is a body entrusted with securing civil and political rights. It is implied in that task to see to it that the rule of law be observed, irrespective of its contents. If the executive branch of government applies the law in force selectively, the foundations of the rule of law are in jeopardy. If, on the other hand, Article 26 is interpreted in a broader sense as requiring that there be equality 'in' the law, the Committee will have to deal with substantive issues in the most varied legal fields, from the law of social security to tax law or the law of state subsidies.[12] Fortunately for the Committee, the opportunities now provided by Article 26 have not yet been fully discovered by lawyers in all the states parties to the Covenant. Otherwise, the Committee might have been overwhelmed by applications, which it could not properly deal with, either quantitatively or qualitatively. Indeed, it should be repeated that the Committee is the main expert body in the field of civil and political rights. Its members are recruited on account of their expertise concerning these rights. Economic and social rights are much more difficult to handle, given their dependence on contextual factors. Thus, on the whole, it was extremely ambitious to

---

[9] Additionally, it should be noted that the Covenant contains a number of other non-discrimination clauses which, on their part, would have little sense if Article 26 had the meaning derived from it by the committee: Articles 3, 4(1), 14(1), 25(1).

[10] *See supra* note 4.

[11] Karagiannis, *loc. cit.* (*supra* note 6), at p. 485, believes that there is no substantive difference between the two articles, except for their different scope of application *ratione materiae*.

[12] In spite of this difficulty, some authors advocated right from the beginning that Article 26 should be generally able to be invoked. Thus, B.G. Ramcharan, 'Equality and Non-discrimination', in: Louis Henkin (ed.), *The International Bill of Rights. The Covenant on Civil and Political Rights*, New York 1981, affirmed that even denial of a 'tax rebate' could constitute a denial of equal protection under Article 26.

claim that the Committee had a right of supervision also in the fields covered by rights of the second generation.

It is amazing to note that Article 2(1) is overlooked in many decisions of the Committee, although according to the structure of the Covenant it is the most prominent provision governing instances of discrimination. Recourse to Article 26 is necessary and indispensable whenever an applicant invokes a violation which lies outside the scope *ratione materiae* of the other substantive Articles of the Covenant; all other claims could be dealt with under Article 2(1). Yet in many instances of the latter class Article 2(1) is not even mentioned. Thus, the cases where French nationals sought to employ the Breton language in judicial proceedings but were unsuccessful in this attempt concerned, on the one hand, freedom of expression, and, on the other hand, the right to a fair hearing in accordance with Article 14. Nonetheless, the Committee focuses exclusively on Article 26 in reviewing the communications brought by the applicants.[13] Likewise, issues of fairness of proceedings were in issue in *Cheban* v. *Russian Federation* (2001), where the Committee had to respond to the allegation of the applicant that he had been unjustly denied a jury trial. Again, although the heart of the matter was located in Article 14 (1), the Committee failed to make any reference to Article 2(1).[14] A similar observation can be made with regard to *Kavanagh* v. *Ireland* (1991), where the complaint was made that the distribution of competences between ordinary courts and a Special Criminal Court could be arbitrarily chosen by the Attorney-General, depending on his political judgment, and that in fact this had happened in the case at hand. In *Debreczeny* v. *Netherlands* (1995) the application of rules on incompatibility between different functions in government had to be assessed: Could a police officer at the same time be a member of a local council? Here, the Committee left aside not only Article 2(1), but also the introductory clause of Article 25, which explicitly provides that the right to be elected shall be granted 'without any of the distinctions mentioned in Article 2 and without unreasonable restrictions'.[15] The research undertaken by the present writer has unearthed just one case where the Committee explicitly states that the same issue as examined under Article 26 could also arise under Article 2(1).[16] In fact, there seems to be a growing tendency among applicants to invoke Article 26 with a view to bringing to the

---

[13] Case No. 219/1986 (*Guesdon* v. *France*), Views adopted on 25 July 1990, UN doc. A/45/40 Vol. II, 61 (CCPR/C/39/D/219/1986) at paras. 10.4, 11; Case No. 221/1987 and 323/1988, (*Cadoret and Le Bihan* v. *France*), Views adopted on 11 April 1991, UN doc. A/46/40, 223 (CCPR/C/41/D/221/1987) at para. 5.8; Case No. 327/1988 (*Barzhig* v. *France*), Views adopted on 11 April 1991, UN doc. A/46/40, 272 (CCPR/C/41/D/327/1988) at para. 5.7.

[14] Case No. 790/1997 (*Cheban* v. *Russian Federation*), Views adopted on 24 July 2001, UN doc. A/56/40 Vol. II, 88 (CCPR/C/72/D/790/1997) at paras. 7.1–7.4.

[15] It could be argued that these two provisions implicitly provide the basis for the reasoning in para. 9.2 of the decision of the Committee.

[16] Case No. 488/1992 (*Toonen* v. *Australia*), Views adopted on 31 March 1994, UN doc. A/49/40 Vol. II, 226 (CCPR/C/50/D/488/1992) at para. 8.7.

attention of the Committee anything that seems objectionable, without bothering too much about its characterization as 'discrimination'.

The uncertainties about the scope of application of Article 26 in the jurisprudence of the Committee have prompted three states to enter reservations. When in 1993 acceding to the Optional Protocol, Germany declared that the competence of the Committee shall not apply to communications

> 'c) by means of which a violation of Article 26 of the [said Covenant] is reprimanded, if and insofar as the reprimanded violation refers to rights other than those guaranteed under the aforementioned Covenant.'[17]

There can be no doubt that the jurisprudence initiated by the Committee in *Broeks* and *Zwaan-de Vries* was the reason for this highly unusual reservation. According to the Committee's General Comment No. 24(52), such a reservation, which had not been made already at the time of ratification of the Covenant itself, is incompatible with the object and purpose of the Optional Protocol.[18] To date, the lawfulness of the German reservation has not yet been tested in a case brought before the Committee. We shall refrain from commenting on this divergence of opinions.

Switzerland, which acceded to the Covenant in 1992, made a reservation on that occasion which foreshadowed what Germany did one year later with respect to the Optional Protocol. [19] It specified:

> 'L'égalité de toutes les personnes devant la loi et leur droit à une égale protection de la loi sans discrimination ne seront garanties qu'en liaison avec d'autres droits contenus dans le présent Pacte.'[20]

Thus, also Switzerland has misgivings about the generous way in which the Committee conceives its mandate under Article 26.[21] Lastly, Liechtenstein followed the example set by its two neighbours when it acceded to the Covenant in 1998.[22] In the circumstances, it is certainly not wrong to say that no other interpretation suggested by the Committee is as controversial as the scope it has assigned to Article 26.

---

[17] Deposit of instrument of accession on 25 August 1993.

[18] [1995] Report of the Human Rights Committee ([1995] HRC Report), UN doc. A/50/40 Vol. I, p. 119, at 122 paras. 13–14.

[19] Deposit of instrument of accession on 18 September 1992.

[20] UN doc. CCPR/C/2/Rev.4, 24 1994, p. 44.

[21] *See also below* (*infra* note 44) the aftermath of the Committee's decision in *Gueye*, where the French Conseil d'Etat flatly stated that the views expressed by the Committee were not binding on France.

[22] Deposit of the instrument of ratification on 10 December 1998. The reservation is worded as follows: 'The Principality of Liechtenstein reserves the right to guarantee the rights contained in article 26 of the Covenant concerning the equality of all persons before the law and their entitlement without any discrimination to the equal protection of the law only in connection with other rights contained in the present Covenant.'

It is the purpose of this article to inquire what results the new jurisprudence on Article 26 has yielded during the fifteen years since the Committee embarked on its current course in *Broeks* and *Zwaan-de Vries*. Without again challenging the well-foundedness of the interpretation adopted in 1987, it will attempt to ascertain whether the extension of the principle of equality and non-discrimination to all fields of governmental activity has proved to be useful for applicants, by being usable as a weapon in cases of discrimination which otherwise could not be combated, and manageable for the Committee itself, since the wide opening of the gates of the Optional Protocol could end up in overburdening it with cases exceeding its working capacity.

III. THE MAIN POINTS OF THE CASE LAW CONCERNING ARTICLE 26

1) Reasonable and Objective Grounds

It is perhaps the central proposition in the *Broeks – Zwaan-de Vries* jurisprudence that not every distinction amounts to discrimination, which is forbidden by Article 26. Indeed, in the modern social welfare state legislation has become the art of distinguishing. Rare are the statutes which are in a real sense addressed to everyone. Mostly, when domestic statutes are adopted today, they are meant to remedy a specific situation which concerns not the entire population, but a specific social group where problems of some kind or another have arisen. The Committee is therefore right in holding that 'a differentiation based on reasonable and objective criteria does not amount to prohibited discrimination within the meaning of Article 26'.[23] This holding has been repeated time and again.[24] Sometimes the formulations vary slightly, but those variations do not mean that the Committee has strayed from its course. It invariably attempts to find whether a distinction made by the legislative or the executive branch of government can be justified within the context of the relevant facts.

---

[23] Case No. 172/1984 (*Broeks* and *Zwaan-de Vries* v. *The Netherlands*), Views adopted on 9 April 1987, UN doc. A/42/40, 149 (CCPR/C/29/D/172/1984) at para. 13.

[24] *See* for instance, Case No. 218/1986 (*Vos* v. *The Netherlands*), Views adopted on 29 March 1989, UN doc. A/44/40, 232 (CCPR/C/35/D/218/1986) at para. 11.3; Case No. 295/1988 (*Järvinen* v. *Finland*), Views adopted on 25 July 1990, UN doc. A/45/40 Vol. II, 101 at para. 6.3; Case No. 516/1992 (*Simunek* v. *The Czech Republic*), Views adopted on 19 July 1995, UN doc. A/50/40 Vol. II, 89 (CCPR/C/54/D/516/1992) at para. 11.5; Case No. 454/1991 (*García Pons* v. *Spain*), Views adopted on 30 October 1995, UN doc. A/51/40 Vol. II, 30 (CCPR/C/55/D/454/1991) at para. 9.4; Case No. 608/1995 (*Nahlik* v. *Austria*), Decision adopted on 22 July 1996, UN doc. A/51/40 Vol. II, 259 at para. 8.4; Case No. 666/1995 (*Foin* v. *France*), Views adopted on 3 November 1999, UN doc. A/55/40 Vol. II, 30 (CCPR/C/67/D/666/1995) at para. 10.3.

2) Equality in the Law

The second element of the conception of Article 26 as adopted by the Committee consists of requiring legislative bodies to act in full respect for equality and non-discrimination. General Comment 18(37) explains that these principles govern 'legislation and the application thereof'.[25] In substance, this is nothing new with regard to an international instrument for the protection of human rights. The Covenant simply enjoins all states parties to comply with the obligations which it sets forth, and in general it matters little which branch of government domestically bears the responsibility for implementing the commands imparted from the international level. However, issues of equality and non-discrimination are particularly sensitive and difficult. Essentially, one can take the view that the task of distinguishing between different groups of persons partakes more of a political than of a legal nature. Consequently, in the past many states, even though permitting judicial review of parliamentary statutes, were reluctant to entrust their tribunals with resorting to equality and non-discrimination as a legal yardstick.[26] This is reflected in all those formulations which speak of equality 'before' the law.[27] Traditionally, this phrase was understood as equality before the courts in a time when judicial review of parliamentary acts was still inconceivable. Although such inhibitions seem to have been overcome by now, in any event in Western democracies, it remains the case that to review whether a given regulation corresponds to the precept of equality and non-discrimination presupposes almost necessarily a value judgment which in many instances is not predetermined by precise legal rules.[28]

3) No Discriminatory Intent Needed

The case law of the Committee has also clarified that discrimination can occur even if there is no intent on the part of the government concerned to discriminate against a given group of persons. Implicitly, this was acknowledged by the Committee in *Singh Bhinder* v. *Canada* (1989).[29] Later, the Committee rejected the defence put up by the Czech Republic in *Simunek* (1995)[30] and *Adam* (1996)[31] by contending that in refusing restitution or compensation to persons whose property had been confiscated

---

[25] *See supra* note 4.

[26] *See* Gerhard Leibholz, 'Die Gleichheit vor dem Gesetz und das Bonner Grundgesetz', *Deutsches Verwaltungsblatt* 1951, p. 193.

[27] Thus, the German Basic Law provides (Article 3(1)) that 'all persons shall be equal before the law'('Alle Menschen sind vor dem Gesetz gleich.').

[28] For a succinct comparative analysis *see* H.-J. Rinck, 'Die höchstrichterliche Rechtsprechung zum Gleichheitssatz in der Bundesrepublik, der Schweiz, Österreich, Italien, den USA und Indien, *Jahrbuch des Öffentlichen Rechts*, Neue Folge, Vol. 10 (1961), p. 269, at 329 *et seq.*

[29] Para. 6.1.

[30] Para. 11.7.

[31] Para. 12.7.

during the communist period it had not pursued a discriminatory aim. Rightly, the Committee stated that 'an act which is not politically motivated may still contravene Article 26 if its effects are discriminatory'. It stands to reason that, for instance, a parliamentary majority, which is not mindful of its obligations under international law may in all good faith adopt a statute which is profoundly discriminatory vis-à-vis a minority group of the population. On this point, the Committee therefore deserves full approval.[32]

4) Inconsistency of Case Law – The Issue of Status

However, the Committee seems to have lost its orientation in developing its case law step by step. Article 26 should be read carefully. Its second sentence contains a list of forbidden grounds of distinction, which corresponds word for word to the list enunciated in Article 2(1). Although the second sentence takes a clear stand against discrimination 'on any ground', it exemplifies what is prohibited by the list just mentioned, which enunciates only stable characteristics of a human person, not just contingent features which may change overnight. In fact, the last two words of the second sentence are particularly revealing. By referring to 'other status', Article 26 makes clear that individuals are protected on account of their 'status', i.e. on account of conditions to which they are irremediably linked or which – as regards religion, political or other opinion – have become part of their personality so that they would have to forego their identity by changing their mind. In fact, concerning all the characteristics enunciated by Article 26 human beings are particularly vulnerable. They are unable to adapt to changing circumstances to follow the *Zeitgeist*. Therefore, it is plausible to argue that they need special protection also in areas lying outside the general scope *ratione materiae* of the Covenant.

To remain faithful to the central concept of status is not something alien to the jurisprudence of the Committee. In one decision, in any event, it was clearly specified that not any legal inconsistency could be deemed to amount to discrimination in the sense contemplated by Article 26. In *B. d. B et al.* v. *Netherlands* (1989) the Committee held that the authors of the communication had not contended that their different treatment 'was attributable to their belonging to any identifiably distinct category which could have exposed them to discrimination on any of the grounds enumerated or "other status" referred to in Article 26'.[33]

The Committee has not followed, however, the direction indicated by the word 'status' in Article 26. It feels that it is entitled to, and should, review any injustice or inconsistency that may be encountered in national law, even if such flaws of the legal regime in issue have nothing to do with the status of the persons concerned. A particularly instructive case is the communication of *Lestourneaud* v. *France*

[32] *But see also* Case No. 295/1988 (*Järvinen* v. *Finland*), Views adopted on 25 July 1990, UN doc. A/45/40 Vol. II, 101 at para. 6.4, where the Committee stated that the impugned legislation 'had no discriminatory purpose'.

[33] Case No. 273/1988 (*B. d. B. et al.* v. *The Netherlands*), Decision adopted on 30 March 1989, UN doc. A/44/40, 286 (CCPR/C/35/D/273/1988) at para. 6.7.

(1999). Lestourneaud had been appointed, within the framework of legal aid, to defend the interests of a minor in a matter before the Assize Court of Haute Savoie. The minor was the civil claimant in a criminal case involving rape and other sexual abuse. The relevant proceeding lasted for two years. After the trial had ended, Lestourneaud sought a higher remuneration than provided for in the legal aid scheme. According to this scheme the defendant's lawyer was entitled to a better remuneration than the plaintiff's lawyer. Lestourneaud felt that this distinction was unwarranted, given the necessity to spend the same time in the proceeding. What was at stake, hence, was the evaluation of the responsible French authorities concerning the value of the work of a defence lawyer, on the one hand, and the work of the lawyer for a plaintiff in a criminal proceeding. To be sure, the Committee dismissed the application as inadmissible. But it did not do so because the complaint did not come within the purview of Article 26. It examined the complaint, finding that 'representation of a person presenting a civil claim in a criminal case cannot be equalled to representing the accused'. It is only because the complaint did not seem to be sufficiently substantiated that it was deemed not to satisfy the prescribed requirements of admissibility. In order to be on the right track, the Committee should have dismissed the application because it did not raise any issue concerning the status of the applicant.

A similar case is that of *G.* v. *Canada* (2000).[34] The applicant, a frustrated academic, holder of a Ph.D. in educational psychology from the University of Toronto, contended that in appointing staff Canadian universities preferred to hire persons with a degree from a university in the United States. Again, this application was dismissed as being inadmissible. But the reasons given for that determination show that the Committee was in principle prepared to consider the allegations in the light of Article 26. The application failed because the applicant had not been able to substantiate that the conduct of the Canadian authorities concerned 'was manifestly arbitrary'.[35] The question is: Can the Committee be really called upon to review whether it is reasonable for an academic institution to distinguish between the quality of diplomas awarded by other academic institutions? It is difficult to see how such a policy could affect the 'status' of a person.

Even worse are those cases where the Committee gets entangled in the complexities of the requirements, which must be met by a person in order for him/her to obtain certain social benefits. Here, the jurisprudence commenced in *Broeks* and *Zwaan-de Vries* has been developed further and further without giving too much consideration to the possible limits of enquiring into the manifold distinctions which legislation in that field necessarily has to make.[36]

---

[34] Case No. 934/2000 (*G* v. *Canada*) Decision adopted on 17 July 2000, UN doc A/55/40 Vol. II (CCPR/C/69/D/934/2000).
[35] *Ibid*., para. 4.2.
[36] For further details *see infra* note 37.

IV. THE AREAS OF APPLICABILITY OF ARTICLE 26

1) Article 2(1) and Article 26

Whenever the centre of gravity of a case is located within the scope *ratione materiae* of Articles 6 to 25 or 27 of the Covenant, Article 26 has no specific role to play. Any dispute of that kind can be dealt with in accordance with the non-discrimination clause of Article 2(1).

2) Social Welfare Benefits

The new course steered by the Committee commenced in the field of social allowances. Both in *Broeks* and *Zwaan-de Vries*, unemployment benefits were in issue. While the applicants were successful in both of these cases, in *Danning*, views handed down on the same day; the Committee dismissed the claim raised by the applicant. In the Netherlands, the first two decisions must have been widely publicized because many complaints relating to the calculation of unemployment payments or pension rights followed. Reference should be made to *P.P.C.* v. *Netherlands* (1988), which again centred on unemployment benefits, *Vos* v. *Netherlands* (1989), where the applicant claimed a disablement allowance, *Sprenger* v. *Netherlands* (1992), a case concerning public health insurance, *Oulajin and Kaiss* v. *Netherlands* (1992), where two Moroccans living in the Netherlands insisted that they were entitled to receive payments under the Dutch Child Benefit Act for foster children living with their wives in Morocco.[37] The high point of that line of cases was reached in *Schmitz-de Jong* (2001), which reflects a mentality of almost shameless plundering of public funds. The applicant, born in 1949, felt violated in her rights under Article 26 because the municipality of her residence refused to issue her a 'partner pass', which gives a right to reduced fees for public transport, social and cultural activities, library services and museum entries. Her husband, born in 1924, was the holder of a pensioners' pass, which every Dutch citizen over the age of 65 can claim. Partners of pensioners have a right to be issued with a partner pass, provided that they have reached the age of 60. When the applicant applied for that pass, she was just 44 years old and obviously did not meet that requirement. Before the Committee she claimed that she was a victim of discrimination on the ground of age. Common sense dictates rejection of such an abusive communication. But the

[37] Further cases: Case No. 418/1990 (*Cavalcanti Araujo-Jongen* v. *The Netherlands*), Views adopted on 22 October 1993, UN doc. A/49/40 Vol. II, 114 (CCPR/C/49/D/418/1990): unemployment benefits; Case No. 425/1990 (*Doesburg Lannooij Neefs* v. *The Netherlands*), Views adopted on 15 July 1994, UN doc. A/49/40 Vol. II, 120 (CCPR/C/51/D/425/1990): social assistance payments; Case No. 484/1991 (*Pepels* v. *The Netherlands*), Views adopted on 15 July 1994, UN doc. A/49/40 Vol. II, 221 (CCPR/C/51/D/484/1991): widower pension; Case No. 477/1991 (*B.-R.* v. *The Netherlands*), Decision adopted on 7 April 1994, UN doc. A/49/40 Vol. II, 294 (CCPR/C/50/D/47): unemployment benefits; Case No. 658/1995 (*Van Oord* v. *The Netherlands*), Decision adopted on 23 July 1997, UN doc. A/52/40 Vol. II, 311 (CCPR/C/60/D/658/1995): retirement pension.

Committee carefully reviewed the complaints, finding that the age limit of 60 years was an objective criterion of differentiation.

It is true that discrimination on account of age raises complex problems. Age is certainly a 'status' from which nobody can escape. However, that status is not mentioned in the list enunciated by Article 26. It would be extremely awkward if the Committee started to examine the issue of age discrimination on the basis of a case-by-case examination in all fields of life. Whether there should exist a compulsory retirement age in any given country is a matter of political determination. The Covenant provides no indication as to how that conflict of interests should be resolved. It stands to reason that there can be no age limit for the rights enshrined in the Covenant. The right to life, freedom from torture and freedom of expression cannot be made subject to any age requirement. But age limits for civil servants or generally for labour contracts in the economy are a different matter altogether. It is precisely this issue which demonstrates on how dangerous a path the Committee has embarked.

The Netherlands is not the only country whose legislation in social matters has been reviewed by the Committee. France was the defendant in the case of *Gueye* (1989), where former Senegalese members of the French Armed Forces complained of being discriminated against as to their pension rights inasmuch as the level of payments had been frozen in 1975. In *Blom* (1988) as well as in *Lindgren and others* (1990) Sweden had to defend itself against the allegation that discrimination was being practiced against private schools. A similar reproach was brought forward against Canada in *Waldman* (1999). Austria was the defendant in *Pauger* (1992), where the issue of a widower's pension rights was in issue, and in *Nahlik* (1996), where distinctions in the calculation of retirement benefits had to be gauged. Lastly, the case of *Drake* v. *New Zealand* (1997) should be mentioned. It concerned the failure to introduce a compensation scheme for civilian victims of Japanese mistreatment during the Second World War. Only members of the Armed Forces of the country receive payments under the War Pensions Act. No remedy has been provided to persons outside New Zealand's armed forces.

Closely related to the class of cases just referred to are those cases where the applicants complained that the contributions they had to make to social security schemes had been fixed at too high a level. Both of the two relevant cases, *B. d. B.* v. *Netherlands* (1989) and *Snijders and others* v. *Netherlands* (1998), were unsuccessful.

3) Property Issues

Property or financial assets are not protected as such by the Covenant. But in conjunction with Article 26 issues of confiscation, restitution and compensation come within the purview of the Covenant. Since 1991, the Committee was seized with a number of communications claiming that the Czech Act 87/1991, which introduced a regime of restitution for property unlawfully confiscated by the communist regime, on condition, however, that the claimant be a Czech national and that he/she reside in the Czech Republic, was incompatible with Article 26 and that, as a consequence, administrative and judicial decisions denying restitution on that ground were at variance with the Republic's obligations under the Covenant. It stands to reason that without the Committee's *Broeks – Zwaan-de Vries* jurisprudence such communications could not have crossed the threshold of admissibility. However, these early cases concerning social security matters had also cleared the ground for an examination as to its merits of the Czech Act 87/1991. In *Simunek* (1995) and *Adam* (1996), the Committee determined that the double requirement of nationality and residence was not based on objective and reasonable grounds, given the fact that through political persecution the former Czechoslovak state itself had driven the claimants out of the national territory. The Czech Republic could not expect persons who had been received as refugees in a foreign country and had eventually taken the nationality of that country, to return to their state of origin.

In the later case of *Blazek and others* (2001), the Committee confirmed its earlier rulings. It noted in this connection that its views in *Simunek* and *Adam* had not been heeded by the Czech Republic (para. 5.3). In the recent cases of *Des Fours Walderode* (2001) and *Fábryová* (2001) it turned out furthermore that the Czech Republic had proceeded to retroactively amending the law or manipulating judicial proceedings in order to frustrate the right of the claimants to restitution of the property which they had enjoyed under the Czech legislation as originally enacted after the fall of the Communist system.

As far as restitution of property of Sudeten Germans is concerned, a claim was also raised by a German citizen that the deadline of 25 February 1948, which excluded confiscatory measures carried out between 1945 and 1948, had been fixed without any good reason and thus amounted to a violation of Article 26. In *Drobek* v. *Slovakia* (1997), the Committee dismissed this claim as being inadmissible, arguing that (para 6.5)

> 'legislation adopted after the fall of the Communist regime in Czechoslovakia to compensate the victims of that regime does not appear to be prima facie discriminatory within the meaning of Article 26 merely because ... it does not compensate the victims of injustices allegedly committed by earlier regimes'.[38]

This line of reasoning was upheld in *Malik* (1998) and *Schlosser* v. *Czech Republic* (1998).[39] Thus, the indirect retrospective effect of the criticism brought under the

---

[38] Dissenting opinion by Committee members Medina Quiroga and Klein, Case No. 643/1995 (*Drobek* v. *Slovakia*), Decision adopted on 14 July 1997, UN doc. A/52/40 Vol. II, 300 at 303 (CCPR/C/60/D/643/1995), who rightly argued that the case would have deserved an examination as to its merits.

[39] Dissenting opinion by Medina Quiroga and Klein, Case No. 669/1995 (*Malik* v. *Czech Republic*), Decision adopted on 21 October 1998, UN doc. A/54/40 Vol. II, 294 (CCPR/C/64/D/669/1995) at 297 and Case No. 670/1995 (*Schlosser* v. *The Czech Republic*), Decision adopted on 21 October 1998, UN doc. A/54/40 Vol. II, 298 (CCPR/C/64/D/670/1995) at 304.

cover of Article 26 was brought to a halt. Only in one case did the Committee go back beyond the cut-off date of 25 February 1948. In *Brok* v. *Czech Republic* (2001), it found that the denial of restitution with regard to Jewish property that had first been confiscated by the Nazi regime during the time of German occupation of Czechoslovakia, was restored to its rightful owners in 1946 and was then nationalized by the Czech state in 1946/1947, amounted to a violation of Article 26. This decision met with resolute dissent by Committee members Scheinin, Ando and Chanet.[40]

The Hungarian legislation on restitution, by contrast, received full approval by the Committee in *Somers* (1996). No distinction was made according to the status of the claimants. Everyone received vouchers with which he/she could participate in acquiring former state property. Even if that method of compensation was disadvantageous for persons not living in Hungary, it could not be objected to as being discriminatory.

4) Alternative Civilian Service

Basing itself on its *Broeks – Zwaan-de Vries* jurisprudence, the Committee has also examined the fairness of legislation setting forth that young men refusing military service have to discharge alternative service of a length considerably more extensive than the military service to which they have objected. Since there is no right to conscientious objection under the Covenant, Article 8(3)(c)(ii) making clear that it is committed to the discretion of states parties to admit 'national service' in lieu of military service, the issue of alternative service lies outside the scope of the Covenant. Hence, Article 2(1) is inapplicable. The Committee has therefore made the comparison between the duration of the two types of compulsory service in the light of Article 26. In a first decision, *Järvinen* v. *Finland* (1990), it found that to increase the length of alternative service to 16 months as compared to eight months for military service can be deemed to be unobjectionable, taking into account the fact that Finland had introduced the regime applicable to the applicant with a view to permitting a free choice of the individual, abstaining henceforth from subjecting conscripts to a painful test of the sincerity of their convictions as conscientious objectors. Curiously enough, however, in *Foin* (1999), *Maille* (2000) as well as *Venier & Nicolas* (2000), it came to a different assessment regarding the French legislation, which also doubled the length of national alternative service, although at a higher level. While military service lasted twelve months, objectors had to serve for 24 months. The Committee did not accept the argument that to prolong the duration of civilian service was the only effective way of testing the sincerity of an individual's convictions. Committee members Ando, Klein and Kretzmer, in the two later decisions joined by member Zakhia, appended a forceful dissenting opinion to these views, arguing that those who perform military service have to shoulder burdens which are not imposed on those opting for alternative service.

---

[40] Case No. 774/1997 (*Brok* v. *The Czech Republic*), Views adopted on 31 October 2001, UN doc. A/57/40 Vol. II, 110 (CCPR/C/73/D/774/1997).

In the case of *Brinkhof* v. *Netherlands* (1993), the Committee noted that regarding exemptions from military service as well as substitute civilian service all religious denominations had to be treated alike. There could be no privilege in favour of a specific religious group. The principle of equality and non-discrimination was of general application. Consequently, Jehovah's witnesses could not claim a special regime just for themselves.

V. THE LEGITIMACY OF GROUNDS OF DISTINCTION

1) General considerations

It is not easy to assess whether all of the decisions by which the Committee has either rejected or accepted a given distinction can on their part be considered objective and reasonable. We shall attempt to review some of these decisions from the viewpoint of our position that the status of a person must be the determinative criterion.

The Committee is certainly on safe ground in holding that the same rules must apply to men and women. Thus, proceeding from the (debatable!) premise that Article 26 constitutes a general clause of equality and non-discrimination, the leading cases of *Broeks* and *Zwaan-de Vries,* which centred on discrimination of women, were rightly decided, and the same can be said of the two cases of *Pauger* v. *Austria* (1992 and 1999), where the applicant challenged the less favourable treatment of widowers in comparison with widows. In fact, equality between the sexes works both ways, in favour of women as well as in favour of men.[41] Likewise, family relations may validly be taken into account. Since the family is placed under the protection of Article 23, social legislation is not prevented from distinguishing between married and unmarried couples when granting financial benefits.[42] On the other hand, no state can be obligated to contribute without any limitation to the upbringing of foster children.[43] As far as nationality is concerned, it certainly defines the status of a person. But the cases of *Simunek* (1995) and *Adam* (1996) have shown that the value of this criterion is a relative one, depending entirely on the context within which it is used. As convincingly pointed out by the Committee in those two cases, nationality cannot be a condition for restitution of property if by measures of persecution the state concerned induced the claimants to flee their home country and to settle abroad where hospitality was granted to them.

---

[41] *See also* Case No. 786/1997 (*Vos* v. *The Netherlands*), Views adopted on 26 July 1999, UN doc. A/54/40 Vol. II, 271, where lower pension payments to married men than to married women were held to violate Article 26.

[42] *See* Case No. 180/1984 (*Danning v.* The *Netherlands*), Views adopted 9 April 1987, UN doc. A/42/40, 151(CCPR/C/29/D/180/1984); Case No. 395/1990 (*Sprenger* v. The *Netherlands*), Views adopted on 31 March 1992, UN doc. A/47/40, 308 (CCPR/C/44/D/395/1990); Case No. 602/1994 (*Hoofdman* v. *The Netherlands*), Views adopted on 3 November 1998, UN doc. A/54/40 Vol. II, 36 (CCPR/C/64/D/602/1994).

[43] *See* Cases Nos. 406/1990 and 426/1990 (*Oulajin and Kaiss* v.*The Netherlands*), Views adopted on 23 October 1992, UN doc. A/48/40 Vol. II, 131 (CCPR/C/46/D/426/1990).

In particular with regard to social benefits, however, the Committee has sometimes got bogged down in details about cut-off dates, periods to take into account for the calculation of certain payments, and other details which any legislation must decide, but which have nothing to do with the identity of the persons concerned. Numerous cases can be adduced to show that the Committee should review the path it has embarked upon. In *Vos* v. *Netherlands* (1989), a woman who had received a disablement allowance before the death of her husband received after that date a widow's pension which was some 90 guilders lower than the former monthly payment. Rightly, the Committee dismissed the complaint, arguing that the unfavourable result simply followed from the application of a uniform rule to avoid overlapping in the allocation of social security benefits. But it still examined the complaints raised under the auspices of Article 26 instead of concluding that the case did not come within the scope of application of that provision. Another case of high complexity is the case of *García Pons* v. *Spain* (1995). The applicant, a civil servant, had been appointed substitute judge but could not exercise his functions. His request to obtain unemployment benefits was not granted since he could return to his former post. The Committee eventually dismissed the communication, but only after having considered the complaint of a violation of Article 26. But is it really the body which should examine such trivial details of national regulations of the civil service? *Cavalcanti Araujo-Jongen* v. *Netherlands* (1993), *Nahlik* v. *Austria* (1996) and *van Oord* v. *Netherlands* (1997) are other cases of the same calibre. The case of *Schmitz-de-Jong* v. *Netherlands* (2001) was already mentioned. In all of these instances, the final outcome is perfectly right. All of the communications were dismissed. But the Committee gets uselessly drawn into examining petty rules, which exist by the thousands in any legal system. Once lawyers will have learned that it is prepared seriously to consider such bureaucratic distinctions, which of course are capable of causing concern to the person affected, it may become flooded by irrelevant communications so that its essential functions in the service of civil and political rights could suffer serious damage.

2) The Difficult Task of Assessing Distinctions

To conclude this analysis, three cases may be mentioned where the review carried out by the Committee gives rise to serious doubts because of the brevity of the reasons given.

The dispute surrounding retirement pensions for former members of the French Armed forces of Senegalese nationality (*Gueye* v. *France*, 1989) has already been mentioned.[44] The Committee found that the freezing of the level of pensions in 1975

[44] *See also* the comment by Gérard Cohen-Jonathan, *AFDI* 1989, p. 424 *et seq.* The critical position taken by Andrew Drzemczewski and Paul Tavernier, 'L'exécution des 'décisions' des instances internationales de contrôle dans le domaine des droits de l'homme', in: Société française pour le droit international (ed.), *Colloque de Strasbourg: La protection des droits de*

could not be reconciled with Article 26. To support this conclusion, it invoked essentially the fact that the Senegalese soldiers had provided the same kind of service as the French soldiers. But it failed to consider in depth the argument that differences in the economic, financial and social conditions as between France and Senegal could be invoked as a legitimate justification. The sentence suggesting that 'if one compared the case of retired soldiers of Senegalese nationality living in Senegal with that of retired soldiers of French nationality in Senegal, it would appear that they enjoy the same economic and social conditions', misses the point inasmuch as retired French soldiers normally live in France and not in Senegal.[45] It is obvious that a person is infinitely better off with a given amount of money in Senegal than in France. It is certainly not unreasonable to adjust pension payments to the general standard of living in the country concerned. However, none of these elementary considerations appears in the reasoning of the Committee. Obviously, the decision would have benefited from a greater deal of expertise among its members. It is no wonder, therefore, that France has refused to comply with the views expressed under Article 5(4) of the Optional Protocol.[46] It is of the view that Article 26 refers only to rights set forth in the Covenant.

The Committee had to enter another difficult field by comparing subsidies provided to public schools with much lesser assistance given to private schools. In *Blom* v. *Sweden* (1988), the applicant complained that education allowance payments were only made to pupils attending private schools if the courses offered by such schools were placed under governmental supervision. This is certainly a reasonable requirement inasmuch as private schools can apply for obtaining such official approval. Public subsidies presuppose teaching that meets carefully determined quality standards. However, the case of *Lindgren and others* v. *Sweden* (1990) is of a different nature. Here, open discrimination was practiced. A number of municipalities in Sweden granted financial aid for the purchase of children's textbooks and for their meals, but only for the benefit of children attending public schools, not for children in private schools. The Committee, however, denied the existence of discrimination contrary to Article 26. It said:

> 'The parents of Swedish children are free to take advantage of the public sector schooling or to choose private schooling for their children. The decision of the authors of these communications to choose private education was not imposed on them by the State party or by the municipalities concerned, but reflected a free choice recognized and respected by the State party and the municipalities. Such free decision,

---

l'homme et l'évolution du droit international, p. 197 *et seq*., at 210, does not seem to be sufficiently buttressed by pertinent arguments.

45 Case No. 196/1985 (*Gueye* v. *France*) Views adopted on 6 April 1989, UN doc. A/44/40 (CCPR/C/35/D/196/1985), para 9.5.

46 Decision of French Conseil d'Etat of 15 April 1996, *see Doukouré* v. *France* (2000), para. 2.6.

> however, entails certain consequences, notably payment of tuition, transport, textbooks and school books.'[47]

This reasoning is of extreme poverty and does not touch upon the real issues involved. First of all, it should have been noted that the choice of a school corresponding to the capabilities of the child concerned belongs primarily to his/her parents. According to Article 5 of the Convention on the Rights of the Child, which reflects a general principle of law, states parties are bound to respect the responsibilities, rights and duties of parents which are intimately connected to freedom of thought, conscience and religion as set forth in Article 18.[48] Thus, to choose a school is not just a discretionary decision, but an exercise of the rights enshrined in Article 18. However, no trace of this legal configuration can be found in the Committee's views. Second, it should also have been taken into account that the parents of children attending private schools are taxpayers like the parents of pupils attending public schools. In other words, these parents are denied equal participation in public expenditure to which they have contributed by their tax money. In Germany, where the right to establish private schools is guaranteed in the Basic Law (Article 7(4), first clause), the Federal Administrative Tribunal has derived from this guarantee a right for private schools to be financed by the state, basing itself on the two considerations just outlined.[49] In the circumstances, we have to conclude again that the Committee was rather unsuccessful in appraising whether the distinctions operated in the Swedish school system were warranted by reasonable and objective criteria. This case is all the more deplorable since it has strong links with the substance of the Covenant, which the Committee failed to discover.[50]

Diergaardt and others v. *Namibia* (2000) is another case where the reader is not satisfied when perusing the relevant paragraph of the Committee's views (para. 10). At stake was the refusal of governmental agencies to reply to questions put, and requests made, in Afrikaans by the members of the Rehoboth Baster Community, whose mother tongue is in fact Afrikaans. The Committee found a violation of Article 26. For it, the decisive argument seems to have been the fact that the relevant instruction imparted by the higher Namibian authorities was to apply even in instances where the officer addressed was perfectly able to provide a response in Afrikaans. Such obstinacy may well amount to discrimination based on language, which is explicitly prohibited by Article 26. But nothing is said in the views about

[47] *Loc. cit.*, para. 10.3.

[48] The Convention, adopted by UN General Assembly resolution 44/25, 20 November 1989, entered into force on 2 September 1990, just two months before the views in *Lindgren* were handed down.

[49] Decision of 11 March 1966, *BVerwGE* (*Entscheidungen des Bundesverwaltungsgerichts*) 23, p. 347.

[50] We agree, however, with the decision in Case No. 694/1996 (*Waldman* v. *Canada*), Views adopted on 3 November 1999, UN doc. A/55/40 Vol. II, 86 (CCPR/C/67/D/694/1996) at paras. 10.5, 10.6, according to which all religious schools must be treated in the same fashion, without any privilege or discrimination.

the relevant coordination with Article 27, which abstains from granting a right to use minority languages in dealing with public authorities, and no account is taken of the relevance of the state's decision deliberately to introduce English as the official (unifying) language of the entire country.[51]

On the whole, the balance sheet of the cases dealt with under Article 26 outside the scope proper of the Covenant is fairly disappointing. It would appear necessary that the Committee review the course it has steered hitherto.

VI. SOME SUGGESTIONS

There can be no panacea for the shortcomings criticized in this Article. It is true also that an outsider may not be able fully to grasp the complexities of a case as it results from the submissions of the parties involved so that one or the other evaluation may appear to be somewhat rash. Nonetheless, it is submitted that the application of Article 26 along the lines pursued by the Committee since *Broeks* and *Zwaan-de Vries* can be put on much safer foundations. The following observations are designed to contribute to such a re-orientation.

1) In the first place, as already suggested, the Committee should again make the issue of status the centrepiece of its interpretation of Article 26. Article 26 does not deal with just any distinction that can be found in national legislation, but focuses on certain types of structural discrimination, where a person suffers injustices because of his/her stable and permanent characteristics.[52]

2) Second, the Committee might emphasize the margin of appreciation, which national authorities enjoy in making the many distinctions which intervention in the modern welfare state requires. Curiously enough, it is only in an individual opinion in the case of *Oulajin and Kaiss* v. *Netherlands* (1992) that this aspect was forcefully highlighted. Committee members Herndl, Myullerson, Ndiaye and Sadi wrote:

> 'Unless the distinctions made are manifestly discriminatory or arbitrary, it is not for the Committee to re-evaluate the complex socio-economic data and substitute its judgement for that of the legislatures of States parties.'[53]

It is submitted that such restraint is a sound device, suited to protect the Committee from being drawn into minuscule or context-dependent details, where different and even opposite solutions can be backed up by good arguments. We may recall, in this connection, that the European Court of Human Rights has evolved a jurisprudence in which the margin of appreciation enjoyed by states parties plays a pivotal role.

3) Lastly, the Committee should be encouraged to continue the course, which it has staked out in a number of decisions, without steadfastly continuing that course. The first one of these determinations was made in *P. P. C.* v. *Netherlands* (1988),

---

[51] *See also* dissenting opinions by Committee members Amor, *loc. cit.*, p. 149; Ando, *ibid.*, p. 151; Bhagwati, Lord Colville, Yalden, *ibid.*, p. 152; Lallah, *ibid.*, p. 158.

[52] Conclusion also shared by Ramcharan, *loc. cit.* (*supra* note 12).

[53] *Loc. cit.*, p. 559.

where the Committee held that the scope of Article 26 'does not extend to differences of results in the application of common rules in the allocation of benefits'.[54] Along similar lines, in *Vos* v. *Netherlands* (1989) it stated that 'differences in result of the uniform application of laws do not *per se* constitute prohibited discrimination'.[55] The general concept hidden in these propositions should be generalized. It is not, and cannot be, the task of the Human Rights Committee to enquire whether legislative bodies have always acted consistently in the most perfect manner. In all countries, tax law, for instance, is a field of state activity where many classes of persons are distinguished, where deadlines and cut-off dates are fixed and where the most divergent aims of public policy are pursued by the competent law-setting bodies. In Germany alone, thousands of cases are fought every year, some of which even end up before the Federal Constitutional Court.[56] We do not doubt that in other countries where the tribunals are allowed to test normative acts, including parliamentary statutes, as to their conformity with the principle of equality and non-discrimination, similar developments can be observed.[57] The fight for social justice may well be pursued in national fora. We repeat our conviction that the Committee should not feel obligated to join that race.[58] Only when structural discrimination is being practiced, based on the status of a person, should recourse to the Committtee be open as an ultimate remedy. If such precautions are taken, the break-through in the interpretation of Article 26 epitomized by *Broeks* and *Zwaan-de Vries* can be prevented from becoming a pyrrhic victory for the Committee.

---

[54] Case No. 212/1986 (*P.P.C.* v. *The Netherlands*), Decision adopted on 24 March 1988, UN doc. A/43/40, 244 (CCPR/C/32/D/212/1986) at para. 6.2. Almost the same formula was employed in Cases Nos. 406/1990 and 426/1990 (*Oulajin and Kaiss* v. *The Netherlands*), Views adopted on 23 October 1992, UN doc. A/48/40 Vol. II, 131 (CCPR/C/46/D/426/1990) at para. 7.5, and in Case No. 478/1991 (*L.-v. d. M.* v. *The Netherlands*), Decision adopted on 26 July 1993, UN doc. A/48/40 Vol. II, 217 (CCPR/C/48/D/478/1991) at para. 6.4.

[55] Case No. 218/1986 (*Vos* v. *The Netherlands*), Views adopted on 29 March 1989, UN doc. A/44/40, 232 (CCPR/C/35/D/218/1986) at para. 11.3.

[56] Recently, for instance, the Federal Constitutional Court had to rule on the different taxation of pensions of public servants, on one hand, and pensions under the general scheme of retirement pensions, decision of 6 March 2002, *Neue Juristische Wochenschrift* 2002, p. 1103.

[57] The Committee had a foretaste of these complexities in Case No. 742/1997 (*Byrne and Lazarescu* v. *Canada*), Decision adopted on 25 March 1999, A/54/40 Vol. II, 354 (CCPR/C/65/D/742/1997).

[58] *See also* the observation by Torkel Opsahl, 'Equality in Human Rights Law With Particular Reference to Article 26 of the International Covenant on Civil and Political Rights', in: *Progress in the Spirit of Human Rights. Festschrift für Felix Ermacora*, Kehl *et al*. 1988, p. 51 *et seq*., at 64: 'One may . . . query whether the Committee is likely to become an effective 'Ombudsman for Equality' in every area covered by legislation of any kind, in every respect, on every criterion . . .'

ANNEX

LIST OF VIEWS UNDER ARTICLE 5 (4) OF THE OPTIONAL PROTOCOL REFERRED TO IN THE ARTICLE

1) Case No.172/1984 (*Broeks* v. *The Netherlands*), Views adopted on 9 April 1987, UN doc. A/42/40, p. 139.

2) Case No. 180/1984 (*Danning* v. *The Netherlands*), Views adopted 9 April 1987, UN doc. A/42/40, p. 151.

3) Case No. 182/1984 (*Zwaan-de Vries* v. *The Netherlands*), Views adopted on 9 April 1987, UN doc. A/42/40, p. 160.

4) Case No. 212/1986 (*P.P.C.* v. *The Netherlands*), Decision adopted on 24 March 1988, UN doc. A/43/40, p. 244.

5) Case No. 191/1985 (*Blom* v. *Sweden*), Views adopted on 4 April 1988, UN doc. A/43/40, p. 211.

6) Case No. 218/1986 (*Vos* v. *The Netherlands*), Views adopted on 29 March 1989, UN doc. A/44/40, p. 232.

7) Case No. 273/1989 (*B. d. B.* v. *The Netherlands*), Decision adopted on 30 March 1989, UN doc. A/44/40, p. 286.

8) Case No. 196/1985 (*Gueye et al.* v. *France*), Views adopted 3 April 1989, UN doc. A/44/40, p. 189.

9) Case No. 208/1986 (*Singh Bhinder* v. *Canada*), Views adopted on 9 November 1989, UN doc. A/45/40 Vol. II, p. 50.

10) Case No. 219/1986 (*Guesdon* v. *France*), Views adopted on 25 July 1990, UN doc. A/45/40 Vol. II, p. 61.

11) Case No. 295/1988 (*Järvinen* v. *Finland*), Views adopted on 25 July 1990, UN doc. A/45/40 Vol. II, p. 101.

12) Cases Nos. 298/1988 and 299/1988, (*Lindgren and others* v. *Sweden*), Views adopted on 9 November 1990, UN doc. A/46/40, p. 264.

13) Cases Nos. 221/1987 and 323/1988, (*Cadoret and Le Bihan* v. *France*), Views adopted on 11 April 1991, UN doc. A/46/40, p. 223.

14) Case No. 327/1988 (*Barzhig* v. *France*), Views adopted on 11 April 1991, UN doc. A/46/40, p. 272.

15) Case No. 415/1990 (*Pauger* v. *Austria*), Views adopted on 26 March 1992, UN doc. A/47/40, p. 322.

16) Case No. 395/1990 (*Sprenger* v. *The Netherlands*), Views adopted on 31 March 1992, UN doc. A/47/40, p. 308.

17) Cases Nos. 406/1990 and 426/1990 (*Oulajin and Kaiss* v. *The Netherlands*), Views adopted on 23 October 1992, UN doc. A/48/40 Vol. II, p. 131.

18) Case No. 478/1991 (*L.-v. d. M.* v. *The Netherlands*), Decision adopted on 26 July 1993, UN doc. A/48/40 Vol. II, p. 217.

19) Case No. 402/1990 (*Brinkhof* v. *The Netherlands*), Views adopted on 27 July 1993, UN doc. A/48/40 Vol. II, p. 124.

20) Case No. 418/1990 (*Cavalcanti Araujo-Jongen* v. *The Netherlands*), Views adopted on 22 October 1993, UN doc. A/49/40, Vol. II, p. 114.

21) Case No. 488/1992 (*Toonen* v. *Australia*), Views adopted on 31 March 1994, UN doc. A/49/40, Vol.II, p. 226.

22) Case No. 477/1991 (*B.-R.* v. *The Netherlands*), Decision adopted on 7 April 1994, UN doc. A/49/40 Vol. II, p. 294.

23) Case No. 425/1990 (*Doesburg Lannooij Neefs* v. *The Netherlands*), Views adopted on 15 July 1994, UN doc. A/49/40 Vol. II, p. 120.

24) Case No. 484/1991 (*Pepels* v. *The Netherlands*), Views adopted on 15 July 1994, UN doc. A/49/40 Vol. II, p. 221.

25) Case No. 500/1992 (*Debreczeny* v. *The Netherlands*), Views adopted on 3 April 1995, UN doc. A/50/40, p. 59.

26) Case No. 516/1992 (*Simunek* v. *The Czech Republic*), Views adopted on 19 July 1995, UN doc. A/50/40 Vol. II, p. 89.

27) Case No. 454/1991 (*García Pons* v. *Spain*), Views adopted on 30 October 1995, UN doc. A/51/40 Vol. II, p. 30.

28) Case No. 608/1995, *Nahlik* v. *Austria*, Decision adopted on 22 July 1996, UN doc. A/51/40 Vol. II, p. 259.

29) Case No. 566/1993 (*Somers* v. *Hungary*), Views adopted on 23 July 1996, UN doc. A/51/40 Vol. II, p. 144.

30) Case No. 586/1994 (*Adam* v. *The Czech Republic*), Views adopted on 23 July 1996, UN doc. A/51/40 Vol. II, p. 165.

31) Case No. 601/1994 (*Drake* v. *New Zealand*), Decision adopted on 3 April 1997, UN doc. A/52/40 Vol. II, p. 273.

32) Case No. 643/1994 (*Drobek* v. *Slovakia*), Decision adopted on 14 July 1997, UN doc. A/52/40 Vol. II, p. 300.

33) Case No. 658/1995 (*van Oord* v. *The Netherlands*), Decision adopted on 23 July 1997, UN doc. A/52/40 Vol. II, p. 311.

34) Case No. 735/1997 (*Kalaba* v. *Hungary*), Decision adopted on 7 November 1997, UN doc. A/53/40 Vol. II, p. 263.

35) Case No. 651/1998 (*Snijders et al.* v. *The Netherlands*), Views adopted on 27 July 1998, UN doc. A/53/40, Vol. II, p. 135.

36) Case No. 669/1995 (*Malik* v. *The Czech Republic*), Decision adopted on 21 October 1998, UN doc. A/54/40, Vol. II, p. 294.

37) Case No. 670/1995 (*Schlosser* v. *The Czech Republic*), Decision adopted on 21 October 1998, UN doc. A/54/40, Vol. II, p. 298.

38) Case No. 602/1994 (*Hoofdman* v. *The Netherlands*), Views adopted on 3 November 1998, UN doc. A/54/40, Vol. II, p. 36.

39) Case No. 742/1997 (*Byrne and Lazarescu* v. *Canada*), Decision adopted on 25 March 1999, UN doc. A/54/40, Vol. II, p. 354.

40) Case No. 716/1999 (*Pauger* v. *Austria*), Views adopted on 25 March 1999, UN doc. A/54/40, Vol. II, p. 202.

41) Case No. 786/1997 (*Vos* v. *The Netherlands*), Views adopted on 26 July 1999, UN doc. A/54/40, Vol. II, p. 271.

42) Case No. 666/1995 (*Foin* v. *France*), Views adopted on 3 November 1999, UN doc. A/55/40, Vol. II, p. 30.

43) Case No. 694/1996 (*Waldman* v. *Canada*), Views adopted on 3 November 1999, UN doc. A/55/40, Vol. II, p. 86.

44) Case No. 861/1999 (*Lestourneaud* v. *France*), Decision adopted on 3 November 1999, UN doc. A/55/40, Vol. II, p. 234.

45) Case No. 756/1997 (*Doukouré* v. *France*), Views adopted on 29 March 2000, UN doc. A/55/40, Vol. II, p. 194.

46) Case No. 689/1996 (*Maille* v. *France*), Views adopted on 10 July 2000, UN doc. A/55/40, Vol. II, p. 62.

47) Case Nos. 690/1996 and 691/1996 (*Venier & Nicolas* v. *France*), Views adopted on 10 July 2000, UN doc. A/55/40, Vol. II, p. 75.

48) Case No. 934/2000 (*G.* v. *Canada*), Decision adopted on 17 July 2000, UN doc. A/55/40, Vol. II, p. 251.

49) Case No. 760/1997 (*Diergaardt et al.* v. *Namibia*), Views adopted on 25 July 2000, UN doc. A/55/40, Vol. II, p. 140.

50) Case No. 819/1998 (*Kavanagh* v. *Ireland*), Views adopted on 4 April 2001, UN doc. A/56/40, Vol. II, p. 122.

51) Case No. 857/1999 (*Blazek et al.* v. *The Czech Republic*), Views adopted on 12 July 2001, UN doc. A/56/40, Vol. II, p. 168.

52) Case No. 855/1999 (*Schmitz-de-Jong* v. *The Netherlands*), Views adopted on 16 July 2001, UN doc. A/56/40, p. 165.

53) Case No. 790/1997 (*Cheban* v. *Russian Federation*), Views adopted on 24 July 2001, UN doc. A/56/40, Vol. II, p. 88.

54) Case No. 747/1997 (*Des Fours Walderode* v. *The Czech Republic*), Views adopted on 30 October 2001, UN doc. A/57/40, Vol. II, p. 88.

55) Case No. 765/1997 (*Fábryová* v. *The Czech Republic*), Views adopted on 30 October 2001, UN doc. A/57/40, Vol. II, p. 103.

56) Case No. 774/1997 (*Brok* v. *The Czech Republic*), Views adopted on 31 October 2001, UN doc. A/57/40, Vol. II, p.110.

57) Case No. 865/1999 (*Marín Gómez* v. *Spain*), Views adopted on 5 November 2001, UN doc. A/57/40, Vol. II, p.198.

PART V

THE INTERNATIONAL COVENANT ON CIVIL AND POLITICAL RIGHTS AND DOMESTIC LAW

THE DOMESTIC APPLICATION OF THE COVENANT IN AUSTRALIA

Ivan Shearer

A constant task of the Human Rights Committee, during its work of the past 25 years, has been to monitor the compliance of state parties with their obligations to ensure that their laws and practices give effect to the rights secured by the Covenant and to provide effective remedies for their violation. Article 2 of the Covenant provides that

> '(2) Where not already provided for by existing legislative or other measures, each State Party to the present Covenant undertakes to take the necessary steps, in accordance with its constitutional processes and with the provisions of the present Covenant, to adopt such legislative or other measures as may be necessary to give effect to the rights recognized in the present Covenant.
>
> (3) Each State Party to the present Covenant undertakes: (a) To ensure that any person whose rights or freedoms as herein recognized are violated shall have an effective remedy . . .'

Where a state party has passed legislation directly incorporating the Covenant as part of its domestic law, or where the constitution of that state gives the force of law to international conventions duly ratified and promulgated, or where the state party's laws contain a Bill of Rights that recognises substantially the same rights as are contained in the Covenant, it can be said that that party's laws fulfil its obligations under Article 2. The concern of the Committee in those cases is then focused on actual implementation in practice. But what of the alternative recognised in the words of Article 2: 'or other measures'? How is the discharge of the obligations under Article 2 to be assessed in the case of a state party, such as Australia, which has not legislated specifically to incorporate the Covenant, which has no Bill of Rights, and which adopts an essentially dualist approach to the place of international obligations in its legal system? Might such 'other measures' include a legal system that provides for the protection of human rights through a combination of unwritten laws administered by the judiciary, and through additional statutory protections in particular areas of the law? In other words, can a state whose legal tradition remains anchored in the common law inherited from England effectively implement the Covenant?

Australia is not only a state of the English common law inheritance. It is also a federation in which powers over certain matters are granted to the federal parliament, the residue of legislative competence remaining with the constituent states. Most of the laws with which human rights are concerned, in particular the criminal law, lie within the power of the states. While the federal power to legislate with respect to 'external affairs' has been given a wide interpretation by the High Court of Australia, and certainly embraces the power to legislate for the implementation of international treaties and conventions throughout Australia, notwithstanding that the subject matter of such treaties or conventions would otherwise belong to reserved domain of the states, political rather than legal considerations have hitherto impeded the enactment of a comprehensive national Bill of Rights based upon the Covenant.

The situation of Australia with respect to the formal incorporation of human rights within its legal system remains essentially the same as that of the United Kingdom before 2000, when the Human Rights Act came into force, and of Canada and New Zealand before they too enacted comprehensive legislation protecting human rights.

There has been implicit endorsement by the Committee of the view that state parties need not necessarily implement their obligations under the Covenant by comprehensive legislation incorporating it into domestic law; that a common law system might, in principle, be sufficient. The Committee, however, in its Concluding Observations on the third and fourth periodic reports of Australia under Article 40 of the Covenant, adopted on 28 July 2000, pointed to the existence of gaps:

> 'The Committee is concerned that in the absence of a constitutional Bill of Rights, or a constitutional provision giving effect to the Covenant, there remain lacunae in the protection of Covenant rights in the Australian legal system. There are still areas in which the domestic legal system does not provide an effective remedy to persons whose rights under the Covenant have been violated.'[1]

This paper explores the reasons for these 'lacunae' and how they might be filled.

1. THE 'DUALIST' THEORY OF THE RELATIONSHIP BETWEEN INTERNATIONAL LAW AND DOMESTIC LAW

Contrasting with the dualist theory of the relationship between international law and domestic law, favoured by states of the common law inheritance, the 'monist' theory derives from natural law theories that see all law as one: human reason, applied to the facts of creation and human nature, yields rules which cannot come into conflict, whether they arise on the international or the domestic law planes, if they are truly law in the sense of being the product of right reason. The dualist view of the relationship is in part a consequence of the decline of the natural law tradition in the 19th century and a product of that legal approach known as positivism. For the English jurist John Austin, writing in the middle of the 19th century, international law was not law at all, having its validity in morality only. While that view was never adopted expressly by the English judges or by the judges of other parts of the common law world, occasional echoes of it were heard in the past; there was a tendency of judges to regard international law as an alien and rather exotic creature,

[1] UN Doc. A/55/40, at paras. 498–528.

to be regarded with extreme caution. More typical of the dualist view is to regard international law as true law but as operating on a separate plane from domestic law.

The Australian courts have accepted the dualist position as the fundamental starting point. The High Court of Australia has repeated on several occasions the dictum of Chief Justice Sir Owen Dixon, in 1948, that 'international law is not a part, but is one of the sources of, Australian law'.[2] In 1992 Justice (later Chief Justice) Sir Gerard Brennan restated this approach in a landmark case concerning aboriginal land rights, but preceded his statement with a recognition of the influence of international law on the development of the common law of Australia:

> 'The expectations of the international community accord in this respect with the contemporary values of the Australian people. The opening up of international remedies to individuals pursuant to Australia's accession to the Optional Protocol to the International Covenant on Civil and Political Rights . . . brings to bear on the common law the powerful influence of the Covenant and the international standards it imports. The common law does not necessarily conform with international law, but international law is a legitimate and important influence on the development of the common law, especially when international law declares the existence of universal human rights.'[3]

The question then is how a particular rule of international law might become incorporated in the common law: whether it can be so incorporated only by a positive act of transformation from the international to the domestic plane by legislation, or whether there can be an indirect form of transformation through the exercise of discretion by the judges in interpreting or applying the existing common law.[4]

2. THE TRANSLATION OF INTERNATIONAL LAW INTO DOMESTIC LAW

It is an almost inevitable consequence of the conception that international law and domestic law operate on separate planes that some formal act of adoption, or transformation, is required in order to incorporate, or make effective, the norms and rules of international law within the domestic legal order. As will appear, however, courts of the common law tradition will regard certain rules of international law as automatically incorporated within the common law.

The requirement of direct transformation is clear where the international law rule is contained in a treaty and owes its origin to that treaty. It is a general principle of constitutional law, known to all countries of the common law world, that treaties

[2] *Chow Hung Ching* v. *The King* (1948) 77 Commonwealth Law Reports 449.

[3] *Mabo* v. *Commonwealth* (1992) 175 Commonwealth Law Reports 1, at para. 42.

[4] For a recent review of *see* Shane S. Monks, In Defence of the Use of Public International Law by Australian Courts", *22 Australian Yearbook of International Law* pp. 201–226 (2003).

cannot operate as law without implementation through legislation because that would be to concede to the executive branch of government the power to make laws. The applicable constitutional principle is the doctrine of the separation of powers: direct law-making power is reserved to the legislature. Where a treaty – and especially a multilateral convention such as the Covenant – either restates an existing rule of customary international law or crystallises a new rule, then that rule should be treated as deriving from custom and not treaty.

Where a relevant international law rule is established in customary international law the attitude of the courts is more nuanced. The constantly evolving body of the common law is capable of picking up and automatically incorporating relevant rules of customary international law, provided that certain conditions are met. In the first place, the rule must be clearly established in customary international law. Secondly, the rule must be essentially self-executing in nature in the sense that it is capable of being applied within domestic law without adaptation or choice of means. Thirdly, the rule must not conflict with existing legislation or with settled judicial precedent. Finally, the rule in question must be broadly in harmony with the existing law so that the judges do not overstep the limits of their leeway of judicial choice by declaring changes to the existing law of a radical or particular nature suited only to legislative prescription.

Some examples of the application of these conditions are furnished by recent cases.

In 1992 the High Court of Australia considered the issue of access by accused persons unable to pay for counsel to free legal counsel as provided in Article 14(3)(d) of the Covenant.[5] The accused had been convicted of serious offences involving the importation of narcotic drugs. He was not represented by counsel at trial because he was indigent and the legal aid authorities had denied him assistance. A previous decision of the High Court had rejected the view that the common law required that an accused be represented in cases of serious offences. The High Court was invited to reconsider that decision in the light of Australia's adherence to the Covenant. Attention was drawn to statements by Justice Michael Kirby in the Australian courts, and by judges of courts in the United Kingdom, that where the common law was uncertain judges could have regard to ratified treaties (and, one should add, established rules of customary international law) as an aid to the development of the common law. In their joint judgment Chief Justice Mason and Justice McHugh said on this point:

> 'Assuming, without deciding, that Australian courts should adopt a similar, common-sense approach, this nevertheless does not assist the applicant in this case where we are being asked not to resolve uncertainty or ambiguity in domestic law but to declare that a right which has hitherto never been recognised should now be taken to exist. Moreover, this branch of the applicant's argument assumes that art. 14(3)(d) of the ICCPR supports the absolute right for which he contends. An analysis of

[5] *Dietrich* v. *The Queen* (1992) 177 Commonwealth Law Reports 292.

> the views of the Human Rights Committee on communications submitted to it relating to art. 14(3)(d) reveals little more than that the Committee considers that legal assistance must always be made available in capital cases (Pinto v. Trinidad and Tobago, CCPR/C/39/D/232/1987.)[6] However, the European Court of Human Rights has approached the almost identical provision in the ECHR by emphasising the importance of the particular facts of the case to any interpretation of the phrase 'when the interests of justice so require' (Monnell and Morris v. United Kingdom (1987) 10 EHRR 205, at p.225; Granger v. United Kingdom (1990) 12 EHRR 469, at pp. 480-482). As will become clear, that approach is similar to the approach which, in our opinion, the Australian common law must now take.'[7]

The Court then proceeded to fashion a new approach within the common law which regarded a right to free legal assistance in serious criminal cases as not a free-standing right but as an aspect of the common law right to a fair trial. Since the courts in Australia do not themselves control the funds from which counsel are paid in legal assistance cases, the Court declared that in serious cases where an indigent accused was unrepresented by counsel, Australian courts must issue a stay of proceedings until such time as legal representation could be provided, by whatever means. Although the High Court seemed to turn its back on the Covenant as a source of this newly created common law right, and did not consider whether the Covenant provision had achieved a parallel status as customary or general international law, it was clearly influenced by it. The approach also illustrates the difficulty of applying directly an international law rule expressed in particular language without adaptation to the local legal system.

The question of possible automatic incorporation of customary law was considered by the Federal Court of Australia in 1999.[8] The applicants were aboriginal Australians who sought a declaration that the Australian government had in the past pursued policies, and engaged in practices, that amounted to genocide under international law. The majority of the Court held that the crime of genocide could not be regarded as part of the common law of Australia in the absence of legislation defining it precisely, giving particular courts jurisdiction over it, and prescribing penalties.[9] A dissenting judge thought otherwise.[10] All judges were agreed, however, that even if genocide as defined in international law were a crime under Australian law, the applicants could not establish that the facts alleged by them amounted to that crime.

---

[6] *See* now General Comment 13 of the Committee, and the jurisprudence of the Committee collected in S. Joseph, J. Schultz and M. Castan, *The International Covenant on Civil and Political Rights: Cases, Materials, and Commentary* (Oxford University Press, 2000) 320–322.

[7] *Ibid.*, at para. 20.

[8] *Nulyarimma* v. *Thompson* (1999) 96 Federal Court Reports 153.

[9] *Ibid.*, Justice Wilcox, at 157–166, and Justice Whitlam, at 166–173.

[10] *Ibid.*, Justice Merkel, at 173–216.

Whether the relevant source of international law is a treaty or customary international law, Australian courts are always open to the argument that an interpretation of a governing domestic statute should conform, so far as its words permit, to international law. In a case before the High Court of Australia in 1997 Justice Kirby expressed this approach as follows:

> 'Australian law, including its constitutional law, may sometimes fall short of giving effect to fundamental rights. The duty of the court is to interpret what the Constitution says and not what individual judges think it should have said. If the Constitution is clear, the court must (as in the interpretation of any legislation) give effect to its terms. Nor should the court adopt an interpretative principle as a means of introducing, by the back door, provisions of international treaties or other international law concerning fundamental rights not yet incorporated into Australian domestic law. However, as has been recognised by this court and by other courts of high authority, the inter-relationship of national and international law, including in relation to fundamental rights, is 'undergoing evolution'. To adapt what Brennan J said in *Mabo v. Queensland (No.2)*, the common law, and constitutional law, do not necessarily conform with international law. However, international law is a legitimate and important influence on the development of the common law and constitutional law, especially when international law declares the existence of universal and fundamental rights. To the full extent that its text permits, Australia's Constitution, as the fundamental law of government in this country, accommodates itself to international law, including insofar as that law expresses basic rights. The reason for this is that the Constitution not only speaks to the people of Australia who made it and accept it for their governance. It also speaks to the international community as the basic law of the Australian nation which is a member of that community.'[11]

For some it may be disappointing that the High Court of Australia has not embraced the automatic incorporation doctrine of the relationship between customary international law and domestic law. Yet in reality adherence to the transformation doctrine has not resulted in a lessening of the impact of international norms and standards, including those of the Covenant, on the interpretation of statutes and the development of the common law of Australia. Indeed, it may be argued that the awareness of the judges, as evidenced in the passages cited above and many other passages that could have been quoted, of the constraints of the transformation approach, in situations where international law and domestic law interact, has resulted in a more harmonious and integrated legal doctrine.

---

[11] *Newcrest Mining* v. *Commonwealth* (1997) 190 Commonwealth Law Reports 513, at 657–658.

3. THE STATUS OF THE COVENANT IN AUSTRALIAN LAW

It follows from what has been said above that treaties and conventions do not, as such, have the force of law in Australia. They are, however, referred to by judges as an influence in the interpretation of statutes and the development of the common law.

The status of the Covenant in Australian law was explained in the joint judgment of Chief Justice Mason and Justice McHugh in a case before the High Court of Australia in 1992.[12] They said:

> 'Ratification of the ICCPR as an executive act has no direct legal effect upon domestic law; the rights and obligations contained in the ICCPR are not incorporated into Australian law unless and until specific legislation is passed implementing the provisions . . . No such legislation has been passed. This position is not altered by Australia's accession to the First Optional Protocol to the ICCPR, effective as of 25 December 1991, by which Australia recognises the competence of the Human Rights Committee of the United Nations to receive and consider communications from individuals subject to Australia's jurisdiction who claim to be victims of a violation by Australia of their covenanted rights. On one view, it may seem curious that the Executive Government has seen fit to expose Australia to the potential censure of the Human Rights Committee without endeavouring to ensure that the rights enshrined in the ICCPR are incorporated into domestic law, but such an approach is clearly permissible.'

The Covenant does, however, have a 'visibility' in Australian law higher than that of most other international conventions. The Human Rights and Equal Opportunity Commission was established by legislation enacted by the Australian parliament in 1986. The scheme of the Act consists principally in giving authority to the Commission (HREOC) to work for the progressive implementation of designated international conventions and declarations through representations to the federal government, through other public awareness activities, and where appropriate through intervention in judicial proceedings. It also has the power to hear complaints from individuals who allege violations of their human rights, but its findings are advisory only. The jurisdiction of the Commission is confined to an examination of federal and Territorial laws and practices only; it does not extend to the laws and practices of the states. The Covenant, together with certain other international instruments, is reproduced in full text in the Schedule annexed to the Act.[13] Despite

---

[12] *Dietrich* v. *The Queen* (1992) 177 Commonwealth Law Reports 292, at para.17.

[13] In addition to the Covenant, the following instruments are also annexed: ILO Convention No. 111 (1958) Concerning Discrimination in Employment, the Convention on the Rights of the Child (1989), and the United Nations Declarations on the Rights of Mentally Retarded Persons (1971), Disabled Persons (1975), and Religious Intolerance (1981). A similar legislative technique is used in the Racial Discrimination Act, 1975, the Sex Discrimination

attempts by counsel in some cases after 1986 to argue that the annexure of the international instruments to the Act amounted effectively to their incorporation into Australian law, it has been clearly established by later judicial decisions that this is not the correct view. In a decision in 1999, in a case in which an aggrieved prisoner was complaining about certain prison conditions, the Federal Court of Australia declared:

> 'Although the HREOC Act was enacted to secure the fulfillment of Australia's obligations under the ICCPR, the Act does not make the provisions of the ICCPR directly enforceable in the Australian courts. Nor have the provisions of the ICCPR upon which the appellant relies been given the force of law by any other statute. It is because the ICCPR does not give rise to rights or obligations enforceable under Australian law that it cannot give rise to a 'matter' which constitutes a 'justiciable controversy' . . . That is, the ICCPR cannot support the making of an order or declaration of the kind which the appellant seeks.'[14]

That decision illustrates the comment in the Concluding Observations of the Human Rights Committee with respect to Australia adopted in July 2000 that there are lacunae in the protection of Covenant rights in the Australian legal system.

An alternative way of treating the Covenant as incorporated in Australian law has been to invoke the doctrine of legitimate expectation in administrative law. In the case of *Minister of Immigration and Ethnic Affairs* v. *Teoh* it was held by the High Court of Australia that, among other matters, treaties and conventions ratified by Australia gave rise to legitimate expectations that executive decision makers would have regard to them in reaching their decisions.[15] But this is a matter of procedural fairness: if the decision maker disregards a treaty or convention the affected person must be given an opportunity to argue against that course. The doctrine does not have the effect of making the provisions of the treaty or convention part of Australian law.[16]

The intention of the Australian government to legislate so as to reverse even this very limited effect of the decision in the case of Teoh drew adverse comment from the Committee in its Concluding Observations on Australia's third and fourth periodic reports in July 2000. The Bill for this purpose was not passed during the last parliament. It is unknown whether the government will re-introduce it.

The provisions of the Covenant have an influential effect on the interpretation of legislation and on the development of the common law in the manner described in

---

Act, 1984, and the Disability Discrimination Act, 1992. The monitoring mechanisms under these Acts have been brought into association with HREOC.

[14] *Minogue* v. *Human Rights and Equal Opportunity Commission* (1999) 84 Federal Court Reports 438. To the same effect is the case of *Collins* v. *South Australia* [1999] South Australian Supreme Court 257 (on-line service).

[15] (1995) 183 Commonwealth Law Reports 273.

[16] *Minogue supra* note 14 at para. 37.

the previous section. Australian courts may also have regard to the decisions of the Human Rights Committee on the meaning of the Covenant.[17]

4. THE SITUATION OF ABORIGINES IN AUSTRALIA

In its Concluding Observations on the third and fourth periodic reports of Australia in July 2000 the Committee set out a number of concerns respecting the situation of aborigines and Torres Strait Islanders. While noting as positive developments the decisions of the High Court of Australia in the cases of *Mabo* and *Wik*, concerning recognition of traditional land title, and the enactment of the Native Title Act, 1993, the Committee was concerned that:

> 'in many areas the native title rights and interests remain unresolved and that the Native Title Amendments of 1998 in some respects limit the right of indigenous persons and communities, in particular in the field of effective participation in all matters affecting land ownership and use, and affects their interests in native title lands, particularly pastoral lands....[The Committee recommends that] the necessary steps be taken to restore and protect the titles and interests of indigenous persons in their native lands, including by considering amending anew the Native Title Act, taking account of these concerns.'

The Committee also expressed its concern regarding the 'continuing effects' of past policies of separating aboriginal children from their families.

In entering upon such sensitive matters the Committee has to tread a delicate line. In the case of some countries, manifest injustices occur as a result of government oppression, indifference, or incompetence. It is then a case of the Committee using its voice and weight to urge necessary change, sometimes in emphatic language. In cases such as Australia, however, these matters have been the subject of intensive debate in an open society, in which all interested groups have expressed their views. There has been exhaustive debate in parliament. It then becomes a question of political judgment whether the right decisions have been reached. Moreover, addressing the situation of indigenous Australians is a continuing process, and no legislative or other prescriptions can be said to be final. There was a sense of irritation in government circles in Australia that the Committee had formulated its observations on the basis of reading the government's reports covering its implementation of the Covenant in general, the reports of NGO's, and after only a short open session.

In defence of the Committee, it should be remembered that these are only 'observations', not decisions of a body of final determination. Moreover, the carefully chosen language of the Committee is not that of outright condemnation. While the recommendation that Australia should consider the further amendment of the Native Title Act, which was arrived at after an exhaustive search for consensus,

[17] *See for example*, *Johnson* v. *Johnson* (2000) 201 Commonwealth Law Reports 488 (Kirby J.).

might be regarded as provocative, this should, in context, be regarded as part of the dialogue between the Committee and Australia, not as a directive. Taken in this spirit, the views of a broadly representative and expert committee can be regarded as a disinterested and possibly useful contribution to the ongoing debate in Australia on such questions, not as a high-handed intervention that forecloses further debate.

5. IMPLEMENTATION OF THE COMMITTEE'S VIEWS UNDER THE OPTIONAL PROTOCOL

Several complaints have been brought to the Committee against Australia under the Optional Protocol to the Covenant, to which Australia adhered in 1991. Mention will be made here of two of those cases.

In *Toonen* v. *Australia* the complainant argued that the criminal laws of the state of Tasmania making sexual relations between consenting males in private an offence were discriminatory and a violation of the right to privacy (Articles 2 and 17 of the Covenant).[18] Australia, as a party to the Covenant, was in this instance the respondent to a complaint made against the laws of a part of Australia over which, in respect of the criminal law, the federal government and parliament had no constitutional authority. In fact, as the correspondence between the Australian government and the Office of the High Commissioner for Human Rights in relation to the case reveals, Australia offered no defence of its own against Mr. Toonen's complaint against the laws of Tasmania. It did, however, forward to the Office the comments and explanations of the government of Tasmania. Following the Committee's finding of violations of the Covenant, the Australian government urged the government of Tasmania to take effective action to remedy the complaint. Tasmania refused to do so. The Australian federal parliament could not legislate directly so as to alter or override the criminal laws of Tasmania. Under the Australian Constitution, however, the federal Parliament has power to pass laws with respect to external affairs, which includes the implementation of treaties. The federal parliament thus passed the Human Rights (Sexual Conduct) Act, 1994 which, specifically relying on Australia's obligations under the Covenant, prohibited arbitrary interference with privacy in relation to consensual sexual conduct, thus indirectly providing for a federal defence to a breach of state laws. In 1997 the parliament of Tasmania finally removed the offensive provisions from its Criminal Code.

In the case of *A.* v. *Australia*[19] a Cambodian asylum-seeker complained of his lengthy detention in custody under the Migration Act. He alleged violation of Article 9(1) of the Covenant in that the detention was arbitrary in the sense of

[18] Communication No. 488/1992 (*Toonen* v. *Australia*), Views adopted on 31 March 1994, UN doc. A/49/40 vol. II, p. 226.

[19] Communication No. 560/1993 (*A.* v. *Australia*), Views adopted on 4 March 1997, UN doc. A/52/40 vol. II, p. 124. The complainant exhausted his domestic remedies in an unsuccessful appeal to the High Court of Australia: *Applicant A.* v. *Minister for Immigration and Ethnic Affairs* (1997) 190 Commonwealth Law Reports 225.

unreasonable, unjust and inappropriate. He also alleged a violation of Article 9(4) in that the extremely tightly drawn Australian legislation respecting unlawful immigrants denied him an effective right of review of his detention by a court. The Committee upheld the complaint on these points. In this case the Australian government refused to implement the Committee's views. The government contested the Committee's interpretation and application of the Covenant in relation to the complaint. In its Concluding Observations of July 2000 on Australia's third and fourth periodic reports the Committee expressed its concern in markedly strong language:

> 'Rejecting the Committee's interpretation of the Covenant when it does not correspond with the interpretation presented by the State Party in its submissions to the Committee undermines the State Party's recognition of the Committee's competence under the Optional Protocol to consider communications.'

In communications brought to it the Committee is not a court of law and it does not hand down binding decisions. On the other hand, state parties accepting the Optional Protocol recognise the competence of the Committee to consider communications and to express its views. Even if not strictly binding, those views represent an authoritative guide for the interpretation of the Covenant by a body designated by the Covenant itself. Those views are therefore not lightly to be disregarded.[20]

The stand-off in relation to this case between Australia and the Committee is most regrettable. It has to do with the most contentious political issue in Australia today: how to deal with the problem of asylum seekers arriving in large numbers by irregular means, and the conditions of their detention. Australia is not alone in facing the problem: indeed in terms of numbers it is not as greatly burdened as many other countries. There is vigorous criticism of the government's policies by NGO's and prominent commentators. The most positive thing that may be said is that, in a climate of free speech and the Australian tradition of robust public debate, the government is constantly under pressure to justify its policies and actions. The Committee's views, rather than being ignored, are constantly being reinforced in the course of this debate.

The Committee has sometimes expressed concern at the apparent lack of any formal procedure in the governmental structures of some state parties to the Covenant for implementing the views of the Committee in cases of individual communications. The position in Australia is as follows. The Office of International Law in the federal Attorney General's Department has the responsibility for responding to all individual communications concerning Australia under the Covenant and also under the Racial Discrimination and Torture Conventions. The Office coordinates with the relevant federal, state, and territory agency (or even

[20] The weight to be accorded to the opinions of expert international bodies has been considered judicially in Australia: *Commonwealth* v. *HREOC* (2000) 180 Australian Law Reports 635, at 643–646 (Katz J.)

private corporation) whose conduct has led to the communication. It coordinates in a similar manner the responses to the views expressed by those committees. Where appropriate, these responses are cleared with the relevant government ministers. The Office of International Law maintains a schedule of communications that is regularly updated.

6. TOWARDS A BILL OF RIGHTS IN AUSTRALIA?

Australia is one of the few countries of the world without a formal Bill of Rights, or an enactment of constitutional or near-constitutional status giving legal effect to human rights, including those contained in the Covenant. Notwithstanding this lack, it can be asserted, without undue hubris, that Australia's record in human rights is better in practical implementation than that of many countries whose fundamental laws purport to protect human rights.

Nevertheless, there are gaps, as pointed out by the Committee, and there is awareness in Australia that improvements must be made. The judges of Australia have proven themselves, especially in recent years, to be both sensitive to international standards of human rights and resourceful in blending them where possible into the common law. Governments too have been active in legislating on particular aspects of human rights, such as discrimination. The work of the Human Rights and Equal Opportunity Commission has been especially noteworthy, notwithstanding its lack of jurisdiction over many matters arising under state (as distinct from federal) law and practice.

In 1973, and again in 1985, a Bill of Rights was proposed by the government of Australia, then under a Labour Party administration. Those Bills were substantially identical with the Covenant. They did not complete their passage through both Houses of Parliament, however, owing to the opposition of the states. The states saw the Bills as a threat to their independence within the federal system. A compromise, reached under a Liberal-National Party coalition administration, was the creation of the Human Rights and Equal Opportunity Commission, described above.

A movement to re-consider a Bill of Rights has gathered strength in recent times.[21] The experience of Canada, New Zealand and the United Kingdom with their different models will be especially influential in this movement, bearing in mind that they too are countries of the common law which not so long ago lacked Bills of Rights. It is to be hoped that suggested models for Australia will keep close to the Covenant, so that the jurisprudence of the Committee and that of Australia and other state parties may be mutually reinforcing.

---

[21] *See for example*, M. R. Wilcox, *An Australian Charter of Rights?* (1993); H. Charlesworth, 'International Human Rights Law and Australian Federalism' in B. Opeskin and D.R. Rothwell, *International Law and Australian Federalism* (1997), chapter 9.